Emotions, Stress, and Health

ALEX J. ZAUTRA

OXFORD
UNIVERSITY PRESS
2003

OXFORD
UNIVERSITY PRESS

Oxford   New York
Auckland   Bangkok   Buenos Aires   Cape Town   Chennai
Dar es Salaam   Delhi   Hong Kong   Istanbul   Karachi   Kolkata
Kuala Lumpur   Madrid   Melbourne   Mexico City   Mumbai
Nairobi   São Paulo   Shanghai   Taipei   Tokyo   Toronto

Library of Congress Cataloging-in-Publication Data
Zautra, Alex.
   Emotions, stress, and health / Alex J. Zautra.
      p.   cm.
   Includes bibliographical references and index.
   ISBN 978-0-19-530798-6
   1. Clinical health psychology.   2. Stress (Psychology)   3. Emotions.
   I. Title.
   R726.7   .Z38   2003
   616'.001'9—dc21   2002001456

Printed in the United States of America
on acid-free paper

To Mom and Dad

For generosity beyond measure

Preface

Though we pursue and can find happiness, neither the world outside nor our world within grants us a life free of difficulty. Our emotional lives are a rich blend of colors, some brilliant, others dark and foreboding. We may wish to follow a path through life that is simple and uncomplicated, and at times we desperately need it to be so. This book recognizes, however, that we can choose another path, a path that acknowledges from the outset that we have both sweet and sad voices within us. These apparent contradictions in how we feel reveal a deeper truth about ourselves. We are complex creatures emotionally, even if we wish it were otherwise.

To deal with this complexity in ourselves and in the world around us, we each develop our own ways of understanding and responding to events. These are our own private theories, and they guide us through life. We revise them along the way to accommodate new information, and sometimes—perhaps more often than we care to admit—we revise the "data" of our encounters so that they fit our preconceptions of how life ought to be. We cope with uncertainty this way: by constructing and, at times, deconstructing our worldviews about health, happiness, and adaptive styles of life.

We behavioral scientists are no different in our uses and abuses of theory. We are in the business of developing models of human adaptation. Although a single model will not describe any one person perfectly, scientists often forgive a few blemishes here and there and continue to hold on to models in science that do not quite fit. This is a "warts and all" approach, and it is sound advice up to a point. Scientists are no different from the rest of humanity, though, when it comes to holding on to out-dated ideas because they fit best with what is most comfortable, most symmetrical. Even when changing our way of looking at things would advance knowledge, we might resist. In this book, I suggest that we do need to change the way we think about our emotions to better understand how those emotions affect our health. Indeed, data from many studies, as well as common sense, dictate that a fresh approach is needed if we are to improve the accuracy of our models of healthy adaptation.

To improve on current models, we first need to know what difficulties arise with them. In psychology, as in all sciences, strong opposing sides are often drawn. Although these positions may help crystallize distinctions between theories, on close inspection the opposing arguments often prove to be based on false dichotomies. This has been the case for two models of human adaptation within behavioral science. A very basic division has emerged in those models: the division between the psychology of defense and the psychology of growth.

One set of models focuses on how we prepare for and adapt to pain, stress, and other features in our lives that threaten our psychological adjustment. I like to refer to the models of defense as the "East Coast theories," because they have their roots in traditional psychodynamic theory, which is taught more frequently in East Coast schools of psychiatry and psychology and which helps shape the psychotherapeutic efforts of many East Coast clinics. Better adjustment comes often through coping with forces within ourselves and learning to employ more mature defenses. Fundamentally, these are models that acknowledge human frailty and seek to promote endurance and hardiness in the face of life's many threats to our well-being.

West Coast psychology looks at human adaptation through a very different lens. In it, personal growth, self-development, and rebirth are the keys to human adaptation. In this collection of models, the focus is on developing the positive, not defending against the negative. These models offer ways to embrace even the most stressful life experiences so as to grow and learn from them. From this perspective, the world offers opportunities embedded within each challenging situation. What we need to learn is how to take full advantage of those situations. Psychotherapy, as practiced within this model, is not really therapy at all; rather, it is guidance toward a more actualized self. If defense against harm is the primary evolutionary principle that governs human striving on the East Coast, then reproductive urges and the nurturing and care of the young that follow are at the root of the West Coast models.

Have I exaggerated the differences between the coasts? Certainly. There are as many exceptions as exemplars among the schools closest to either ocean. Nevertheless, these two approaches represent fundamental differences in how psychological theorists and educators approach the task of defining psychological health. It is this tension between the need to anticipate and cope with adversity by engaging our mature defenses and the desire to develop ourselves, find intimacy, and pursue happiness that frames the debate not only among theorists but also within our families and within ourselves.

Modern health psychology texts often represent these two views as points along a continuum from illness to wellness. At one end of the continuum we cope with pathological conditions, mental as well as physical, that need corrective therapy. If we are not suffering from illness, we can extend ourselves beyond normalcy toward some ideal or optimal state of mental and physical conditioning. We do so to prevent illness and to promote psychological and physical well-being. Abraham Maslow (1968) was one of the first to present such a model of human functioning. In his framework, individuals focus first on survival needs, and as those needs are met, new, higher order needs emerge, such as a need for social ties and finally for fulfillment and self-actualization. Maslow tried to build a bridge between East and West by making growth contingent on taking care of survival needs first.

But Maslow's model cannot be right, at least not in its purest form. Not because psychological growth is an illusion, and not because we can ignore threats to our well-being, but because positive strivings do not depend on the satisfaction of more basic needs. We struggle for survival to meet basic needs every day, and we also strive for happiness, seek excellence, and hope to learn and develop ourselves, and we may also do these things every day if we are fortunate enough. We attend to both sets of needs. On the same day on which we struggle with anxiety over a delinquent bill, we might recall with pride the day we brought a child into this life or have a good laugh with our colleagues over a scene from a risqué movie such as *The Full Monty*. What we do when we wrestle with demons, both those within ourselves and those from without, represents one important part of life's drama. But the dance we do to fulfill our desires, our goals and ambitions for ourselves, represents another, altogether separate part of the drama that occupies our consciousness. Our quality of life depends on how successfully we conduct both missions.

Fred Herzberg, a renowned industrial psychologist, was one of the first to recognize that people had dual purposes at work: to minimize dissatisfaction from the many potential sources of job stress and to maximize job satisfaction, which arises from opportunities for accomplishment. Indeed, he challenged Maslow's model on these same grounds, citing the example of the "starving artist" as someone who can strive for fulfillment even when basic needs are not met (Herzberg, 1966). He once told me that Maslow, on his deathbed, whispered to him, "Fred, you were right all along."

Is that story true? Maybe not. But whether or not Maslow confessed to the shortcomings of his model, there is considerable evidence to support two-dimensional models of psychological well-being. This book is written as an invitation to readers to engage in two-dimensional thinking about themselves and others. Keeping these two dimensions of human motivation separate can lead to a fuller understanding of human strivings to sustain and enhance the quality of life. This view also can eliminate travels down many blind alleys—a consequence of trying to live only in accord with either the West Coast's model of growth or the East Coast's model of defense. It offers a "new math" for measuring the "goodness" of one's life that goes beyond the simple addition and subtraction, the weighing of good feelings against the bad, that so often characterizes one-dimensional thinking.

In the chapters that follow, I present the research evidence for a two-dimensional view of health and well-being, along with its implications for how we think about everyday events, cope with difficulties, and find sources of satisfaction and meaning in our lives. Indeed, the two-dimensional view of emotions is a fundamental part of the story I tell in this book.

There is a second part to this story as well. Our lives and our models of ourselves are not divided in two at all times. Rather, over the course of daily life the degree of independence in our judgments about our emotions shifts dynamically in response to demands of the situation. Under stressful conditions, demands for a more unified response to the threat can change the dynamics of the inner discourse between negative and positive emotions. During these times, positive feelings can erase negative feelings from consciousness, and negative affects can overwhelm positive ones. In many ways this is an adaptive response to stressful situations. During combat, falling in love, or even while wrestling with your steering wheel on a icy street to avoid skidding into a parked car, we do well to focus on the affective information necessary to make decisive judgments. These are often defining moments in our lives, when our primary beliefs about ourselves, our capacities for life, our vulnerability, and our resiliency are forged. The fusion of affective states, however, is neither ordinary nor a desirable condition for the preservation of psychological well-being most of the time. As I describe in detail later in this book, narrowing the bandwidth of emotional experience will get us in trouble if it is prolonged, and when misapplied, it will inevitably lead us to mistaken judgments at critical junctures. Indeed, individuals differ in how well they can restrain the impulse to oversimplify their emotional lives.

Richness in emotional experience is central to quality of life. We need to be capable of feeling joy and grief, anger, and also humility and gratitude. But to ask how one set of emotions influences another is a much more complex question than people have cared to consider before. This book describes how thinking about emotions and fully embracing emotions in all their complexity changes the meaning of adaptation to stress and offers a broader and more differentiated understanding of the dynamic role of emotions in health and psychological well-being.

I present this emergent view, drawing in part on an analysis of empirical studies that my colleagues and I have conducted and in part on the work of other research teams. My aim is to provide an integrated perspective on stress and adaptation that highlights the role of emotions in the preservation of health and recovery from illness.

Organization of the Book

In the first chapters I set out some basic definitions of emotion and stress. I ask, What are emotions and where do they come from? I offer a brief review of the scientific literature on these questions and present my forecast of where the fields of emotion and stress are heading. I annotate the chapters with notes and references that may interest readers who wish to obtain a more comprehensive grasp of the work in these fields. From the start I try to alert the reader to the complex interplay between emotions, stress, and health.

Chapter 4 is the turning point in this book, because it is in this chapter that I first lay out the foundation for understanding how stress influences our experience of emotions. The research evidence clearly points to significant changes in the contours of our affective consciousness during stressful times. Here, and in a later chapter on attention, I point out how a dynamic model of emotion helps us understand how our minds adapt in times of difficulty.

At this point in the book, a critical question arises. If positive emotions are indeed independent of negative emotional states, of what benefit are those emotions? Chapters 5 and 6 address this question. Chapter 5 focuses on the influences of positive emotions on mental health, and chapter 6 focuses on physical health. A second, much broader question arises in chapter 7, namely, how we define optimal emotional health. In that chapter, I urge that we broaden and deepen our understanding of what constitutes emotional well-being beyond the conventions of coping and adjustment that are in vogue today.

My intent in the subsequent set of chapters is to demonstrate that a full understanding of the dynamics of emotion and stress has broad reach. I provide an analysis of several public health problems to illustrate the applicability of the approach, including separate chapters on the problems of chronic pain, child abuse, and addiction. In mental health domains, I focus on depression and anxiety, which are among the most prevalent forms of psychopathology. I discuss how attention to the dynamics of emotions and stress can help us understand these conditions better and offer new ways to intervene therapeutically. Finally, I briefly examine how the understanding of the dynamic relationships between emotions and stress may inform us about broader social concerns with chapters on work, marriage, aging, and community.

This is not a self-help book, so the reader will not find a prescription for a happier life contained between the covers. However, it does offer a novel perspective on the many problems in everyday life and encourages the reader to examine his or her own life in new ways.

It is book for people who are mindful of the psychological dimensions of life. It will be of greatest interest to those who have a penchant for reading about the inner workings of people. The book will be of special interest to those in the helping professions, such as psychologists, counselors, psychiatric nurses, and social workers. Educators teaching undergraduate courses in abnormal psychology, the psychology of adjustment, human motivation, and health psychology may find the book a useful supplement to a primary text. In courses on emotions and health, it could serve as the main text around which a course may be organized. As a researcher, as well as an educator, I also hope to stir up interest among behavioral scientists and graduate students who are investigating how stress and emotions influence health.

Acknowledgments

Many people have contributed to this work. Although citations allow me to reference the published work of scholars, my colleagues, friends, and students at Arizona State University have provided me with much more. Through discussions and debates on the role of emotions in stress and health, the members of our Cognition and Affect Research Team have guided my work. John Reich, my lifelong collaborator in research, has inspired me with his energy and convictions regarding how cognitive processes shape our emotional experiences. Mary Davis has brought her perceptiveness of the inner experiences of men and women to our many discussions of emotions and health. Her close reading of my early drafts helped improve the clarity and organization of many of the chapters. One of my students, Phil Potter, by virtue of his quiet yet compelling intellect, brought me back to the twin themes of emotions and stress that I had once abandoned. This book would not have been written without his influence. Another former student, Bruce Smith, has made key contributions through his own research on the role of emotions in resilience and vulnerability to chronic stress, as well as in our work together. Both undergraduate and graduate students who have been members of my class on "Emotions, Stress, and Health" have made many of the ideas presented here come to life. Some have provided examples from their own lives, and others have taught me lessons from philosophies of social science that cast the themes of this book into a broader context. Last, I owe much gratitude to two colleagues who helped edit this work, Benjamin Gottlieb and Howard Tennen, who devoted many hours to reading an earlier draft of this manuscript. Their challenges to my thinking, as well as my grammar, added substantially to the quality of this work.

Early in my career, three wise men guided me through my studies: Ernst Beier, Bruce Dohrenwend, and Fred Herzberg. Each had his own gifts, and each followed his own star, but together they offered a view of stress and emotions with a depth, clarity, and scope that I could not have thought possible. I have had such good fortune to have been mentored by not just one but three masters within the psychological disciplines. They have taught me to look to both the pursuit of happiness and the defense against threat as guides to understanding human adaptation. I invite you to do the same.

Contents

Emotions, Stress, and Health

1   The Nature of Emotional Experiences

Our mind is capable of passing beyond
The dividing line we have drawn for it.
Beyond the pairs of opposites of which the world consists,
other, new insights begin.
                    —Hermann Hesse, "Inside and Outside"

I watched my 4-year-old son approach some waves one day. We were at a water park in the desert, so the waves were made, not by the pull of the moon, but mechanically, with levers instead. Even though it is not the ocean, people flock there just the same. It is an oasis of rhythms: a large body of water rising, falling, and rising again. My son approached these waves with delight, eyes sparkling, and voice pitched high. Yet he stood back a bit, not quite ready to jump in, a bit apprehensive. He was displaying two basic emotions: joy and fear. He seemed to experience them nearly simultaneously, even though they are very different feeling states. Where did he get such a rich feeling repertoire? Allow me to review some possibilities. First, we might consider emotions to be a sensory experience, like hearing, sight, smell, taste, and touch. It could be a sixth sense, focused not on the detection of external events but on internal states, not so different from sensing muscle tone within our bodies. Though part of what we mean by *emotion* may be captured as a sensory experience, there are a few difficulties with this idea. First, anatomically, no specific area exists in the cortex for an emotional sense, as exists for the five senses. Emotions appear to be more centrally located. In fact, emotions pervade all our sensory experiences to a great extent and give those sensations meaning. When a man looks at what he believes to be a beautiful woman, his emotions are focusing this gaze, shaping the image he sees. The same inner excitement he feels focuses other senses as well. Emotions are not one of the senses. They appear to be better described as organizers of meaning, providing direction to our senses.

This quality of emotions brings up a second fundamental distinction between emotions and our sensory experiences. Emotions often urge certain sets of actions. Some emotion theorists have defined emotions as just that, "action-tendencies,"[1] like the desire to run away from something we fear. These feelings not only orient us to what we see, hear, smell and taste, but they also direct our behavior to a large extent. So in a way the cortex's motor strip, as well as the other sensory organizers of our experiences, are governed, at least in part, by our emotions.

William James and his colleague Carl Lange came up with a different view of emotions.[2] They saw emotions as a consequence rather than a cause of our reactions to stimuli. We observe ourselves behaving in some way, having certain patterns of physiological arousal, and arrive at a label for that experience. Thus we do not run because we are afraid, but rather we are afraid because we run. This work extends to facial movements as well. So we do not smile because we are happy, but we are happy because we smile.

Researchers who failed to find sufficient specificity in physiological responses to differentiate among emotional states in response to events discredited this model, at least in part.[3] Most human behavioral responses do not correspond to one and only one emotional display. When we are running, is it away from something or toward something else? How then do we know what we feel if we cannot infer it from our behavior?

Perhaps we just figure out how we feel logically. Stanley Schachter and Jerome Singer's (1962) research ignited a wave of interest in cognitive models of emotion.[4] From their perspective, feelings arise from how we appraise or interpret bodily sensations. If these states are undifferentiated, as physiologist Walter Cannon (1927) suggested, then information about what we are feeling must come from elsewhere. Schachter and Singer (1962) posited that specific emotions were determined by cognitive processing of contextual cues. So, after seeing a bear, we interpret our arousal as fear because we know that bears are potentially hazardous to our health and well-being. Then we run.

Many psychologists (myself included) accepted this cognition-first model as gospel when it came to defining emotions. Appraisal theories of emotion became the most popular. One appraisal theorist who has been especially influential is Richard Lazarus (1982, 1984).[5] He proposed that mechanisms of appraisal of the potential for harm, loss, or benefit from events are at the heart of many of our emotional reactions. In early versions of his model, these appraisals were seen as thoughtful, deliberate evaluations of events. There are two types of appraisals in Lazarus's model: *primary* appraisals, which are initial judgments of adaptation demands of the event, and *secondary* appraisals, which constitute evaluations of the ability to cope with the event. The better equipped we are to respond effectively, the more benign the resulting emotional reaction to the event will be. In his early experiments, Lazarus showed students movies of rather grisly events, such as subincision, an Australian aborigine rite of passage in which the young male of the tribe has the tip of his penis sliced. Emotional reactions, both self-reports and physiological recordings of heart rate and blood pressure, varied as a function of the sound track: high reactivity and negative emotions were seen when the act was described as painful and unhealthy, low reactivity was evidenced when the subincision was described as a bold symbol of emergent manhood.

The cognitive model for understanding emotion has reigned supreme for 25 years because of its broad applicability. However, there were many defects in the model, and these defects have led many researchers to question the usefulness of the model altogether. First, it is well known that we often react to fear-producing stimuli before we are aware that we are afraid. So there is a timing problem. That problem suggests that both analysis and response to threat could be independent of conscious appraisal and are quicker, more automatic, and even more effective than appraisal-based emotional responses.

One major challenge to the appraisal-first theories of emotion arose from the research of Robert Zajonc (1980, 1985).[6] Zajonc reasoned that if at least some emotional responses to stimuli could be shown to occur without awareness, then the cognitive model could not be right, at least not exactly right. Zajonc searched for a way to display a stimulus to participants in his experiments without the participants being aware of the display. He found an answer in an old technique thought to induce what is called subliminal perception. He projected a series of images onto a screen but did it so quickly that the participants in the study could not actually recall that they had seen the images. He varied the number of times he projected these images, all the while checking his data to make sure his participants did not guess at better than chance levels that they actually saw the image. After presenting the images, he asked the study participants which of them they liked best. He reasoned that people would prefer the familiar to the unfamiliar, all else being equal. Play a record over and over and it becomes popular. (By the way, this principle was at the root of the payola scandal in the late 1950s, when rock and roll was taking hold. Radio station disk jockeys would take bribes to play someone's music over and over, giving those songs an advantage on the Hit Parade.)

Zajonc's results confirmed his suspicions. The images presented more frequently were preferred over those presented infrequently. Further, the participants had no idea whether the image had actually been presented at all. Their emotional reactions to the images were generated unconsciously. Or, as Zajonc (1980) phrased it in the title of his work, "Preferences need no inferences." A door was opened by Zajonc's work, a door to understanding emotions as something more than mere products of the mind. Emotions appear to have meaning and purpose independent of what we think of them.

Emotions as Fundamental Processes

As clever as Zajonc's experiments were in pointing out the tears in the cognitive fabric, there is even more convincing evidence that emotions are not mental constructions. This evidence comes from the many cross-cultural studies of the communication of emotions. Those studies reveal that basic human emotions are hardwired to a great extent. Ask an expressive person to make a face that shows anger. Take a picture of that face and show it around. Do you think people will accurately identify that emotion? They can. Are the rules for identifying emotion via facial expression universal? Suppose these pictures were shown to villagers from tribes in the jungles of New Zealand or Borneo, people who have had little or no experience with our culture. Would those people correctly identify basic emotions such as anger, fear, joy, and sorrow? Those studies have been done, and the evidence is in. Basic emotions are communicated via the face through universal symbols (Ekman, 1994a, 1994b; Izard, 1994; Russell, 1994). What about other channels of communication, through sound, for instance? Will someone from the South Bronx interpret the sound of happiness in the same manner as someone from Poland or Japan? It turns out that they do (Scherer, 1986).[8]

Just how basic are these neurological programs for expression and recognition of emotions? A neuroscientist with an ear for the melodies of emotion, Manfred Clynes (1978), has demonstrated just how hardwired we are through an instrument called the sentograph. The sentograph is a very simple device. It records the amount of pressure exerted by an index finger pressing on a button. There are two dimensions of pressure—vertical (up and down) and horizontal (forward or back)—and both are recorded by the sentograph over very brief time intervals, usually around 2 seconds. The device averages between 30 and 50 repeated expressions of the same emotion to produce two summary waveforms. These waveforms, or sentograms, depict the amount of finger pressure up or down and forward or back for the average of each person's set of 30 to 50 two-second expressions.

What do these sentograms have to do with the fundamentals of emotion? It turns out that even by altering the simple pressure of a finger, we display emotions, and we do so in the same way, no matter which side of the globe we live on. Clynes (1978) has shown that certain patterns of fingertip pressure are understood universally as distinct emotions. To prove his point, he trained people to reproduce certain patterns and then asked them what emotion they would assign to that pattern. With a very high degree of consensus, around 80% for most patterns, people rated just the pattern of movement of their fingers as indicative of distinct emotions.

In figure 1.1 I have reproduced his sentograph depictions of two positive emotions: nonerotic love and sexual feelings. Note the smooth, gentle

A. Love expressed as finger pressure

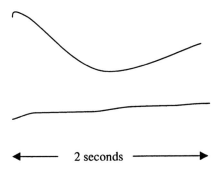

◄——— 2 seconds ———►

B. Sexual feelings as expressed by finger pressure

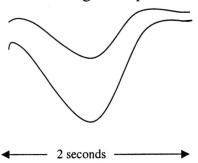

◄——— 2 seconds ———►

Figure 1.1. Clynes' sentograph depictions of two positive emotions.

patterning of the expression for love in the top graph. By closing your eyes and pressing your finger onto a semifirm surface with the same pattern in mind, you can get a feel for the emotional message embedded within this figure. Now look at sexual feelings: There is excitement built into that form through the sharp angle of descent in horizontal pressure. The shape of these forms of emotion produced through finger pressure is also consistent across cultures. Clynes believes they are built within our nervous systems. They are universal rhythms of the mind.

Clynes (1982) has found these same patterns in music, based on changes in frequency of the sounds over time. Sadness issues forth in the blues, and sexual excitement jolts us in hard rock (mom was right about that all along). To Clynes, music pieces are stories of emotion told in all their complexity, with feelings layered over other feelings, some lasting, others fleeting, still others developing in sequences that connect us all through universal codes for the experience and interpretation of emotion. These forms of emotional expression are embedded within us and provide a fundamental basis for understanding and communicating with one another. They are not only on our faces or in our voices, hearts, or our gut; they emerge from every pore. To appreciate just how central these emotion programs are, I turn next to some of the latest developments in studies of the brain.

The Neuroscience of Emotions

At the start of the last decade of the twentieth century, then President George Bush declared that the 1990s would be the "decade of the brain." Few could have anticipated that the emphasis on the brain would lead us to discoveries that would put us so much in touch with our emotions. Neuroscience has indeed blossomed over the past decade, with the annual meetings of the Society for Neuroscience now attracting more than 40,000 participants, the largest scientific meeting in the country. From 1990 on, brain-behavior researchers have captivated us with discovery after discovery about how behavior is linked to neural processes. New techniques of brain imaging give us photographs of the brain in action, and not only in response to motor movements. These brain images appear to capture our thought processes as well. The resolution is not very clear at present. It is like the movie *Photographing Fairies*. We see smudges on the video screen, and those smudges change when we ask our participant to recall a word or phrase. We know something is happening because we can detect a change in the image. Is it really a thought we have spotted on the brain scan? Maybe it is. And that's pretty exciting. And if we can see thoughts, why not go deeper? Why not see if we can locate emotions as well?

One popular theory places the experience of all emotions on the right side of the brain.[9] There have been many popular accounts of this theory, as well as empirical studies that have found evidence of emotional reactivity most prominently on the right side, particularly in the dorsal-lateral frontal cortex. One key structure that underlies this region is the amygdala, which is seated centrally within the brain just below the cortex. This almond-shaped brain structure is the Grand Central Station of fear. In fact, people with brain lesions only in the amygdala find themselves rather fearless.[10] By the way, being without fear does not mean that one loses other negative emotions. And the person can still be hurt. Pain, for instance, is still experienced by those who have lost their amygdalas. Only the anticipation of future pain is lost. Although the loss of anticipatory reactions to negative events would certainly reduce the experience of pain, we would not know enough to avoid pain in the future, and plans to protect ourselves from any number of possible harms would fall on fallow ground without these emotional warning signals. No, we would not function well without an amygdala.

Fear is only one of several negative emotions that scientists have attempted to map within the brain. Different patterns of neural activity underlie different emotions.[11] It is fair to say that there is not just one center for emotion but many centers; each is devoted to mounting adaptive responses, but for different purposes.

The new direction in neuroscience has been to study emotional processes such as fear as an integral part of our thinking rather than to attempt to segregate thoughts from feelings. Antonio Damasio called the separation of mind from emotion Descartes's error (1994).[12] René Descartes was noted for separating mind from body, postulating that the study of the mind should proceed without reference to the mechanics of the body. This was quite a liberating philosophy of science, allowing biomedical science to advance unconstrained by the force of theological arguments over such matters as the location of the soul within the body. Mind-body dualism also allowed psychological sciences to emerge without having to provide some physical manifestation for every construct under study. One could study anger, for example, without seeing red, and one could measure intellectual functioning without resorting to phrenology. Cognitive sciences grew out of this mind-body tradition and have made extraordinary advances in understanding how the brain works as a computational device, processing information, reducing uncertainty, and guiding decision making.

However, like all models, the computational model does not fit the data of everyday experience all that well. The problem is that the brain is not just a high-speed computing device; it is more like a gland: wet with neurochemical signaling of approach and avoidance, pleasure and pain, anger, fear, joy, and various combinations of these states and signals (Sapolsky, 1994). These emotions provide the context within which we process information, evaluate events, calculate our odds, and act on those calculations. As much as we might like to think otherwise, the mind, it seems, is really still in the body.

One of the prominent neuroscientists dedicated to the study of emotion is Joseph LeDoux (1996). LeDoux first became interested in emotion while studying patients with brains severed by injury or from needed surgery so that their left and right brains could no longer communicate through the usual pathways. In the course of this work, he encountered a patient with a split brain who could visualize words presented to either the left or the right hemisphere of the brain (it is possible to do this by presenting images to certain visual fields on the retina but not others). As in most of us, the centers for language comprehension and speech were located in the patient's the left hemisphere, so the patient could speak about events that gained entry to the left side of his brain. Without connections across hemispheres, he was at a loss to report on what he had seen on the right side. The classic problem for these patients is being able to name an object they pick up with the left hand (which sends signals to the right hemisphere). Even though they can manipulate it correctly in that hand, they cannot identify the object. Imagine holding the winning *Reader's Digest* sweepstakes entry in one hand but not being able to tell yourself what you are holding, let alone tell anyone else about it.

LeDoux (1996) showed the patient words that had definite emotional connotations. *Mom* was one of the words, *Devil* another. When LeDoux displayed these words to the patient's left hemisphere, the patient could read and report what he saw, as well as evaluate whether the word referred to something good or bad. When the words were presented to the right hemisphere, however, the patient could not report what word was presented, because this information could not cross over to the left side of his brain where language was available. What he could do, surprisingly, was report on whether the word carried the connotation of a good or a bad emotion. The routes of transmission of emotional meaning were different from those carrying verbal meaning. LeDoux (1996) thus saw evidence early in his career that emotions could be felt independent of verbal meaning structures in the brain.

Emotions are systems of neurophysiological response, according to LeDoux (1996). Many emotion researchers, including Carroll Izard (1971) and Silvan Tomkins (1962, 1963, 1984, 1991) share this view. In Le-

Doux's (1996) model of the brain, the thalamus and the amygdala play key roles in processing inputs, responding to potential threats, and also sending signals along for further processing by the neocortex. He sees the basic patterns of emotional response as universal not only for humans but also across many vertebrate species. In evolutionary terms, this makes sense. The processes of adaptation started long before *Homo sapiens* arrived on the scene. Emotions are systems that aid adaptation in all animals. They provide a powerful means of integrating responses to the pressures from the external world with the needs of the inner world. And if the emotional processing systems worked well for other animals, why change them when it comes to humans?

Paul Ekman has reissued Charles Darwin's classic text, *The Expression of Emotion in Man and Animals* (Darwin, 1872/1998).[13] As Darwin and many others have reported, the biomechanics of emotional expression are highly similar across species, as well as within a species. Those pictures of man and chimp baring teeth are uncanny in their likeness. So too are the lowered brow and downward pulse on the face of sorrow in both. Given the evidence, the conclusion seems inescapable that many expressions of emotion are molded within our minds from genetic material. When those responses are elicited is largely, but not completely, a product of cultural rules governing the expression and interpretation of feeling states. Some stimuli are likely to have universal appeal and others will likely provoke near universal disgust.

Some emotions are indeed fundamental. Carroll Izard (1971) has identified 10 basic emotions, which may mix together like primary colors to give us many different feelings. Two of the ten are positive emotions: interest/excitement and joy. Seven others are negative emotions: distress/anguish, anger/rage, disgust/revulsion, contempt/scorn, fear/terror, shame/humiliation, guilt/remorse. Only one emotion, surprise, does not carry either a positive or negative valence by definition.

Many other classification systems for emotion exist. Interestingly, they all identify more negative emotions than positive ones. Based on his work on mapping unique emotional expressions in the human face, Paul Ekman (1982) has made a list of 17. Seven of Ekman's "basic" emotions are clearly positive, but he reports that the positive emotions, unlike negative emotions, do not differ as much from one another in expression. Although each negative emotion has a unique signature when expressed on the human face, positive emotions all share a single set of facial muscle movements that together portray a genuine smile.[14]

John Cacioppo and colleagues (Berntson, Cacioppo, & Gardner, 1999; Cacioppo & Berntson, 1994) remark on the evolutionary significance of what they call the "negativity bias" in taste as well as other perceptual systems. Our taste buds can detect sweetness at 1 part per 200 but bitterness in 1 part per 2,000,000. From the point of view of survival, it is more important to detect toxins (many of which do taste bitter) than to ensure a proper balance of carbohydrates in our diets.

Suppose two people are standing side by side across the room. One is a smiling, attractive member of the opposite sex, who appears to be beckoning to you to come closer. The other has a menacing look, hot with anger, and appears to be leering just at you. To whom would you pay more attention? I posed this question to members of my class on emotions. Everyone agreed. The menacing look holds our attention more. Our bias in attending to negative affects more than positive ones can be attributed to the simple fact that death has to win only once. It also makes sense for our bodies and minds to come equipped with the capacity to distinguish among more types of negative emotions than positive ones. Natural selection favors those who develop a greater appreciation for what might harm them.

We can distinguish among our feelings to the extent that we are conscious of these emotional rumblings throughout our brains. And it pays to be aware of those feelings, because awareness allows us to amplify those feelings that we prefer and to quiet those emotional responses that threaten us. But how much control do we really have? Researchers differ considerably in the extent to which they grant people much influence over their emotional destinies. LeDoux (1996), for example, believes we have few effective ways to manage our emotions. This raises an interesting question, however. If we could not exercise control over our emotions, then why would we have developed such a keen capacity to be aware of what we feel? The cerebral cortex may have evolved for just that purpose: to regulate our emotional responses. In fact, our feelings provide not only a window to our emotions, but the first stage of feedback to ourselves about how well we are doing in managing our interactions with the world. The information contained in those feeling bundles keeps us alert to possibilities for changing things, perhaps by regulating how much we will listen to those pulses from within and take action on the world around us.

In sum our emotions are dynamic systems that guide our adaptations to a complex and changing environment. These systems serve us well by providing mechanisms of response to life's many opportunities and its many threats to our well-being. Our emotions operate within the context of the personal meanings that we assign events. Richard Lazarus (1991), in a restatement of his model, reminds us that emotions are complex cognitive-motivational-relational systems of evaluation and intention.[15] Indeed, reformulated cognitive approaches have demonstrated that appraisals play a prominent role in shaping the full expression of emotions by evaluating events in light of our own goals, standards, and relationships (Clore & Ortony, 2000, Frijda, 1993; Stein, Trabasso, & Liwag, 1993). But it would be a mistake to see these emotional systems as simple by-products of our goals and plans, rising up like the tides to defend our interests only when needed. It is much more interesting than that. Our emotions also shape the very goals that we develop for ourselves. They provide the basic motivational templates from which we find purpose and meaning.

Our emotional responses are complex, sometimes even contradictory. Indeed, their origins may be best understood by invoking a fundamental evolutionary principle: *Form follows function*. The form that our emotional systems take was not preordained; it is the result of millions of years of test drives on the savanna. Those systems that functioned well survived. New systems that also worked well were added on. We might hope to find a blueprint that maps out exactly how each neuromodulating molecule fits into a grand scheme of emotion regulation. But such a blueprint does not exist. We have evolved a set of systems full of repeats, confounds, disjunctions, and conjunctions. It appears a bit messy on the surface, but it works splendidly out on the open road.

One of the implications of an evolutionary approach is that we have evolved not just one emotion system. My son shouts with glee but stands back from that wave, not because he is ambivalent. He displays no discomfort at feeling two emotions at the same time. That is because he, like all of us, has evolved more than one system of emotional response in order to handle a complex world adaptively.

In the chapters that follow I develop this idea of separable emotion systems. I focus on two systems in particular, and they provide a framework for much of the discourse of this book. One of those systems takes care of those survival needs by responding adequately to threat. This is LeDoux's (1996) defense system. It goes by other names as well. The other system is that of enjoyment, psychological growth, and positive affective action. There may be more systems, as well, but in this book I emphasize those two. Each has been built with evolutionary clay and formed and hardened by repeated testing. The two systems arose to fulfill different functions and so evolved separately. One is not more or less mature than the other. Rather, each represents different motivational principles of living. When we say, "I am of two minds about that," we can sometimes hear them both calling for our attention. We have spent much time within psychology studying the processes of coping with and adjusting to harm. We have attended, foremost, to the resolution of the negative emotions, perhaps because they appear so dangerous, and have discounted positive emotions as less immediate concerns. Now it is time to approach the understanding of our emotions with both agendas in mind.

2   Emotions in Two Dimensions

> Was he free, was he happy, the question is absurd
> Had anything been wrong, we should certainly have heard
> —W. H. Auden, "The Unknown Citizen"

In this chapter I develop the idea that emotions are best understood from a two-dimensional framework. To understand these two faces of emotion, we could start with the question Auden poses in his poem about the Unknown Citizen. When he asks, "Was he happy?" he challenges us to think beyond life's problems when seeking to understand one another. If you have ever asked yourself, "Am I really happy?" you know just how complex such a simple question can turn out to be.[1] It turns out that there is more than one answer to this question. This, in a nutshell, is the lesson that a two-dimensional approach provides.

"Is my cup half full or half empty?" Here, again, we are struck with a question far more complex than it appears on the surface. The question also seems to pose a paradox. There is no single correct reply. Only by taking a point of view can we answer the question at all, and our choice would appear purely subjective. When optimistic, we see the cup as half full, and when pessimistic, we see the cup as half empty. This is hardly satisfying. As I discuss in this chapter, our error is in searching for a single answer. By doing so we miss the obvious and correct response to the question: Our cups are *both* half full *and* half empty. One part of us attends to what we have gained, but another part of us is keenly aware of what we may have lost. To resolve paradoxes such as these about what we feel, we need to look critically at some of our basic assumptions regarding positive and negative emotions.

Most of us believe that to feel good means not to feel bad, that positive feelings are incompatible with negative feelings. These statements are simple truths built from the language of feelings, affects, and emotions that are as commonsensical as one plus one equals two. But in fact, performing even such simple arithmetic on our emotions is tantamount to adding apples and oranges, particularly when it comes to comparing many positive and negative affective states. Indeed, it appears that much of the time, positive and negative feeling states are not opposites at all. They represent distinct emotional forces in our lives. Consequently, we can and do feel good even though we are feeling bad. We can have bittersweet memories of past innocence or anxious excitement about the prospects of a new romance.

This simple idea about how people experience affects has some extraordinary implications for how people's needs and problems are assessed and how effective various therapeutic interventions will be. By allowing for the existence of multiple conflicting emotions, we can stop worrying about whether we are happy or not. We are probably both. We do not have to solve every riddle over our mixed emotions. How often is it that we do not know how to describe our feelings? I suspect at least some of those times we are searching unsuccessfully to find the single best emotion with which to understand ourselves. But we are often "of two minds" about things, and what we lose in simplicity we can gain in clarity.

Our language does not always help us think about emotions in all their complexity. The classic model of emotion dimensions was based on judgments of words that describe feeling states. Through analyses of ratings of degrees of difference between affect-laden words, Charles Osgood and his colleagues (Osgood, Suci, & Tannenbaum, 1957) identified three primary dimensions of judgment: evaluation, activity, and potency. The dimension of *evaluation* ranges from highly positive to highly negative along a single continuum and is the most salient of the three. *Activity* refers to the level of arousal or energy that the word connotes. For example, *sleepy* would be low and *alert* high on this continuum. *Potency* refers to strength or, in some contexts, control. Words that connote power are potent, and those that suggest weakness are not. With some methodological improvements,[1] these dimensions of affective judgment are still considered to be primary in the classification of emotive aspects of language. When we sit in summary judgment about important events in our lives, including our feelings about those events, we employ these dimensions. Indeed, we often place events along a continuum from bad to good, as well as using the other dimensions that Osgood et al. (1957) had identified to classify our experiences.

Norman Bradburn (1969) and his colleague David Caplovitz (Bradburn & Caplovitz, 1965) uncovered something quite unexpected when they asked people across the country to report on what they actually experienced, not just how they judged their experiences. As part of a national survey of happiness, they asked literally thousands of people whether they had experienced feelings such as "depressed or unhappy" and "very lonely, or remote from other people" over the previous few weeks. They also asked about positive feelings, such as being "on top of the world" and "particularly excited or interested in something." When they asked the questions in this way, they found that the number of positive emotions the person experienced was independent of the number of his or her negative emotions. In other words, one could not predict how happy the person was from how unhappy he or she was.

Bradburn (1969) went further with these analyses and asked whether differences in social conditions influenced positive and negative feelings in the same way. Interestingly, different conditions influenced different dimensions of affect. People who were financially strapped generally had more negative affect but not less positive affect than those with average incomes. Those people who participated most in social groups had the most positive affect, but they did not have less negative affect. Thus some experiences led to more joy but not less sorrow, and other experiences led to more anxiety but no less excitement.

The idea that one type of experience can enhance positive feelings without influencing negative feelings and that another can enhance negative states without lowering positive ones had been anticipated several years before Bradburn's (1969) now-classic work by Fredrick Herzberg. Herzberg and his colleagues (Herzberg, 1966; Herzberg, Mausner, & Snyderman, 1959)[3] asked midlevel managers to report on critical events that represented a significant change for the better or for the worse in their working lives—events related to either increases in job satisfaction or job dissatisfaction. When the researchers analyzed the data, they found that managers reported one set of events when discussing times of high job satisfaction and an entirely different set of events when describing events that contributed to their job dissatisfaction. Events that derived from the work itself were sources of job satisfaction. Among these were events classified as "achievement" and "personal growth." The managers did not mention the lack of opportunity to achieve as sources of job dissatisfaction, however. Events that were sources of job dissatisfaction arose from supervision, pay, and other aspects of the job environment. Interestingly enough, material rewards, such as increases in pay and bigger offices, were rarely mentioned as critically satisfying events (Herzberg, 1966; Herzberg et al., 1959).

The works by Bradburn and by Herzberg and colleagues were similar in two important respects. First, they introduced the idea that many positive affective states were not simply the opposite of negative states. Second, and in many ways more important, they found evidence to suggest that different features of the person's experiences in the world were responsible for these affective states. Their findings are not limited to community and work life. Researchers studying the joys and sorrows of raising children, the vicissitudes of friendship, and the attraction and fears of intimacy have found worlds divided into positive and negative spheres. Knowledge of the positives tells us little about the extent of the negatives. Likewise, knowledge of the negatives does not predict the positives. In life we are dealt both winning and losing hands.

To understand the significance of this point, it might be useful to contrast it with a fairly well-accepted model of how life circumstances influence a person's sense of well-being: adaptation-level (AL) theory (Helson, 1964; Frederick & Loewenstein, 1999).[4] In this model, emotions are experienced along a continuum of positive and negative, and our scales of judgment adjust to each new input by resetting the neutral point for rating new events based on the goodness and magnitude of prior events. Many highly positive experiences would lead us to reset our neutral points so that each new event would be evaluated less positively because of the resetting of our adaptation levels. Thus all happiness is relative and can bring about unhappiness through these changes in the adaptation level. AL theory is a sour-grapes model of happiness; it predicts more trouble sustaining happiness among those who attain extraordinary rewards than among those who do not.

From Bradburn's (1969) perspective, events influence emotions differently. A highly positive event would increase positive affect, and its impact may influence how other affective experiences influence happiness according to AL dynamics; but that event may have no effect on negative affective states. Thus, in Bradburn's (1969) model, lottery winners do not eventually become unhappy with their everyday lives as a natural consequence of winning big in the lottery, but in Helson's (1964) and other unidimensional models, they would.[5] Philip Brickman, Dan Coates, and Ronnie Janoff-Bulman (1978) interviewed a group of winners of the Michigan lottery to see how much they were enjoying their everyday lives a year or two after winning. All participants in the study had to have won at least $50,000 dollars, a fairly large sum in those days, and most had won substantially more money than that. The researchers selected a matched control group of nonwinners from among those who also bought lottery tickets. The results showed that the lottery winners were not happier with life than the nonwinners were, but, contrary to AL theory, they were not more unhappy, either (Brickman et al., 1978)

Life experiences often carry more than one emotional message. When we treat events as either positive *or* negative, we often miss the full meaning of those experiences. A study by Mary Westbrook (1976)[6] provides an illustration. Westbrook was concerned that that a simple 10-item scale, such as Bradburn (1969) had used, probably missed much of the meaning of experiences. She also worried that such questions might foster biases in reporting, such as the desire to look good (social desirability) or the tendency to be more agreeable, and thus to say yes to any question. Note that this bias would operate such that the person would say yes to questions about both negative and positive affect.[7]

To investigate positive affect without these biases, Westbrook (1976) developed trace measures of affects. A trace measure is an indirect method of observing a phenomenon by measuring its by-products. Electrons, for instance, leave a trail of disturbance behind them that is easier to detect with an electron microscope than is the electron itself, which is darting in and out of existence during the measurement interval. Westbrook (1976) recorded verbal samples from participants as they described important events in their lives. After transcribing those speech samples, she coded each clause for the presence of positive affect in each bundle of words, then summed them to get a total score, correcting along the way for the total number of words spoken.

This technique had already been perfected for detecting traces of a number of negative affects. Westbrook (1976) was the first to measure positive affect in this way. She collected data from a number of samples, but one stands out: 200 mothers recalling childbearing 2 to 7 months after giving birth. For that sample, Westbrook did not code only positive affect from the verbal samples. She also scored the same transcripts for a host of negative affective states, such as separation anxiety, death anxiety, mutilation anxiety, hostility expressed inward, and hostility expressed outward. Then she compared each person's positive affect score with her negative affect scores.

There was no relationship between a mother's reports of positive aspects of childbearing and her reports of any of the various forms of anxiety or hostility. The amount of positive emotion was independent of the negative emotions. This makes perfect sense once we stop to think about it. But no one collecting and coding these verbal affect traces had thought about it before Westbrook (1976) did. Conventional wisdom was that the most, perhaps the only, relevant aspect of childbearing was that it was stressful. But in fact, the joys of this emotional experience are at least as important as the sorrows. As Westbrook put it, "If childbearing is considered only in terms of women's negative affects, it is indeed a time of anxiety, depression and crisis" (1976, p. 718).

Since these early investigations of bidimensional models of emotion, a number of studies have been conducted on these issues with increasing precision in measurement and statistical analysis. For instance, David Watson and Auke Tellegen (1985; Tellegen, Watson, & Clark, 1999b) selected six published studies of transient self-reported affect, subjected the individual correlation matrices to factor analysis, and discovered that two principal dimensions consistently emerged: one positive and another negative. Other researchers have reached similar conclusions on the basis of factor analyses of emotion items: Positive affect terms and negative affect terms identify distinct dimensions of emotional experience.

This two-dimensional structure of emotion also holds across cultures. Most cross-cultural studies have simply translated items from English into another language. Church, Katigbak, Reyes, and Jensen (1999) took a much deeper look at structure by building a vocabulary of emotion words drawn from the Filipino culture they were studying.[8] Analyses of ratings of 147 emotion-laden adjectives revealed a similar two-dimensional structure of the words Filipinos use to express emotions. The overlap between the positive and negative emotion dimensions was about 4%—even smaller than what is often observed in the United States.

Watson, Weise, Vaidya, and Tellegen (1999) have recently updated their two-dimensional model of affective experiences. In doing so, they clarified the ways in which their model is different from the models which place positive and negatives at opposite ends of a single continuum. Rather than refer to these emotions as affects, they suggest that we refer to them as positive and negative *activation states*. By substituting this terminology, they are focusing attention on the presence, as opposed to the absence, of positive and negative emotions. Degree of excitement, interest, activity, and attraction fit as positive activation states, and these terms are on their list of positive states. However, *calm* and *relaxed* do not fit there, and are left off the list. On the negative side, fear, distress, and anxiety fit as negative activation states, but *tired* and *fatigued* do not (Watson et al., 1999).

One advantage of this classification scheme is that it provides greater clarity in defining emotional states. Highly arousing emotions are less ambiguous than low-arousal affects. There is little doubt that fear is a negative affect. But consider the emotion-laden term, *calm*. Does this refer to the presence of a positive state or the absence of an anxious state? Probably a bit of both. There is also an important issue of reliability of ratings. People are more likely to correctly identify the presence of something than its absence. When people have to make judgments about attitudes they do not hold, there is no telling what they might say. This principle is well established in attitude research but often is overlooked by otherwise sophisticated methodologists in research on self-reports of affect. People can rate how nervous and tense they feel much more easily than they can rate how free they are of tension or nervousness.[9]

One way to organize the many types of emotional states is to consider them as belonging to different families, as Paul Ekman (1982) suggests, or, more formally, as modes of activation. Here is where David Watson and colleagues (1999) model applies, and they are not alone in advocating separate systems for positive and negative activation. Other researchers refer to these two families as *appetitive* and *defensive* motivational systems. Still others use terms such as *approach* versus *avoidance* motivational systems. Although all our emotions do not map onto these various two-dimensional grids in exactly the same way, they have much in common.

Are there more than two families of emotion? That depends, at least in part, on what we consider to be a member of the family. Although positive and negative emotions appear to form primary dimensions, how do we account for the many distinct forms of emotion that lie within those two dimensions? Interest and joy, for example, may be like sister and brother, but they are certainly not the same feelings. Contentment is at least a cousin of joy, but probably not a member of the immediate family. What about the emotions that feed the "dark side," such as fear and anger? There are many members of these two families that deserve separate attention, even if the members within a family tend to show up together. I deal with some of these distinctions later. They become especially important when understanding clinical problems such as addiction and social problems such as violence in the community.

The Circumplex Model of Affect: An Alternative View

There is still controversy over how best to represent two dimensions of affect. Some maintain that positive and negative emotions are on separate dimensions and others argue that they are on opposite ends of the same continuum. The alternative model, proposed by James Russell and others (Feldman-Barrett & Russell, 1999; Russell & Carroll, 1999a, b), is called the circumplex model.[10] This model also classifies affects with a two-dimensional grid, but the axes have different labels. One dimension extends from positive to negative. The other extends from high arousal to low arousal. Indeed, this is a productive way to think about the ingredients of various affects: a certain amount of arousal plus a certain amount of pleasantness or unpleasantness. To illustrate the differences between Rus-

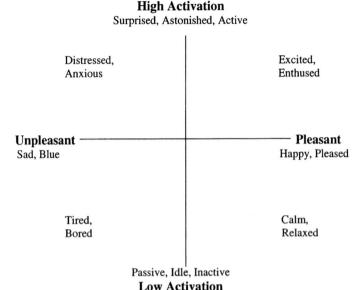

Figure 2.1. Russell's circumplex model.

sell & Carroll's (1999a) and Watson et al's (1999) models of emotion terms, we reproduce them here.

Both models have two-dimensional axes. Each axis represents a separate dimension, with affect words falling along these axes based on how related they are to each dimension. In figure 2.1, for instance, the word *surprise* is high in activation, so it is at the top of that dimension; but because *surprise* is neutral in its degree of pleasantness, it is placed at the midpoint of that scale. The word *excited"*, on the other hand, is both high on the activation dimension and highly pleasant, so it is placed to the right of *surprised*. *Happy* is less activating than *excited* but still high in pleasantness, so it is placed lower on the activation dimension, halfway between the high and low ends of that scale. Watson and colleagues (1999) also use a two-dimensional framework, but the axes refer to different dimensions. In this scheme, shown in figure 2.2, each word is placed on the graph based on two ingredients: the degree to which it activates positive emotions and the degree to which it activates negative emotions. Unlike in Russell's scheme, the opposite end of the high positive dimension is not high negative but the lack of positive emotion. So his scale classifies words such as *excited* at the top of the positive dimension and words such as *bored* at the bottom. On the negative dimension, the opposite of *distressed* is not *happy* but *calm*.

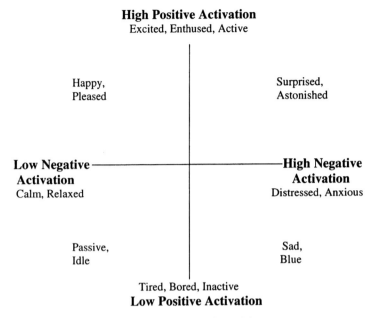

High Positive Activation
Excited, Enthused, Active

Happy,
Pleased

Surprised,
Astonished

Low Negative
Activation
Calm, Relaxed

High Negative
Activation
Distressed, Anxious

Passive,
Idle

Sad,
Blue

Tired, Bored, Inactive
Low Positive Activation

Figure 2.2. Watson's two-dimensional model.

Which model fits the data better? Neither model fits the data exactly. Positive affects are not completely independent of negative affects. At any given moment, can we really experience positive feelings as readily when we are feeling upset as we can when we are feeling calm? For instance, except perhaps for James Bond, it is physiologically impossible to be simultaneously sexually aroused and intensely anxious. This means that the two-dimensional space for positive and negative emotions is warped. Just how it is warped is a point discussed at some length later on.

But is arousal really independent of emotion? Consider the word *active*. This word should fit in as having medium to high arousal with neutral valence. But Watson's team (1999) has shown that this adjective correlates strongly with positive emotions. Indeed, these findings fit well with the logic of positive activation. The term implies approach rather than withdrawal. The converse applies for some low-arousal affect terms such as *uninterested*, which imply negative affect. Some researchers have suggested that the circumplex should be curved more, like a banana, to reflect a significant relationship between valence and arousal at the extremes; very high arousal is often negative, as is very low arousal. Indeed, most positive emotions are not located at the extremes of arousal.[11]

So what has this debate on the labeling of dimensions taught us? On the surface, there does not seem to be much to the debate. To argue that words such as *bad* and *good*, *happy* and *sad*, *anxious* and *calm* must be opposites seems to come right out of a page from Gertrude Stein: "Yes, an opposite is an opposite is an opposite." This is the semantic structure that guides our connotative language and, to some extent, our appraisals of how we feel. But consider this question: Is the experience of joy the opposite of the experience of sorrow? Do these emotions motivate the person to opposing thought and action that are directly contradictory?

Take ambient temperature, for example. I live in Phoenix, Arizona. It is a rather hot climate, as climates go, especially in the summer. We often pray for relief from the ovenlike temperatures that greet us whenever we climb in our cars after letting them sit in uncovered parking for 30 minutes or more. We want, even crave, a cool day. Now, cold is the undisputed opposite of hot. The physics of this are clear; cold is not only the opposite of heat, it is the absence of heat. If ever there were a clear bipolar dimension, it is temperature. In fact, the researchers who are most critical of the study of positive and negative affects as separate domains use temperature as an illustration of what they mean. Cold is the other end of the heat continuum from hot. This seems undeniable, does it not?

Manfred Clynes (1978) disputes such unidimensional thinking when it is applied to the neurobiology of experience. Although cold technically is the absence of heat, it is not experienced as the absence of heat stimulation but as the presence of cold. The math and physics of temperature do not guide our experiences. Biological systems do. As Clynes (1978) notes, there is a world of difference. Biological systems inform the judgment of temperature (and emotion) through dynamic changes in the activation of various molecular systems. Cold induces changes in our bodies that are unique beyond just the withdrawal of heat. Likewise, positive emotions are the result of a set of neurochemical events that are not simply the absence of neurochemical events that bring on negative emotions.

A circumplex model may provide the best coordinates for locating emotions in two dimensions, yet it may still miss the mark. An emotion provokes actions that take place in the body and follows biological rules, not trigonometric ones. As Clynes (1978) would say, our mathematics may produce a scale to measure emotions that goes from +3 to −3, but within the body there are no negative numbers, no way to subtract an action, except through another action.

I once asked my 4-year-old son to tell me whether the water in our swimming pool was warm or cold: a simple question that seems to have only one answer. There is, after all, only one temperature. People might disagree about how comfortable the temperature is, depending on their degree of sensitivity to cold. But they still can make only one evaluation of temperature, right?

My son gave me an unexpected response, however, one that I should have guessed all along. To explain his response you need a little background, particularly if you do not have young children. As of this writing, one of the best deals in town for kids (and their parents) is a soft ice-cream cone served at the drive-up window at McDonald's. You can get vanilla, chocolate, or a combination. When you get both, it comes out of the machine in two separate streams intertwined on top of the cone. It is called a "twist."

And that was my son's answer to the question about the pool water's temperature. "Twist, Dad," he said. "It's twist." He wrapped the two separate concepts of hot and cold around one another, just like chocolate and vanilla that are braided together at McDonald's. And when I stop to think about it, he is right. We do have two separate registers for temperature within us, one for hot and one for cold, even though the mercury in the thermometer rises and falls along a single dimension.

At a deeper level, the essential difference between these two models is that one is a top-down approach to emotion and the other a bottom-up approach. The top-down approach emphasizes higher-order cognitive processes in the experience of emotions. Dating back to experiments by Schachter and Singer (1962), this approach posits that emotion is a consequence of cognitive labels that we place on aroused states. The bottom-up model, illustrated by the work of Robert Zajonc (1980), focuses on ways that affect, not cognition, is primary. It is this model, with its strengths in the neuroscience of affect and motivation that I elaborate on next.

The Neurology of Positive and Negative Activation Systems

Activated states of positive and negative emotions appear to have separate neurobiological functions and perhaps even distinct anatomical structures. Different neurochemistry underlies the experience of positive feelings compared with the experience of negative emotions. Although we cannot designate a single chemical messenger in the brain (neurotransmitter) as the carrier of negative or positive feelings, the presence and/or relative absence of some neurochemicals have been correlated with good and bad feeling states. Considerable work has been done, for example, on the association between depletion of serotonin in the brain and the presence of negative emotion (Malenka, Hamblin, & Barchas, 1989; Panksepp, 1998). Biological psychiatry has relied on this principle in developing drugs designed to treat depression and other affective disorders. Another neurochemical, dopamine, has been linked to states of positive activation (see

Wise & Hoffman, 1992). Indeed, the dopamine system of neural connections in the brain is thought to underlie much of what we view as goal-directed behavior, through what Jaak Panksepp (1998) has referred to as the "seeking system."[12] The opioid system has been associated with pleasure and the relative absence of pain. Different drugs used for the control of pain, and at times abused for the pursuit of pleasure, have relied on emerging knowledge of the opioid family of neurochemicals. Another neurotransmitter, corticotropin-releasing hormone (CRH), increases significantly when we are under stress and mobilizes a number of neuromechanisms associated with emotions such as fear and anxiety. Every month new discoveries are made in the neurochemistry of emotion. Along with these investigations has come a new respect for the differences between positive and negative emotional states.

More intriguing still have been attempts to show that positive and negative emotions activate different brain structures. The first evidence of this came from research on differences in left- and right-brain reactivity to emotional stimuli. For instance, early studies showed that when emotionally disturbing films were projected only to the left visual field (which then transmitted them to only the right cerebral hemisphere), higher ratings of negative affect were produced than was the case when those same films were projected solely to the right visual field (and transmitted to the left hemisphere). Dimond, Farrington, and Johnson (1976) used the same methodology of projecting affect-laden images to left and right visual fields, except that they measured heart rate changes instead of self-reports of emotion. Amusing cartoons projected onto the left visual field provoked larger heart-rate changes than cartoons projected to the right side. However, with threatening films, the participants' heart rates sped up the most when the images were projected onto the right side of the brain.

Richard Davidson and his colleagues (Davidson, 1992; see Davidson, 2000, for a recent review) have advanced these initial studies using direct measures of brain activity. Their early work was done before modern imaging methods such as positron emission tomography (PET) and functional magnetic resonance imaging (fMRI) were available. Prior to the use of imaging, most neuroscientists relied on recordings of electrical activity taken from the surface of the human skull through the use of the electroencephalograph (EEG). (With nonhuman animals, researchers would sink electrodes into structures within the brain and stimulate various sites to locate sites for specific functions. People would not let you do that, and if they did, you would have to question their brain functioning.)

Davidson (1992, 2000) was among the most thorough of research scientists using EEG, mounting as many as 100 electrodes on the scalp. These

listening devices could detect and to some extent integrate the signals coming from electrical impulses within the brain. The stronger the signal coming from a given location, the more likely it was that many brain cells were
firing in the structures underneath the electrodes. The integration of all
these signals itself looks like a cloud of electrical activity. One could not
make out much detail, and the technique does not have any depth perception to speak of. In short, it is a blunt instrument, as far as brain imaging
goes, but for a while it was all we had to go on.

Davidson asked the following question: Would those with positive
emotions show different patterns of EEG activity than those who were
experiencing more negative emotions? He started with the idea that people
differed in what one psychologist once called "joy juice." Some people
always seem to be bubbling over with positive emotions, whereas others
cannot seem to utter a single encouraging word about themselves to
anyone.

Davidson (1992) asked groups of undergraduate volunteers to read
over a series of affect terms—some positive, such as *excited, active, interested*, and some negative, such as *unhappy, depressed, anxious*. Their task
was to select the emotions that best described themselves. Most people
would pick predominately positive words, mixed in with one or possibly
two negative affects. Davidson wanted to identify so-called "pure" groups,
those who rated themselves at the extremes of positive and those
who rated themselves at the extremes of negative emotion: the top and
bottom 5%.

Once he identified these extreme groups, he invited them into his
laboratory and hooked them up to his EEG equipment. Those who saw
themselves as experiencing the extreme of positive emotion also had more
left frontal brain activity. Those who saw themselves as experiencing the
extreme of negative emotions were more likely to show activation of the
right frontal area of the cortex. Emotional processes appeared to find their
home in cortical regions and in different regions for positive and for negative emotions (Davidson, 1992).

Another admittedly crude way to identify functioning in different parts
of the brain is through the study of clinical cases of brain damage. Whether
the result of a stroke or gunshot wound, loss of function is paired with loss
of brain tissue, and attempts are made to infer the function of the damaged
sections of the brain through a careful assessment of the functions that
were lost. Following the logic of his EEG work, Davidson (2000) expected
that damage to the frontal regions of the brain would lower positive emotional experience. Davidson found support for his predictions in a study
of people who had suffered strokes or lesions on one side of the brain or

the other. Those with left-sided damage were much more likely to be depressed. Those who had damage to the right side were more likely to show mania, but not depression.

Can we say with any assurance that Davidson is right, that positive emotions are expressed on one side of the brain and negative emotions fall primarily on the other? Not everyone agrees. Indeed, some neuroscientists challenge the notion that emotions can be located in specific geographic locations. They see these states as processes that draw on information from the whole brain, rather than stimuli or responses with specific anatomical sites. Even if we posit that emotions do have physical representation at specific sites, there is considerable debate about the exact location of those sites.

One alternative involves hemispheric inhibition (Turner, 1981). In this model, one of the roles of each hemisphere of the brain is to control or inhibit the neural activity on the other side. Damage in one side of the brain lowers the amount of inhibitory control exercised by neurons from the damaged side on the neural firing of neurons from the undamaged side. Note that this model then takes the same data that Davidson (2000) presents on stroke patients and finds evidence for emotions on opposite sides of the brain. Damage to the left side reduces inhibition of the right hemisphere, so what we observe with left-sided damage is not the absence of positive emotion neurons but the freedom (disinhibition) of neurons on the right side. Disentangling these pathways is tricky business, and for good reason: There are billions of neural connections between left and right hemispheres alone, and that does not count the billions of synapses within each hemisphere.

Winning and Losing

Imagine that you are playing a game of chance. The dealer holds up a card, the back side facing you so that you cannot read it. Your task is simple: Guess whether the dealer is holding up a red card or a black card. If you guess right, you get a dollar. If you guess wrong, you lose a dollar. You buy in with a stake of 20 dollars and hope for the best. You know that your odds of guessing right are 50/50 each time you guess, provided that you do not think you are clairvoyant and that the dealer does not employ some sleight of hand such as drawing cards from the bottom of the deck. Anyone who has gambled knows that even with less than 50/50 odds, you can go on winning streaks in which your guesses pay off several times in a row. This is a time of no mild positive emotion. Your world is full of joy; you can do no wrong. However, you can also go into a tailspin at the card table, losing money left and right across several consecutive rounds. The feelings then are also quite strong, but this time they are of opposing valence. Some describe it as "getting beat up inside."

Rebecca Elliot and her colleagues (Elliot, Fristo, & Dolan, 2000) were the dealers in one such experiment. Unbeknownst to the volunteers in the study, they stacked the deck to create periodic winning and losing streaks for each of the nine volunteers in their study. They did not use actual cards but rather projected the card image on a screen to the participant, who was confined within a magnetic brain-imaging chamber. The participant could press a button to indicate his choice: either black or red. Meanwhile, for each victory or loss (called "reward" or "penalty" by the researchers), fMRIs were taken to record changing patterns of activity in segments of brain tissue during winning and losing streaks.

Careful analysis of multiple trials revealed distinct patterns of brain activity for each. Different brain structures appeared to be involved for winning versus losing, although they did not conform to a "left- versus right-brain" emotion grid, as some might expect.[13] Although it appears that a definitive map of positive and negative emotional responses within the brain is likely to elude us for some time to come, these data are nevertheless instructive. To the brain, positive and negative experiences are not opposite ends of a single continuum. They generate distinct patterns of neural activity.

The work of locating brain regions associated with specific emotions continues vigorously, but I suspect that pinpointing emotions within the brain will be an elusive enterprise. These brain patterns within us are more than inner sensations; they are also our inner voices. Emotions provide us not only with information but also with direction, even advice, on how to think and how to behave. As such, emotions are signals that motivate, as well as represent states of mind. Their usefulness to us depends on both of these functions, and they communicate with many different neural structures to fulfill those tasks.

Another prominent neuroscientist, Jeffrey Gray (1982), uses behavioral systems to describe the inner workings underlying human action and reaction. His work in specifying the neuropathways of two such systems, behavioral activation and behavioral inhibition, is particularly relevant to our discussion of the separation of affects. These systems translate loosely into two forms of motivation: approach and avoidance. These two systems indeed map well onto positive and negative affective domains. Approach motivation is strengthened by positive affective information, whereas avoidance is strengthened by negative affects.

Peter Lang (Lang, Bradley, & Cuthbert, 1998) has devised a similar two-dimensional structure for emotions based on two primary motive sys-

Table 2.1. The Dynamic Components of Two Emotion Activation Systems

Components	Negative affective dynamics	Positive affective dynamics
Motives	Reduction of aversive states	Promotion of positive states
Behavior	Avoidance, retreat, defense	Approach, goal pursuits
Emotions	Fear, anxiety, anger	Interest, excitement, joy
Thoughts	Pessimism, worry	Optimism, hope
Hopes	Freedom from fear	Happiness
End-State	Security, safety	Fulfillment

tems: defensive and appetitive. When we engage one system, we also suspend attention to the other system. Even very basic reflexes can be sorted into these two camps: defense or desire. We blink when startled, as a primitive defense against possible harm; we salivate in anticipation of pleasure. Our actions are shaped by these two separate motives, and even our reflexes are "primed" to respond one way or the other depending on our motives. The startle response is a case in point. When we are in a defensive mode, the startle reflex is quicker and of greater magnitude. But in a reward condition, our startle reflex is slower and of lower magnitude. Show a person pleasant pictures, and the startle response slows; but show him or her unpleasant pictures, and the startle response speeds up.

When faced with uncertainty, we find ourselves at a critical choice point: either to advance, perhaps out of interest and curiosity, or to retreat, out of apprehension and the need to protect and defend against possible harm. Of course, we may also do both, take two steps forward and one step back and so on. Most complex situations present reasons for caution, as well as boldness.

What Gray (1982) and Lang et al. (1998) both emphasize is that these two systems that govern our behavior are not mirror images of one another. They are separate systems of neuroendocrine activation, located in different regions of the brain, stimulated by different neurochemical interactions, and leading to clearly distinguishable patterns of neuroelectrical activity. Again, we need to think about our actions as not simply either *approach* or *avoidance* but rather as *degrees* of approach and *degrees* of avoidance. Many of our problems may be thought to arise from the inability to synchronize these systems that regulate our personal and interpersonal thoughts and actions. In chapter 7, when I discuss common maladaptive forms of emotional regulation, I describe further how these systems can go awry.

In table 2.1, I have summarized the basic components of these two emotion activation systems that highlight the distinctions embraced by many researchers who have adopted a two-dimensional perspective. The distinctions begin with motivation. Negative affects provoke needs to lessen aversive states leading to avoidance, retreat, and defense. Positive affects, on the other hand, promote active engagement in pursuit of goals. The emotional states are different, as are the cognitions that accompany those states: fear and worry on the one hand, interest and hope on the other. Success is measured as security and safety in one dimension, fulfillment in the other.

Some Initial Implications

The two emotion systems outlined in table 2.1 appear self-evident to many of us. In practice, however, our beliefs about human motivation are often surprisingly single-minded. In my field of clinical psychology, many theorists have labored under the assumption that a single dimension underlies human behavior: that of defense against threat. This assumption has led to enormous difficulties at times and sometimes to downright silliness in our attempts to understand why a person does what he or she does. For example, why do people work? To avoid starvation. Why do people compete with one another? To avoid feeling inferior. Why are some people so dedicated? They might fear (irrationally) that they will not measure up otherwise, or they may simple be obsessive, workaholic types, defending against anxiety. But why do people engage in intellectual pursuits and appear to enjoy it? It is a defense, a sublimation of other needs that are frustrated, primarily sexual ones. Why do people steal from one another? Because they are afraid that they will be left with nothing. Why do men rape women? Because they are angry over past hurts, suffer feelings of rejection, or see themselves as inadequate lovers. All these explanations focus on defense against harm as the primary motive of human behavior, missing an entire dimension of human thought, feeling, and action that is based on active pursuit of desirable goals. Is it really too great a step in our thinking to say that some people do these things I just mentioned simply because they enjoy them?

What are the implications of this two-dimensional view for understanding psychological well-being? The first important message is that positive states are *not* the opposite of negative states. Therefore, an adequate assessment of well-being needs to include both, measured separately. To fully judge a person's status, we need to ask two questions about emotional health, not just one.

In later chapters in this book, I review in greater detail how two-dimensional thinking can clarify our understanding of positive mental health, as well as two of the most prevalent psychopathologies: depression and substance abuse. Before covering that material, I find it valuable to present a few introductory illustrations of the usefulness of my model. At present, mental health problems such as depression are being treated by both pharmacological and behavioral approaches. Suppose you were selecting from among different antidepressant medications and that the person you were treating not only displayed a vulnerability to experiencing greater negative affect but also was bereft of positive emotions. You suspect a neurochemical disturbance rather than an environmental deprivation. In this case, it would be very important to know which medication influences both affect systems.

The same principle holds true for behavioral prescriptions. Suppose you wanted help someone you loved because she is depressed. It would be important to know whether the person suffers from deficits in positive mood, as well as from excessive negative emotions. In addition, it would be of paramount importance to know whether the type of therapy you might employ would influence the positive, the negative, or both emotion systems. At this point, we can only speculate how exercise, cognitive therapy, psychoanalytic treatment, or popular programs such as meditation and goal-setting workshops might influence a person's emotional health. Few studies have addressed these questions in a way that allows us to discriminate between influences on positive and negative emotions.[14]

Dynamic systems of emotion underlie not only how we feel but also how we think about events. Some researchers who seek to preserve Descartes' mind-body dualism react as though our cognitive processes have been invaded by aliens when rational thought shows an emotional side. Yet such an invasion appears undeniable, given the evidence. Even simple cognitive judgments such as "liking" have two underlying affective dimensions: "liking" and "not disliking." More complex cognitive judgments, such as expectancies for future events, also show a bifurcated structure. The purely cognitivist models are ill equipped to deal with the reasons that a person can hold optimistic beliefs about future events and yet retain pessimistic beliefs about the same future. After all, what is pessimism if not the opposite of optimism? Logically they should be opposites, just like happiness and sadness, or, for that matter, hot and cold. If expectancies were constructed from pure reason, it would be just that way: a simple one-dimensional world. Alas, emotional dynamics do invade our expectancies, and they do so not just once but twice.

Robinson-Whelen, Kim, MacCallum, and Kiecolt-Glaser (1997) provide us with an example of these dynamics. They conducted a prospective study of the psychological and physical health of 224 older adults. They studied two groups of elders: one group with healthy spouses and another group with spouses who had a major physical infirmity. These researchers employed the best optimism scale available at the time with which to study an individual's expectations for the future.[15] The scale measures what are called "generalized expectancies" with questions such as, "Overall, I expect more good things to happen to me than bad" and "I always look on the bright side of things."

When the researchers examined the older adults' responses to these optimism items, they found that older adults could be both optimistic and pessimistic at the same time. For those without caregiving burdens in the home, optimism and pessimism were virtually independent, with only a 6% overlap between the two.[16] This makes sense only if we allow two sets of emotional experiences to influence the development of expectations. Optimism is built on our experience with positive events and our interpretations of them. However, pessimism is built up through our encounters with adversity and our interpretations of the feelings that resulted from those negative events. As a consequence, we can hold two sets of expectancies even about the same future if we have a mixture of past experiences to draw on.

Robinson-Whelen et al. (1997) went on to analyze how these two sets of expectations predicted future distress. They found that those who expressed a great deal of pessimism became increasingly anxious and depressed, reported more stress, and were more unhealthy 1 year later. In other words, pessimism predicted future distress. However, the "spring in their step," that is, their degree of optimism, did not predict less depression and anxiety or better health the following year. The newspapers spun the following headline from this article's results: "Pessimism harms more than optimism helps" (*Star Tribune*, 1998, E3).

What is wrong with this picture? The missing piece is an account of the positive emotions experienced during those times. As the authors acknowledged, optimistic people may indeed end up happier, even if they are no less anxious than less optimistic people are. Unfortunately, they did not include a measure of well-being, so we cannot tell whether prior avowals of optimism increased the chances that the person would be happier 1 year later, regardless of how anxious they felt.

But that is not the whole story. Robinson-Whelen and her colleagues (1997) found something else important. The relationship between optimism and pessimism was not the same for everyone. I mentioned earlier that half the sample was drawn from elders who were devoting a considerable number of waking hours to caring for another person. The members of this group were of comparable age and were matched on gender to the group that did not have someone to look after. The researchers referred to the caregiver group as being chronically stressed, which is appropriate given the considerable demands on their time, energy, and emotional stamina compared with those who were not in a caregiving role. When the researchers analyzed the relationships between optimism and pessimism, they found one very important difference between these two groups. Compared with noncaregivers, caregivers' expectations were not divided neatly into two independent dimensions. Instead, there was substantial overlap between the absence of optimism and the presence of pessimism: about 36% for the caregivers. The stressful caregiving situation appeared to compress the judgment processes governing their expectations for future events such that they did not or could not hold both optimistic and pessimistic expectancies in their minds. This qualification to a two-dimensional framework is a theme I return to many times in the chapters that follow.

In this chapter I have begun to lay the foundation for one central point: We understand ourselves and others much more clearly when we treat our positive and negative emotions as complementary rather than opposing forces. In the work of adaptation, it is most useful to see our emotional world in two dimensions. In response to life's opportunities and its challenges, we rely on both our desires and our fears as guides, and we need to listen when both happiness and sorrow call. Again, Clynes (1978) provides a metaphor for these two systems. It is like holding the reins of a horse-drawn carriage: You can pull to activate, but you cannot push to get the opposite; you need another rein to pull the horse on another side to guide its course. These two systems operate in parallel most of the time, with some very important exceptions. One of the key exceptions occurs when we are under stress: Then that carriage is careening down the hill out of control. I focus on these processes in the next two chapters.

3   Stress and the Eyes of the Beholder

An unspeakable horror seized me. There was a darkness; then a
dizzy, sickening sensation of sight that was not like seeing; I saw
a Line that was no Line; Space that was not Space: I was
myself, and not myself.

—Edwin Abbott, *Flatland: A Romance
of Many Dimensions*

Stress plays the spoiler in our emotional lives. Each stressful
experience reminds us that our world is not altogether stable and that, no
matter how well we fortify our defenses, the unexpected, even the un-
thinkable, can happen. As Bob Dylan sings it, "The times, they are
a-changin'." Change breaks up the rhythms within our minds and our bodies. It is this disruption of mind and body that constitutes stress in our
lives. Buddhist teachings refer to this experience as "dukkha"—the pain
that arises out of the ungovernable nature of events. Our adaptations to
life, as well as our theories of how people sustain emotional well-being,
must be dynamic ones to accommodate these inevitable disruptions in lifestyle routine.

   To begin, we need an adequate definition of what constitutes stress.
This is no easy task in itself. The term is a slippery one, and we need to
get a grip on a way of defining stress that distinguishes it from emotions,
particularly negative emotions. But before offering a definition here, I want
to discuss some commonly used definitions of stress that have caused more
than a little confusion. After offering a more useful definition of stress, I

review two of its principal domains: the psychological and the physiological. Each of these domains has a unique perspective to offer on the nature of stress and our means of adaptation to stressful experiences. The first problem we encounter in defining stress is the unrestrained usage of the word in the language of everyday life. We have woven *stress* into our conversations about nearly every encounter with negative feelings. Whether we are angry, anxious, depressed, defiant, defensive, challenged, or defeated, it has become commonplace to talk about how stressful life is and how we must guard against its adverse effects. Like microwave radiation from the Big Bang, stress is the ever-present tension within our minds that has been with us since awareness first broke through our neural circuits.

When the word *stress* is used in this way, it does not help us to understand one another or ourselves very much. And when stress becomes synonymous with any unpleasant emotion, information is actually lost, not gained. Because of this, some researchers (see, e.g., Kasl, 1987) have argued that it might be better to dispense with the concept altogether. For concepts to be useful in science, or for that matter in any context, they have to be informative, adding to what we already know. The ubiquitous *Stress* with that capital "S" does not really provide much added value, and it may obscure important differences in our emotional reactions to events.

One approach to defining stress that practically everyone has embraced at one time or another is to let each individual define for himself or herself what is stressful. This is to say that stress, like beauty and almost everything else that is important, is in the eye of the beholder. Indeed, if a person does not recognize his or her experience as stressful, then is it really appropriate to refer to the experience as stress producing? If this seems like a convenient ploy to escape the hard work of defining what is stressful, then you have already guessed the punch line here. But let's pursue this line of reasoning for a while and see how far we get.

There are at least two problems with letting a person determine what is stressful for him or her. First, if the defining feature of the stress experience is subjective, we are left without any firm boundaries around the construct making it impossible to differentiate stress from such other phenomena as tension, nervousness, and anxiety. Investigators in the field of health psychology have developed scales to measure perceived stress in their research (see Cohen, Kessler, & Gordon, 1995).[1] These scales are brief, highly reliable, and consistently correlated with measures of depression, anxiety, and symptoms of ill health that are thought to be consequences of stressful situations. Indeed, many researchers adopted this easy approach to assessing stress and continue to do so to this day. The problem is that these measures assesses tendencies to perceive events as stressful, as well as how much stress is in people's lives, thereby confounding stress as the stimulating event with the person's anxiety in response to the event.

The second problem with using perceptions to define stress is that we would not be able to define what stress is and what it is not independent of the person's emotional reactions. If the person is a reliable reporter of his or her internal state, this might not pose too great a difficulty. Or, failing that, if everyone were equally reliable (or unreliable) in their reports about themselves, we might be persuaded to live with a subjective definition of stress. However, people are not particularly reliable as reporters of their own emotions. Furthermore, people differ in how much they are willing and able to reveal about their feelings.[2]

A branch of interdisciplinary inquiry called *psychosomatic medicine* is devoted to the study of the inner mechanisms involved in the processing of emotions, including feelings of stress, and their role in physical health. One of the major tenets of this perspective is that people who fail to acknowledge their inner emotional conflicts may suffer dire health consequences due to unhealthy physiological sequelae of emotional inhibition.[3] The sheer volume of studies that support various aspects of this hypothesis governing mind-body relationships should give us pause about the usefulness of self-reports as the basis for our assessments of stress. If those who do not reveal their emotions are more prone to illness, and if we are attempting to test whether stress is also related to illness, we are up the proverbial creek when we rely on self-reports to define the "stressfulness" of an experience. What would we say? Is the person who does not report stress the most stressed?[4]

Many investigators have found it most useful to separate the person's perceptions of their life experiences from the experiences themselves, labeling them as part of the person's *stress response*.[5] The stress response has many diverse meanings; it can refer to behaviors and thoughts during and following a stressful event, or it may refer to coping efforts employed as a means of handling stressful situations. In addition, the stress response has also been used to characterize physiological changes, such as increases in blood pressure and heart rate, and cognitive appraisals of the various attributes of the stressful experience, such as whether the event threatens self-esteem and the person's beliefs in their own capacity to cope effectively with the stress. I discuss many of these stress responses later in this chapter.

Now many in the field may stop here, claiming that we have gone as far as we can in identifying what constitutes stress. They may say that we can depend only on the individual's appraisal of events to define the nature of stress in that person's life. But what if we wish to go further into the "science" of stress? Can we define stressful experiences apart from the person's response?

At this point we must rely on our theories about behavior to define those aspects of life experience that are most likely to disturb the normal ebb and flow of human activities. Notice that I just sneaked in a working definition of stress: that which disturbs the norm, upsets our equilibrium, overturns the apple cart.

One of the most ingenious definitions has been offered by two European health psychologists, Holger Ursin and Miranda Olff (1993). They suggest that stress is best defined as an information gap, something that is either missing presently or is about to disappear. The disruption of homeostasis is due to the absence of expected inputs, too little or too much. This is certainly different from defining stress as the presence of an undesirable event! But it also makes a great deal of sense, particularly if we put this definition together with Manfred Clynes's (1978) ideas about emotions. If we accept emotions as rhythms of the mind, then stress arises from premature departures from, delays in, or disruptions of those rhythms. We are temporarily lost, disoriented in a sense, when we do not hear the next note that we expect in our interactions with the world outside. This is the formal definition I have adopted in this book: Stress represents an increase in the *degree of uncertainty* experienced over an important aspect of life (see Cassel, 1975).

One way to think about uncertainty is in relation to the probability of some future event. Figure 3.1 shows how these two ideas are related. First, uncertainty is at its lowest point on two occasions: when you know for certain that an event will occur and when you know for certain that it will not. These two points are depicted on the graph as the end points, at which the likelihoods are 0% and 100%, respectively. Uncertainty at the apex when the chances are 50/50 that the event will occur. It is during those times when we are least informed. It is also a time when even a little information can have considerable influence on our decision making.

I have added another dimension to this graph, because uncertainty alone does not capture a key ingredient of the stressor: the degree of change or disruption in patterns of thought and behavior that are caused by the event. This is a dimension that defines the meaningfulness of the change to the person—the depth of the stress experience. Unpredictable events that do not disturb our patterns of life are only mildly stressful, and even relatively certain events, such as an upcoming divorce, can be stressful if they would not just overturn, but crush, the apple cart.

What kinds of experiences fit this definition? The list is a long one. They include experiences involving loss, failure, threats of and actual physical harm, uncontrollable and unanticipated events, role conflicts, role am-

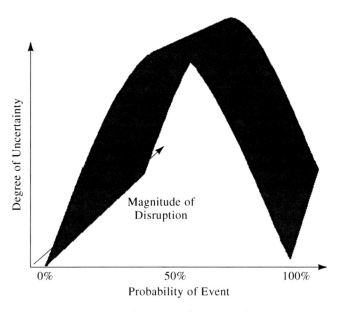

Figure 3.1. Stress as a function of degree of uncertainty
and magnitude of change associated with the event.

biguity, role transitions, task demands, and loss of autonomy. Investigators
have attempted to come up with a few salient dimensions of the stressful
experience, and there are many useful classification schemes (Thoits,
1983). I use a structure that draws on the properties of the events themselves as much as possible and that relies as little as possible on emotional
responses for determining what constitutes a stressful event.

When it comes to disruption, size certainly ought to matter. That is
to say that major events have a larger impact on our behavior than everyday events. However, on another dimension, everyday events have an important edge in their disruptiveness compared with major events. Many
events are more disturbing than a few. And everyday events happen with
much greater frequency than major events. We might experience 10 or 15
truly major events in our lifetimes, but we could easily experience that
many small events in just one day. Though the number of everyday stressors may usually be quite low, just by chance they can occur so closely
together in time as to cause considerable distress.

These are the days when nothing seems to go right. The events may
all be relatively trivial, like spilling coffee on one's clothing, the extra credit
card charge that shouldn't be there, or the $20.00 ticket for parking 5
minutes overtime at a meter. Any one of these events would be a minor
blip on life's radar screen. Put together a string of mildly distressing events,

however, and it feels is if the whole world is bent on ruining our lives (Zautra, Guarnaccia, & Dohrenwend, 1986).

A string of bad luck does not happen often, but when it does, nearly everyone is distressed by it. There is a game my father-in-law played with my children one day. He asked them to guess something, such as a number he was thinking of. After they guessed, he told them whether they were right or not. Invariably they guessed wrong, or at least he would tell them so. After guessing wrong five times in a row, every child felt distressed. For some children, only three wrong guesses were enough to depress them; others could hold out longer, maybe up to seven wrong answers. But we all have limits on our capacity to cope with adverse news. The point is that we have common reactions to adversity. Unsettling experiences that introduce uncertainty about our past, the present, or our future livelihoods are stressful for just about everyone.

Degree of control and predictability of events are central to the experience of the stressfulness of events. If you can predict an event, you can prepare for it, and, in doing so, reduce its impact. For those of us who remember the shock of hearing of President John F. Kennedy's assassination, at least a part of that stress was a direct result of the suddenness of the experience. Similarly, people who lose loved ones as a result of tragic and unexpected circumstances are more affected than people who lose a loved one due to chronic and progressive worsening of diseases such as cancer. By and large, the research evidence supports the view that sudden events pack a stronger wallop than expected events.[6]

This is likely true for major events, but is it also the case for everyday troubles? One study by van Eck, Nicolson, and Berkhof (1998) provides an answer. They recruited 91 men for a 5-day diary study of the effects of stressful events in their daily lives. Each participant was given a self-report booklet for each of the 5 days and a pager. The experimenter would page the participants 10 times each day at random intervals to signal the participants to complete a short questionnaire as soon as possible following the beep. The questionnaire contained several inquiries about stressful events that may have occurred since the previous beep, such as whether the event was expected, whether it was a chronic source of disruption, and whether the person thought the outcome was controllable. In addition, there were questions that asked the participants for ratings of their positive and negative mood at each time.

The authors were interested in how the person's ratings of the occurrence, predictability, chronicity, and controllability of the events were related to negative emotions at the time the events were occurring. With 10 ratings per day, 5 days per person, and 91 participants, this amounted to 4,550 observations to draw on to study these relationships.

Unpredictable events were rated as significantly more unpleasant than events that were predictable. Furthermore, events that had happened previously did not increase negative affect as much as did events that were novel stressors. There was one seeming contradiction, though. After accounting for unpleasantness and prior occurrence, the predictable event elicited a stronger negative reaction than unpredictable events. Why would this be so?

Imagine you are in one of Edgar Allen Poe's torture chambers. The torture is relatively benign: a drop of water on your forehead while you lie strapped down on a padded table. The drops of water come with precise regularity, every 30 seconds. Does prediction help you cope with the stress? In fact, the regularity itself may make it even more distressing. It signifies the total lack of control over the environment. Indeed, helplessness in the face of even the smallest of nuisances can be highly distressing if the event is likely to recur. Thus hidden within some predictable stressors is the fact that you have no control over the event. You can see it coming, but you can do nothing to stop it.

There is another kind of control that comes into play in the face of those stressors that cannot be avoided: control over the outcome. How many times have you heard someone say, "I just won't let it (him or her) get to me"? By controlling the response (by humming a refrain of "sticks and stones," for instance), the person minimizes the impact of the stress. Of course there are many ways to do this, and only some of them work some of the time. "Stonewalling" might be an effective response unless the stress refuses to go away, as former President Nixon and his coconspirators learned after Watergate. Reviewing one's own feelings and making them public might help, or it might make matters worse. The underlying principle is that those events for which the person does not have an effective coping response are the most stressful. This control was of primary importance to the men in the pager study. Stressful events had their most adverse effects on the emotions of these men when they could not influence the course or outcome of the experience. These events threatened adjustment to a much greater extent than other unpleasant events.

Glass, Singer, and Friedman (1969) provided one of the first convincing demonstrations of the influence of perceptions of control on the stressfulness of events. They recruited undergraduate women from Hunter College and the City College of New York, put them in a laboratory room, and gave them two tasks to complete while wearing headphones. They had to proofread an article for errors and solve a puzzle. The puzzle actually could not be solved, so performance was scored based on the number of attempts. The number of times they missed identifying an error in the proofreading assignment was used as an index of poor performance on that task. In the first study the experimenters delivered blasts of white noise up to 110 decibels to their participants and examined whether the noise affected their performances. If blasts of noise came at standard intervals so that the college students could predict when they would get an earful, there was little if any decrement in their performances. When the noise was presented at random so that the participant could not predict the next occurrence, their tolerance for frustration on the insolvable puzzle was low, leading to significantly fewer attempts. Further, they made twice as many mistakes on the proofreading task as those who received noise at predictable intervals.

In the second study, the researchers made one small but important change to the procedure: They added a button. They told half their participants that if they pressed the button, they could shut off the noise. This was the perceived-control condition. The other half of the participants had no button to press. It turned out that none of the women in the first group actually pushed that button. But just knowing it was there had profound salutary effects on their performances. They tried harder to solve the puzzle and missed significantly fewer errors when proofreading. What is more, they rated the noise much less aversive than those participants without a button to press (Glass et al., 1969).

So far, I have reviewed several dimensions of events that could be used to rate their stressfulness: the number of the events; their magnitude or size; and their degree of unpredictability, uncontrollability, and chronicity. These experiences are most likely to disrupt homeostasis, and it is not hard to see that they do so through adding uncertainty to our own lives. They represent experiences with the external world that do not behave according to plan.

A number of approaches have been developed to translate these ideas into reliable methods of assessing stress in everyday life. Although it is impossible to review all the potential solutions at this stage, there are some well-established approaches to the assessment of major and minor events that deserve mention. George Brown (1989) has developed what he refers to as a contextual approach to the assessment of *long-term threat* from major life events. Using 20 questions in a clinical interview, Brown invited people to recall their most troubling events concerning their families, romantic relations, and work lives. He asked the participants to provide approximate dates for the events, to discuss what was happening at the time, and how they reacted to the event. These remarks formed the context. They were recorded and rated by trained experts in terms of the severity of the "contextual threat" to the person's adjustment. Brown's (1989) system for rating the degree of threat from stressful life events is highly reliable when used by well-trained observers. Also, many studies have shown that people who have experienced highly threatening events are more likely to suffer physically, as well as psychologically.

Which is worse: to suffer a major calamity, or to live with a chronically troubling situation that periodically erupts into a burst of small undesirable events that are out of your control? The major event may temporarily threaten your way of life, but those episodes of small events are in a way worse; they demonstrate fundamental flaws in your way of life. Brown and his colleagues (1989) developed a method for characterizing these situations by assessing what they called *long-term difficulties*. These difficulties are patterns of everyday life that have troubled the person for 2 years or more. Indeed, the presence of such ongoing adversity is highly disturbing, equal in magnitude to major stressors, yet qualitatively different from them.

Bruce Dohrenwend and his colleagues (Dohrenwend et al., 1993) have created a different method for judging the stressfulness of events. They take issue with methods of assessing stressfulness of events that rely on judgments of the personal context surrounding the events. The context not only contains elements of the stressor itself but also depends on the abilities of the person to mount an effective defense against the stressor. For example, in Brown's (1989) rating system, other stresses occurring at the time of the event are included as part of the context, and those data are used to gain a fuller appraisal of the severity of the stress.

Dohrenwend et al. (1993) favor keeping the ratings of the event itself distinct from ratings of context. Their approach relies on systematic structured probes of major events to identify major dimensions of stress, such as predictability, controllability, and "fatefulness": the degree to which the event was independent of the person's actions. Dohrenwend et al.'s approach is most useful for identifying key dimensions of the stress experience that shape the severity of the stressor independently of personal and social contexts. Brown's (1989) approach comes closer to defining stress in terms of the strengths and vulnerabilities of each person, but it does so at the cost of blending in contextual features, along with the actual stress event, to determine the severity of threat.

My colleagues and I have also developed a set of methods for assessing the degree of stress in everyday life.[7] We prompt the person to report daily difficulties by presenting lists of commonly occurring troubles. There are 13 classes of events in the full inventory: schooling; recreation; religion; transportation; finances; crime; relationships with friends, family, spouse/ significant other, extended family; work; household maintenance; and health-related events. Under schooling, one of our items is, "Could not take a course you wanted." For spouse/significant others, we ask questions such as, "Were you criticized by your spouse/significant other?" By asking the person whether one or more events occurred in each of these aspects of daily life, we can get a fairly accurate picture of the number and types of stressors that have occurred to the person over the past day or week (see Zautra et al., 1986; Zautra, Schultz, & Reich, 2000). The value of our methods (and those of other researchers who have developed similar approaches) is that it is possible to obtain estimates of stressful events occurring over short periods of time and to relate increases in stress to changes in health and well-being prospectively. Changes in the level of everyday stress one day can be used to predict changes in positive and negative affects the following day.

Thus far in this chapter I have identified those characteristics of the life experience itself that are stressful and reviewed some of the principal ways in which researchers measure these stressors. This is the stimulus side of the stress equation. There is a response side as well, fortified by careful investigations of physiological changes that accompany stressful events. In fact, scientists have made more progress to date in mapping the physiology of the stress response than they have in identifying the physiological routes to emotion. I turn next to a discussion of this side of the stress equation.

Stress Response Physiology

Researchers in disciplines such as microbiology and endocrinology have a very different approach to defining stress than behavioral scientists do. In fact, stress researchers from biological and psychological disciplines often have great difficulty understanding one another. This breach in communication is due in part to fundamental differences in their definitions of phenomena such as stress and distress. A colleague of mine at Arizona State University is a reproductive endocrinologist. We once taught a class together on stress, and when she got up to define stress in that class for the first time, she presented an overhead. In her picture, many of the endocrine pathways were listed: Estrogen, prolactin, testosterone, and cortisol all had links to neural and glandular structures in her chart. What about the psychological aspects of stress? For this she drew a small cloud at the top of her chart with the word *stress* written across it and a single arrow from that cloud to the brain. Like the Eskimo words for snow, each discipline has its penchant for detailed inquiry on its own terms but has little knowledge of the complexities that exist in other disciplines. This is another meaning of the phrase, "Stress is in the eye of the beholder."

Important physiological changes do occur in, during, and after stressful experiences. These responses originate at a number of sites in the brain, including the hypothalamus, the locus coeruleus, and the amygdala.[8] These structures in the brain send and receive feedback signals from two stress-response systems: the sympathetic-adrenal-medulla axis (SAM), which responds within seconds, and the hypothalamic-pituitary-adrenal cortex (HPA axis), which is fully activated about 10 minutes later. These systems are the brain's agents of influence and communication with the rest of the body about how to respond to the stressor. Each system changes the way other systems in the body function, stimulating activity in one, such as the cardiovascular system, and inhibiting activity in another, such as the digestive system. The feedback from these physiological changes gets back to us as well and generates those "stressed-out feelings" that we all have experienced at one time or another. In figure 3.2, I have tried to give a parsimonious rendering of some of the major systems and hormones involved in the stress response.

The figure shows the two major stress response systems emanating from a cluster of brain structures, often referred to as the limbic system. These include the locus coeruleus, located at the top of the brain stem, a neural structure that precipitates a stress response through its release of norepinephrine and that changes the chemical balance favoring excitation versus inhibition of various neurons throughout the limbic region. The limbic region includes the thalamus, the hypothalamus, the hippocampus, and the amygdala, as well as other adjacent structures such as the anterior cingulate (not shown in the figure) that play pivotal roles both in the stress response and in the regulation of emotions. In fact, the limbic system is often described as the source of all emotion, a designation that is not really accurate. Limbic structures are certainly central to the experience of emotion, but both lower and higher cortical regions also participate in the regulation of emotional experiences.

There are two principal regions within the hypothalamus that translate limbic system messages into stress reactions. The lateral hypothalamus is one of them. When stimulated from limbic structures, this region infuses our adrenal glands with norepinephrine, activating the SAM system. When the adrenal medulla gets the signal, it secretes epinephrine, and we are off and running, sometimes quite literally. By the way, epinephrine has a half-life of only a couple of minutes, so without continuing stimulation, the SAM system activity will fade away rather quickly.

The periventricular nucleus of the hypothalamus secretes key neuro-hormones that work in concert to activate the HPA axis: corticotropin-releasing hormone (CRH) and arginine vasopressin. These hormones stimulate the pituitary and also help keep the SAM system primed with norepinephrine. The anterior pituitary, when stimulated, lets loose a number of key hormones. Adrenocorticotropic hormone (ACTH) is among

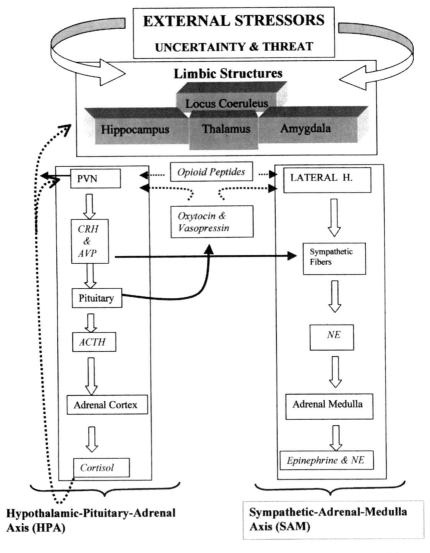

Figure 3.2. Two stress response systems: HPA and SAM. Note: Dashed lines signify inhibitory feedback. PVN = periventricular nucleus; Lateral H = lateral hypothalamus; NE = norepinephrine; AVP = arginine vasopressin; ACTH = adrenocorticotropic hormone.

them, and that hormone stimulates the adrenal cortex to release glucocorticoids, such as cortisol, into the bloodstream.

Wouldn't it be better to find a way to extinguish, or at least blunt, the stress response and avoid all these complex physiological responses, let alone the emotional discomfort that accompanies them? Modern medicine could certainly find a drug we could take so that we would not have to experience either the rapid increase of unwanted arousal every time we got on the freeway at rush hour or the slow burn we feel while waiting overtime for our partner to show up for dinner. To answer this question, it is most useful to ask another question first: What does the stress response accomplish? What good *is* it?

There are two answers, and both tell us that we cannot do without a stress response, or at least that we should not try to eliminate it until we consider the consequences. First, the stress response is needed to provide sufficient energy to take action, whether it is to confront the challenge or take flight. Sympathetic arousal means increases in catecholamines, such as epinephrine and norepinephrine, that mobilize glucose stores in the body, raising heart rate and blood pressure to speed delivery of those sugars to locations throughout the body. Unnecessary systems that require energy are shut down in the process. Growth, reproduction, and digestion are put on hold to maximize available energies. The HPA-axis plays a major role in suspending functions not currently in demand through the secretion of cortisol and other glucocorticoids, including a dampening of the immune system to save energy and slowing down inflammatory responses to injury (Chrousos & Gold, 1992; Sternberg, 1992).

Cognitive processing changes as well in response to stressors. Information processing is more focused, allowing for quicker response times, and pain sensations are blunted, at least at first, so that we are not overly attentive to wounds that may distract us from fight or flight (Sapolsky, 1994). Stress also influences how we experience our emotions, a point I return to later.

These physiological responses to stress are not harmful most of the time. Our bodies (and minds) have evolved to adapt well to most stressful situations. For every rise in a stress peptide, there are countermeasures that arise to down-regulate that stress response and allow the body to restore a homeostatic balance physiologically. Initial increases in prolactin, for example, give way to increases in cortisol, which down-regulates prolactin (see Kelley & Dantzer, 1991). Increased cortisol in the bloodstream crosses the blood-brain barrier to influence CRH in such a way that dampens stress reactivity, lowering further cortisol releases. Figure 3.2 illustrates some of the key feedback mechanisms. They are represented as the dashed lines with arrowheads pointing upward rather than downward. A case in point is the opioid system. Opioid release into the central nervous system follows stress. This action not only reduces pain that might accompany stress (one would not want to be licking wounds during fight or flight), but the peptide may also down-regulate other actions of the stress system, including releasing factors within the brain associated with stress reactivity. Oxytocin is included along with vasopressin in the figure. They are known to be released under stress (as well as at other times). In sufficient quantities, they can also be "stress busters." As far as feedback systems, I have only scratched the surface here. There are many ways in which the stress response self-regulates. It is a marvelous system of checks and balances (see Charney, Grillon, & Bremner, 1998a, 1998b).

The key fact, often lost in the shuffle, is that the stress response has to include a way to shut itself down. Without a shutdown valve and a stress "thermostat" to control that valve, we would most definitely overheat, boil over, so to speak. Failure to turn off the stress response can have rather devastating consequences. A temporary loss of bodily restorative functions through a slowing of immune cell activity is tolerable but unhealthy if sustained.

Chronic elevations in cortisol could reflect chronic stress but could also be due to a failure of the feedback mechanisms to properly down-regulate physiological activity. In either case, chronic elevations in cortisol can lead to failure of numerous organs throughout the body, as well as premature cell death in key sectors of the brain.

Through his focus on the HPA-axis, Hans Selye (1973) introduced modern medicine to the idea that the stress response could be damaging to health. He saw this response as a nonspecific physiological reaction to events that tapped the body's energy reserves. Selye identified three stages of the stress reaction: alarm, adaptation, and exhaustion. Alarm reactions orient us to what is new, different, and a potential threat to our way of life. Adaptation is the body's work to regain homeostasis. Exhaustion is refers to a response system that is too tired to mount an adequate defense. Post-Selye models of the stress response tend to deemphasize this last stage. It turns out that most of the problems that arise from stress are not due to a worn-out response but to a failure of our bodies and minds to properly regulate the stress response (see Sapolsky, 1994, chapter 2).

Current models of the harmful effects of stress focus on problems in recovery of homeostasis following a stress response. Bruce McEwen (1998) and his colleagues have developed one of the most interesting of these models.[9] They have been interested in the long-term effects of repeated stressors, such as the ongoing difficulties that I discussed earlier in this chapter. McEwen (1998) notes that chronically stressful situations often do not permit full recovery, either physiologically or psychologically. Without recovery the person may have chronically elevated stress hormones, and those hormones can do considerable damage to intellectual, as well as emotional, functioning. Also, these systemic problems can result from our own biological propensities. In some of us, the biological triggers are wired to ignite physiological responses that overwhelm our bodies. Alternatively, some systems do not ignite rapidly enough, leading to an inadequate response, prompting other hormonal responses to expand without the usual and necessary counterregulation.

If you think of our biological response to stress varying along a normal curve, this formulation makes the most sense. Most of us fall somewhere in the middle of the curve in terms of intensity, but there are some with blunted responses at the low end and others with highly reactive responses to stress at the other end. These differences arise from constitutional factors; they may develop early, through childhood experiences (such as abuse and neglect, discussed in a later chapter); later, through traumatic events in adult life; or they may be shaped over time by chronically stressful situations. The individual's unique patterns of stress response may be particularly useful in some cases. For example, some situations call for vigilance, others require rapid responses, and still other situations are best left unattended, lest we make matters worse. However, those responses at the extremes of the continuum are less likely to lead to regained equilibrium following stress and can be unhealthy in the long run.

McEwen (1998) defines adaptations to stress as forms of allostasis: the ability to achieve stability through change. He has coined the term *allostatic load* to refer to the burden of stress adaptation. The consequences of heavy allostatic load are not immediate, but they are severe, including hypertension and atherosclerosis, rheumatoid arthritis, and even cell death in the hippocampal region, harming storage sites for long-term memory.

There are four types of conditions that are associated with heavy allostatic load. One condition arises from repeated stress. Suppose that every day of the month and every month for a year you faced a threat to your well-being. Soldiers on the front lines faced this kind of stress. In his novel *Catch-22*, Joseph Heller gives us some excellent examples of the stress experienced by fighter pilots who faced life-threatening events during each sortie. Even if you were prepared, your blood pressure would rise, and your heart rate would soar. These physiological responses alone could cause significant wear and tear on the cardiovascular system.

Most of us do not face life-or-death threats every day, but McEwen (1998) presents other scenarios that may apply to many of us. In a second condition, high allostatic load results when the person fails to find a successful adaptive response to a repeated stressor. McEwen uses the example of public speaking for someone who develops a chronic anxiety reaction to standing in front of an audience. In this case, the repeated events are not stressful for everyone, but they turn into chronic stressors when the person cannot find an adaptive response.

A third cause of high allostatic load is the failure to shut down the stress response. The homeostatic mechanisms responsible for returning the body and mind to a resting state do not function adequately. The body does not fare well under conditions of sustained arousal. If the cortisol response to stress does not abate, for example, the body's organ systems may age prematurely and alter brain chemistry, resulting in significantly impaired memory. Another potential consequence of chronic elevations in cortisol and other glucocorticoids is immune suppression. Lower levels of immune response leave the body more susceptible to cold viruses and other pathogens. More frightening still are the potential effects of stress-related immune suppression on cancer survival. A reduction in the number of circulating natural killer cells can allow tumors to grow more rapidly and hasten the course of the disease.

Ron Glaser, Janice Kiecolt-Glaser, and colleagues have conducted a series of experiments on the effects of psychological stress on wound healing.[10] In these studies, the experimenters actually wounded their volunteer participants slightly: by lancing the forearm with a biopsy tool in one study, by making a slight cut around the gums in a dentist's chair in another, or, in third study, vacuuming the skin for an hour or so until small blisters formed. Though wounding sounds like an invasive technique, there was an important purpose to this experiment that justified the bodily insult. The researchers wanted to see whether stress influenced the body's ability to repair itself. In one of the studies, conducted with dental students, they compared how long it took for a wound to heal during final exams versus over the summer break. The wounds during final exams took 40% longer to heal than they did during vacations. In another study, the researchers tracked down some of the physiological changes that might account for these differences. Women who were more distressed at the time they were given forearm blisters showed higher cortisol levels and lower levels of cytokines that promoted inflammation at the site needed for wound healing. The implications of findings such as these are significant, whether applied to recovery from surgery or gang warfare: distress interferes with wound healing.

A higher level of cortisol during stress is often thought to be the principal cause of stress-related illnesses. But it is not the only way in which adaptation can fail us. The body can also respond with too little cortisol, or another arm of the stress response may be out of balance. McEwen (1998) discusses the consequences of a blunted response, that is, when one member of the stress response team fails to react sufficiently. This is the fourth problem associated with allostatic load. Many physiological responses to stress act in concert, even serving to regulate one another, and depend on adequate feedback from one another. Without cortisol, for example, proinflammatory cytokines might overwhelm the body's defenses, leading to errant attacks against the body's own tissues. This is what appears to happen in autoimmune diseases such as rheumatoid arthritis, lupus, and multiple sclerosis. Our body needs to find the middle ground in immune responding, but chronic stress, as well as catastrophic events, can upset that balance.

It would be wrong to think that our adaptation is a delicate balancing act, easily cracked open by the slightest stress. The systems that govern our bodies are wonderfully responsive to disruptive events, with many ways to restore equilibrium. McEwen (1998) alerts us, however, to failures of adaptation due to extraordinary stressors in vulnerable systems. These failures, once initiated, can spin out of control to such an extent that our bodies' defenses may never be the same again.

Two factors contribute mightily to our vulnerability to allostatic load, according to McEwen (1998). On the physical side, unhealthy habits, such as poor diet, lack of exercise, and (over)use of products such as nicotine and alcohol, are major risk factors. His second vulnerability factor is more interesting from a psychological standpoint. McEwen calls it the *perception of stress*, referring to the same aspects of the stress response that were discussed earlier: a perception of threat, anticipation of harm, and a lack of control. McEwen (1998) does not elaborate on the various types of stress perceptions, perhaps because they fall outside of his discipline and within the domain of the psychological sciences.

Suffice it to say that our emotional responses to stress are central mechanisms of adaptation and maladaptation. We develop patterns of thinking over time, habits of feeling in response to everyday stress, and healthy and unhealthy behavioral accommodations to stress. Under extraordinary circumstances, we may develop these patterns in response to single traumatic events as well. The relationships between stress and health are complex to be sure, and our bodies and our minds play a major part in how well we are able to keep ourselves together during times of stress.

How do we lighten our allostatic load? Run daily, eat broccoli, stop drinking too much, and calm ourselves during stressful times. "Just play it cool, boy," as one of the gang leaders in *West Side Story* tells his troops. Later in the play, Tony and others in the gang learn just how difficult it is to follow this advice during a "rumble" (gang warfare). We ourselves know just how easily we are provoked in our everyday lives at work, at home, and even on the road. In models of stress and ill health such as McEwen's, our initial reaction is not what usually gets us into trouble. To prevent stress-related illness, we need to pay greater attention to how our bodies (and minds) recover homeostasis.

There is another aspect of Hans Selye's original formulation that has been improved on. Selye (1973) characterized the stress response as a general activation of a host of regulatory systems. It turns out that it is possible to identify specific stress responses. In fact, a number of scientists have suggested that the stress response can be divided into two distinct patterns: one that is characterized by strivings to assert control and a second that describes attempts to cope with a failure to control. Bjorn Folkow (1993) has labeled the first as an *active adaptive defense* and the second as a *defeat reaction*. The active defense system is loosely identified with the activation of the SAM-axis, whereas defeat has been linked to HPA-axis activation, especially cortisol. Do these dimensions map onto the two sequences of approach versus avoidance/withdrawal that were discussed previously in the context of emotions? Yes, they do, at least in part.

Rotenberg, Sirota, and Elizur (1996) provided one of the most insightful discussions of these two systems of stress response. In presenting their model of adaptive versus maladaptive tensions, Rotenberg and his colleagues suggest that two behavioral reactions typify stress physiology. They call one *search activity* and the other the *renunciation of search*. According to Rotenberg et al., search activity is championed by the SAM system, and renunciation of search is accompanied by increases in HPA-axis activity. When the organism engages in search activity and does not attempt to disengage from the challenging situation, Rotenberg et al. (1996) state that it has "stress without distress." The ratio of norepinephrine to cortisol is a marker of this kind of stress response, and it is considered more adaptive than the other, in which the person gives up, swallows hard, and attempts to live with defeat.

Renunciation of search is considered the hallmark of some forms of depression, but there is something altogether too Western in the belief that these coping strategies are always maladaptive. There are situations in which continued striving is maladaptive and acceptance of loss of control is most efficient for the conservation of resources, even if it means relinquishing hope for a positive outcome. Depression is a natural consequence of loss (Klinger, 1975). It is the premature renunciation of search due to feelings of helplessness that we need to guard against.[11] There are not many of us who, like Don Quixote, can dream the impossible dream and never be disillusioned by failure.

The Psychology of Stress Responses

Rothbaum, Weisz, and Snyder (1982) provided a new understanding of how people sustain themselves even in the most unsettling of circumstances. They proposed that when direct means of gaining control over life events fail, people would often resort to what they referred to as *secondary control strategies*. These strategies vary widely depending on the situation and the person's resources, but they have one thing in common. They all focus on coping methods other than finding a direct solution to the problem. They might include avoiding disappointment from failure by expecting less from oneself, relying on more powerful people to help solve the problem, and seeking to understand and accept the current situation rather than trying to change it. Rothbaum et al. (1982) suggest that optimal adaptation occurs when we take a balanced approach, using primary control methods when there is hope for their success and secondary control strategies when there is more to be learned by accepting defeat and disengaging from Promethean efforts to resolve the irresolvable.

In truth, both engagement and disengagement are engines of response available within us. The psychophysiology of each response pattern is different, and the consequences for health and illness are also different. The stress responses correspond to emotional states, and this is perhaps what is most surprising and most interesting. Rather than one general reaction, we have two different response systems. We use each as the need arises, and the balance we strike between striving to take control and efforts to disengage and accept depends both on the types of stresses we are confronted with and the resources we can muster at the time.

Roth and Cohen (1986) have captured the psychology of these stress responses in their identification of two separate methods of coping: approach and avoidance. We use approach coping to seek better control over what has happened and to gain a better understanding of the nature of the stressor. We use avoidance coping to manage the threat to our way of life that the stressful situation provokes.

In real life, we often vacillate between approach and avoidance, especially in response to complex stressors such as a job change, divorce, the loss of a physical function due to a chronic illness, or the sudden death of a loved one. Indeed, if you asked people to describe how they have been coping with a difficult situation, you would find that they engaged in both forms and that one form negates neither the use nor the potential value of the other.

Does active approach coping reduce distress from upending events? Certainly most models of stress and coping are predicated on this proposition. In fact, this prediction is a fundamental tenet of some coping models of mental health. Findings from empirical studies are often disappointing on this point, showing little or no benefit of active coping on negative affect and other indices of psychological distress.[12] Often overlooked in these models is that affective health is two-dimensional. The benefits of adaptive coping responses cannot be fully assessed by relying on a single dimension for evaluation of our feelings. Approach coping may be thought of as a means to activate positive emotive forces, in essence to feel effective once again. Even if this form of coping does little to resolve negative emotional reactions to stress, it is still valuable as a means of promoting positive reengagement.

Avoidant coping is a very different response to adversity. This coping dimension is employed most as a means of gaining some control over negative emotions through a retreat to safer ground. When we study people who are distressed, we often find that they are employing avoidant coping more than those who are not distressed. Some students of coping have jumped to the tenuous conclusion that the avoidance was the cause of the distress. Those interpretations reverse the true cause-and-effect relationships in many cases between psychological distress and the need to withdraw from situations too difficult to face directly (Zautra, Sheets, & Sandler, 1996).[13]

This misinterpretation is the consequence of applying a faulty paradigm—a paradigm that sees emotional responses to stressful situations in only one dimension, considering approach as adaptive and withdrawal as maladaptive, when both have their places, depending on the circumstances. This one-dimensional paradigm urges people to confront all problems rather than avoid some, sometimes causing even more grief along the way. Indeed, these faulty applications of coping theory have been more than a little unkind to those who are struggling to adjust to adversity.

This struggle is most painfully evident in those who are attempting to come to terms with highly traumatic events that defy comprehension, such as a child's drowning in the backyard swimming pool, or the collapse of the World Trade Center Towers. These upending experiences may be so horrific that just the thoughts of the event are too threatening and painful to bear. Horowitz, Field, and Classen (1993)[14] have found that many people who have had traumatic experiences develop what they called "stress response syndromes." People with these syndromes find themselves preoccupied with images of the stressful experience, yet at the same time, they are trying to push those thoughts out of consciousness. According to Horowitz et al. (1993), the minds of some trauma victims vacillate rapidly between the fulfillment of two different needs: the need to find a coherent explanation of the stressful experience and the need to avoid the overwhelming threat to the person's beliefs about himself and his social world. It is as if the mind is locked in a wrestling match between approach and avoidance, two coping processes that are fused into one reverberating circuit by the force of the traumatic experience.

In this chapter I have attempted to show that, like emotions, stress responses are complex and multifaceted, both in their physiology and their psychology. At the core of that complexity are two important and distinct methods of recovery from stress: mounting efforts to restore the positive and to defend against harm. In the next chapter, I draw stress and emotions together to examine how they interact. I show that the processes of stress reactivity and recovery are made both simpler and more dangerous by the changes that stress creates in the fabric of the emotional experience itself.

4 The Effects of Stress on the Experience of Emotions

Saltwater snails
Have three neurons: one
To turn them toward the light
One to tell them to stay put
And one to override when
It's best to hold tight
Despite the evidence.
                    —James Armstrong,
          Monument to a Summer Hat

Have you ever had a close call, a brush with death or some other near disaster, and, looking back, realized that the odds were not much better, perhaps less than 50/50, that you were going to make it? In a split second's time your fate was decided. Perhaps too there was even a choice you had to make. A left turn or a right? And you made the right choice. Do you remember what you were feeling at the time? Not afterward, but right then?

For me, it was speeding up a hill on a country road outside of Grass Valley, California, on a motorcycle. At 50 mph, I was definitely going too fast. Just over the rise, there was a boy on his bike stopped in the middle of the road waiting for the traffic to clear so he could turn left for home. There was not enough road for both of us, and at my speed, I knew I would hit him.

I had to leave the road, and I remember deciding to do so just when

I saw a row of mailboxes along the side of the road, each resting on a frame of 1" cast iron piping. It was raining at the time, and I knew I had to ditch my motorcycle or suffer severe injury ramming into those metal pipes. Sure enough, my bike slammed right into the pipes, bending the handlebars up 90 degrees. Aside from a few skin burns, I was fine, rolling to a stop behind my motorcycle.

During the 1 or 2 seconds it took this accident to unfold, my mind was focused on one aim only: escaping injury.

In chapter 2, I described how positive and negative emotions are independent of one another. There are many reasons that this separation is adaptive, but perhaps the most obvious benefit is in terms of depth of information processing. As long as we retain two separate registers for emotional information about our experiences, we can make richer and more complex evaluations of ourselves and our motivations, and how our interactions in the world affect us. We can weigh the good with the bad before deciding what action to take. And most important situations in our lives require careful appraisals because they contain both costs and benefits, risks and the promise of adventure and good fortune.

Information processing requires cognitive resources, however, and when we process positive and negative affective information separately, it is more expensive in terms of these resources than when we process them as opposites. In many demanding situations, the benefits of fuller information are more than offset by their costs. For one thing, information processing takes time. In the motorcycle accident I just described, a threat of harm focused the emotional experience to permit a rapid and unified response.

The stress need not be life threatening, however, to challenge us emotionally. Everyday events that alert us to unresolved difficulties also can change how we respond. It may be a notice of a bounced check a week before the next payday, a troublesome quarrel with a teenage daughter, or a smile missing at the bedpost from one's partner of many years. There are many ways that such events upend us emotionally. Such experiences can put us on edge, leading us to react with irritation at the slightest bump in the orderly progress of any other part of the day: impatience in traffic, anger at an innocent mistake of an employee, readiness to slam down the phone on the marketer who calls during dinner. Suddenly thin skinned, we misinterpret innocent jokes as malevolent put-downs. What is happening to our processing of emotional experiences during these times?

As the previous chapter reveals, a defining characteristic of stress is that it increases uncertainty about the sustainability of our way of life. And uncertainty increases information demands. Under stress, we do not have as much cognitive capacity to process affective information as we have when our lives are calm. As a consequence, emotion processing is compressed. Our field of vision is narrowed,[1] and our judgments turn more black and white, more definite and less tentative; in a word, simplified.

There is perhaps no better example of this than people's emotional reactions during the presidential election at the turn of the century. For 5 weeks after the election, the vote count was too close for either candidate to declare victory. It was a time of great uncertainty for the whole country, or at least for those voters with a strong interest in the results of the presidential race. A virtual tie, the media said. One candidate won the popular vote, another was poised to win the electoral college count and assume the presidency, ahead by a mere 960 votes out of the 6 million cast in the state of Florida. The race was so close that the network coverage actually called the race in favor of one of the candidates, only to withdraw that projection less than an hour later. One of the candidates called to concede, only to call back and retract his concession a few minutes later.

I remember driving to work listening fervently for news. I was interested in nothing else. My whole focus was on that race. I switched channels whenever the news station I was listening to switched to a different story. My attention had narrowed dramatically. There was other news, some of it of considerable importance, even momentous. Bill Clinton became the first U.S. president to visit Vietnam since the war. I ignored it. Israeli school buses were now the targets of Palestinian terrorists, and Israeli gunships began firing rockets again in Gaza, killing civilians. There was increased bellicose posturing by the Taliban leadership in Afghanistan. Small potatoes compared with the court's decision about whether to allow a hand count of dimpled ballots.

It was like the Super Bowl with the teams tied and the game thrown into perpetual overtime. Court filings, late returns, court judgments, and new injunctions punctuated the news every day for weeks, alternating between favoring the candidacy of one or the other. With each possession, the team with the ball would march down the field, only to see its game-winning field goal blocked.

For many people, it was not just a game. Emotions did not just run high; they were increasingly polarized. The rhetoric escalated to a breaking point. Each side accused the other of trying to "steal" the election. People talked openly about how "disgusted" they were by the process and how much contempt they held for the other side. Even news commentators began taking sides. Few people were listening to any point of view other than their own. The space available in their minds for processing opposing thoughts and emotions was shrinking fast. One of my colleagues said that, in order to carry on in the face of this uncertainty, he had to imagine himself sealed inside a soundproof cylinder made of Plexiglas through which the word "vote" could not pass.

Plexiglass did not hold back the volatile protests at the Miami-Dade County Court House. "The fix is in!" were the words of Republican partisans as they stormed the headquarters of Miami-Dade County election officials. Ironically, those very actions fixed the result. Partly in reaction to the press of the crowd, the canvassing officials in Miami-Dade reversed their earlier decision and stopped the recount of some 10,000 disputed ballots. The election was decided, at least in part, by a cascade of strong emotions rushing through people's minds that would fill the void and put an end to uncertainty.

The Narrowing of Emotional Space

Suppose we could represent the potential range of our emotional experiences on graph paper—the kind of paper with lines criss-crossing on the page. We could chart the extent of our positive emotions using the lines that run along the vertical axis, and the extent of our negative emotions using the lines that run along the horizontal axis. When stress is low, our emotional playing field would be a broad, flat Cartesian space, with the vertical and horizontal lines crossing at right angles, perpendicular to one another. On this two-dimensional graph paper, there would be plenty of room to represent level of positive emotion along one axis, independent of the level of negative emotion along the other axis. Figure 4.1 presents one graphic illustration of what our emotional space might look like under stressful conditions. A stressful event disturbs our neat, two-dimensional maps of emotions. Like gravity curving the fabric of space stressors impinge on our awareness to cause the grid lines for positive and negative emotions to bend toward one another. It is no longer how good and bad we feel, but how much we feel good *or* bad.

With uncertainty high, the presence of one type of emotion can offset or interfere with the experience of another type of emotion to a significant degree. Spatially, I have drawn this as a curve in the geometry of emotions. We do not know the exact shape, though the evidence collected thus far has made it clear that the affective dimensions are curved inward to reflect an increasing inverse relationship between positive and negative emotions.

These stress-related emotional dynamics can be highly adaptive. First, a smaller condensed affective space allows for more rapid and adaptive responses during times of threat. When a tyrannosaurus rex is chasing you,

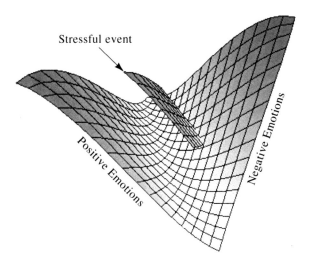

Stressful event

Positive Emotions

Negative Emotions

Figure 4.1. A collapse in affective space following stress.

it does not make much sense for you to wonder what is for dinner (you already know). Second, internal resources, both physical and mental, are better focused under stress, allowing for more efficient use of energy stores. Consider your thinking when trying to decide which wire to cut to defuse a time bomb with 10 seconds left. You think, "red or green?" as you are trying to recall your training at the School of Bomb Disassembly. You do not want any irrelevant memories to intrude on your consciousness at this point of choice. What if, as in the movie *Ghostbusters*, the Pillsbury dough-boy popped into your mind, just as it did in Dan Aykroyd's? The more uniform and regimented your thinking, the quicker and more accurate your appraisals are within a single dimension. You may be missing the subtleties, but they are best appreciated on another, less alarming day.

Del Paulhus and David Lim (1994) have given us a good example. These investigators studied whether judgments of photographs were affected by what they called arousing events.[2] They asked college students who were about to take a test to rate the likability of 50 photos of famous people, such as Adolf Hitler and Mother Theresa. They compared their ratings to those of a control group that did not have an imminent exam. To balance things, they used an equal number of photos of people who generally evoked positive emotions and photos that typically evoked negative emotions. Those students with an exam to worry about did not make more negative ratings or more positive ratings on average. Instead, they made more extreme ratings. They rated the positive photos more positively and the negative photos more negatively than those students without an upcoming exam. In reaction to the exam stress, the students' emotional minds narrowed to give simpler, more definitive judgments.

In the previous chapter I introduced a study of working life conducted in the Netherlands (van Eck, Nicolson, & Berkhof, 1998). For that study, white-collar workers made ratings of how they felt each day for 5 consecutive work days. Using what is known as experience sampling, these men were beeped 10 times at random intervals throughout each day, 50 times in all. At each moment, they rated how they felt, using adjectives supplied by the investigators. Some of these feeling words were positive in valence, such as *cheerful*, *relaxed*, and *satisfied*. Summing these ratings of these positive emotions provided scores for each person's positive affect at each beep. Items identifying negative emotions, such as *depressed*, *anxious*, and *worried*, were used similarly to indicate each person's negative affects at each beep.

The employees also reported how much stress they were experiencing, so we decided to examine how the workers' emotional lives changed during stressful times (Zautra, Berkhof, and Nicolson, 2002). We analyzed the responses to see whether there were differences in the degree of independence between positive and negative emotions during stressful as opposed to nonstressful moments.[3] The analyses revealed a set of findings that fit the Venn diagrams shown in Figure 4.2. When stress was low, the employee's positive feelings were almost entirely independent of their negative feelings. But when stress was high, positive and negative emotions were not independent of one another. The direction of that relationship was inverse: The more negative feelings the person expressed, the fewer positive feelings he or she had. In fact, under stress, there was a 25% overlap between positive and negative feelings. Good feelings were less likely in the presence of negative emotions. The space in the workers' consciousness for experiencing both emotions appeared to have shrunk an average of one-fourth of its previous size.

Here is another example, this time from our own laboratory. Phil Potter (1999) studied people in chronic pain from arthritis. In that study, 190 arthritis patients had weekly telephone interviews, and they reported on their positive and negative emotions and level of pain from their arthritis during those interviews. During most weeks, their disease activity was moderately low, and the patients' levels of negative affect and positive affect were independent of one another. The scales formed two separate dimensions. In those weeks when their disease activity was high, however, there was a significant shift in these correlations: Higher inverse correlations were found between positive and negative affect. Potter (1999) argued that the disease activity constituted a major source of stress for those

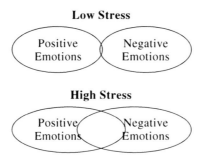

Figure 4.2. Stress and emotions.

with arthritis, leading them to react more narrowly to everyday experiences; they felt either "good" or "bad," not "good and bad."

For the same study population (Potter, 1999), my research team recorded weekly levels of interpersonal stress in the lives of these arthritis patients and also in a group of healthy older adult women who were similar in age but did not suffer from chronic pain. We estimated both the number of stressful events they reported each week and their perceptions of change in the stressfulness of the week compared with the previous week. The interpersonal events we inquired about were grouped together in four different domains: friends, spouse/significant other, family, and work. Table 4.1 lists some sample items from each of these domains to give you an idea of the nature of this inquiry.

We identified a highly stressful week for our participants if they reported twice as many stressful events within a domain than previously, if they rated the previous week much more stressful, or if they recorded a combination of both more events and higher ratings of stressfulness. Once we identified a stressful week, we arranged for a home interview within the next day or two. We had already conducted an assessment during a week in which the participant's life was relatively stress free and his or her arthritis was relatively inactive. That baseline week provided a good contrast to the high-stress week.

About 180 of the people in the study had high-stress weeks. The participants were interviewed in their homes during the following day or so, which gave us an opportunity to conduct a powerful test of whether the degree of independence in the ratings of positive and negative emotions changed when a week of relative calm was compared with a highly stressful week.[4]

At baseline, there was only a 9% overlap in the level of positive and negative affects. The correlation was negative and significant, meaning that when a person reported negative feelings, he or she tended to report fewer

Table 4.1. Sample Events from the Inventory of Small Life Events

Undesirable Events	Desirable Events
• Had an argument with partner	• Praised by family member
• Met an unfriendly person	• Visited with a friend
• Criticized by family member	• Child did something nice for you
• Argument with boss	• Completed work assignment

positive feelings. Still, over 90% of the scores for one emotion could not be accounted for by the other. In contrast, during the high-stress week, the degree of overlap increased to slightly more than 25%. Again, the relationship was inverse, meaning the more negative affect, the less positive affect. But during the high-stress week, negative affects crowded out the positive feelings to a much greater extent than they did during a non-stressful week[5] (Potter, 1999).

Do these types of changes in the structure of emotions following significant stress apply to other populations as well? We (Zautra, Reich, Davis, Nicolson, & Potter, 2000) recently examined whether older adults would fit the patterns we observed for arthritis patients. For this study, we asked men and women between 60 and 80 years of age to report on their emotional health. Twenty-nine of these elders had recently lost a spouse, 25 were physically disabled, and 60 were healthy nonbereaved controls. The bereaved participants had experienced the death of a spouse between 7 and 9 months before the assessment of positive and negative affect. All disabled participants had moderate to severe activity limitation and had reported a new illness or injury or a significant worsening of a preexisting condition within 6 months of the initial screening. The healthy participants were in the same age group as the other older adults, but they had not experienced the death of a spouse within the previous 2 years, or a disabling illness or injury within the previous year.

As one might expect, positive affect was lower and negative affect was higher for bereaved and disabled participants compared with the healthy elders. More important, the correlation between positive and negative affect was significantly higher for the bereaved and physically challenged older adults: .52 for the highly stressed elders and .13 for those without either major calamity (Zautra et al., 2000).

These data are useful because they show effects that are due to real-life experiences rather than experimentally induced stressors that might not provide as accurate a portrayal of the person's response. But this "real life" aspect can be limiting as well. Participants could not be randomly assigned to major stressors such as these. The lack of random assignment leaves open the possibility that something other than the stress experiences may have differed between these groups. Whatever it might be, that difference could be responsible for the results. The groups are comparable in age, gender, number of children, and other characteristics, so we doubt that any biases were introduced in the selection procedures. But we cannot be certain that the groups did not differ in some other important way that we did not measure.

To resolve these concerns, we (Zautra et al., 2000) also analyzed data from another study of older adults. In this study, the experimenters "stressed" each participant, but not until they had gathered prestress measures on mood and emotion. The stressor amounted to a speech the participants had to give while being videotaped in which they described their best and worst personal qualities. Twenty-six men and 30 women (average age of 65) participated in the study. They answered questions about their positive and their negative emotions four times: once before the speech, a second time immediately after the speech, and two more times, 40 minutes and 60 minutes after the baseline assessment. Once again the findings conformed to the patterns we observed in other studies: a sharp increase in the inverse correlation between positive and negative affects during stress, returning to baseline levels during recovery. Stressful experiences seemed to modify the structure of affective experiences, increasing in the degree to which negative emotions would cancel out positive feeling states.

In the studies reviewed thus far, it appears that stress poses serious threats to positive affective health by reducing the boundaries between negative and positive affect. But our model does not preclude the opposite: a significant decrease in negative emotion coinciding with increases in positive feelings during times of stress. These are the opportunities for improving well-being that stress affords, and we are often unaware of these forces at work. During stressful times, our attention is drawn to the crisis. But what if something wonderful occurs: A caring friend reaches out to us for the first time, or, after a lengthy deliberation, a supervisor at work, faced with making an "up or out" decision about us, chooses promotion over dismissal. The experience can be exhilarating. Pain and pleasure combine in these defining moments of crisis in which positive and negative emotions are intertwined.

John Reich and I (Reich & Zautra, 1981) conducted a study to see if these effects could be reproduced, not by manipulating the level of stress but by introducing more positive events. We recruited 141 college students and asked them to report the number of stressful events they had experienced recently and to rate their levels of life satisfaction and psychological distress. Then we asked one-third of the sample to engage in positive activities, telling them to "go do 12 pleasurable things, in addition to what you would do normally." We gave them 2 weeks to comply. They returned to fill out the posttests after that time. That, in essence, was our experimental manipulation. Two groups served as controls. One group was given no instructions but simply returned 2 weeks later. To control for any bias introduced by simply telling college students to do something positive, we asked the remaining one-third of the sample to do two pleasurable things over the following 2 weeks. We hypothesized that only the group given instructions to do 12 pleasurable things would show the benefits of positive events.

Those students given the push to do 12 pleasurable things reported an increase in life satisfaction, and even those with instructions to do just two additional pleasurable activities increased their positive moods. The pleasurable activities did not lower distress, however, with one key exception. Those college students who reported many stressful events at the time at which they were engaging in pleasurable activities showed a significant drop in psychological distress. Stress provided an opportunity for students to lower their negative affects through engaging in activities that would boost their positive emotions.

Laughter and Stress

Events that boost positive states come in many forms, and one that has just begun to receive scientific attention is laughter. Norman Cousins's story (1981) stimulated this interest in humor. This former editor of *The Saturday Review* developed a rare skin disease that inflamed connective tissue just beneath the skin's surface. The condition was very painful, and Cousins was hospitalized. Even with all the care and attention he received at the hospital, his health did not improve. On the contrary, he found the conditions of in-patient care sterile and smothering: *Iatrogenic* is the medical term for the situation in which doctors and nurses do what they think is best for you but their efforts make matters worse rather than better.

Cousins (1981) described his flight from the hospital as if it were a prison breakout, escaping from suffocating confinement to take charge of his own care in a hotel room across the street. There, with the help of understanding nurses, he entertained himself by playing his favorite Marx Brothers' movies, and engaging in other merry-making sight gags. As a result, his condition improved dramatically. Medically speaking, it was a minor miracle.

Does this mean that laughter is better than modern medicine? Not in the least. In fact, we all need to be wary of using testimonials as valid scientific evidence. There are other potential explanations for Cousins's recovery. Since Cousins's book appeared, however, a number of research- ers have begun to examine the benefits of laughter.[6] Academic journals dedicated to this research agenda have sprung up as well, including *The International Journal of Humor Research* and one simply titled *Humor*.

Kuiper and Martin (1998) have been examining the role of laughter in response to stress as part of a research program dedicated to understand- ing individual differences in "sense of humor" and the value of laughter to our well-being. They asked whether laughter would interrupt the usual negative affective responses to everyday life stress. Eighty men and women completed laughter diaries for 3 days, monitoring their levels of stress and their positive and negative emotions. Consistent with their hypotheses, laughter did not reduce negative emotions most of the time. But for those who had had a particularly stressful 3 days, laughter was associated with fewer negative feelings (Kuiper & Martin, 1998).

How do we understand these results? The authors offered a number of alternative explanations, including a common favorite among many stress researchers: that positive emotions provide a buffer against stress. But that proposition is more of a description than an explanation of the findings. Stress-related changes in the relationship between positive and negative emotions provide the mechanism that may underlie the effects that Kuiper and Martin (1998) observed.

One way to understand laughter is to see it as a consequence of odd combinations of affects, like putting two ideas together that do not usually go together: the proverbial "good news" and "bad news" sequence.[7] Now, I do not think that this definition fits all types of humor, but my aim here is to identify one facet of jokes that makes us laugh: finding something pleasurable in something painful. Those who laughed more in Kuiper and Martin's (1998) study kept their positive affect levels unharmed or even elevated while encountering stressors. By finding something comical during times of stress, the study participants sustained positive affects that could reduce negative emotions. Perhaps, too, those people who hold more com- plex schemas for emotional awareness are more apt to laugh in difficult situations and thus to find ways to keep their positive emotions protected from anxiety and other negative emotions that may arise during times of stress.

Can laughter ever be harmful? In our culture there is one occasion on which laughter is definitely not sanctioned: when grieving the death of a loved one. We wear black both as a symbol of the loss of the positive force of that relationship and also to signify the absence of joy. What happens if you smile, or worse yet, laugh, when mourning the loss of your partner? Some approaches to understanding the healing process have taken a rather dim view of the expression of positive emotions during grief "work," arguing that we may unconsciously wish to avoid the pain of fully experiencing the loss. Jocularity under these circumstances is thought to betray a desire to divert attention from "working through" the loss experience; it is believed to subvert the human need to fully experience the painful emotions associated with the death of a loved one.

Not all cultures share the view that sorrow and pain need to be expressed and that merriment during this time of grief is salt in the wound. The small island nation of Bali provides a study of contrasts (Wikan, 1989). The Balinese believe that laughter aids the healing process and also prevents the spread of negative emotions to other members of the community. For them, laughter makes the blood flow more freely in the veins and calms our hearts.[8]

George Bonanno and Dacher Keltner (1997) tested one of the predictions of the "laughter as denial" model.—the prediction that those who laugh during grief work would take longer to recover.[9] They recruited 38 men and women from the San Francisco Bay area who had lost a spouse between 3 and 6 months earlier. To track the course of their recovery, Bonanno and Keltner (1997) conducted clinical interviews with these volunteers at 6, 14, and 25 months after the death of the spouse. They also conducted what they called a "narrative interview" in which the bereaved person was asked to "relate as openly as possible whatever comes to your mind" about two persons: their deceased partners and the most important living person in their lives currently.

The interesting part of this study is that, instead of just asking the study participants to report how they felt, the researchers filmed the participants and then coded their facial expressions for the display of various emotions while they talked about their late spouses. They coded the expression of a number of negative emotions, including anger, contempt, and sadness, but they also coded positive emotions, such as enjoyment and amusement. They then examined whether the extent of expression of these various emotions predicted grief-related mental health symptoms.

The bereaved who expressed anger, contempt, and fear during their narrative interviews had the worst prognosis of all participants. They were still showing problems of adjustment 25 months after their partners' deaths. Not all negative emotional displays showed these patterns, however. Expressing sadness did not influence adjustment for better or worse. Those who expressed positive emotions, especially full open-mouthed laughter during their discussions of their partners, showed better adjustment at every assessment than those who did not laugh. Both the expression of anger and the absence of positive emotion predicted poor adjustment 2 years after the spouses' deaths. To answer the question I posed earlier, the evidence indicates that even in grieving, and maybe especially during this time, the expression of strong positive emotions assists recovery from stress. When our emotional lives are constricted, it appears that laughter can transform our experiences by liberating positive feelings from the bleak prospects conferred on us by negative emotions.

Fredrickson and Levenson (1998) have suggested that one of the principal roles of positive emotions is the "undoing" of negative emotions. They provide some convincing evidence that physiological responses to stress are altered by positive emotions. To demonstrate their point, these investigators showed one sample of participants an amusing movie right after they showed a distressing one; they recorded participants' cardiovascular activity during both movies. They were interested in the rate of recovery in the cardiovascular response following the rise during the initial stressful film. In one comparison condition, participants watched a second movie that was neutral in emotional content, and others watched a sad movie. There was a second positive emotion condition as well: a movie that generated feelings of contentment. The two groups that recovered most quickly to baseline levels during the second movie were those people who watched the amusing film and those who watched the film that generated contentment.

Do our natural responses to stress have effects similar to those induced experimentally? Fredrickson and Levenson (1998) did a second study to address this question. They observed the facial expressions of the participants who watched a very sad film and recorded cardiovascular responses simultaneously. Some people were caught on camera smiling occasionally while watching the film. Others sat grim-faced throughout. Both those who were smiling and those who were grim were equally saddened by the movie and showed elevations in cardiovascular response consistent with a stress response. The cardiovascular response returned to normal much more rapidly in one group. You have probably already guessed who recovered most quickly: those who smiled.

In sum, these studies indicate that positive events and emotions have their greatest influence on negative emotions and cardiovascular health when the person is under stress. This pattern of results closely fits the model of compression of affective space that we have introduced.

In essence, we find that stress provides the third force in life's triangle, defining the range and depth of our positive and negative emotional experiences. To understand our emotions, we need to attend to both positive and negative states of consciousness. These are not static structures but fluid representations of our responses to the world in which we live, shaped by the degree of stress in our lives. Dynamic forces influence our experience of our emotional states and ultimately how our emotions influence our behavior. Full understanding of the impact of our emotions on our physical and mental health requires knowledge of the demands placed on us to act and react, both to rare catastrophic events and also to upending experiences in everyday life. In the next two chapters, I apply these principles and take a fresh look at the evidence for the ways in which positive emotions influence mental and physical health during times of stability and times of upheaval in our lives.

5   Positive Emotions and Mental Health

Are We Chasing the Rainbow?

In a dark time, the eye begins to see.
—Theodore Roethke,
"In a Dark Time"

"My daughter took my pain with her." One of our rheumatoid arthritis patients said that to us. We were marveling that the pain due to her disease had suddenly dropped to 0 from moderately high levels of 60 on a 0-to-100 scale. She saw this change as her body's reaction to the death of her daughter. Actually, this woman had lost her father and daughter within the same 2 weeks. It happened by chance to be a time at which we were monitoring her stress and disease activity with weekly interviews, so we were able to detect these changes in disease occurring in concert with the deaths in her family. We also were able to confirm a clear reduction in clinical signs of inflammation following those deaths by physician joint examinations (Potter & Zautra, 1997).[1] The major losses she experienced had unintended benefits to her health. In fact, those benefits lasted about 6 months, the usual period of time associated with grieving over the death of a close family member.

This is an unusual case example. The more common assumption is that stress is usually bad for our health but potentially good for us in other important ways. Stressful events may give way to responses that are transforming, providing opportunities for us to learn and become stronger psychologically as a consequence. In the next two chapters I review the evidence for this "silver lining" in adversity. This chapter focuses on mental health, and chapter 6 examines studies of physical health outcomes. Allow me to forewarn the reader, though: The results are not exactly what you might expect.

Among the first to suggest a salubrious consequence of stressful experiences was Hans Eysenck (1983). He proposed that adverse life experience could "inoculate" a person against future calamities. Initial exposure to a specific type of stressor would allow the person to acquire coping responses useful in defending against a similar stressor in the future. This is analogous to the way in which the immune system develops memory cells following initial exposure to pathogens, cells that make the organism better equipped to respond effectively to a second exposure. There has not been a great deal of evidence supporting or refuting Eysenck's claim (however, see Guarnaccia, 1990[2]), but it certainly is a model worth keeping in mind during difficult times.

"If only it were this simple!" some of my colleagues in the psychological sciences would say. Indeed, most stress researchers would agree that major stressors such as a death in the family place a person at risk, making him or her more vulnerable to psychological, as well as health, problems.[3] This way of thinking derives, at least in part, from Hans Selye's model (1973) In principle, Selye believed that we all have limits as to how much stress we can tolerate before the regulatory systems in the body which preserve homeostasis break down. More up-to-date models focus on contrasting maladaptive stress responses such as "learned helplessness" with more adaptive ones such as "learned resourcefulness."[4] Stressful events threaten our beliefs in our ability to cope with life's challenges. If, as a consequence of traumatic events, we think of ourselves as failures and believe that we have little influence over the course of our lives, we may respond with feelings of depression, become demoralized, and stop caring for ourselves. Divorce has been known to affect people in just these ways, and for some, the death of a loved one can have similar effects.

Most researchers would argue that our responses to stressful events are the keys to successful adaptation. As I discussed in chapter 3, there is also ample evidence that some ways of reacting create many more problems than they solve. In the final analysis, there is little doubt that people differ in how they cope with stressful events and that those who cope poorly clearly suffer the consequences in terms of poor mental health. The $64,000 question is whether we can end up better than we were before it all started as a consequence of our own efforts. In short, can we become stronger from these experiences? Can we turn swords into ploughshares?

Significant events in our lives may be thought of as turning points.[5] Crises make us stronger when resolved successfully and make us weaker when unresolved or resolved poorly.[6] There are many factors that might influence how well we cope, including our own mental health at the time of the stressful event. Also, the responses of important people in our lives, such as our parents, children, spouses, and supervisors at work, all can help tip the balance in terms of success or failure in adaptation.

Do people find ways of transforming stressors? It turns out that they do, and frequently. In my own community studies, I ask people to report what they do to help themselves cope with difficult situations in their lives. Without prompting, one response that people offer about 20% of the time is that they "look for the silver lining."[7] Coping inventories usually contain a set of questions to probe this transformation, typically referred to as *cognitive restructuring.* For example, the items might ask whether the person would "Try to learn or grow from the experience" or "Try to find the good in what has happened." People in stressful situations frequently report these kinds of thoughts. When prompted by questions such as these, more than 50% of adults state that they rely on these transforming thoughts to help them through the situations they find stressful (see Schaefer & Moos, 1998; Smith, 2000).

Does mental health actually improve through coping in this manner, or are the people who cope this way just painting over difficult times? The evidence is not so straightforward. In fact, to answer this question at all requires an answer to another question first: What do we consider to be evidence of better mental health? Let us assume that what we mean by improvements in mental health are reductions in psychological distress. Then the surprising answer is no; mental health *does not* improve from such transforming experiences.

It is useful to examine those studies that have looked at this question with the thoroughness needed to uncover evidence on this very important question. Darlene Goodhart (1985) tested whether there would be improvements in mental health among those people who reported what she called "positive conversions." These conversions were gains resulting from the stressful life experiences. These gains included personal growth consequences such as, "Developed greater trust in personal judgment," and "Became more of the kind of person I wanted to be," and social relationship gains such as "Got involved in more satisfying relationships." Her inventory was extensive, containing 53 kinds of positive outcomes. She asked 175 college students to report on stressful events and the outcomes of their efforts to cope with those stressors and then examined the relationship between their mental health and the degree to which they reported positive conversions. As a counterweight to these conversions, she also collected data on 51 potentially negative outcomes, such as, "began feeling less capable of handling things," and other indicators of a failure to cope successfully with the stressful event.

The results were quite consistent across a number of indicators of psychological distress. *Positive conversions had no effects*, whereas negative outcomes were strong predictors of continuing distress for these students. A result such as this is disappointing, to say the least, for those who expect to see strong gains in mental health following such conversions.

Goodhart (1985) went further, asking the same students to report on new stressors and their mental health after a 2-month hiatus. If positive conversions made the student more resilient then, Goodhart argued, those with a greater number of positive conversions at the first assessment ought to show less distress when facing reported new stressors when they were assessed a second time, 2 months later. They did not show any evidence of this. Breaking the conversion measure into components such as personal growth versus social relationship improvements did not make a difference either. Transforming stressors was striking out left and right as a means of improving mental health.

There is an incongruity here, though. On the one hand, there is ample evidence that people believe that they can transform the meaning of calamities so that they benefit emotionally. Yet, these conversions of bad to good appear to hold little solace for them when coping with distressing events. How do we resolve these apparent contradictions?

One might first look for problems in the researcher's methods. There are limitations in any study and Goodhart's (1985) is no exception. One may question whether there was sufficient time between the first and the second assessments to detect benefits of this transformational coping. The stressful events they converted may have been relatively inconsequential, and those events may have been quite different from those that the person reported at the second assessment. Indeed, positive conversions of more central events in the people's lives might make more noticeable differences in their mental health.

Folkman, Chesney, Collette, Boccellari, and Cooke (1996) examined the benefits of transformational coping for people contending with the illnesses and eventual death of their partners who suffered from acquired immune deficiency syndrome (AIDS). In periodic interviews, Folkman et al. asked those caregivers to relate how they coped with the suffering and death of their loved ones. Indeed, she found that many of her participants found ways to transform their experiences that were uplifting emotionally.

Because not everyone reported transformational coping, it was possible to inquire whether those who employed those strategies were better off psychologically. Further, because the caregivers reported their coping strategies during each interview, it was possible to observe shifts in ways of coping over time and to ask whether changes toward more transformational coping would make a difference in the person's level of distress. Did

Folkman and her colleagues observe better adjustment following transformational coping? No. Their findings were similar to Goodhart's (1985) results with college students in this respect. There were no differences in levels of psychological distress between those people who found some good in living through the experiences of suffering and death of their loved ones and those who did not.[8]

Recently, Bruce Smith (2000) examined the data from the 18 published studies that addressed the question of whether people who reported benefits arising from stressful experiences had lower levels of psychological distress than others who experienced similar stressors but did not report benefits.[9] When he computed an average effect based on these studies, using a scale that ranged from $+1$ to -1, he found that the relationship hovered close to 0.

How are we to understand these results? Are people simply deceiving themselves by reporting benefits in misguided attempts to feel better about calamities that befall them and their loved ones?

The fault really lies with social scientists' (mis)conceptions about what constitutes mental health. The focus has been on psychological distress: feelings of anxiety, depression, and other states of unrest within the psyche. However, the benefits of transforming stressful experiences do not lie in this realm of mental health.

Where, then, might we look for evidence of improvements in mental health, if not in reductions in the levels of anxiety and depression? One central need is to sustain interest in life's tasks in spite of distressing experiences. At the core of such motivations are expectations for positive emotional outcomes. As I have suggested, evidence from a number of sources suggests that, without such nourishment, we lose incentive to carry on with life at all.

Is there evidence that transformational coping influences these positive affects? Both Goodhart (1985) and Folkman et al. (1996) included measures of positive emotions, as well as negative emotions, in their studies. Both found evidence that those positive emotions increased in concert with these transformational forms of coping. People who speak of silver linings are not deceiving themselves. It is the narrowness of our definitions of what constitutes mental health that has been misleading. A sustained positive engagement with life results from these particular coping efforts, even if the distress the person experiences does not subside.

Here, Smith's (2000) review is helpful again. In 6 of the 18 studies he reviewed, the authors had recorded evidence of positive mental health, along with reports of benefit finding. In those studies, Smith found a consistent pattern. People who found benefits were happier.[10] In fact, when he ran a statistical test that compared distress versus well-being outcomes for those studies that assessed both, he found an important difference: Benefits boosted positive emotions more strongly than they ameliorated distress (Smith, 2000).

How significant is this benefit in the scheme of things? Certainly, the addition of moments of joy enriches life, even if briefly. Few mental health experts would consider this result satisfying, however, without a demonstrable reduction in distress. Is our search for more profound mental health benefits tantamount to chasing rainbows? Do the positive emotions that derive from transforming stressful experiences translate into any more important mental health benefits than these boosts in positive emotion?

The answer depends on how you ask the question. The research literature is replete with findings similar to Goodhart's (1985).[11] Active coping efforts that transform stressful experiences into opportunities for growth usually are not associated with less psychological upset in the long term. A telling example is a very carefully designed study of bereavement conducted by Darrin Lehman and his colleagues (Lehman et al., 1993). They examined the positive changes reported by those who experienced a sudden loss of a close family member. The number of benefits that arose from the deaths was unrelated to psychological distress 4 to 7 years later. One may question whether any stress-induced changes would be expected to last for so long a time. But other changes did have lasting effects. Although there were no reductions in distress from positive changes, the number of negative changes was associated with poorer mental health over the long term. Certainly this would be a bitter pill to swallow: that we can learn what *not* to say or do to harm oneself any further but not how to help ourselves or those we love feel less pain?

Some models of mental health offer a broader perspective on adaptation than one that is focused solely on resolving emotional distress. One of these approaches focuses on our view of ourselves as effective agents in this world, another on the factors that underlie meaningful social relations, and a third on our search for coherent themes and deeper meaning in our lives during troubling times. If we consider how these aspects of positive mental health are fortified by positive emotion, then we may better understand how moments of joy during difficult times may strengthen us even if they do not improve our defenses against psychological upset.

Stress as a Kiln for the Development of Self-efficacy

Robert White (1959) described a motivational principle that underlies much of our behavior: the need for effectance.[12] Unlike other needs that diminish when satisfied, this need grows stronger when exercised. Simply put, people strive to be effective in what they do, and the more successful they are, the more they want to do. Success in the face of adversity is a special case. It is a time at which positive feelings of accomplishment occur within the context of troubling events. Whether effectance is exercised by taking an action that solves the problem or by finding meaning and a greater good in the experience, the positive emotions that result may lead to a strengthening of personal efficacy and a broadening of the capacity for resilience.

One of my favorite children's stories, *The Little Engine That Could* (Piper, 1984), provides a good illustration. It is a simple story. A small engine is asked to take on a task usually reserved for larger engines: hauling a group of boxcars over a mountain pass. It is a stressful time. If the train does not arrive at the other side soon, many children will be without their toys for Christmas. It is a tough assignment, and the engine almost does not make it over the top. What gives our little guy the needed energy to succeed? A simple mantra he repeats to himself over and over as he chugs along: "I think I can, I think I can, I think I can." That thinking process is what a personal sense of efficacy is, in a nutshell.

More formally, coping self-efficacy is a set of beliefs concerning one's abilities to cope successfully with adverse circumstances. The importance of expectations in the governing behavior has a long history in cognitive psychology, and expectations of oneself, referred to as self-efficacy, have been developed as a focal point of adaptation from a cognitive perspective (Bandura, 1992a, 1992b).[13] Even if a stressful event gives rise to considerable emotional upset, a person can still feel able to resolve the crisis successfully. There is no doubt but that the Little Engine suffered on the way up the mountain. But that stress can provide a fire that tempers the individual's capacity to adapt to stressful events. The blend of distressing circumstances and positive affects gained by small wins along the way can create a unique product: an increased sense of personal efficacy. Those beliefs in oneself strengthen resolve and enhance adaptation.

Such beliefs may be particularly valuable when people are coping with chronic stressors such as an ongoing illness or a troubled interpersonal relationship. The stressful circumstances are likely to recur, and efficacy beliefs are likely to reduce both anticipatory anxiety and the psychological distress that accompanies the stressors. Indeed, there is now extensive evidence in the literature that efficacy in coping serves as a protective factor against loss of morale among older adults who become disabled (Zautra, Hoffman, & Reich, 1997; Zautra, Reich, & Newsom, 1995).[14]

To what extent are these efficacy judgments influenced by the coping efforts the person actually employs in response to stressful life events? We have found that some coping responses enhance a person's beliefs that they can make an effective response to the stressor. Active forms of coping may be especially likely to enhance self-efficacy. The benefits that accrue from active, mindful approaches to problem resolution may be found in the person's beliefs about his or her own capacity for resilience in the face of future calamities.

My colleagues and I (Potter, Engel, Hamilton, & Zautra, 2002) examined the benefits of self-efficacy beliefs among arthritis sufferers who were attempting to reduce pain and improve their physical functioning by undergoing total knee replacement surgery. We enlisted the help of orthopedic surgeons who performed total knee replacement surgeries for men and women with severe pain and functional limitation due to osteoarthritis of the knee. The surgeons allowed us to conduct assessments of the arthritis patients' psychological status during preoperative appointments and then to reassess the patients at 4 weeks and at 6 months after surgery. Nursing staff rated the patients' pain and physical functioning once prior to and twice after surgery. We also asked the patients to tell us what steps they took to cope, how effectively they thought they were dealing with their knee pain, the expectations they had for the success of their surgery, and their judgments of their own mental and physical functioning before and after knee replacement.

Presurgery functioning and postsurgery coping were used to predict who would show the greatest improvement in quality of life from the knee replacement 6 months afterward.

Figure 5.1 shows what we found. Each arrow represents a relationship with functional health 6 months after surgery above chance levels of association. The top arrow shows that presurgery functioning was a clear predictor of how well the person could use the knee 6 months afterward. The arrow just below that one shows that patients with pessimistic expectations for successful outcomes had their prophesies come true to some extent. Those who had fewer hopes for recovery actually did less well than their counterparts who had greater hope and less pessimism regarding the likelihood of surgery success. After accounting for these expectancies and presurgery functioning, we turned next to assess the independent contribution of efficacy beliefs on surgery outcomes.

We found that those who felt that they could be effective in coping with knee pain after surgery showed the greatest gains from their surgery. They had less pain, and showed the greatest gains in functional health. In the final analysis, these "I think I can" beliefs were the most important factors in determining who improved most following surgery. Active coping efforts, including problem solving, exercise, and use of pain management techniques such as relaxation, were responsible, in part, for those efficacy beliefs.

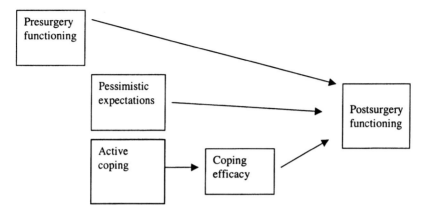

Figure 5.1. Factors in knee replacement surgery outcomes.

What makes a person likely to pursue recovery with the most vigor? We also assessed whether the patients had a strong "sense of purpose" in their lives prior to surgery based on how they answered such questions as "I have a sense of direction and purpose" and "I enjoy making plans for the future" (Smith & Zautra, 2000). We found that those surgery patients who had a strong sense of purpose, with plans in mind for the use of that new knee, were the most active following surgery. They also showed the greatest gains in psychological functioning. The physical aspect of replacing worn-out knees was not the whole story, by any means. Maximum gains in psychological and physical functioning accrued to those patients with a forward-looking approach to a better life, expectations for success, and strong beliefs in their capacity to recover rapidly.

The Formation of Social Bonds under Extreme Stress

There are other ways in which our responses to stress may lead to lasting adaptive transformations of our emotional lives. One way is through changes in our readiness to form new bonds and strengthen existing relationships during times of extreme social upheaval. These are the crises around which images of the adaptive self and sense of community are formed and stored for future stressful times. And if adaptation efforts fail to quell the emotional storm, these traumas may scar the affect system, leaving positive and negative emotions fused, perhaps permanently.

Elder and Clipp (1988) examined the effects of combat on social relationships among veterans of World War II and the Korean conflict. Physical combat is one of the most stressful situations we can face in life. Not only do we encounter the threat of imminent death but we may also experience physical injury, exhaustion, and loss of comrades and friends. In many cases, combat veterans witness the deaths of their closest friends. It is hard to imagine anyone surviving such extreme stress without emotional scars. When Elder and Clipp (1988) interviewed 149 veterans 30 years after the wars, the posttraumatic symptoms of nightmares and flashbacks had subsided for the most part, but many still had traumatic memories of the wartime events.

Elder and Clipp (1988) were interested in the bonding that occurred between comrades during the war and the extent to which those relationships became lasting friendships. In particular, they wanted to examine the role of combat-related stress in the formation of these ties. To investigate these phenomena, the researchers first grouped the veterans based on their degree of exposure to combat stress. They placed those who had had no actual combat experience in one group, those who had been in combat but not exposed to death in another, and a third group comprised those who had been exposed to deaths of members of their platoons. When the investigators compared these groups' recall of posttraumatic stress, only 15% of those soldiers who had seen no combat reported symptoms such as nightmares, sleeplessness, and irritability, compared with 54% of those who had witnessed death in combat (Elder & Clipp, 1988).

Did those soldiers who had witnessed death in combat avoid or embrace social ties with members of their platoons after the war? The investigators found that those who had witnessed death in combat were much more likely to have stayed in touch with members of their platoons. They report that "the loss of one or more comrades in combat intensifies ties to surviving mates." Sixty percent of those combat veterans who had lost a comrade reported continuing ties with at least one friend from the service, compared with 30% of those in combat who did not lose a comrade.

The social bonds created in battle were helpful in healing emotional wounds as well. Those who had had signs of posttraumatic stress at the end of the war more often attended reunions with their comrades. And those who went to reunions did not show those stress symptoms at the 30-year follow-up. In contrast, those with stress symptoms when the war ended who did not attend reunions continued to experience those symptoms 30 years later. The authors put it this way: "Traumatic experiences destroy and impair, but they also produce relationships that enrich and sustain life."[15]

Thus the most devastating stress of combat leads to very special relationships. It is a case in which strong positive regard for another is paired with surviving some of the most compelling negative experiences imaginable. The contrasting emotions are experienced under conditions of life or death, leading to the close conjunction of the extremes of positive and negative through the embrace of one's surviving comrades during the pain of loss. We have few such experiences in our lifetimes, but those we do experience play a central role in defining who we are in relation to others in our social world (see Simpson & Rholes, 1994). The bonds formed during extreme stress may not release us from the burdens of mental distress, but they do provide lasting experiences with complex emotions and perhaps a critical lesson: that strong positive emotional attachments may arise not in opposition to negative emotions but because of them.

Finding Meaning

The Austrian psychiatrist Victor Frankl (1963) was among the first to describe man's valiant efforts to find something of value in even the most desperate of circumstances. A survivor of the German concentration camps during World War II, he wrote of what he learned from his experiences there in a classic book titled *Man's Search for Meaning*. During forced marches, he would contemplate his wife, and those imaginings sustained him during some of the most difficult ordeals. He found that those who could find a purpose, even in the smallest of activities in their daily lives at the camp, were able to retain a semblance of hope. Those who could not find meaning were broken early in spirit and physically by the horrors of the camp.

Is the search for meaning a natural adaptive force within us that arises in response to stress? I believe it is. Rothbaum's notion of secondary control (Rothbaum et al., 1982), which I introduced in chapter 3, applies here. Our minds appear organized to propel us forward toward finding sources of positive emotion, even in the face of the worst imaginable conditions. The mind and body rebel against the suppression of positive emotions under stressful conditions. Aleksandr Solzhenitsyn (1974) writes of experiences in the Russian gulag, "It was only when I lay there on rotting prison straw that I sensed within myself the first stirrings of good (p. 615)." And Tony Blair, prime minister of Great Britain at the time of the terrorist attack on the World Trade Center and the Pentagon, led the peoples of the world to recovery from those traumatic events with these words: "Let us re-order this world around us and create lasting good out of the shadow of evil."[16]

Is this goodness a medicine that heals wounds? In this chapter, we have seen that the distress often remains within the confluence of silver linings. The experience of positive emotions when things fall apart is essential evidence, nonetheless, that life is not one-dimensional, after all.

Even in the worst of times, when our lives appear shattered into a thousand pieces, piled like rubble on the hard ground, these blades of life shoot through. I suspect that this gentle force of positive emotion does have hidden healing powers. However, this power is manifested in ways other than in the elimination of psychological distress. Evidence for the effects of the positive on physical health is the focus of the next chapter.

6 The Role of Positive Emotions in Health

There is just this for consolation: an hour here or there when our lives seem, against all odds and expectations, to burst open and give us everything we've ever imagined, though everyone but children (and perhaps even they) knows these hours will inevitably be followed by others, far darker and more difficult. Still we cherish the city, the morning; we hope, more than anything, for more.

—Michael Cunningham, *The Hours*

This chapter focuses on how positive emotions may benefit physical health. However, there are problems in associating health with happiness that might give us pause to begin with. First, there is our Puritan morality warning us that anything that feels good is probably bad for us. This dictum then is reinforced by many examples of how human pursuits all too often pose threats to public health. Before getting any further in examining the evidence for the benefits, I first want address how positive emotions are viewed as hazardous to public health.

I recall my own Puritanical views coming into focus when I saw the film *The Man Who Skied Down Everest*. In this movie, people risk their lives so that one fellow can ski down the slopes of the highest peak in the world.[1] In the end, the skier bails out halfway, tumbling down the icy slope, skis and poles flying every which way. He lives on, proud of his accomplishment, whereas others in his party suffer from frostbite and other maladies. What human folly, I told myself.

Public health researchers often take a dim view of such risky human strivings. Boxing, football, drinking, smoking, and our never-ending affection for speeding through yellow lights are more examples of an endless array of human passions that translate into needless injury and untimely death. Consider human sexuality. There probably is no greater risk to public health and stability in community life than our sexual appetites. Transmission of disease, including the most deadly virus yet known to man; male violence directed at other men and at women; family discord provoked by jealousy; and sexual transgressions are at the top of a long list of physical health problems that result from people seeking pleasurable sexual experiences.

Thus far, we have seen that positive emotions do not deter negative feeling states most of the time. Now we add to this the many public health calamities that have resulted from human desires for happiness. What good *are* these feelings? Many researchers would dispense with the study of positive emotions altogether, viewing them at best as part of the great human comedy and, at worst, as a cause of much human suffering. These social scientists would admonish us to refocus research efforts on the identification of health risk and personal vulnerability, including the risks that result from chasing after rainbows. Others are even less sanguine about our pursuit of happiness, viewing positive emotion as the enemy of reason and the harbinger of human folly. There is much evidence to support both of these views.

Early in the year 2000, there was a headline in *The New York Times* (Hershey, 2000) that reported an increase in deaths following the celebration of the new millennium. The city's health department reported a 50% increase in deaths during the first week of the year 2000, compared with the first week of 1999. Did people overdo their millennium celebrations? By coincidence, I met a funeral home director while traveling home from a meeting. He was no ordinary Charon (the ferryman of the dead in Greek mythology). He owned funeral homes in four different states. When I met him, he was puzzling over his own statistics: a 20% drop in business during the last month of 1999. The problem was not confined to one location: All his funeral homes had reported less business during the waning months of 1999. Now this is very unscientific evidence, but it raises an interesting question: Were some people able to wait until they reached the new millennium before dying? And if they were able to do this, how did they accomplish this feat? Is there a hidden role that positive pursuits play here, perhaps through promoting optimistic expectancies and a desire to extend life, that triggers health-sustaining physiological processes?

Norman Brown (1959) spoke of a human "life force,"[2] and positive emotions probably come as close as one can to a measurable property of that internal engine that propels us through life toward goals of self-realization. Fredrick Herzberg (1966) saw the satisfaction of these needs as the fuel for human motivation.[3] Unlike hunger or thirst, these positive strivings are not diminished with attention to those needs. Indeed, the drive toward self-fulfillment intensifies with successes in our strivings to achieve in areas of life that we value. For quality of life, these positive emotions are central to what is commonly referred to as "the good life."

To what extent do these human strivings fulfill human needs? That is, do we suffer from disengagement from goals? Csikszentmihalyi (1975) devised an experiment to address this question[4] by studying how people react when they were deprived of pleasurable experiences in their daily lives. He recruited a group of 20 undergraduate students at the University of Chicago and instructed them to "act in a normal way, doing all the things you have to do, but do not do anything that is play, or non-instrumental" (p. 162). Even little pleasures, like enjoying a glance at a beautiful sunset, were to be avoided. Many reported strong adverse reactions. Headaches, fatigue, and tension were common physical symptoms. Feeling less creative, angrier, and less reasonable were emotional costs of this deprivation. It seems that we need a steady diet of even these small pleasurable events to sustain us. It is a set of needs that is rarely acknowledged in the scientific study of life events. Yet the data clearly demonstrate that small pleasurable events sustain us through the course of everyday life, even if those experiences do nothing to solve the larger problems in our lives.

So perhaps it is true that we cannot do without positive emotions. Still the question remains: Are they good for us? As I discussed in chapter 2, these emotions arise mostly out of the satisfaction of a separate set of needs from the needs for self-defense and recovery from painful and otherwise distressing experiences. In the previous chapter I presented evidence of their value, primarily in positive mental health, not in alleviating psychological distress. We need to consider an important qualification introduced in chapter 4: There are times, particularly under stress, when attention to positive emotions may improve our prospects for health and recovery from illness. In fact, the evidence points to just this kind of influence: a strong physical health benefit, even when there is no reduction in symptoms of mental distress.

One of the places to look for such benefits is in studies of cardiovascular health. There is mounting evidence that positive emotions have an important role to play in protecting us from high blood pressure and other heart ailments. Affleck, Tennen, and Croog (1987) found these benefits in their study of 287 men who suffered heart attacks.[6] They interviewed these patients 7 weeks after their heart attacks and asked them whether they found any silver linings in that experience. About half of all participants acknowledged some benefit from the experience. Some reported that the heart attack led to a change in philosophy of life, including becoming more in touch with their values; others reported that they learned the value of healthy lifestyles; 25% reported that they modified their ways of doing things so that they could enjoy life more.

Affleck et al. (1987) tracked these patients for 8 years after their initial heart attacks, recording how many had another heart attack over the 8 years and how many reported physical impairments that limited their return to fully active lives. Those who had found some benefit from their brushes with death that first time had less disability and also were less likely to experience another heart attack than were those men who could find nothing good in what had happened to them. We do not know from Affleck et al.'s (1987) study whether those men who reported benefits actually carried out their plans to modify their lifestyles, nor do we know whether there were physiological changes that might explain the health benefits accruing from perceiving positive gains. The findings are intriguing nevertheless, for they suggest a direct link between positive benefit finding and cardiovascular health.

Helgeson and Fritz (1999) found direct evidence that positive beliefs influenced recovery from coronary heart disease.[8] They studied a group of 199 men and 99 women who had just undergone angioplasty. Angioplasty is a surgery frequently performed on patients with coronary heart disease. Its purpose is to unblock arteries, and in this purpose the surgery is highly successful, with 90% or more of surgical patients showing substantial reduction in arterial blockage, at least at first. However, within 6 months, many patients find that their heart problems return. The most frequent cause of that relapse is what is called restenosis, a return of the blockage in the coronary artery.

Helgeson and Fritz (1999) met their participants as they were leaving the hospital after successful angioplasty and recruited them into the study. Nearly 90% of those asked agreed to participate, which means that the study sample is likely to be representative of the population of patients who receive that procedure. The investigators gave the patients questionnaires to complete and then followed them over the next 6 months to see who would show a recurrence of cardiac ailments. The criteria included death due to a heart attack, another angioplasty, bypass surgery, and/or progression of disease as judged by the physician based on stress tests that revealed evidence of additional cardiac events. Twenty percent of the recruited patients had one of these cardiac events. The question the researchers asked was whether they could predict whose hearts would stay healthy after angioplasty, based on responses to the questionnaires completed just after surgery.

Helgeson and Fritz (1999) gave the heart patients three psychosocial measures: (1) measures of negative emotional states such as depression, hostility, and anxiety, (2) measures of healthy behaviors such as regular exercise, low-fat diets, and time for relaxation, and (3) a cluster of positive mental health measures they referred to as *cognitive adaptation*, including self-esteem, optimism, and sense of mastery. After ruling out any effects on angioplasty success from income, education, and other sociodemographic indicators, they tested whether these three variables would predict who would have adverse coronary events in the 6 months following surgery.

Only the measures of cognitive adaptation reliably predicted who had sustained recoveries following surgery. All other effects were marginal at best. When the investigators broke apart the measures within the adaptation index and tested them against one another, they found that self-esteem and optimism—states of mind saturated with positive emotion—were responsible for the effects. When they classified high, medium, and low scores on cognitive adaptation, they found that those low in these attributes were three times more likely to have a coronary event than those scoring highest on these indicators of positive mental health.

What mechanisms might be responsible for these protective effects of self-esteem and a positive outlook? One possibility was that those who were more upbeat led healthier lifestyles. In this study, however, they found no relationship between the health behavior measures and coronary events, ruling out those variables as a putative mechanism. Helgeson and Fritz (1999) suggest that self-esteem and optimism may lower blood pressure and heart rate directly through neuroendocrine mechanisms and lead to a less abrupt change in heart rate and blood pressure during stress, including, perhaps, the stress from the surgical experience itself.

Scientists have uncovered more evidence of the connection between positive emotions and health through the study of the neurophysiological effects of exercise on cardiovascular fitness. Exercise is something we know is good for us, at least in moderation. It also brings "runner's high" and other positive feelings. James McCubbin (1993; see also Dishman, 1997)[5] has been studying the physiological processes thought to be responsible for such positive feeling states. McCubbin (1993) has focused on a class of opioid substances in the brain known as beta-endorphins. As yet, researchers cannot directly observe the ebb and flow of these peptides within brain tissue. So experiments to examine the effects of neurochemicals such as endogenous opioids must assess those effects indirectly. They do this by administering a drug that is known to affect the chemical being studied. Sometimes an agonist is given, which is a substance that potentiates (or elevates) the response. Alternatively, an antagonist that blocks the biological response of interest is sometimes given.

McCubbin (1993) and his colleagues have done most of their work using antagonists. They provided aerobic training to a randomly chosen group of volunteers. Half of those who received training and half of the controls without training were given an opioid antagonist, a drug called naltrexone. The researchers administered this drug just prior to laboratory tests used to evaluate the effects of the cardiovascular training on blood pressure and heart rate reactions to stress. In the study, the stressor was a series of complex mental arithmetic problems presented under severe time pressure, a procedure known to elevate anyone's blood pressure and heart rate.

When the researchers compared those with exercise training to those who did not receive the training, there were clear differences between the groups. Having to solve complex math problems raised the blood pressure less in those with the exercise training. What happened to those participants given the drug that blocked opioid secretions? Interestingly enough, the beneficial effects of exercise disappeared. This evidence suggests that a signal from the opioid system is essential for the lowering of blood pressure responses following physical training.

These effects are not confined to those changes induced by exercise. McCubbin's research team has also found that relaxation training can have the same beneficial effects on stress reactivity (McCubbin, et al., 1996). So the physical conditioning does not appear to be the critical factor here. Instead, positive emotions, whether induced through training or relaxation and meditation, appear to be the keys that open a healthier blood flow. These results are not found just in laboratory studies. Investigators report similar findings when they have participants wear blood pressure gauges as they go about their daily routines.

Do these health benefits of positive emotions extend to other health problems? Cohen, Doyle, Turner, Alper, and Skoner (2002) investigated whether people with many positive and/or negative emotions were more susceptible to the common cold. Adult men and women, recruited with advertisements in the newspaper, first rated the extent of their everyday positive and negative emotions. To obtain this information, the investigators conducted telephone interviews on three evenings a week for 2 weeks, asking the participants whether they felt negative emotions such as depression, unhappiness, nervousness, tension, hostility, or anger during each day. They also asked participants about positive emotions. They constructed a separate index using adjectives such as *lively, happy, cheerful, calm,* and *relaxed* (Cohen et al., 2002).

Following these assessments, the investigators gave the participants nose drops with one of two types of rhinovirus and quarantined them for several days. To determine objectively whether the participants contracted colds, the researchers measured both the antibody response to the rhino-virus and the amount of nasal mucus during the 5 days after exposure. They also asked participants to report cold symptoms to obtain a subjective estimate of cold symptoms.

By objective criteria, slightly more than one-third of the participants got the flu following exposure to the virus, and the investigators then sought to predict who became ill from the reports of emotion provided during the telephone interviews. Those participants with high levels of positive emotion on the days before exposure to the virus were less likely to have the flu than participants with lower levels of positive emotion. In contrast, individual differences in negative emotion were unrelated to flu symptoms. These findings held for both objectively defined flu symptoms and subjectively defined symptoms. Tense and angry people were no more vulnerable to the flu than people who were not tense or angry. The vulnerable people were those who were not cheerful and energetic (Cohen et al., 2002).

Recovery from Traumatic Life Events: A Role for Positive Emotions?

Thus far, I have discussed the role of positive emotions in the ebb and flow of daily life. It may be instructive to extend this discussion to major, even traumatic, events, such as an untimely death of a close family member, to see what has been uncovered regarding health effects. Traumatic events are among the most studied and the least understood experiences. There is no doubt that these experiences can have profound effects on our psychological well-being. Janoff-Bulman (1992) has studied traumatic events extensively. Although traumas differ from one another in many ways, she has identified one unifying experience among those coping with these unexpected calamities: a shattering of fundamental assumptions. She notes that certain beliefs sustain us in our everyday lives. Prominent among those beliefs is that the world is a benevolent place, a place in which things happen for a reason. Traumas challenge those assumptions and at times even raise doubts about our self-worth.

The assumptions we have about the world allow us to maintain an orderly view of our relationship to events and reduce uncertainty about the future. The arbitrariness of traumatic experiences, however, lifts the curtain on our lives to reveal chaos where there had been order and un-certainty where there had been faith and trust. The stress is often severe, and the need for recovery of a coherent view of one's place in the world is great.

The healing process itself may take many forms, but there is one form that is the most popular: talking about one's emotional reactions to the event with someone who cares. It is called *self-disclosure*, and it has an extensive following among those who teach, perform, and engage in psychotherapy.

There are many theories concerning why self-disclosure may be helpful in recovery from major traumas. One popular model is that some people inhibit their expressions of negative feelings following severe crises. This inhibition bottles up those emotions, and such constraints on emotional expression are considered harmful not only to psychological adjustment but also to physiological adaptation. People may inhibit their self-expression because they are afraid of the powerful emotions they harbor, but, according to some theorists, failure to "get it out in the open" may leave an open wound, delaying the cognitive processing needed to come to terms with the experience and to reach closure. A failure to talk about what has happened may lead to rumination over the events, perhaps even with recurring mental images of the trauma. When people talk about traumatic experiences, they are reopening channels of communication between their emotions and processes of cognitive adaptation, allowing for better understanding of the event and a recovery of beliefs of fairness and other fundamental assumptions that had been challenged by the traumatic experience.

Pennebaker (1990) has designed studies to put these theories to empirical test. He asked college students to write about a stressful experience that was very meaningful to them, and he instructed other students to write about something else unrelated to events in their past. Those students who wrote about their traumas had fewer subsequent visits to the student health center and were happier, when assessed a month or two later, than those given the task of writing about something inconsequential. This result has been replicated numerous times with different groups and different measures of outcome, ranging from better work attendance to greater immune cell activity in the presence of a pathogen. Beneficial health effects also have arisen from talking, as well as writing, about the events. The key appears to be the expression of thoughts and feelings about the stressful experience.

How are we to understand the mechanisms of adaptation involved in recovery from these traumas? After 10 years of research and considerable success in reproducing these beneficial effects on health due to self-disclosure, Pennebaker, Mayne, and Francis (1997) examined some of the potential mechanisms that they believed were responsible for these effects. They analyzed the words people use to express themselves. In this case, the language people use is thought to be a window into their thought processes. Pennebaker et al. (1997) reasoned that the use of language containing strong negative feelings in the self-disclosing essays would be an important indicator that the person was allowing the expression of hidden emotions. Such expressions of negative emotional states would then lead to more accurate cognitive processing of the trauma and its impact and to better integration of the experience and a more coherent structure of meaning. In contrast, the expression of positive emotions would distract from the primary task of self-disclosure and recovery. Therefore, the researchers predicted that those people with many negative and few positive affect-laden words in their disclosures would benefit the most from telling their stories.

But the mechanisms of healing may be quite different than those identified by Pennebaker et al. (1997). From a two-dimensional view of emotional health, one of the potentially damaging effects of traumatic events is a loss of complexity in our emotional lives. Traumatic events not only raise negative affects but also reduce positive affects, and they may do so dramatically. These events disturb the normal wide berth between negative feelings and the capacity to experience positive emotions. Such is the subtext of "grief" following the death of a loved one and of being "paralyzed by fear" following a severe threat to life or livelihood. Positive emotions disappear, and the capacity to experience and express these feelings may be recovered only slowly for some, after weeks or even months. Usually when we think of the impact of trauma on health, we think of the impact of negative affective states over an extended period of time. But when we dissect the impact of these traumatic events, we see that two processes are occurring: the increase in negative emotions and the loss in the ability to experience positive feelings due to the collapse of affective dimensions following stressful events. After the terrorist attack on September 11th, 2001, many of us went through the succeeding days grim-faced, humorless, stone-cold in affect. It is this loss of positive capacities that may be the most disruptive to adaptation and health in the longterm: not the inhibition of expression of negative feelings but the inhibition of positive feeling states.

Let us return to the research on expression of emotions about past traumatic events to see how this model predicts different results from Pennebaker's (1990, 1997). Essentially, we argue that a return to health would be marked by a return to the relative independence of positive and negative affects. Those people who are able to reestablish a connection to positive emotion when reviewing the traumatic experiences should be most likely to show health benefits. In short, the more the person expresses positive emotions while retelling the story, the more he or she should find health benefits. The benefit would extend, however, only to those who reexamine the events fully enough to make the transformation real. Those who fail to reveal any negative emotions in the stories of their stressful experiences may still be in an emotional straitjacket, unable to allow coexpression of positive and negative feelings. Without this emotional richness, self-disclosure may not be beneficial.

These predictions, derived from our dynamic model of stress and emotions, were substantiated. When Pennebaker and colleagues (1997) counted the number of times the study participants expressed various emotions in their narratives, it was the number of positive affect expressions, not the number of negative affective words, that predicted better health. Some expression of negative feelings was useful, too. In fact, the people with the best health outcomes fit the profile we identified: Their disclosures of traumas included many positive emotion-laden words and a few negative affect words.

I do not pretend that this set of findings will be the last word on how people benefit from talking about difficult life experiences. This area of research is rich in complexity. Nevertheless, we are again alerted to how positive emotions emerge, when we might least expect them to, as a key benefit to adaptation and health.

A striking illustration of the life-sustaining properties of positive emotion comes from the "nun study" (Danner, Snowdon, & Friesen, 2001), an intensive examination of the health and longevity of 180 Sisters of Notre Dame conducted in the 1990s. These Catholic nuns were born prior to 1917 and ranged in age from 75 to 95. Over the course of the 9-year follow-up, 42% of these women died, and the researchers sought after variables that would predict survival.

It turned out that, when the nuns took their vows for the order, they were asked to write autobiographies. The researchers found these hand-written documents, many over 50 years old, in files kept in the rectories. Danner et al. (2001) wondered whether the emotions these nuns expressed in their autobiographies would predict who was still alive at the end of the study.

Each word was coded for the presence of negative emotion, positive emotion, and the absence of emotion. Then each sentence was scored in a similar way. Multiple raters were used to ensure reliability in these judgments, and the researchers were indeed able to confirm high levels of agreement among raters on the levels of emotion expressed in the autobiographies.

The investigators summed up the number of positive and negative emotion words and the number of positive and negative emotion sentences and then ranked each nun on her emotional expressiveness. The researchers then tested whether nuns who ranked high in emotional expression lived longer.

The number of negative emotions that were expressed did not predict who would stay alive. But the presence of positive emotions in the writings was strongly associated was longevity. Chance of survival across the 9-year study was 2.5 times greater for the 25% who expressed the greatest number of positive emotions. The researchers estimated that nuns in the top 25% in their use of positive emotions in their storytelling lived an average of 10 years longer (Danner et al., 2001).

By what route can positive emotions preserve our health and make us more resilient in the face of difficult, even traumatic, experiences? Let us return to the physiological model examined earlier for positive emotions generated from exercise: the opioids. Among their many actions, opioid systems are known to play a key role in regulating neuro-endocrine responses to stress, and in turn, to stress-related down-regulations of the immune system. Could gains in positive emotion lead to longevity through promoting a healthier immune response?

Even speculations about such a relationship would have been scoffed at 5 years ago by cancer researchers. Now there are some data, not in themselves conclusive but nonetheless suggestive, that this may well be the case. Researchers followed the lives of 40 gay men who had tested positive for HIV infection (Bower, Kemeny, Taylor, & Fahey, 1998; see also Folkman & Moskowitz, 2000). These men were part of Folkman et al.'s (1996) study study, reported on earlier. Each of these men had experienced a death of a close friend or partner due to AIDS. Bower et al. (1998) scored the transcripts of their interviews with these men to judge whether or not the men had found some meaning or purpose in the deaths of their friends and loved ones. Sixteen or 40% of the group did discuss finding meaning. Some reported important lessons, such as spending more time with people who they cared about and living life in the most satisfying way possible.

One marker of disease progression for those who are HIV-positive is the rate of decline in CD4 cells, which are key cells in immune function lost over time to the AIDS virus. Those partners who found meaning in the deaths of their loved ones had a slower rate of decline in circulating CD4 cells. Further, more of those partners who found meaning were alive 3 years later than those who had not found some benefit (Bower et al., 1998).

Some researchers are skeptical of findings that come from observational studies such as these. From a methodological point of view, only those investigations that manipulate the independent variable are "true" experiments. In Folkman et al.'s (1996) study, finding meaning was the key measure, and it defined individual-differences in how the HIV patients coped with bereavement. No matter how carefully any study is done, there is always some question that can be raised about whether other, unmeasured differences between patients that were hidden from the investigators could account for the findings. Only by experimentally inducing "meaning" in some way can researchers eliminate these uncertainties.

Cruess et al. (2000) encouraged a group of women with breast cancer to find meaning, with interesting results. They enlisted 34 women who had just had surgery and randomly assigned them to one of two conditions: a 10-week cognitive-behavioral stress management program or a waiting-list control group that would receive the same treatment but only after the experiment was completed. The investigators monitored two key outcomes from women in treatment and control conditions: degree of psychological distress and levels of cortisol in circulation in the bloodstream. The researchers expected to see treatment effects on psychological and physiological health. They reasoned that cortisol was a good marker for stress responses that suppress immune function. High cortisol levels would be particularly dangerous to breast cancer patients, who must rely on a responsive immune system to arrest further spread of malignant cells.

When Cruess et al. (2000) examined changes pre- to post intervention, they found no difference between groups in level of psychological distress. The intervention apparently did not influence the patient's experience of negative emotions. However, they did find differences in cortisol; the treatment group had lower levels of this immune-suppressing hormone in their bloodstreams than did the control group.

The cognitive treatment had emphasized patients' finding new and more positive interpretations of their illness as ways of transforming the stresses that this illness had brought about. When the investigators compared groups, the treatment group was, in fact, much more likely to report finding benefits from their experiences with breast cancer. Some remarked, for example, that their illness "brought the family closer together." Others reported a new appreciation of themselves and their lives with comments such as, "my illness made me more accepting of things."

The treatment lowered cortisol levels and increased benefit finding. The next and final step was to see if benefit finding lowered cortisol levels. It did. Those participants in the treatment group who showed lower levels of this stress hormone after the treatment were those who were able to find benefits from their experiences with cancer. The engagement of positive emotions through benefit finding appeared to be the key ingredient in improvements for these women, not a reduction in distress (Cruess et al., 2000).

These findings are dramatic illustrations of the potential links between immune system functioning and positive emotions. As it turns out, this finding is becoming increasingly commonplace. No one expected it, least of all those researchers investigating the role of stress hormones on immune processes. The focus on negative affective states has left many feeling blind-sided by these findings and more than a little reluctant to delve into the realm of positive emotions. It has been a place where angels fear to tread. In fact, scientists in such novel mind-body fields as psychoneuroimmunol-ogy[6] have been particularly reticent, fearing the huckster label—a designation that has been applied so aptly in the past to many who have promoted various snake oil preparations that promise to cure all that ails.

All the pieces of the puzzle are not in place. A biological mechanism by which positive emotions can turn on the immune system and thereby foster healthier and longer lives has not been identified. There are some candidates among the many chemical messengers, such as neuropeptide Y (Zukowska-Grojec, 1995), but to date, the absence of attention to this area leaves us with few careful experiments that are grounded in sound theoretical work. Nevertheless, empirical demonstrations of the effects of positive states on immune function are dotting the landscape with increasing frequency, as predicted by pioneers in this field (Melnuchuk, 1988; Panksepp, 1993).

Of late, considerable attention has focused on those immune processes involved in natural killer (NK) cell activity. These cells' ability to proliferate in response to the presence of cancer cells is frequently used as a measure of immune system health because such activity directly parallels a key immune function: protection against cancer cell growth. Valdimars-dottir and Bovbjerg (1997) conducted a straightforward study of the relationship between positive emotion and NK cell activity, with intriguing results. They recruited 48 healthy middle-aged women, asked them questions about their positive and negative feelings at the time, and drew blood on 2 consecutive days. They found that women who reported more positive mood had higher levels of NK cell activity than women with less positive mood, but not always. Only those women who reported negative mood got an immune system boost from positive mood. Those women who reported no negative emotions during those 2 days were unaffected by their positive moods. The presence of psychological distress appeared to have created a physiological context that favored the influence of positive states on immunity. It suggested that stress-related processes may trigger the healing properties of positive states.[7]

Another example comes from the work of Segerstrom, Taylor, Kemeny, and Fahey (1998). They studied changes in NK cell activity in 50 students in their first semesters of law school. At the beginning of the semester the researchers drew blood and asked the students to report on their degree of optimism. Segerstrom et al. (1998) used two measures of optimism in this study. One measure focused on the students' global beliefs and expectations about the course of their lives by asking them questions such as, "In uncertain times, I usually expect the best." Another measure focused more on their immediate beliefs in themselves with questions about current situations, such as, "It's unlikely I will fail (at law school)." Segerstrom et al. (1998) referred to this measure as situational optimism, as opposed to the other, global measures that they called "dispositional optimism." The interesting aspect of this study was that the researchers took advantage of the students' midterm exams as a naturally occurring stressor. They asked whether these two forms of optimism would influence change in immune activity identified from assays of the initial blood drawn at the start of the semester compared with the immune assays on blood drawn during midterms.

A global optimistic outlook had no effect on changes in NK cell activity during the stress of exams, so "Pollyanna" models of health received no support. However, there was a strong and reliable relationship between situational optimism and immune activity among these law students. Those students who were optimistic about their success in coping with the stresses of law school also had immune systems better prepared to engulf and destroy cancer cells than those who were not as optimistic. Two factors were important: (1) They were under stress, and (2) the positive state had relevance to the stressful situation.

For many illnesses such as cancer, we assume that greater immune system activity is beneficial. Yet autoimmune conditions such as rheumatoid arthritis result from overabundant immune responses that cause abnormal joint inflammation and pain. For people with autoimmune disorders, the effects of positive emotions may be quite different from those observed in cancer patients. Health from the standpoint of the immune system may be defined best by using theories of adaptation such as Bruce McEwen's (1998) model of allostatic load. As discussed in chapter 3, the key issue is not whether there is a sufficient immune response to stress but whether there is adequate homeostatic regulation of both the initial response and recovery. An imbalance in either direction can be harmful to health.

Yoshino, Fujimori, and Kohda (1996) and Nakajima, Hirai, and Yoshino (1999) have conducted two studies with rheumatoid arthritis patients to examine the effects of positive emotions on autoimmune processes. They brought groups of patients into a lecture hall after lunch and showed them an hour-long video of traditional Japanese comic stories. In the first study, they compared the patients' arthritis pain levels before and after the video and drew blood before and after to test for changes in levels of interleukin 6 (IL-6), a proinflammatory cytokine associated with autoimmune disease processes in rheumatoid arthritis. In a second study, the researchers compared the IL-6 levels of rheumatoid patients who saw the video with a control group of rheumatoid patients who were randomly selected not to see the video.

Both studies showed significant effects of humor on disease processes for patients in pain. Not only was the pain substantially lower, but also IL-6 levels were reduced significantly for those rheumatoid patients who watched the video. Increasing positive emotions in both studies reduced the production of immune products responsible for inflammation, pain, and damage to the body's joints.[8]

Do the studies on cancer and rheumatoid arthritis provide any clues as to mechanisms by which our bodies convert a positive emotion into better health? One aspect appears especially important, and that is the timing of the emotion. The positive emotion, when present at the time of stress, appears maximally effective in strengthening resistance. The stress can be an actual event, a painful episode, or the memory of a stressful time, as exemplified by the intrusive thoughts of those recalling traumas in their pasts.

In sum, these studies provide convincing evidence that positive emotions are a key ingredient in the preservation of health. They suggest a separate hidden dimension of influence on health that has been overshadowed by the focus on negative emotions. Attention to reduction of stress and psychological distress, however palliative, does not provide the only focus for preserving physical health. Repair of the boundaries between happiness and distress through a renewed openness to the experiences of positive emotions such as joy and contentment even in difficult times may be the type of healing that we need most to recover physical, as well as emotional, health. And if retaining emotional complexity is central to our health and well-being, we will need to reexamine our assumptions concerning what constitutes good mental health.

7　Emotional Intelligences

> *Negative Capability*, that is, when a man is capable of being in uncertainties, mysteries, doubts, without any irritable reaching after fact and reason.
>
> —John Keats, letter to his brothers,
> George and Thomas.

People differ in their emotional capacities, just as they differ in intellectual capacities. This chapter is devoted to exploring such individual differences in emotional intelligence. But what does it mean to be intelligent with emotions? Many in the behavioral sciences have grown up shouldering the philosophies of René Descartes and Immanuel Kant, who taught that emotion is the antithesis of reason. Logic, hard-nosed thinking, and high-speed analysis are thought to be the keys to the sublime when it comes to intellect. From this perspective, emotions are at best a nuisance, at worst a source of bias, irrationality, and error in information processing and decision-making. For some, emotional intelligence seems to be an oxymoron, like "kind terrorist" or "idiot savant."

Somewhere along the way to the end of the twentieth century, however, we turned away from processing speed as the sine qua non of intelligence. Perhaps it is the result of high-speed computers such as Deep Blue checkmating Garry Kasparov, the best human chess player at the time of the match. We talk of the need for good judgment, as we can no longer compete in computational tasks. Perhaps we can blame the baby boomers; according to some commentators, the boomers are talking about the need for wisdom just to compensate for the slowing of their intellectual skills. Whatever the cause of this new emphasis on emotional smarts, it is apparent that people differ in their capacity to experience, understand, communicate, and manage their feelings and in their ability to understand the feelings of others.

Together, these kinds of individual differences have come to be known as *emotional intelligence*.[1] However, just as there are many forms of intellectual prodigy, there are also many ways for us to be smart (and dumb) about our feelings. There may well be a general emotional quotient, an EQ, analogous to the "G" factor in general intelligence; but we also have unique strengths and personal shortcomings in these emotion-processing abilities. We have not one, but several, emotional intelligences.

For the sake of clarity, I have ordered these many facets into three basic ways in which individuals differ in their emotional abilities: (1) the ability to effectively perceive, communicate, and manage negative emotions, (2) the ability to experience, communicate, and sustain positive emotions, and (3) the capacity to preserve the boundaries between positive and negative emotions in order to understand the complex emotions in oneself and others. People differ dramatically from one another in their skills in each of these domains, and success in one domain does not guarantee success in another.

In keeping with the bias in the psychological sciences toward the study of what goes wrong in life, most investigations of individual differences in emotional health have focused on how well people regulate their negative emotions (but see Ryff & Singer, 1998).[2] Individuals differ dramatically in the amount and types of negative emotions they experience. It is easy to demonstrate this. Ask several groups of people to report on their feelings of unhappiness every day for a month. These groups may be college students, older adults in a retirement community, or middle managers at an electronics firm. It does not matter from where you draw the sample; the results will be the same. Some members of the group will consistently report more unhappiness than their counterparts. The degree of stability in these reports is striking. Even if this diary study were extended for a year, there would still be ample evidence that those people identified as the most unhappy today would be the same people reporting the most unhappiness tomorrow, next week, or even next year.[3]

Studies of individual differences in personality have shown that those people with the highest average negative affect also get the highest scores in neuroticism (Watson, Clark, McIntyre, & Hamaker, 1992).[4] Although Hans Eysenck (1967) developed this personality dimension to capture individual differences in emotional volatility, the use of the term *neuroticism* has become synonymous with high negative affectivity. Ask yourself the following questions: Do you sometimes feel happy, sometimes depressed, without any apparent reason? Are you inclined to be moody? Does your mind often wander while you are trying to concentrate? Are you frequently lost in thought even when you are supposed to be taking part in a conversation? These are all items from Eysenck's inventory. The more "yes" answers you give to those questions, the higher your score on neuroticism.

Besides saying yes to questions such as those just posed, what distinguishes a neurotic from others? Actually, rather than trying to single out the stereotypic sourpuss, we all could be described as having stronger or weaker tendencies to behave neurotically. Neurotic responding is characterized by over-attention to what has gone, or might go, wrong. Within the coping framework of approach/avoidance, the neurotic answer is avoidance, and that orientation colors much of what neurotics do. It is like a cloud over one's head; I picture Eeyore in the Winnie-the-Pooh books, walking around in the rain. The rain cloud is only over *his* head, and that fact makes him all the more miserable.[5]

Gross, Sutton, and Ketelaar (1998) investigated whether those high in neuroticism would exhibit disproportionate sensitivity to negative material. He showed students a 1-minute film on amputation of an arm. The film has a high disgust quotient. What Gross did was compare students high on neurotic responding with those who were not neurotic on their levels of negative affects before and after the film. Those high on neurotic responding showed not only greater negative affect to begin with but also greater increases in negative affect following the film.

The influence of neuroticism extends beyond reports of negative feelings to significant differences in brain activity. One research team (Canli, Zhao, Desmond, Kang, Gross, & Gabrieli, 2001) use fMRI to record brain activation patterns from women who were presented a series of pictures of angry and crying faces, spiders, guns, and cemeteries, known to evoke negative emotions. The higher these women scored on neuroticism the greater was their brain activity in frontal and temporal regions in response to the negative imagery.

Those of us scoring high on this dimension of emotional ill health also tend to process information about our worlds differently. We view the glass darkly. Rusting and Larsen (1998) have been investigating the cognitive processes and have detected strong evidence for bias in favor of the negative associated with neuroticism. In one of their studies, participants were asked to fill in the letters to complete a word; some words could be either positive or neutral, and others could be either negative or neutral. Word fragments such as *"ORROW" and "TEN"* were used as potentially negative emotion words. Others, such as *"JO,"* were used as potentially positive emotion words. Those participants who were high in neuroticism showed a preference for completing the word by filling in the letters to spell negative emotions such as *sorrow* and *tense*, as opposed to neutral terms such as *borrow* and *tenth*. What about the positive-leaning word fragments? Did neurotics tend to find fewer positive words as well? They did not.

To understand the role of personality in positive emotions, we need to consider another term, also introduced by Hans Eysenck (1967): *extraversion*. People with high scores on this personality characteristic tend to be more outgoing, social, and sensitive to rewards than those who are more introverted. Here are some of Eysenck's questions about extraversion: Do you prefer action to planning for action? Are you happiest when you get involved in some project that calls for rapid action? Would you rate yourself as a lively person? Would you be very unhappy if you were prevented from making numerous social contacts? If you thought most of these questions described you, then you would get a high score on extraversion, at least according to Eysenck. Interestingly enough, people vary in how extraverted they are, quite independent of their levels of neuroticism. We can be both neurotic and extraverted. We can also be neither, which might be described as mild-mannered but a little boring, as temperaments go.

Are extraverts happier than nonextraverts? In the study I just reviewed, Rusting and Larsen (1998) measured the degree of extraversion among his participants, along with neuroticism. Although the extraverts did not report more negative words, they did identify more words that were positive than introverts did. On average, extraverts also report more positive affect than introverts do; they also are engaged in more rewarding social activities. Perhaps extraverts enjoy many pleasures but do not enjoy them as much as introverts, who report fewer pleasurable engagements. Are extraverts on a kind of hedonic treadmill, seeking more and more pleasure but gaining less and less? Gross et al. (1998) checked this possibility by comparing the reactions of extraverts and introverts to the comedy strips. They found no evidence that extraverts were less responsive to comedy. On the contrary, after watching the comedy film, extraverts showed a significantly greater boost in positive affect than introverts.

In the fMRI study I discussed earlier, Canli and colleagues (2001) presented positive images as well as negative images to their participants, and assessed extraversion as well as neuroticism. The positive images included pictures of cute puppies, ice cream and brownies, a happy couple and sunsets, all proven to evoke positive emotions. Neural activation during the presentation of positive images was highest among the women high in extraversion, and these effects were observed across a number of limbic structures. The influences of the two personality indices on brain activity were distinct. Women high in neuroticism did not respond with more or less brain activity when presented with positive images, and extraverts did not react more or less to negative images. Self-report and brain activation studies show, nonetheless, that extraverts had more happier moments than introverts.

This pill is perhaps the hardest to swallow. To say that some people are more distressed than others most of the time is not easy to accept. However, to accept the fact that some people enjoy life a lot more than others so seems even more unfair, and we often resort to calling those grapes sour to disguise our feelings. The interpersonal consequences of uneven distribution of pleasurable experiences are potentially grave; concerns for others' reactions provide much of the subtext that underlies the inhibition of people's expressions of joy within social groups and help explain why communities with profound resource inequalities are unhealthy places for all who live there (Wilkinson, 1996). I discuss these points further in chapter 15.

Neuroticism and extraversion influence how much positive and negative affect we experience in everyday life. Elements of neuroticism also figure prominently in other related concepts. Scales that measure hopelessness, helplessness, depression, anxiety, and even general psychiatric distress also detect neuroticism to some extent. Extraversion has fewer linkages to other measures of personality than neuroticism, but some links include important concepts such as vigor, interpersonal engagement, and incentive motivation (see Depue & Collins, 1999).

The underlying themes of adaptation to negative and positive emotion find expression in personality attributes other than neuroticism and extraversion. On close analysis, even personality variables conceived of as unidimensional constructs often reveal two factors, one focused on positive themes and another on negative. Optimism, beliefs about internal and external control over life's events, and attributions we make over responsibility for events are some examples (Zautra, Potter, & Reich, 1997). People can be optimistic but also pessimistic, perceive themselves as in control of negative but not positive events, and attribute positive events to themselves, but not negative events to others. All of personality is informed by our emotions. When separate domains of emotion are tapped by the personality construct, separable dimensions of personality arise.

Bruce Smith (2002) demonstrated this point convincingly. He administered a wide-ranging battery of personality and coping measures to a sample of 172 older adult women coping with moderate to severe pain from either osteoarthritis or rheumatoid arthritis. A number of these measures assessed what Smith (2002) referred to as *vulnerability factors*: personal dispositions that placed the person at greater risk for adaptation difficulties. His list included neuroticism, anxiety, depression, feelings of helplessness over arthritis pain, an avoidant style of coping, and a pessimistic attitude.

This cluster of personality features is most relevant to the first dimension of emotional intelligence I introduced in this chapter: the capacity to regulate one's negative emotions.

Smith (2002) did not stop there in his examination of key individual differences. He identified a separate positive set of personal dispositions which he called *resilience*. To test this concept he used a cluster of measures representative of the second domain of emotional intelligence: the capacity to find and sustain positive emotional health. Included in Smith's list were measures of extraversion, optimism, purpose in life, and how much the person copes actively with stress.

Each of the women completed these personality measures and then answered questions about their emotional well-being each week for 12 consecutive weeks. The question that Smith asked was whether those women who were more vulnerable were also more likely to report increases in negative affect and decreases in positive affect from one week to the next. He also wanted to know whether the attributes of resilience helped lower negative affect and raise positive affect week to week.[6]

What did he find? If you bet that vulnerability factors predicted greater negative affect week-to-week, you would be right. But the degree of vulnerability did not predict positive affect from one week to the next. The resiliency scales, such as optimism, extraversion, purpose in life, and growth-oriented coping, were the key to elevations in positive emotions week-to-week. Consistent with a two-dimensional model, people with these positive attributes were nether hurt nor helped in their struggles to regulate negative emotions. Resiliency did not predict less negative affect from one week to the next, only greater positive affect. Smith (2002) concluded that vulnerability and resilience defined two ways in which people differ in their capacity to regulate their emotions, each with different attributes and each influencing different feelings. In sum, when we consider how emotionally intelligent we are, we need to consider two parts to the question: How well do we contend with negative emotions in all their facets, and how able are we to regulate and sustain our positive feelings?

Dual Motivational Systems

Sometimes emotions are best thought of as the feelings we experience, but they are also motivational states, and some of the work on these aspects of emotional intelligence has been particularly revealing. In chapter 2, I discussed how prominent neuroscientists such as Jerome Gray and Peter Lang have split the emotion atom in two. Lang et al. (1998) sees all emotions as organized around two motivational systems, a *defensive system* and an *appetitive system*. Gray (1982) refers to two motivational systems within the brain as fundamental to emotional experience: the *behavioral inhibition system (BIS)* and the *behavioral activation system (BAS)*. There is increasing evidence to suggest that people differ in the degree to which they rely on each of these systems. It turns out that to define people's motivational dispositions we need to know both how much they retreat from potential harms and also how often they vigorously search after and find sources of joy. These differences can be captured to a great extent by measures designed to identify the extent to which a person tends toward a defensive posture, characterized by "fight or flight" and behavioral inhibition, versus the extent to which they strive to fulfill interests and desires, characterized by behavioral activation.

Charles Carver and Teri White (1994) constructed an inventory to capture these tendencies. Below are some of the key items in their scales:[7]

Behavioral Inhibition Scale	Behavioral Activation Scale
1. If something unpleasant is going to happen, I usually get pretty "worked-up."	1. When I get something I want, I feel excited and energized.
2. I worry about making mistakes.	2. When I want something, I usually go all-out to get it.
3. Criticism or scolding hurts me quite a bit.	3. I will often do things for no other reason than that they might be fun

For each item in the scale, the person rates how much he or she agrees with the statement, and a total score is computed by summing the items in each scale. People who score high on behavioral inhibition also tend to score high on measures of neuroticism, show more anxiety, and report more psychological distress. They ruminate about potential sources of harm and are more dependent on feeling safe and secure in order to feel satisfied with their everyday lives. People who score highly on behavioral activation are more extraverted, seek novel situations, display more vitality, and tend toward the active (perhaps even hyperactive) side of the spectrum. If you are like me, you are trying to locate yourself, your family, and your friends on these scales.

There is, however, one important attribute of these scales that you might easily overlook when you think about where you and others fall on these aspects of emotional regulation: Level of behavioral inhibition is independent of behavioral activation tendencies. People can be high on both or low on both, and those people can be found within our society just as readily as people who are high on one and low on the other. The scales are not just uncorrelated with one another; they are not even related to the same emotional health indices. For example, people low in behavioral inhibition do not report more (or less) positive affect, more extraversion, or more vitality than those high in the construct. Likewise, people high in behavioral activation do not show less anxiety, less negative affect, or less avoidant styles than those with low scores on behavioral activation. These motivational tendencies follow a two-dimensional path, just as measures of affect do.

Gambling with Emotion

Thus far we have discussed studies that build a case for separable dimensions of inhibition and activation based on correlational analyses. Here is an illustration drawn from research using an experimental paradigm. Imagine the following computer game. The screen flashes with five elements supposedly in a sequence of some kind and then flashes another element. Your job is to decide whether this last element fits in the sequence. You have to indicate "yes" or "no" within 8 seconds. It sounds easy enough; but suppose, further, that the pattern is not recognizable (by experimenter design) and that you are told that you have to use your intuition to decide whether or not the sixth element fits the sequence of the other five. Carver and White (1994) used this game with undergraduate students who volunteered to be in a study. But they arranged some devilish twists in the game to see whether students high in behavioral-inhibition acted differently from those low in inhibition and also whether students high in behavioral activation differed from those low in activation.[8]

The experimenters manipulated the consequences of this gamble: threat of punishment in one study versus expectation for reward in the other. In the punishment study, they had their participants plunge an arm into ice water and hold it there as long as possible. Then they told the participants that some people need "reticular activation" in order to do well in the game and that, if they did not get enough sequences right in the first part of the game, they would need another reticular wake-up call: the ice-water plunge (Carver & White, 1994).

Now imagine that you are told this and then, as you start playing the game, you realize that you cannot identify any of the sequences presented—you are guessing on that sixth light every time. Would this make you nervous? In truth, the experimenters presented the elements in random sequences so that there was no pattern to any of them. What they wanted to find out was whether the game would increase anxiety and whether that increase would be greater for those highest in behavioral inhibition. No one actually got the second cold-water plunge, but some participants were much more nervous than others. As predicted, those highest in behavioral inhibition approached the game with the most trepidation (Carver & White, 1994).

With another group of volunteers, Carver and White (1994) manipulated reward instead of punishment for performance in the same game. The participants were told that if they did well in the game by intuiting the sequence, they would gain extra experiment credits to use toward fulfilling a course obligation. The researchers then gave those in the study false feedback, telling them they were doing very well at the game, assuring them that they would be rewarded with extra credits (in keeping with ethical principles, the participants did get the extra credits after the study was over). Now everyone felt good when they were told that they were performing well, but some were happier than others. As predicted, those higher in behavioral activation were the happiest (Carver & White, 1994). I should note here that no amount of behavioral inhibition affected the participants' happiness. Likewise, no amount of behavioral activation protected the participants from feeling nervous about the ice water plunge.

The latter studies bring experimental rigor to the examination of how separate motivational tendencies influence two fundamental emotional responses: how anxious we become under the threat of punishment and how excited we are by promises of reward. However, their methodological strength is offset somewhat by the artificiality of the situation. Not many of us would define life as a game of pattern recognition in which the object is to guess the right answer rather than figure it out.

Gable, Reis, and Elliot (2000) studied these questions in real-life situations. Working with undergraduate student volunteers, these experimenters asked their participants to complete daily diaries, recording positive and negative events for 14 days and their positive and negative emotions on each of those days.

In all, 88 students participated in this study. Their behavioral inhibition and behavioral activation scores ranged widely, as did their levels of positive and negative affect. Those with greater behavioral inhibition experienced the highest average level of negative affect over the 14 days. They also showed the most reactivity to negative events; the analysis of these results required an examination of days on which negative events were higher than usual so that the amount of increase in negative affect could be compared with that on a less troubling day. As predicted, the most negative affect was reported by those participants who scored high on behavioral inhibition and who were having a particularly rough day at school. Did the disposition toward behavioral activation matter? No, it did not. There was no difference in level of negative affect or in reactivity to negative events as a function of behavioral activation. But those high in behavioral activation did show more positive affect over the 14 days, and in one comparison, more positive events (Gable et al., 2000).[9]

Is a disposition toward activation or inhibition embedded within our gray matter? In chapter 2 I introduced Richard Davidson's model of emotion activation, with approach on the left and avoidance processes on the right side of the prefrontal cortex. As you may recall from chapter 2, Davidson (2000) developed a neural model of affective style that is based on differences in EEG firing on left and right sides of the prefrontal lobes. Through the measurement of brain wave activity,. Davidson relied on the well-established method of identifying extreme groups. A small proportion of those people he tested showed extreme right-sided asymmetry, which means much greater EEG activation on the right versus the left side of the prefrontal cortex. There are also people who show asymmetry favoring left-sided activation. It turns out that those with high behavioral inhibition show greater right frontal asymmetry and those with high behavioral activation show greater left brain asymmetry (Sutton & Davidson, 1997).

Emotional Complexity as a Form of Emotional Health

Thus far, I have discussed individual differences in two emotional regulation abilities: dealing effectively with both negative and positive emotions. What of the third kind of emotional intelligence—the ability to retain perspective during difficult times and to recover emotional complexity following stressful events? Differences in this type of emotional intelligence may not be important in defining the level of positive and negative emotions the person experiences or even in predicting sensitivity to emotion-laden material. Rather, this realm of emotional intelligence focuses on key individual differences in the way positive and negative emotions are understood in relationship to each other. Although no researcher has yet attempted to classify individual differences of this sort rigorously, there are a number of promising attempts to measure this form of affective complexity.

A good starting point for understanding how people may differ in this form of emotional intellect is to study individual differences in their abilities to recognize emotional complexities embedded within everyday life events. Richard Lane (2000) has developed such a test of *emotional awareness*. As data, he uses a person's own descriptions of how he or she would feel if certain hypothetical events occurred. Embedded within each event are some interesting emotional twists, such as losing an important race to your best friend. To score high in emotional awareness, respondents need to acknowledge the emotional complexities in their descriptions of events.

To construct criteria for evaluating emotional awareness, Lane and his colleague Gary Schwartz (1987) relied on a model of intellectual development first proposed by Jean Piaget. In Piaget's model, stages of development are distinguished along two key dimensions: degree of differentiation and level of integration. Lane sees emotional awareness along similar lines: progressively more highly differentiated and integrated. Physical sensations are at the lowest level of awareness. At this level the person is aware only of bodily changes associated with emotionally charged events. At the second level are action tendencies. At this level the person can identify how events promote certain behavioral reaction patterns. The person might say, "It made me want to cry," in response to a sad event, or "I just wanted to beat him to a pulp" following events that provoke anger. Awareness of discrete emotions is the next level. At this level, people can identify a specific set of feelings they would have if the event happened to them. In this case, they might say, "I felt sad," or "I was definitely angry," along with reporting the action they might take. According to Lane and Schwartz (1987), the fourth level of awareness is the recognition of blends of emotions, seeing more than one feeling, even contradictory ones, arising from events.

Here is an illustration of that fourth level. "I know I was upset that I lost. Maybe I could have done better. But when I saw her face, and how happy she was, I must say it brought joy to me, too. We have been competitors to be sure. But we're also friends." The world-renowned figure skater Michelle Kwan said this just after the award ceremony for the women's figure skating competition at the Winter Olympics in 1998. Michelle Kwan sees and allows herself to express both her own disappointment and her happiness for the success of her friend.

There is also a fifth level, at which the person not only reports complex sets of emotions but also observes and integrates how those feelings fit with the emotions of others at the time. Kwan's comments are suggestive of that depth. If the interviewer had probed further for level 5 awareness, she might have heard Michelle talk about her friend feeling sad, as well as overjoyed, because her victory meant that others had to lose.

Emotional health depends on one's level of emotional awareness, in Lane's view. Why would this be so? According to Lane and Swartz (1987), people with high levels of awareness are more accurate in their perceptions of their own needs, can empathize with the feelings of others more readily, and, in doing so, are less likely to overreact in complex social situations and more likely to exercise better judgment overall.

Salovey and Mayer (1990; see also Salovey & Sluyter, 1997) suggest that one of the ways in which emotionally intelligent people differ from others is that they are able to identify how they feel, even when the situation is complicated by many contradictory feelings. Salovey and Mayer (1990) examined whether this aspect of emotional intelligence can aid in recovery from negative feelings. After assessing mood clarity and other aspects of emotional intelligence for each of their study participants using measures they developed in prior research, Salovey and Mayer (1990) showed each participant a movie about drinking and driving. The show included a graphic depiction of an automobile accident and was emotionally upsetting to most of the audience. Those movie watchers who were exceptional in their skill in identifying their own emotions and the feelings of those around them were able to regain the positive mood they had at the beginning of the study faster than those who were below average in those abilities. The authors took the additional step of evaluating how much the participants were ruminating over aspects of the film. They asked participants to identify their thoughts every 60 seconds for 10 minutes and to rate those thoughts according to how intrusive, negative, and uncontrollable they were. Those who could identify their moods clearly were less likely to have ruminative thoughts following the film, providing further evidence that awareness of complex emotions is an important and adaptive attribute (Salovey & Mayer, 1990).

Those effects were observed while people watched a movie. Would similar effects be found when reviewing one's own experiences? DeVellis, Carl, DeVellis, Blalock, and Patterson (1998) addressed this question. They asked a group of older adults with osteoarthritis to describe a recent troubling life experience and how they felt about it. As expected, this instruction led to a temporary increase in negative mood. Positive mood was also diminished while the participants in the study recalled the negative experience. Not everyone reacted the same way, however. Those who scored high on Salovey and Mayer's (1990) mood clarity scale showed little loss in positive mood. Amount of negative mood was the same, but those with greater emotional clarity were better able to preserve their positive emotions throughout the exercise.[10]

Our research team has investigated whether people high in emotional clarity can keep positive emotions separate from negative emotions in everyday life (Zautra, Smith, Affleck, & Tennen, 2001). We interviewed older adult women by telephone each week and asked them to report on their positive and negative emotions. We constructed two separate indices of their weekly emotional health: one a measure of amount of positive affect and the other a measure of amount of negative affect. We also administered Salovey and Mayer's (1990) mood clarity scale to obtain an estimate of this aspect of emotional intelligence. We were not interested in whether mood clarity led to more or less negative affect overall or to more positive affect overall. Instead, we wanted to know whether changes in negative emotions from one week to the next would be linked to changes in positive emotions. Indeed, in weeks in which positive emotions increased, there was a tendency for negative emotions to decrease. But again, as DeVellis et al. (1998) found, positive and negative emotions were not linked to the same degree in everyone. For those older adults with greater mood clarity, the linkage between emotions was loosened considerably. Positive emotions during a given week did not protect the person from negative emotions, but negative emotions did not rule out positive experiences.

At the core of these differences in capacity to distinguish among emotions is the complexity of the individual's judgments of his or her emotional experiences. Researchers have created some promising approaches to identifying these judgments. Patricia Linville (1985) has reasoned that people are better protected from emotional ups and downs if they have many distinct aspects to their identities, so that they are able to maintain positive feelings about some aspects of themselves despite negative feelings about other aspects. To assess complexity, Linville (1985) asked participants to sort a deck of 33 cards into as many stacks as they felt they needed to describe themselves. The cards contained positive and negative attributes such as lazy, impulsive, affectionate, and relaxed. The person could create as many stacks as desired and place as many cards on a stack as they wished. The number of stacks and the degree of independence among the ideas represented by the stacks gave Linville (1985) a way of estimating the complexity of the person's self-concept.

Showers (1992) has investigated the degree of integration versus compartmentalization of positive and negative attributes. Showers used the same card-sorting techniques that Linville (1985) used to identify the extent to which the person segregates positive from negative attributes in the piles they form to describe themselves.[11] For example, one person may build several piles with only positive attributes, a kind of Pollyanna collage, reserving a single last pile for all negative aspects of themselves. This organization of the self creates opportunities for higher positive emotions following positive experiences. However, the person with a compartmentalized self is also prone to lower and more lasting negative emotions following negative experiences. Showers (1992) argues that if the person has no redeeming positive attributes embedded within a negative pile to interrupt the activation of negative affects, eventually there will be a virtual avalanche of negative self-thoughts.

Thus far, I have focused on those personality traits that attempt to measure how much people either blend or compartmentalize positive and negative aspects of the self. Another way to look at this phenomenon is to ask whether overall desire for simplicity and the avoidance of complexity may influence affect dimensions. Reich, Zautra, and Potter (2001) studied students with high versus low needs for structure (see also Neuberg & Newsom, 1993). Those with high needs for structure dislike complexities and seek order in their everyday lives. We found that those who disliked complexities and desired simplicity were significantly more likely to report less positive affect along with more negative affect. They were also likely to report more positive affect with less negative affect. In other words, their affect dimensions were less differentiated.

To test a real-world group, in a second part of this research we studied members of the community who suffer from a chronic pain syndrome called fibromyalgia (Reich et al., 2001). We found that those in pain had a greater need for structure on average than healthy college students did. Once you factor in the stress caused by chronic pain, it should come as no surprise that these patients would show greater needs for structure in their everyday lives. Not everyone showed this pattern, but those who did need more structure also showed a simpler affect structure. Like the college students, pain patients with a high need for structure had less room for multiple emotions; they tended to have high levels of affective simplicity along with high levels of cognitive simplicity.

Some Benefits of Emotional Complexity

What benefits accrue from living complex emotional lives? Clearly, there is a cost to complexity. We are not allowed to extinguish negative feelings with a burst of positive experience, for example. What do we gain? From our model, the gain is in resiliency, the capacity for a full recovery. That is the key value of a highly differentiated affect system. With independent sources of positive affect, there is less chance of sustained negative affect following a stressful experience. Our model predicts that the recovery of positive feelings, as well as repair of negative states, is more rapid for those who can experience life as both positive and negative, not simply either positive or negative. F. Scott Fitzgerald (1945) came closest to what I mean here when he wrote, "The test of a first-rate intelligence is the ability to hold two opposed ideas in mind at the same time and still retain the ability to function. One should, for example, be able to see that things are hopeless and yet be determined to make them otherwise" (p. 69).

The field is moving rapidly to develop new and better measures of emotional complexity and intelligence. One approach we are likely to hear much more about focuses on the extent and depth of positive affect expression following a traumatic event. Some call this research "meaning making," which refers to the person coming to terms with tragic circumstances by developing a new understanding of the experience (Tedeschi & Calhoun, 1995). It is what Rothbaum, Weisz, and Snyder (1982) called a secondary control strategy. Those individuals with the capacity to find that "silver lining" may be better equipped to recover rapidly and more fully from stressful events.

In the previous chapter, I discussed Pennebaker's (1990; Pennebaker, Mayne, & Francis, 1997) surprising findings that people were healthier when their stories about stressful events were infused with much positive emotion, as well as some negative feelings. People may differ in their capacity to express both positive and negative emotions about prior events, and those differences in complexity may be especially important in predicting psychological recovery from difficult circumstances.

Bauer and Bonanno (2001) provide intriguing evidence in support of this reasoning. They examined the stories told by bereaved men and women about their relationships with their deceased spouses. They recruited 67 young adult and middle-aged men and women who were recently bereaved and asked them to talk into a tape recorder for 6 minutes about their past relationship. The self-evaluative comments on these tapes were then coded by expert raters to obtain a count of the number of times people made positive remarks about themselves and the number of times they made negative remarks. For example, the comment, "I think I helped make her successful" was coded as a positive self-statement. On the other hand, the remark, "I made a lot of money, but the effort it took ruined our lives" was coded as negative.

The researchers then arranged for clinical interviews of the bereaved sample at 6, 14, and 25 months after the deaths of their spouses in order to gauge the degree of recovery from their losses over time. Then they examined whether the number of positive and negative self-evaluations in the speech samples predicted recovery.

Indeed, these self-evaluations did matter, and those with more emotionally complex stories had the highest recovery rates. Nearly every story had at least one positive self-statement, but some stories had no negative emotions expressed. People who told stories that were exclusively positive did not recover as rapidly as those with many positive statements and at least one negative self-statement. Those who proved to be the most resilient were predominantly positive in their self-evaluative comments, with approximately five positive statements for every negative statement (Bauer & Bonanno, 2001).

Epel, McEwen, and Ickovics (1998) tested the usefulness of another new measure of meaning—making. The measure derives from an inventory of "posttraumatic growth" that assesses how much the person is capable of experiencing psychological growth after facing stressful experiences (Tedeschi & Calhoun, 1996). The inventory has subscales that assess individual differences in Appreciation of Life, Spiritual Growth, New Possibilities, and Relating to Others following stressful events.

Epel and her colleagues (1998) had female volunteers undergo 3 hours of laboratory stress each day for 3 consecutive days. The volunteers did a variety of stressful tasks, such as solving difficult math problems and giving a hastily prepared speech. While the women were engaged in these activities, the investigators drew their blood and analyzed the level of cortisol coursing through their veins each day. A growth orientation did nothing to reduce cortisol levels during the first day, but by the third day, women who reported being able to experience more spiritual growth and appreciation of life following stress showed a significant shift toward less cortisol secretion than other women in the study did. Thus the capacity to think about gains, as well as losses, following traumatic experiences appears to speed adaptation, effectively reducing the physiological burden of stress.

Cole, Kemeny, Fahey, and Naliboff (2000) reported on the healing benefits of another dimension of personality related to emotional complexity: namely, openness to experience. The researchers studied 55 gay men who were HIV positive and were receiving a powerful new antiretroviral therapy that has been highly successful in arresting the disease course. The researchers noted that, although the new drug combination therapy was rather potent in reducing viral load, the rate of recovery of immunity, particularly T-helper cells, was highly variable following this therapy. Cole et al. (2000) reasoned that personality differences might predict who recovers helper cells most rapidly. Based on prior research, they examined five dimensions of personality thought to be the primary ways in which we differ from one another: neuroticism, extraversion, openness, agreeableness, and conscientiousness. Of these five personality dimensions, two proved to be significantly related to T-cell recovery. Neuroticism was not one of these, nor were extraversion and conscientiousness. The key factors were openness and agreeableness. Those men who were more open to experience and more agreeable in their interpersonal relations were more likely to show higher counts of T-helper cells in circulation throughout their bodies following therapy.

The veil has lifted on the study of personality profiles of positive emotionality. My belief is that social scientists will waste little more time in plowing this virgin field in the next millennium.[12] To fully understand and appreciate the findings that will result from these new initiatives, we need to be alert to the mechanisms that underlie positive, as well as negative, emotions. Further, this review indicates that we need dynamic approaches that examine emotional complexity not only when life is calm but also during times of stress to see how well people preserve the boundaries be-tween their positive and negative emotions.

If our thinking is correct, we need to look for not only a broader def-inition of emotional health but also a deeper one. We need to consider whether people possess that "negative capability" that Keats wrote of. In the final analysis, character is not defined by how much positive or how little negative emotion we have but by our capacities to hold both emo-tions up to the light. The ability to sustain attention to positive emotions when coping with highly stressful events and the honesty to acknowledge the presence of negative emotions even as we rejoice may be the highest points of emotional maturity that we can hope to attain.

8   Attention and Pain

The Role of Emotions

I'll kiss you over the eyes till I kiss you blind;
If I can—if any one could.
Then perhaps in the dark you'll have got what you want to
    find.
>   —D. H. Lawrence, "A Spiritual Woman"

My youngest son does not like to get ready for preschool. He does not want to put his pants on, he does not want his shoes and socks on, he does not want to wash his face, comb his hair, or blow his nose. All these things are chores, part of the hassles in a 4-year-old's life he would rather do without. He resists any of my attempts to persuade him to do these things. To say, "Dad has to get to work," or "Dad has to make money to put food on the table," or even to tell him that Dad will have a nervous breakdown if he doesn't hurry is useless. These tactics all fall on deaf ears. As he shakes off any of my attempts to put his pants on, he is in distress management mode, and no argument about how he is making things worse for him, for the family, or for the whole country would convince him to behave otherwise

How do I persuade him to get ready? Force certainly does not work, except the first time, as any parent knows. Threat of punishment is similarly ineffective. But I do know something he wants. At school there is a special place in the refrigerator to store his lunch bag. It is a square-shaped shelf on the door with a lift-up plastic lid. Open that plastic lid, put the lunch box in, close it up, and your lunch has the best seat in the house.

My son has a friend named Max at school who tends to arrive a bit earlier and who also covets the refrigerator door location for his lunch. So, I say, "We had better hurry if we want to get that lunch box spot before Max does." My son wheels around and says, "Dad, what's taking you so long?"

What has happened here? From a cognitive perspective we may try to argue that different words for the same behavior can evoke different emotional responses. But the words I used to encourage my son to get ready for school were not arbitrary choices. The shift in his behavior depended on a shift in his motives. And although there are many possible explanations for his about-face, a model built with multiple affect systems does a better job of explaining my 4-year-old's change in attitude than cognitive models that either ignore affect altogether or simply view positive emotions as the opposite of negative ones. This chapter begins with an examination of how different emotions influence what we attend to and what we ignore. I end with a discussion of one especially relevant aspect of this relationship between emotions and attention: how our feelings influence our ability to adapt to chronic pain.

Michael Posner and colleagues (Harman, Rothbart, & Posner, 1997; Posner & Rothbart, 1998) demonstrated that strong emotions are not easily extinguished by cognitive means. In their experiment they sought to soothe the distress of 3- to 6-month-old infants through a cognitive coping device called distraction. To gather data on distress, the researchers distressed the infants slightly by overstimulating them with certain lights and sounds. Next, they soothed the child with interesting sights and sounds. In this case, the children stopped crying because they immediately oriented to the interesting stimuli. The interesting part is what happened after the novelty wore off. Did the child go on as if nothing had happened? That would be the prediction of purely cognitive models of affect regulation. But it turned out that the child is not really relieved of distress as a consequence of the distracting events. Posner and Rothbart (1998) found that once the new orienting stimulus stopped, the child returned to nearly the same level of distress he or she had experienced before the distraction. Apparently, there is a storage site for this distress, a "distress keeper" that is retained even during the young child's distraction to the novel sounds. The distress was not transformed into another form of affective energy via the manipulation; it was just set aside. To explain this result, one needs to assume that there are at least two "bins" that store emotional information. Posner and Rothbart (1998) found such storage capacities in children after only 6 months of life.

Gordon Bower (1995) has found pervasive evidence that these emotional storage bins, when active, permeate our thought processes. In what he has coined *mood congruent* effects, Bower (1995) has demonstrated that people in positive moods think and behave differently from those in negative moods. The approach he and other researchers have used to investigate the influence of mood is called *mood induction*. The experimenter induces a mildly positive or negative mood and then asks the participant to perform a task of some kind. To induce mood, the experimenter may do one of a number of things: play music, arrange for the person to succeed or fail at some task, or read a story that is happy or sad. Because the participants are randomly assigned to either positive or negative mood induction, differences between groups can show us the effects of mood.

Bower's (1995) first studies were on mood congruent memory. Induction of negative mood led participants to retrieve memories of unhappy events more easily, and positive mood induction made past positive events easier to recall. Two separate registers for memory stores appear to operate, coding key events as either positive or negative. Moods appear to shift our attention from one store of memories to another. Moods affect not only our reconstructions of past events but also the shapes of our imaginations. In some studies, Bower (1995) gave participants a set of pictures from a standardized set of materials known as the Thematic Apperception Test (or TAT). After inducing either happy or sad moods, he asked the participants to tell stories about what they imagined was happening in those pictures. Happy storytellers told happy stories, and sad storytellers told sad stories.

Forgas and Bower (1987) teamed up to study how mood influenced judgments about other people. They induced happy or sad moods, then asked participants to read statements about someone they had never met and form an impression of that person based on what they had read. Sad participants spent more time reading the negative attributes of the person, and happy participants spent more time reading the positive attributes of the person. Needless to say, those in positive moods developed more favorable impressions and remembered more positive attributes of the person during a recall task later. As Forgas (1995) would put it, our judgments are infused with affect.[1]

These mood effects extend to evaluations of oneself. Forgas (1995) led a study in which the participants watched a videotape of themselves after receiving either a positive or a negative mood induction. Those induced into positive moods liked what they saw in themselves. Those in negative moods found much to criticize.

The point here is that positive and negative moods can have powerful effects on what we attend to. Are the effects for positive and negative mood mirror images, or is there something unique about the two mood states in terms of their effects on processes of thought? One pervasive difference should not be overlooked. Unlike people in positive moods, people in negative moods are usually motivated to find a way to recover from their moods. This search for a means to recovery could lead to new learning and other unexpected "benefits" from attending to negative emotions. However, there is a seeming paradox here. If people in negative moods are more highly motivated to change that state, then why do they recall more negative experiences, expect more negative events, and see themselves and others in more critical terms?

Bower (1995) would say that they are not aware of the bias that has resulted from their negative moods. Forgas (1995) has pointed out that the research evidence suggests further that people in negative moods may be motivated both to find congruent experiences and also to repair their negative moods. Mood congruence may be best thought of as an adaptive response, rather than as a mistake. Certainly, staying congruent reduces any dissonance. Consider also the role of control in coping with unpleasant experiences. When I am in a sad mood, I sometimes play the sound track to the movie *Philadelphia*. I get in touch with the depths of my sadness by listening to these songs. I induce my own sad mood, and by doing so, I may actually feel more sorrow. But I begin to feel good as well. I have transformed the experience. As I approach rather than run from the sadness, I am more in control, more alive. So the key question for research is not whether I feel more or less sad when inducing my own moods, but whether other feelings arise as a result of that process.

In chapter 3, I introduced two contrasting responses to stress: active restructuring versus avoidance and resignation. Different responses to negative emotions may arise depending on which of these responses to stress predominates at the time. Richards and Gross (2000) examined how well people remembered scenes from a distressing film clip, based on how they dealt with their negative emotional reactions to the movie.[2] Some people were instructed to try to suppress those negative feelings. A second group was told instead to think about what they saw as if they were medical professionals viewing the movie with detached interest. They called the first strategy *expressive suppression* and the second *cognitive reappraisal*. Those who were instructed to actively suppress their negative emotions remembered less about the scenes when quizzed about them later. It was as if they had partially succeeded in their task of suppressing their feelings by forgetting aspects of the film clip that generated those emotions in the first place. In contrast, those who thought about the clip in a different way switched perspectives, away from negative emotion and toward a positive goal. In so doing they could recall their experiences more clearly than those told to suppress their emotions.

Positive mood primes us in ways that negative mood does not. One difference that has been studied thoroughly has been the effects of mood on creative problem-solving. Alice Isen and her colleagues (Ashby, Isen, & Turken, 1999; Isen, Daubman, & Nowicki, 1987) have studied changes in cognitive performance following positive, as opposed to negative, mood induction.[3] In one study (Isen et al., 1987), for example, the experimenters boosted positive emotions by playing a brief section of a videotape showing bloopers from TV shows. For a neutral mood condition, they played a videotape segment on how to solve math problems. For negative mood, they showed a 5-minute segment of a documentary about the Nazi con-centration camps.

Following mood induction, Isen et al. (1987) provided the participants with some puzzles to solve. One task was candle making. They gave par-ticipants a candle, a book of matches, a box of tacks, and a corkboard with the instruction to figure out how to affix the candle to the corkboard so that they could light the candle and have it burn without dropping wax on the floor. To solve the puzzle, the participants had to use the materials in a new way. They had to empty the box of tacks, tack the box to the corkboard, and then put the candle in the box.

After watching the blooper tapes, 60% to 75% of the participants solved the puzzle. By comparison, only 30% of those people who saw the Holocaust film solved the puzzle. Negative mood induction did not impair creativity; the success of that group was no different from that of the group in the neutral condition. As Isen and her colleagues (1987) have argued, positive mood brings unique benefits to us. Among those benefits is an enhancement of our creativity in problem solving.

Emotions as Information

Our emotions confer some important benefits on information processing. Our feelings focus our attention and provide boundaries to thought and action. Gerald Clore and his collaborators (Clore & Ortony, 2000; Ketelaar & Clore, 1997) have fashioned a theory of affect from these principles, defining *affect* as *information*. What this means is that the emotions we feel provide us with information about our interactions. For example, when we feel negative affect, we know something is amiss. Further, the emotions associated with negative feelings, such as anger, remorse, disgust, sadness, and fear, all are directed toward someone or something. Emotions focus our thoughts, shape our perspective, and help direct our actions.

When affect is understood as information, a number of observations begin to make sense. For example, Clore's model explains why negative emotions seem to capture our attention more than positive emotions do.

Apart from any increase in threat that negative feelings may imply, they also inform us that some corrective or evasive action needs to be taken. In fact, the negative affect often points out where to begin searching for new information to solve the problem. Positive affect often informs us that we are indeed already headed in the right direction.

One of the less understood aspects of emotion is how our feelings communicate information, not only to ourselves but also to those around us. Feelings are powerful, sometimes hidden, persuaders. Beier and Young (1998) discuss emotions as forms of communication that subtly shape the context of an interpersonal exchange. Not only can you not kiss someone who disgusts you, but also the person to whom you communicate disgust is hardly going to want to touch his or her lips to yours. Even if the person wanted such closeness, the powerful message of rejection that accompanies the negative emotion would be extremely difficult to override. Emotional displays regulate the information flow and also create a climate for relating to others. This climate may be warm and sunny, or it may be chilly.

How is this emotion information used under stress? I have defined stress as an increase in uncertainty about what has or will happen. Uncertainty bears a special relationship to information. Shannon and Weaver (1949), two scientists from Bell Laboratories, were the first to examine this relationship. They were interested in setting out equations that would define how much information could be transmitted via telephone lines. They pointed out that information provided by each syllable over the wire was at a maximum when the person listening on the phone was maximally uncertain about what was said. The more the listener knew or could guess about the conversation, the less important any new information bit (or byte) was. With this theorem in hand, the telephone company could estimate just how great a portion of a message could be lost in transmission before it lost its meaning. If we can receive only 20% of a message and still hear it as a whole without loss of information, the phone company can put five times as many messages on a given telephone line, saving money on phone lines and making more profits for "Ma Bell."

Shannon and Weaver's (1949) theorem has significant implications for how emotions influence us. As a source of information, emotions have much greater impact under times of uncertainty. We could think of stress creating a vacuum within us, with our emotions rushing in to fill the void. We are most vulnerable to emotional appeals in times of upheaval in our lives, when we are unsure of our direction, of our future. When we do not understand our own feelings, we are at an especially susceptible moment. In a sense, during stressful times, our cognitive antennae are searching for emotional information to bring the world around us into focus.

It is within this context that we can best understand the results of the famous set of experiments by Schachter and Singer (1962; see also Griffiths, 1997) that I introduced in chapter 1. Recall that these two researchers set out to demonstrate how cognitions influenced our emotions. When they reported the results of their studies in 1962, they put cognitive models of emotion on the map. Perhaps the time was ripe for these models; new theories were needed to fill the void created by growing dissatisfaction with a purely behavioral approach.

The study (Schachter & Singer, 1962) examined the conditions under which people would acquire the feelings expressed by another person whom they were paired with during the experimental session. Unknown to the study participants, their partners were confederates, working for the experimenter, and were trained to act in one of three ways: happy and engaging, angry and unfriendly, or neutral. By luck of the draw, each participant interacted with one of these three people. Before they did that, however, they were given an injection. In the needle was either a saline solution or a form of epinephrine, a central nervous system stimulant.

The key to this experiment is what Schachter and Singer (1962) told—or did not tell—the participants about the injections they received. Some were told exactly what they should expect to experience: more rapid heart rate, increase in nervous tension, and greater overall physiological arousal. But two other groups were randomly selected to receive *false* feedback about their injections. One group was told to expect no change in bodily sensations, and a third group was actually told to expect to feel greater relaxation and a sense of calm.

The participants who received no active drug were not influenced by the behavior of the confederates they talked with after the injections. Those given the arousing drug and told it was arousing also were not influenced by the interaction styles of their confederates. The participants in those conditions showed no change in their own feeling states regardless of the antics of the confederates.

The story was different for those who were given false feedback about their physiological state. They mirrored the feelings of their confederate partners. If the partner was angry, they became angry. If the partner was happy, they reported being happy.

At the time, these results (Schachter & Singer, 1962) were used to support the notion of the plasticity of feelings. Cognitive theorists were especially gratified because this experiment demonstrated how readily people could be influenced to label their own emotions. From the same internal states, some participants in the study inferred that they were feeling happy, but others inferred that they were feeling angry.

Are emotions aroused just by the labels that we place on physiological arousal? I think that a more complete explanation may be found by inspecting the dynamics of emotions under stress. The key to the effects Schachter and Singer (1962) observed lies in the uncertainty—the stress— created by the false feedback. Without an adequate explanation for the arousal produced by the drug, the person was left adrift without an emo- tion to anchor the aroused state. That vacuum was quickly filled by the behavior of the confederate, who provided meaning. If the researchers had looked, I would expect that they would have found that those who were aroused but given false feedback were more likely to show a unidimen- sional structure to their emotions and that those who were aroused by the drug and given correct feedback were not. When the attention is focused on uncertainty, affective information becomes central to us as a means of reducing that uncertainty. In dynamic terms, the emotions spiral in to fill the information void with such force that their multidimensional form collapses. We are left feeling simply good *or* bad as our attention narrows to secure a frame of reference for understanding our own emotions.

Chronic Pain and the Regulation of Attention

Chronic pain also shapes the structure of our emotions. Indeed, nothing rivets our attention faster than pain. Touch a hot plate, get bit by a scor- pion, or bang an elbow down on a slab of concrete while in-line skating, and the reaction is nearly instantaneous. Our sensory systems are well equipped to carry information about damage to our bodies. Doing so quickly allows our nervous systems to mount a swift defense: First, move away from the site of the injury; second, overtake awareness with an over- powering emotional message so as to recruit more deliberate efforts on what to do next to protect oneself from further harm. Pain carries infor- mation that may be crucial to our survival. No wonder we have evolved such a marvelously direct, rapid, and powerful set of signals. Pain is our friend.

In all regulatory systems there are counterregulatory forces, and it is no different with pain. Opioids are activated centrally to blunt the pain and raise the pain threshold for additional pain-inducing events. In a sense, the body begins to accommodate to the pain and also to reduce its influ- ence from the start of the pain experience (Watkins & Mayer, 1982). Sci- entists who study the biology of pain at first saw pain as a closed system governed by homeostatic principles. The body (and mind) would return to normal as soon as the nervous system adapted to the stimulus. This simple model posits that the more instances of pain we experience, the less reactive we would become physiologically, because balancing "oppo- nent" processes kick in. We know now that it is not that simple. Sometimes we do not adapt. Sometimes our bodies leave us in chronic pain. This pain is not a friend.

To understand chronic pain, medical researchers had to change the way they thought about it. From a biomedical standpoint, pain emanates from the site of the tissue damage. Repair that damage and the pain is alleviated. There should be a simple one-to-one correspondence between the presence of some damaged tissue and the pain experience. Further, the body should feel less and less pain over time as adaptation processes kick in. It turns out that on both counts, this mechanistic model does not hold.

The most dramatic example of the failure of this model is the phenomenon that pain researchers refer to as the "phantom limb." Approximately 70% of people who lose an arm or leg from a traumatic injury still sense the lost limb as part of their bodies. What is more, 50% of those who lose a limb feel pain from that limb, and that pain can be excruciatingly real. But there is no arm (or leg), and no nervous impulses firing from that appendage any longer. Where is that pain?

Melzack and Wall (1965) introduced a new model of pain that they called *gate control theory*.[4] According to this model, the experience of pain is controlled by a combination of nerve fibers, some of which stimulate and some of which inhibit the firing of nerves responsible for the pain sensation. The researchers found that there were different kinds of pain transmission fibers and influences that arose not just from the bottom up but also from the top down. Cortical processes, including those in regions of the brain associated with planning and executive functions, contributed descending fibers that could influence the opening and closing of the gates of pain. The pain from the phantom limb does not come from the nerve fibers of the missing arm but from the mental image of the arm that still resides in the memory cells of the somatosensory cortex (Melzack, 1993).

The phantom-limb phenomenon is just the most dramatic example of the contribution of central processes to the experience of chronic pain. Chronic pain is a common problem, estimated to affect 25% of the adult population. Some of this pain has no known medical explanation. Other pain arises from chronic diseases such as degenerative arthritis but can be only partially explained by the underlying disease processes. What has gone wrong for those in chronic pain? Does our two-factor model help understand the problem of pain in people's lives?

Although pain researchers have not found the definitive answer to chronic pain, psychologists and neuroscientists have focused on a set of attentional processes gone awry that might be one of the principal culprits: the anticipation of harm. Like many other things, this makes perfect sense once we think about it. Pain does not just stimulate reactions; pain is also a basis for learning. We learn to anticipate when and from where pain may come, in hopes of avoiding future encounters. Recent brain imaging studies suggest further that different regions of the brain are responsible for the *anticipation* of pain versus the *experience* of pain.[5]

My wife tells me that I am a wimp when it comes to pain. This is, of course, not an uncommon remark in the debates between men and women about who has it hardest. Especially when the woman involved has gone through childbirth, men do not have much of a chance to claim greater suffering in these gender debates. But my wife introduced a new angle in her claims for the superiority of women when it comes to coping with pain. She claims that I never really even experience pain. "You cry out even before it hurts!" she exclaims. And as much as I hate to say it, she is right about that. I find myself reacting to the anticipation of pain so strongly that I often am able to avoid the actual pain experience altogether. The shower turns cold; I scream and jump out, soaking the carpet. On reflection, I realize I experienced less than a second of cold water, and I actually did not experience any pain, just the anticipation of pain. So, technically, my wife is right; I complain even when pain was not part of the subjective experience.

However, I certainly did experience considerable anxiety and perhaps even feelings close to panic. Those emotions were strong adverse experiences comparable in intensity to pain. Chronic pain sufferers experience both the anxious anticipatory response and the pain itself. It is this anticipation of pain that may be a major source of misery for many in chronic pain. People can suffer a long time waiting for that other shoe to drop.

The unpredictability and uncontrollability of chronic pain are two of its most unsettling ingredients. These conditions provoke uncertainty and all the problems with emotions that accompany this stress. Grau and Meagher (1999) have uncovered clear evidence that repeated exposure to pain often sensitizes the body, leading to increased rather than decreased distress following painful stimulation. The stress of not knowing when the pain will arise, how long it will last, and whether one can do anything to control the pain produces an anxiety that may indeed provoke sensitivity, not just at the psychological level but at the actual site of the nerve transmission of pain.

The challenge posed by chronic pain is to learn how to reduce hypervigilance and overconcern about the potential for harm. These anticipatory responses might be highly adaptive in acutely painful situations, but they do not help us when coping with unpredictable episodes of chronic pain. In fact, the stress involved in anticipating pain plays on our emotions in ways similar to other stressful conditions. The uncertainty narrows our range of options for emotional response. When repeated efforts to control the pain are unsuccessful, our focus narrows to attend to that "distress keeper" that Harman et al. (1997) identified. Though we think we are finding a way to anticipate and thus avoid future pain, we do not realize that the more we focus exclusively on distress, the greater our discovery of new sources of misery.

The solution is to think in two dimensions rather than one. Quality of life depends on our capacity to sustain positive affective health, as well as to avoid or otherwise cope with negative affects that challenge our well-being. What happens during the stress of anticipating chronic pain is that the person views pain or its absence as defining the whole of emotional life. This unidimensional thinking, acquired in response to the stress of unpredictable and uncontrollable bouts of pain, is a major source of the problems of recovery from chronic pain. In a sense, what the person must do is to let go of attempts to find *the* answer to pain and allow into conscious attention other ways of engaging with the world. Comedian Tim Allen read this from his script on a recent TV sitcom: "The pain may be mandatory, but the suffering is optional."

Therapeutic Interventions

In cognitive therapies for chronic pain, attention (re)deployment is the key to pain management. In this approach, the patient learns that attention is like a searchlight (Turk, Meichenbaum, & Genest, 1983). When the light of our conscious awareness illuminates one feature, by necessity, other features are cast into darkness. The sensation of pain and other feeling states is no different. A focus on one emotional state tends to turn out the lights on the other emotions. Drawing attention away from pain ushers the pain away for as long as the person can turn attention elsewhere.

Attention does need to be directed somewhere. Consider the parental advice: "Just don't think about it. Just put it out of your mind." This is impossible to do unless you have advanced training in Far Eastern forms of meditation that give form and structure to "nothingness." The practical value of two-dimensional thinking is that it provides a place to put attention that is beneficial to us, namely to positive, as well as painful, states of mind.

Attention redeployment is useful as a short-term strategy for pain management, but it is often not enough. Medication is a necessity for many people in chronic pain. In fact, in 2002, the most frequently prescribed medication in the United States was an anti-inflammatory drug for the treatment of pain in osteoarthritis that has fewer of the painful side effects of previous preparations. Another popular drug in 2002 has been time-release capsules that deliver morphine-based medicines for use in treating

severe cancer pain and also chronic pain from arthritis and other musculoskeletal disturbances.

On the surface, it would appear that these drugs are effective because
they block neural pathways regulating pain transmission. But it would be
a mistake to attribute their success solely to the neurochemistry that occurs
at the receptor sites of neurons responsible for pain signaling. The truth is
much more interesting than that.

Pain medications also can have profound psychological benefits. I am
not talking about the mildly euphoric "buzz" that we get from taking co-
deine or other opioid-related pain killers. When people have access to medications that they can use to help control pain, fundamental changes take
place in the psychology of the pain experience. They are no longer helpless.
They have a response that is effective, at least in part, thereby reducing
their anticipatory anxiety. With less uncertainty about whether the pain
will be unmanageable, people in chronic pain no longer have to hold their
breath, waiting with anticipation and dread for the next round.[6]

Self-efficacy beliefs can benefit pain tolerance even when the beliefs
concern some aspect of life other than pain management. Albert Bandura
and his colleagues (Bandura, Cioffi, Taylor, & Brouillard, 1988) investigated whether efficacy training would influence pain tolerance for a group
of 40 college students.[7] Half the study participants were led through a
series of efficacy-enhancing exercises designed to bolster their beliefs in
their abilities to solve math problems. The other half was led through the
same math problem sequence but at a rate that exceeded their capacity to
solve the problems, leading them to feel ineffective. Before and after the
math exercises, all the men and women were tested for pain tolerance.
They put their hands into a vat of freezing water, and the investigators
recorded how much time elapsed before they withdrew their hands.

The students who were given efficacy training had greater pain tolerance than those who received inefficacy training. But there was more to
the study than that. Half the college students were given an injection of
naloxone, a drug that blocks the analgesic effect of opiates. Those injected
with this opioid antagonist did not show the gains in pain tolerance from
the receipt of efficacy training. In conclusion, it appeared that self-efficacy
beliefs increased pain tolerance but not simply by increasing the person's
psychological stamina. Changes in opioid levels appear to underlie these
gains. These last two studies show that both behavioral and pharmacological interventions can influence pain levels, and they may do so by influencing the same psychological and the same biochemical mechanisms.

Programs focused on enhancing efficacy beliefs have become the main-
stay of psychosocial approaches to pain management put forth by the Arthritis Foundation. As useful as these programs have been in reducing pain,

they often have little or no effect on the emotional struggles of chronic pain patients.[8] How might these programs be enriched by a dynamic two-dimensional model of emotions? Junghaenel and Broderick (2001) have investigated one interesting approach designed to help those with fibromyalgia, a generalized pain syndrome characterized by noninflammatory pain in the soft tissue throughout the body. In addition to the usual self-help course that instructs patients in ways to manage their pain effectively, these investigators asked group members to write about prior traumatic experiences. These writing assignments, built on Pennebaker's (1990; Pennebaker, Mayne, & Francis, 1997) methods, encourage emotional disclosure concerning prior stressful events and provide opportunities for the patients to gain greater understanding of the emotional complexities involved in those experiences.

When Junghaenel and Broderick (2001) compared the outcomes of the self-help groups with and without emotional disclosure, they found significant differences between them. Those patients who engaged in the writing exercises showed significantly greater improvement in cognitive functioning, had less fatigue and more energy, and were happier with their daily lives than patients given the standard treatment.

These kinds of therapeutic interventions offer a refreshingly different approach to pain and other stressful experiences. Instead of relying solely on attention diversion tactics such as distraction or depending exclusively on medications to blunt pain sensations, these methods encourage disclosure and acceptance of adverse emotional experiences as a way of opening the patient's mind to a more enriched daily life.

McCracken (1998) has taken the lead in studying the consequences of one of the key ingredients in these approaches: pain acceptance. He interviewed a group of 160 patients in pain management programs concerning their degree of acceptance of pain and then examined how much their acceptance influenced their adjustment. To assess acceptance, he asked the patients whether they agreed with statements such as, "It's okay to experience pain," "I've done my best to control my chronic pain, and it looks like it won't change," and "It is not necessary for me to control my pain in order to handle my life well."

On the surface, agreeing with these statements suggests that the person has surrendered control of his or her pain. In Western societies, that might be considered failure. But McCracken's findings contradict that Western view. Acceptance was one of the best things pain patients could do to improve their sense of well-being. Not only did those patients with high levels of acceptance show less pain-related anxiety, but they also were less depressed and reported more uptime during which they could participate in life and less work disability. In an important sense, acceptance lowered their stress response to their pain and, in doing so, uncoupled their positive feelings from their pain experiences, allowing them a freedom to be happy, even when it hurt.

Those in chronic pain often rebel against the advice that acceptance of pain is good for them. The reason for this resistance is that they see acceptance as a form of resignation: a passive avoidant response. Acceptance is anything but passive, though. It requires active restructuring of one's thinking about the situation and is likely related to the emotions of approach, not avoidance. The reason for misinterpretation of acceptance as a passive response is, in part, cultural. American society has few, if any, heroes who emerged victorious by showing restraint and patience. Herculean efforts that are active, physical, and masculine are championed in the West. In contrast, Eastern cultures have long seen strength in self-regulation of emotional responses; calmness and serenity in the face of danger are seen as highly valued attributes.

The value of Eastern ways is vividly illustrated in the application of a form of meditative therapy called *mindfulness* (Kabat-Zinn, 1982).[9] In this approach, pain and other negative emotions are allowed in, rather than fought. By meditating, we gain a fuller awareness of all experiences, negative and positive, and thus become increasingly mindful of the rich and varied texture of our emotional lives.

Pain diminishes in importance because it is no longer an obstacle to experience. No longer is it something to battle against. Training in being mindful helps us learn to place the experience of pain alongside feelings such as contentment, sorrow, and joy. Doing so gives us a greater tranquility and freedom from the emotional burden of a never-ending struggle for that elusive state of happiness. Here is how Jon Kabat-Zinn (1990, pp. 297–298)[10] puts it:

> It may also strike you at a certain point, particularly if there is a moment of calmness in the midst of the inner turmoil, that your awareness of sensations, thoughts and feelings is different from the sensations, the thoughts, the feelings themselves—the part of "you" that is aware is not itself in pain, or ruled by these thoughts and feelings at all. It knows them, but is itself free of them. In this stillness, you might come to know that whatever you are, "you" are definitely not your body. . . . It is a very convenient and miraculous vehicle, but it is hardly you.

There are theological points of argument about the role of pain in our lives that I have not tackled here. But they are instructive nonetheless, for they often provide another window into the world and ourselves, a different perspective. C. S. Lewis (1962/1996), best known for his book series

The Chronicles of Narnia, attempted to address a fundamental question that haunts the faithful: Why is there so much suffering in the world? The answer he gives is a complex one, but it boils down to this: Pain reminds us that we do not have all the answers; that we need more than ourselves to reach a state of grace; that surrender of the self requires labors in life that are not of one's own choosing. As he put it, "The human spirit would not even begin to surrender self-will as long as all seems to be well with it" (p. 82). Thus pain is an invitation to humility and a requirement that we look deeper than our bodies for meaning in life. Are pain and suffering needed to initiate a search for meaning?

An ancient Chinese proverb states, "A gem cannot be polished without friction." Significant gains in positive mental health may depend on the presence rather than the absence of pain. For Lewis, our best emotions are coupled with negative emotions, but not at all as opposites; pain and suffering are prerequisites for the development of the most positive features of our identities. The gains are not in self-fulfillment but in the wisdom of surrender.

In his examination of the theological implications of human pain and suffering, Harold Kushner (1981) offers another point of view.[11] He suggests that we expect too much of our Creator to think that He or She could have prevented our pain and suffering or that those experiences have some divine purpose. In his view, God created order out of chaos, but we ought to consider that achievement as a work in progress. The catastrophes that befall us arise from disorder in the world, not from a preordained plan or lesson. Kushner (1981) urges us not to try to search for the cause of our suffering but to ask where the tragedy leads us: not "Why me?" but rather, "What am I to do now?" It is during the pursuit of life in the midst of pain and suffering that we may receive divine inspiration. Kushner (1981) urges us to find meaning in the positive by letting go of our attempts to resolve our suffering. In this sense, he too advocates keeping our emotions separate: Suffering is not an instrument of joy, and joy is not a harbinger of suffering. Our lives are endowed with experiences of both kinds.

9 Depression and Anxiety

Two Frequent Disturbances of Emotion under Stress

Poor Silas, so concerned for other folk,
And nothing to look backward to with pride,
And nothing to look forward to with hope,
So now and never any different."
                    —Robert Frost, "The Death of
                                the Hired Man"

Depression

Thus far in the book my focus has been on the experiences of positive and negative emotions that we all have in common. In this chapter I discuss two types of emotional disturbances that, when severe enough, are diagnosed as affective disorders: depression and anxiety. Just about everyone has had the most prominent symptoms of depression: loss of pleasure in everyday life events, feelings of profound sadness, and hopelessness. There are other symptoms also, ranging from loss of appetite (or overeating) to sleep disturbance and suicidal thoughts. If these symptoms last day in and day out for at least 2 weeks, the person could receive a diagnosis of major depression, unless he or she has experienced a precipitating event such as the death of a loved one or a major physical injury that provoked the depressive symptoms. Community studies have estimated that 24% of women and 15% of men will, at some time in their lives, be clinically depressed (Kessler et al., 1994). About 10% of the adult population are clinically depressed at any one time, even without counting those who disguise their depressive illness by denying the symptoms and self-medicating with alcohol or another drug. There is no doubt that depression is a major mental health problem in our communities.

The losses in quality of life and productivity due to depression are enormous. Current estimates run in the millions of lost workdays per year solely as a consequence of depression (Kessler, DuPont, & Wittchen, 1999). If that were all that depression might do, it would be sufficient to warrant our attention. But depression does much more than harm mental health. When we feel depressed, we are detecting troubled emotions within ourselves, and emotions are in the body as well as the mind. The physiological concomitants of chronic depression are dangerous to our physical health, as well as to our emotional stability.[1]

"Are you hopeful about the future?" Stern, Dhanda, & Hazuda (2001). posed this "Yes" or "No" question to 1,247 middle-aged adult men and women in San Antonio.[2] Then, approximately 10 years later, they checked to see how many of the participants were still living. They found that 1,077 were still alive, and 170 had died since the initial assessment. Ten percent of those initially hopeful had died, but 28.8% of those who had professed to be hopeless were dead at the follow-up.

Musselman, Evans, and Nemeroff (1998) have reviewed the epidemiological evidence concerning depression's influence on cardiovascular health. Their results are startling. Depression appears to double the risk of heart attacks.[3] The effects do not end there. The fate of those who have already had a heart attack is also significantly influenced by depression. Denollet and Brutsaert (1998) followed patients who had sustained myocardial infarctions for 6 years. They found that the chances of dying from heart disease were substantially higher for those who were depressed.[4]

Everson, Kaplan, Goldberg, and Salonen (2000) recently found evidence of a specific link in the chain of events from depression to heart disease.[5] The researchers asked 616 middle-aged men from Finland to indicate whether they felt hopeless using standard assessment techniques. All the men had blood pressure in the normal range at the time they entered the study. Four years later, 20% of the men showed elevations in their blood pressures high enough to classify them as hypertensive: greater than or equal to 165mm Hg systolic or 95 mm Hg diastolic. Needless to say, hypertension is a major risk factor for heart attacks and death from cardiovascular disease.

Everson et al. (2000) first compared those who developed hypertension to those who stayed in the normal range on a host of factors known to be associated with risk for heart disease, including age, physical activity, smoking, alcohol use, education, and parental history of hypertension. After accounting for these factors, they then tested how individual differences in hopelessness predicted hypertension 4 years later. The findings indicated a significant role for hopelessness. Twice as many men who scored high on hopelessness initially developed hypertension as those who were low in hopelessness.

How does depression adversely affect the vascular system? There is no single satisfactory answer to this question, but several theories have been proposed, primarily based on the influence of depression on physiological responses to stress. Elevations in blood pressure from higher sympathetic nervous system activity, increases in ACTH, and chronic elevations in cortisol lead to higher cholesterol and higher concentration of triglycerides in the blood, both risk factors for heart conditions. There are other possibilities that are still under investigation, such as activation of platelets in the blood vessels that can promote fibrogen deposits on the vessel walls, cause actual ruptures in the wall membranes, or both (Musselman et al., 1998).[6] When we feel brokenhearted, our hearts might not actually break, but they could start leaking.

The immune system is also sensitive to depressive symptoms. Researchers have investigated the high death rates among those grieving after the death of a loved one. For 2 to 6 months following a wife's death due to natural causes, the husband is at a significantly higher risk of dying himself (Schwarzer & Leppin, 1992). When investigators looked into this question, they began to find evidence that key components of the immune system were no longer as responsive to pathogens. The immune system appeared to be suppressed by hormonal responses that accompany profound grief.[7] The story, however, turns out to be a bit more complicated, and some doubts have been raised about whether the immune changes are large enough to actually increase the body's vulnerability to diseases. Nevertheless, the evidence for perturbations in immune regulation during depressive episodes is incontrovertible.

Maes et al. (1992) found another type of immune fluctuation that occurs with depression: elevations in interleukin-6 (IL-6), a chemical messenger that stimulates inflammatory processes by up-regulating production of certain immune cell networks. This finding is important because abnormal levels of this cytokine are associated with autoimmune diseases such as rheumatoid arthritis as well as cardiovascular disease. Indeed, rates of depression are higher among those with rheumatoid arthritis when compared with the general population (Pincus, Griffith, Pearce, & Isenberg, 1996; Katz & Yelin, 1993).[8] It is likely not to be such a coincidence that the incidence of both depression and autoimmune disorders such as rheumatoid arthritis occur at a greater frequency among women than men.

Zautra, Hamilton, Potter, and Smith (1999) investigated this link in a study of disease progression among 87 older women with rheumatoid arthritis compared with a control group of 101 women with similar levels of pain who had osteoarthritis. We reasoned that stress and depression might affect the pain reports of both arthritis-affected groups but that depression may have stronger effects on the participants with rheumatoid arthritis. Because of their autoimmune status, we hypothesized that the women with rheumatoid arthritis would be more likely to show a systemic inflammatory response to stressful events than the women with osteoarthritis, who did not have an autoimmune disease.

After assessing their level of depression in that study, we interviewed the participants through weekly telephone calls to gather data on their levels of pain and interpersonal stress each week. Altogether, we collected 2980 weeks of data. We then related changes in level of stress from one week to the next to changes in pain from one week to the next. Both rheumatoid arthritis and osteoarthritis groups reported more pain during stressful weeks, but the group with rheumatoid arthritis showed a much stronger reaction to the interpersonal stresses. When we added depression to the equation we found out why. Those women in the study who not only had rheumatoid arthritis but also were depressed had significantly higher pain levels during stress. In contrast, participants with osteoarthritis who were depressed were not more sensitive to stress. We suspect that the difference was in part due to elevations in IL-6 following stress among those with rheumatoid arthritis. Depression is bad for us when it is chronic, and it is especially destructive for those with an autoimmune disease such as rheumatoid arthritis.

How does a two-dimensional model of emotions help inform us about conditions such as depression? In brief, both affect systems are often derailed in those who are depressed. Both low levels of positive affect and high levels of negative affect characterize most depressed patients. Indeed, these levels of positive and negative feelings define the disorder. Loss of pleasure in life is a hallmark of the depressed person, along with feeling sad and blue. For many, depression may be thought of as a state of inner turmoil. During bleak periods, negative affects predominate, and positive feelings may all but disappear. In sum, depression is an extended period of disturbance in both positive and negative affect systems: a black period in a person's life with much negative emotion and little positive emotion.[9]

Depression as a Response to Stress

There are many paths to depression. Given its many forms, it should come as no surprise that the illness has many causes. There are vulnerabilities to this condition due to differences in genetic endowment, to be sure. Traumatic childhood experiences also contribute to increased risk, and I discuss those contributions to vulnerability in chapter 11. Loss is a common theme in many stories of depression. We all know that depression follows predictably soon after the death of a loved one. The same depressive symptoms that lead to a diagnosis of major depression are referred to in the diagnostic manuals as uncomplicated grief for those suffering from the recent death of a loved one.

Other scenarios besides profound loss can provoke depression. Many of these seem as though they have been lifted right from the Book of Job. Here is one illustration. A woman who has faithfully cared for her husband and two young children develops an intractable cancer. Her husband, frightened of the thought of being alone at midlife, abandons her, throwing himself into the arms of another woman. The no-fault divorce that ensues leaves the divorced woman with half her former income, half as much time with her children, and full time with a malignant tumor. If this woman did not become depressed, we would question her sanity.

Life's indignities need not be as dramatic as this to provoke depression. Everyday stressors can also lead to feelings of hopelessness if we can do nothing to prevent them from recurring. Financial struggles represent some of the more insidious conditions that erode our sense of well-being. Time and again, a day or two before payday, the bank stops honoring your checks, and then your credit card payments are late again. You are charged extra processing fees at the bank, late fees by your creditors, and a resubmission fee every time each check is recycled for payment to an overdrawn account. It does not take many months of a cycle of woes like these for us to throw our hands up in despair.

If these examples sound similar to those I wrote about in describing stressful experiences in chapter 3, you are right. Either a highly stressful event or a series of events are seen as triggers for depressive episodes in many theories of depression. One popular model of depression, for instance, sees repeated exposure to unpredictable and uncontrollable aversive events as a major cause of depression.

Martin Seligman (1975) is often associated with some of the early experimental work on this model of depression.[10] He and his colleagues placed animals, usually rats, in conditions of maximum uncertainty. They shocked the animal in the foot at random or varied the length of the shock pulse in a totally unpredictable fashion. The animals soon learned that nothing they did made a difference. After trying hard at first to control the aversive stimulus, the animals would end up cowering in their cages, avoiding human contact, appearing to lose all interest in their surroundings. According to Seligman (1975), they had learned to be helpless.

Paul Willner (1997) has developed a model that focuses on chronic stressful situations that provoke a loss of interest and pleasure. Rather than introducing a brief series of highly aversive events, such as shock or loud bursts of unpredictable noise, Willner and his colleagues began testing the effects of milder stressors that occur over an extended period of time. To produce what they referred to as chronic mild stress, the researchers arranged a variety of unpleasant experiences for each of their animals. They left the lights on in the cage overnight for a couple of nights, "forgot" to provide food or water for a day, changed the animal's social encounters by housing it with a group of other rats, soiled the animal's cage with wet sawdust, delivered occasional irritating blasts of 85-decibel noise (just a bit lower than a teenager's stereo), tilted the cage at a 45-degree angle for several hours, and, finally, delivered three periods of low-intensity strobe light at 300 flashes a minute for 7, 9, and 17 hours. The animals could not predict or control what was happening to them. For the 3 weeks during which they received this treatment, they could never be certain just what their world would look, sound, or feel like.

It turns out that these chronic mild stressors have lasting effects on the animals' interest in pleasurable experiences. They become impervious to such casual pleasures as sipping on sugar water. Scores of studies provide additional evidence to support the idea that these chronically stressed animals lose much of their interest in their surroundings. They engage in less sexual activity, are less likely to explore open fields, and even show less motivation to pursue self-stimulation of "pleasure" centers in the brain. The effects last for months. Interestingly enough, these patterns are reversible by giving the animals a regimen of antidepressive medications equivalent to what a person might take for major depression.

These models implicate chronic adverse circumstances as key contributors to depression. Humans are different from other animals, though. We have a much greater capacity to think ahead and figure out what is happening. For us, affective disturbance goes hand and hand with cognitive processes. Cognitive models of depression are among those best supported by empirical work, and there are several theories that offer different but related ideas about how thought processes increase vulnerability to depression.

One of the most popular models is called the *reformulated learned helplessness theory*. According to this model, depressed feelings arise not only from failure experiences but also from how we think about those events, in particular our attributions about the causes of such experiences. These causal attributions play a critical role in determining how quickly we recover from those depressed feelings. As I mentioned in an earlier chapter, Lynn Abramson, Martin Seligman, and John Teasdale (1978) introduced this attributional model of depression in the mid-1970s. Since then, other researchers have developed the model even further (Abramson, Metalsky, & Alloy, 1989).[11] In essence, the model defines the kind of causal thinking that is associated with long bouts of depressed states: finding fault with oneself for the failure experience, seeing that fault as a stable or recurrent theme, and believing that the fault is pervasive in its influence, affecting many aspects of the person's life.

The model initially included attributions for positive experiences as well. Depressed people were expected to attribute successes to causes other than themselves, and to see the sources of those positive experiences as fleeting rather than stable and as specific to the situation rather than pervasive. In other words, they would make just the opposite attributions about positive events as about negative events.

Zautra, Guenther, and Chartier (1985) questioned whether attributions for positive events produced negative affects. We asked college students to evaluate their successes and failures using the Attribution Style Questionnaire, a common device for assessing causal beliefs about hypothetical events such as losing a job. In addition, we extended this method by asking the students to keep daily diaries for 2 weeks. In those diaries they reported on their everyday successes and failures and rated the causes for those events using the same questions as those on the Attribution Style Questionnaire. We also asked the students to rate their depressive symptoms using a scale developed by the renowned depression researcher Aaron Beck, called the Beck Depression Inventory, or BDI. We then correlated attributional ratings of real and imagined positive and negative events with depressive symptoms. We also included a measure of self-esteem as one indicator of the positive side of mental health.

The first surprising result arose from our preliminary analyses of the Attribution Style Questionnaire. This measure was supposed to produce a coherent estimate of depressive attributional style. It did not. In fact, attributions for positive events, whether real or hypothetical, were unrelated to attributions made about negative events. This finding alone is important because it suggests that the causal thinking involved in understanding positive experiences is different from the causal thinking involved in understanding disappointments, failures, and other negative life experiences. More to the point, we found that the attributions a person made about positive life experiences were unrelated to their symptoms of depression. Only causal attributions concerning negative events went hand in hand with depressive symptoms. Our study was with college students, not with people diagnosed with the disorder. Other researchers have found similar results among those clinically depressed. In sum, stable, global, and internal attributions for failure make a person more vulnerable to depression, but positive event attributions do not decrease vulnerability. Interestingly enough, attribution researchers have quietly dropped these attributions for positive events from their assessment batteries when examining cognitive factors that place a person at risk for depression.

Maybe they should not have been so rash. Most measures of depression do better at detecting the presence of negative or distressed states than they do at capturing the absence of positive states. For instance, saying that one has unhappy thoughts is like saying that one is depressed. It appears to follow logically. But saying that one has no happy thoughts does not mean *depression* in our everyday use of that term. It means that the person is emotionally neutral: Nothing good is happening, but maybe nothing bad is, either. Most measures of depression reflect this bias toward detection of the negative as well. So the lack of relationship found between positive event attributions and depressive symptoms may be more a function of the limitations in our methods of assessing depression than in the contributions of positive event attributions.

In our study, attributions about positive events were related to outcomes other than depression. Those college students who took credit for the successes and attributed those events to a stable and pervasive personal characteristic had the highest self-esteem. A sense of self-worth is lacking in people with chronic and severe forms of depressive illness. And looking back to Frost's poem, "The Death of the Hired Man," self-esteem is certainly something that Silas lacked

Needles and Abramson (1990) have rekindled an interest in these positive attributions. They suggest that attributing positive events to oneself is important in recovery from depression. They reasoned that beliefs about one's ability to make positive things happen would lead the person to feel hopeful about the future, even when faced with the burden of depressive feelings. Attributions for positive events do not prevent depression from occurring, but causal thinking about positive events can hasten recovery.

Johnson, Crofton, and Feinstein (1996) tested this idea with a group of 52 depressed inpatients at a psychiatric hospital. The patients reported on their attributions for positive and negative events at the start of their hospitalization and later were tested for levels of depression while still in the hospital. Only patients who took antidepressive medications were studied in order to hold constant the effects of drug therapies. Those patients who took credit for positive events and viewed those causes as stable and pervasive showed significantly less depression at posttest. They were significantly more hopeful about their futures than their counterparts were. Remarkably, the attributions the patients made about failure experiences did not predict recovery. This is quite a turn of events. Two separable processes, one dealing with positive experiences and the other with negative experiences, each play a role in clinical depression: One appears to make the person more vulnerable to depression but is unrelated to recovery. The other appears to play no role in the onset of a depressive episode but allows the person to recover more rapidly.[12]

Fava, Rafanelli, Cazzaro, Conti, and Grandi (1998) designed a well-being therapy for depressed patients that focused on removing cognitive barriers to positive states. This approach is in contrast to the more typical one of trying to modify cognitions associated with negative emotions. The researchers then tested the efficacy of their approach as a means of preventing relapse of depressive symptoms for a group of patients who had been successfully treated for a major depressive disorder, either by behavior therapy or antidepressant medication. For comparison purposes, Fava et al. (1998) randomly assigned half of their patients to the standard cognitive therapy methods that focused on eliminating ways of thinking associated with depressive affects. The investigators collected before and after measures on a range of outcomes, including self-reports of positive mental health and psychiatric symptoms and clinical ratings of depressive symptoms made by a clinical psychologist who conducted in-depth interviews with the patients.

Both treatments were effective in reducing self-reports of psychiatric distress. But in the most critical comparison that was based on clinician ratings, patients who had received the well-being therapy showed significantly greater improvement than those who had received standard cognitive therapy. Fava et al. (1998) caution that the study provides only preliminary evidence of the efficacy of their new therapeutic approach. Nonetheless, the findings are surprising. The comparison group received a standard treatment that has been well established as a successful treatment of depression. Indeed, the findings indicate a significant improvement in functioning for those receiving the standard cognitive therapy, as well. The well-being therapy focused on removing barriers to psychological well-being and appeared to be equal to if not better than the standard treatment in preventing depressive symptoms, even though that therapy did not intervene with patients' thoughts concerning their negative emotions. Findings such as these indicate that we need to attend to thoughts and actions that promote positive emotion, if we are to find secure paths to recovery and prevent relapse into depression.

Psychopharmacological Aspects of Depression

Depression has a neurochemical substrate, as well as cognitive and behavioral ones. This is particularly evident in the increasing success of drug therapies that treat clinical and also subclinical levels of depression. Although we cannot identify a single neurochemical as the source of depressive states, the presence and/or relative absence of some substances have been associated with depression (Checkley, 1996). For example, there is evidence that the depletion of serotonin in the brain is one source of negative emotion, particularly depressed states. Other work has pointed to the relative absence of norepinephrine in key brain structures associated with the regulation of negative affect. Modern medicines for depression have relied on these findings to develop drugs designed to treat depression and other affective disorders. One effect of the newer line of anti-depressants is to block the reuptake of serotonin at selective synaptic sites in the brain, thus they are called *selective serotonin reuptake inhibitors*, or SSRIs. How might these medications influence positive and negative emotions? If we think of positive and negative states as opposites, then the answer is clear; the SSRIs should lower negative and increase positive feelings. If they are not opposites and have different neurobiological substrates, however, then the answer to this question is not so simple; it depends on the neurotransmitters that are actually affected by the SSRIs.

Knutson et al. (1998) addressed this question. They gave an SSRI (Paxil) to a group of 26 normal volunteers and a placebo preparation to another randomly selected group of 25 volunteers. Then they examined the effects over 4 weeks of daily drug administrations. What they found was startling. Those on the active drug were less hostile and less irritable and, in general, reported significantly less negative affect. But there was no change in their experience of positive emotions. Although all the data are not in on this question, evidence such as this is consistent with the presence of separate neurochemical pathways for the experience of positive and negative emotions related to depression. This is only one study, and the sample was college students, not clinically depressed patients. Nevertheless, the study is provocative because it suggests that this SSRI, and perhaps the others as well, may reduce negative states without having any beneficial effects on positive states.

What is the future for pharmacotherapies in the treatment of affective disorders? Nemeroff (1998) admires the success of the recent SSRIs but cautions that around 30% of those who try these medications do not improve significantly. There are also a number of unwanted side effects for some people, such as sexual dysfunction.

Nemeroff (1998) urges the development of future depression medications that target the stress-distress brain circuitry. Nemeroff (1998) cites evidence from a number of studies that suggest that hyperreactivity to stress underlies depressive disorders. In particular, abnormalities in corticotropin-releasing hormone (CRH) have been implicated in studies of depressed patients compared with controls. He envisions drugs that will regulate the cellular interactions responsible for physiological reactivity to stress as the twenty-first century's approach to the treatment of depression. Although this may indeed be a useful approach, it is still focused on the alleviation of the negative affective dimension of depression. Based on our review of the work of Needles and Abramson (1990) and others, Nemeroff's (1998) approach may not really speed recovery for many people with depression if their disturbance is characterized primarily by a lack of interest and loss of capacity for positive emotion.

Does this mean that drug companies ought to consider a "depression cocktail" that includes ingredients that boost positive mood, as well as lower negative mood? Not necessarily. Treatments are needed that acknowledge the importance of problems in positive affect and cognition. These problems are not addressed when tackling the causes of high levels of negative affect among those who are depressed. The answer may not be more or different medications. Medications that attempt to accent the positive may even backfire. In chapter 10, I discuss evidence from addiction research on how drug-induced highs may lead to misinterpretation of feelings and behavioral excesses, including drug overuse and abuse.

There may be a built-in limitation to the usefulness of medications to treat deficits in the domain of positive emotion. It is the events that people see as coming, as least in part, from their own efforts that are the most satisfying. Events that do not arise from the person's own actions carry much less punch and may not have lasting salutary effects on well-being. Further, the studies by Needles and Abramson (1990) and by Johnson et al. (1996) suggest that the attributions of success to oneself are a central ingredient in recovery from depression. Is taking a pill effortful enough to lead to those favorable attributions?

These questions are part of the ongoing dialectic between psychology and psychiatry concerning how best to treat depressive disorders. If we take a dynamic view of emotional regulation, there are certainly at least two legitimate sides to this debate. Allow me to expand on one aspect of this debate that concerns the importance of control. Ordinarily, strengthening personal control beliefs would fall naturally within the province of psychotherapies, not drug treatments. But there are exceptions. One of the most troubling aspects of any mental health problem is that feelings, thoughts, and behaviors are no longer under the same degree of executive control. In thought disorders, the person thinks, even hears, things that have no basis in reality. When depressed, the person is not in control of his or her feelings. The person may cry uncontrollably; he or she may have suicidal thoughts that suddenly enter consciousness. Even though people can learn to recognize these thoughts and feelings as a part of their depression, they often can do little to control them. This is a very stressful aspect of disordered affective states that cannot be overlooked. Uncertainty and fear reactions that arise from uncontrollable symptoms create a more intense, stressful, internal context within which emotions are experienced.[13] Any therapy that helps to eliminate this inner emotional chaos would increase personal control, whether the help came from a behavioral or pharmaceutical prescription.

Anxiety

Anxiety disorders are also common in our nation. Approximately 30% of women and 19% of men experience a diagnosable anxiety disorder at some time in their lives. Anxiety has many forms, including panic attacks, phobic reactions, obsessive-compulsive conditions, and post-traumatic stress and generalized anxiety disorders. In addition, it is common for people who are depressed to also exhibit considerable anxiety. Kessler et al. (1999) found that approximately 17% of those adults with enough symptoms to quality for a diagnosis of major depression also had a generalized anxiety disorder. Two larger scale population studies found that 50% to 70% of those with an anxiety disorder were also depressed (Kessler et al., 1999). Even without depression, anxiety constitutes a serious mental health problem can increase the risk of physical health problems.[14]

Anxiety symptoms mimic those that people experience when under stress, only without the precipitating external stressor. Take a panic attack, for example. A man is waiting patiently for a subway train to arrive, along with a hundred other passengers. Suddenly, his heart begins to beat harder, and he begins to breathe rapidly and in shallow gulps. The walls of the station appear to close in; he feels he is suffocating and rushes up the stairs to the street. This person is experiencing an internal state of siege.

Barlow, Chorpita, and Turovsky (1996) define anxiety as a structure "composed primarily of high negative affect, of which the most prominent component is a sense of uncontrollability focused on possible future threat, danger, or other upcoming, potentially negative, events." Unlike responses to stressful events, anxiety is a response to a future event. But according to Barlow et al. (1996), anxiety prompts a narrowing of cognitive perspective similar to that found in stress reactions as the person focuses attention on potential sources of threat or danger.[15] Is it possible, then, that anxiety, like stress, shrinks the emotional landscape, leading to less differentiation between positive and negative emotions?

Williams, Peeters, and Zautra (2002) examined whether anxious people were different in the structure of their affective experiences. We gathered data on the levels of positive and negative affect among two groups of adult men and women: people who were diagnosed with anxiety and people who were diagnosed with depression.[16] When we compared these two groups, at first glance, the depressed patients looked to be the most disturbed, clinically. They reported significantly more negative affect and significantly less positive affect than the anxiety patients did. But when we compared the two groups in terms of the relationship between positive and negative affect, we found a problem for the anxious patients that the depression patients did not have. Anxious patients were much more likely to report a one-dimensional world of emotions than the depressed patients. If they had many positive feelings, anxious patients usually had many fewer negative feelings. When they had many negative feelings, they had few positive ones.

These findings have important implications for treatment of depression and anxiety. Both pharmacological treatment and cognitive therapies focus on increasing the client's sense of control over the depressive symptoms and anxious thoughts. In doing so, they not only reduce negative affective states, but also allow the person to breathe in some positive affect independent of their negative affective experiences. This lowers the stress that comes from feeling out of control and increases a sense of hope. What may be needed most for some problems is the uncoupling of our positive emotions from our negative ones.

Could it be that some treatments already do this? To check on this possibility, we reexamined the data in the Knutson et al. (1998) study on the effects of Paxil on positive and negative affect. The correlations between positive and negative affect before and then after treatment for both the placebo controls and those who received the active drug were inspected. Not only had negative affects been reduced as a consequence of the medication, but also the negative correlation between positive and negative affects, present before medication, disappeared for those taking Paxil. The independence between affects appears to have been restored. By using medication that controlled their negative emotions, the study participants also broadened their emotional awareness.

There is no study as yet that has investigated similar effects due to psychotherapy. However, some suggestive evidence may be found in experimental investigations of self-disclosure. In these studies, some participants are asked to write down their deepest thoughts and feelings about a stressful event. The control group is typically asked to perform a less meaningful writing task of some kind. The disclosure condition is analogous to psychotherapy in that the person is often revealing thoughts and feelings about stressful experiences that they have hidden from themselves, as well as from others (Pennebaker, 1995).

Studies of the health benefits of emotional disclosure are too numerous to report here, but there is one study that stands out as an illustration of how writing about stress may be liberating emotionally. Stephen Lepore (1997) examined whether college students benefited from expressing their "deepest thoughts and feelings" about a highly stressful event in their lives: Graduate Record Examination tests. Students suffer from many depressive symptoms around the time of these exams. One of the reasons for their distress is that the upcoming tests prompt students to ruminate about their performances. These intrusive thoughts break into consciousness for college students, just as they do for others suffering from other anxiety-provoking experiences—thoughts that are often accompanied by high levels of depression.

Lepore (1997) had one group of test takers write about the stress of the exam, whereas a randomly selected control group wrote only about their activities on the previous day. The students were given the writing assignments after the initial assessment but before the second. It was this period of anxiety leading up to the exam that Lepore (1997) was most interested in, not reactions to the exam itself. Because each person's actual experience with the exam would be different, depending on factors such as how well they performed, the methodologically "cleaner" comparison was between groups before they actually took the exam.

Those who wrote down their feelings about the exam showed fewer depressive symptoms before the exam than the controls. Those who disclosed did not ruminate less about the exam. The frequency of their intrusive thoughts increased, just as that of the controls did, as they approached the date of the exam. How this group differed from the controls was in the relationship between intrusive thoughts and depression. Students in the control group who ruminated more about the exam had significantly higher levels of depression than those who did not ruminate. However, rumination did not lead to depression for those students instructed to self-disclose. In short, emotional disclosure uncoupled worrying about the exam from the depressed (and anxious) feelings.

Psychotherapy does not always broaden one's framework for experiencing emotions. Most therapies do not focus on increasing emotional complexity as an explicit target for change, though some do so implicitly (Wiser & Goldfried, 1998).[17] Given what we have learned about the dynamics of emotional health, repair of the constriction in affective space would be an important component of any therapy for people with anxiety disorders and anxious forms of depressive disorder. Indeed, the evidence suggests that explicit attention to the restoration of emotional complexity would be an important advance for psychological, as well as drug, treatments for many mental health problems. With this in mind, I discuss ways that these same principles may be useful in understanding substance abuse problems in chapter 10.

10 Addiction and Emotions

"Perhaps, long since, there was a land beyond
Westward from death, some city, some calm place
Where one could taste God's quiet and be fond
With a little beauty of a human face;

But now the land is drowned. Yet still we press
Westward, in search, in death, to nothingness."
—John Masefield, "The Lemmings"

There is now a Web page with an addiction questionnaire about the Internet. It contains questions that ask whether the person finds relationships with others in cyberspace more satisfying than those of "flesh and blood" at home, whether the person has virtual sex on the internet, how often, and so on. The Web page even offers to find counseling for those afflicted. Where does the virtual addict get this help? It's on the Net, of course.

What are the right questions to ask to understand this addiction? Is the key some kind of pleasure seeking that is out of control? Is it too much of a good thing, a form of hedonistic satisfaction empty of any real intimacy with others, a cheaper but less enduring form of happiness? This is the moral view, a favorite of political conservatives.

There are other questions on the "virtual reality" addiction test that take on a different tone. "Do you find yourself avoiding problems at home by retreating into cyberspace?" "Do you stay on the net to keep from being depressed?" This angle on addiction is that, like alcohol,[1] the Internet is taken for medicinal purposes, as a salve that covers psychological wounds and provides respite, but no cure, for emotional ills. This might be termed the liberal, or as some would say, the bleeding heart, view.

How do we become compulsively drawn to activities such as gambling, or ingesting drugs such as nicotine, alcohol, and cocaine? These puzzling behaviors have occupied the attention of some of the most talented behavioral scientists of our time, and for good reason: The costs in human life and suffering due to addictions are truly staggering. Scientists from the National Research Council and the National Academy of Sciences recently teamed up to estimate the costs of addictions in the United States (McGinnis & Foege, 1999).[2] In 1995, they estimated that 590,000 deaths, one-fourth of all deaths that year, could be attributed to at least one addictive substance. In addition, an estimated 40 million illnesses and injuries each year are attributable to addictions.

For those of us interested in understanding the interplay between stress, emotions, and health, addiction provides many important lessons. This chapter is devoted to uncovering some of those lessons through an examination of how our behavior can spin out of control under the influence of powerful drugs. Substances laced with morphine or other opiate compounds give us emotional highs but can also have powerfully adverse effects on behavior. These paradoxical effects stand in stark contrast to the many beneficial effects of positive emotions on health and well-being that I discussed in chapters 5 and 6. In alcohol abuse, as well, emotional (dys)-regulation is a central theme. We often have high expectations for the mood enhancing benefits of drinking (Lindman, Sjoholm, & Lang, 2000).[3] We take a "little something" to feel good and to lubricate our social interactions. The buzz we get drowns out both the internal censors and also our awareness of the complexities of our social relationships, liberating us from harsh realities and permitting us to enjoy life, at least briefly. But when frequent use shifts to abuse, our emotional lives are transformed in ways we could not have anticipated.

Some commentators would argue that it is the extremes of pleasure itself that take us down: being so hooked on the highs that we lose sight of the negative consequences for ourselves and those people dear to us. Is addiction really the ultimate hedonic treadmill? Many self-help texts would suggest as much. The titles are revealing: *Craving for Ecstasy: How Our Passions become Addictions* (Milkman & Sunderwirth, 1998) is one. In another popular book, author Irving Cohen (1995) called addiction the *High-Low Trap*, a roller-coaster ride that afflicts many non-suspecting people.

What does the framework for understanding emotions that I have presented in this book have to contribute to understanding the apparent dangers of a hedonistic psychology? There is great promise in applying dynamic models of emotion to drug and alcohol addictions, though much of that promise has yet to be realized. Researchers have begun to ask the right questions, focusing on two important issues. First, investigators are now looking at cause-and-effect relations in drug use and abuse with more than one dimension of emotion in mind. Second, addiction researchers have become increasingly interested in dynamic changes in the nature of the emotional experience. In current models, attention has focused on how emotional responses to drug taking change over time as the person's attachment to the drug turns from exploration to habit, to dependency, and to addiction.

Earlier in this book, I questioned whether the model of pleasure dynamics known as adaptation-level (AL) theory fits our everyday experience (see Frederick & Loewenstein, 1999; Helson, 1964). A model of addiction has also been fashioned from AL-theory dynamics by Richard Solomon and John Corbit (1974). They proposed what they called an opponent-process model to describe how seemingly pleasant events turn sour. According to these researchers, initial exposure to experiences often promotes emotional reactions; these stimulus-response patterns they call the A process. Elevations in emotion from the A process automatically lead to another, B process, a kind of internal governor, that introduces an opposing affective state that neutralizes the A state and leads the person to regain affective neutrality. A useful process for negative emotions, you might say, but why does it have to blunt positive emotions? The principle here is conservation of resources. If we did not down-regulate the pleasure we feel from repeated positive events, the accompanying physiological arousal would continue unabated. It would be a clambake with our internal organs.

The opponent-process theorists proposed something very interesting about the workings of these processes over extended periods of time. According to the model, the A response habituates, and over time, the B response begins earlier in the cycle as the person accommodates to repeated exposures. After a while, the person experiences very little pleasure and even a slight discomfort. The model explains why many continue to seek drugs even though they gain little pleasure from those drugs. Over time, the B process takes over, and the person requires more and more of the drug to achieve a good high. In fact, it appears that the person increasingly craves the drug not for the high but to escape the lows. A desire has been converted to a demand.[4]

In opponent-process theory, there is only one emotion system involved with addiction. The B process is not an independent process that governs emotional experience. Solomon and Corbit (1974) called it a slave to the *A* process; it only functions in response to *A* and it does not have a life of its own.

Is there support for the opponent-process model of addiction? A key question to ask is whether a unidimensional model of affective responding can account for our behavior toward substances of abuse, such as alcohol, morphine, and cocaine. Much of the basic research on this question has been conducted on animals, usually rodents.[5] Scientists can get approval to administer addictive substances to animals and at the same time directly manipulate their brain chemistry, things that they would never do with human samples. The researchers attempt to isolate a single molecular response at the nerve endings of key brain structures that may account for addictive behavior.

The dopamine system has been the leading candidate for designation as the pleasure molecule that underlies habitual drug use. This neurotransmitter is found throughout the brain, and there are receptors for it on neurons in most, if not all, key limbic areas (Panksepp, 1998). When scientists injected animals with substances known to block dopamine transmission between nerve endings in the brain (dopamine antagonists), these animals no longer pressed a bar to obtain food, water, or opiates, let alone cocaine and amphetamines. Another behavioral test besides bar pressing seemed to substantiate the rewarding role of dopamine. When given multiple environments to choose from, animals would usually select those areas in which they had previously received the drug; but they did not if they had been previously injected with a dopamine antagonist. As Nader, Bechara, and van der Kooy (1997) noted, these same effects were reversible by giving the animals dopamine agonists: substances that increased the amount of dopamine available at receptor sites.

As you might have guessed, it turns out that reward chemistry is not reducible to a such a simple model. Just when a solution to our search for the pleasure molecule seemed at hand, two separate groups of neuroscientists came up with contradictory evidence and two different two-dimensional models.

Bechara and colleagues (Bechara & van der Kooy, 1992; Nader & van der Kooy, 1997) have reviewed the many papers that have kept the dopamine flagship afloat and noticed something that these studies had in common. All the experiments were carried out with the animals in a state of deprivation. It is standard practice to deprive the animal prior to the start of conditioning trials. The standard pellet food and slugs of water from a nippled bottle are not especially tempting unless the rat is extremely thirsty or starving. So most studies need to starve the rodents first just to get them interested. Bechara and colleagues wondered whether the deprivation context might influence the animals to travel down one motivational path but not others.

The researchers reasoned that the influence of rewards might be quite different when the animals were not deprived. Morphine and other opiates are sought without prior learning, and an animal's appetite for these drugs does not depend on a state of deprivation. This property of the addictive drugs allowed Bechara and his colleagues to examine whether dopamine was a necessary ingredient for reward-based learning in the non-deprived as well as the deprived animals (see Nader, Bechara, & van der Kooy, 1997).

To investigate these processes, the researchers used an experimental procedure called the *conditioning of place preference*. Simply put, what this method attempts to do is to repeatedly pair a physical location with a rewarding (or aversive) stimulus of some kind so that researchers can observe whether the animal comes to prefer or avoid that place. Here is a brief synopsis of one of their experiments (Bechara & van der Kooy, 1992).

They injected one group of rats with morphine several times prior to the conditioning task, to make them dependent on it. This group was called *morphine-dependent*. A second group, called *morphine-naïve*, received no morphine prior to the experimental trials. The rats from these two groups were then given morphine injections during half the ensuing trials and saline (distilled water and salt) during the other half of the trials. This went on for several days.

To examine the rewarding properties of the drug, the experimenters varied the places in which they put the rats after injection. Some rats from each group were put into a special compartment after their morphine shots but put back in their home cages when receiving saline. The experimenters figured that this procedure would make this compartment more rewarding and that the animals would prefer to spend more time there, compared with another compartment not paired with any injections. This condition is labeled "Big-M" for morphine in Figure 10.1. In contrast, some animals were not put there after getting their injections; they were just dropped gently back into their home cages.

After the saline injections, some of the animals were placed into a different compartment. This compartment was being paired with the failure to receive an injection, and the experimenters thought that this place would be more aversive than a different compartment, as it was associated with the failure to attain the drug. This condition is labeled "Big-W," for withdrawal. When these animals received the morphine injections, they were placed back in their home cages.[6] Figure 10.1 shows the various conditions of this experiment, with the results appearing in each box.

After the morphine injections had been stopped for several days, the

	Big M	**Big W**
Morphine Dependent	Little Place Preference	Strong Aversion to Place
Morphine Naive	Strong Place Preference	No Aversion to Place

Figure 10.1. Conditioning results of place preference experiment.

rats were given a choice of two compartments as places to spend their time. The naïve rats in the Big-M condition spent most of their time at the place in which they had received the morphine injections, showing a conditioned place preference. Naïve rats in the Big-W condition did not show any aversion to the room in which they were placed following saline injections. Only the rewards of the drug affected their place preferences.

The morphine-dependent rats behaved differently. They reacted most to the withdrawal condition. They avoided the room in which they had not received morphine but did not show a preference for the room in which they had.

In another study (Nader & van der Kooy, 1997), the researchers gave the animals a drug that blocked the dopamine circuits prior to the conditioning trials. No place preferences developed for the animals dependent on the drug, but the naïve animals did show place preferences. Dopamine appeared necessary for the morphine to have rewarding properties only with the animals who were dependent on the drug and in a state of deprivation. A different neural pathway provided the rewarding effects of morphine for those who were not hooked on the drug. Nader and van der Kooy (1997) followed up with another experiment that gave some rats neurosurgery to destroy that part of the brain identified as the main conduit for reward in non-deprivation conditioning. As expected, the surgery wiped out the place preferences of the naïve rats but not the morphine-dependent rats.

These studies demonstrated that these animals had not one but two separate motivational systems: one that responded to rewarding (pleasurable) properties of the stimulus and another that responded to the need to reduce the aversive (distressing) properties associated with deprivation. The occasional users get the pleasure, but those who are dependent are driven to reduce the pain of deprivation that develops with powerful drugs such as nicotine and cocaine. Over time, the emotional dynamics appeared to change—not along a single continuum from pleasure to no pleasure but in a shift from one dimension to another: from one emotive system involved with approach and reward to another involved with avoidance of distress.

Berridge and Robinson (1995, 1998; Robinson & Berridge, 1993) have taken a different approach that questions whether the dopamine circuitry in the brain really regulates pleasure at all. They reasoned that nearly all the studies of dopamine's reward value have evaluated the chemical's effects on conditioned behavior, measuring the behavior by the number of times the animal would press a bar for the food or drug. They questioned whether the absence of these presses following the administration of a substance that blocked the actions of dopamine (a dopamine antagonist) really meant that the animal no longer found the substances pleasurable. They decided to look at evidence of affective reactions other than the counting of approach behavior through the bar press.

Instead, the researchers looked at the animals' facial expressions. It turns out that both rats and monkeys stick out their tongues when they eat something tasty. Give the animals a drug that removes the effect of the dopamine (an antagonist), and they stop pressing the bar for the food they like. What Berridge and Robinson (1995, 1998; Robinson & Berridge, 1993) found, however, is that the animals do not stop liking the food. The animals' tongues still protrude when tasting it. They still "like" it; they just do not want it as much.

Although wanting and liking are normally linked in our behavior patterns, Berridge and Robinson (1998) argue that the appetite for, the "wanting," and the pleasure in consumption, the "liking," are regulated by separate neurological systems and that it is possible to turn off, even to overly sensitize, one without affecting the other. Their view of addiction is just this: a sensitization of the "wanting" side of the incentive system to the point that it becomes detached from "liking." People have objects they desire and seek them compulsively, even without finding much pleasure in their attainment. On the face of it, this seems strange, but then so is addicted behavior. How many people who are smoking report receiving great pleasure from the smoke? Compulsive behaviors seem to fit this category as well. The person eats massive amounts of food when bingeing. Is the food really that enjoyable? Probably not.

Revealing as these studies are about basic mechanisms of addictive cycles of behavior, we need to turn to human studies to see their relevance to substance abuse. Some of the most interesting studies have been those that have attempted to capture the ebb and flow of emotions in the daily lives of substance users. Kaplan (1992) reports on a study in the Netherlands that examined the daily lives of a group of 20 men and women addicted to heroin. Because drug use is decriminalized in the Netherlands, the investigators were able to easily recruit volunteers from the community to gather information about drug use from a broad spectrum of heroin addicts, not just those already in the criminal justice system. All study volunteers were given beepers that they could wear like wristwatches. These beepers went off 10 times a day for several days. At each beep, the participants reported their drug cravings using a questionnaire designed especially for this study. They also reported on their feelings, health symptoms, the degree of stress they were experiencing and whether they had "gotten high" since the previous beep.

By analyzing the daily accounts of heroin users, Kaplan (1992) and colleagues found that drug cravings were best defined along two dimensions. One set of items defined what they called an *acquisition factor*. This factor defines the frantic seeking of a "fix" that characterizes heroin addiction. People with high scores report "needing dope quickly" and frequently "thinking about using." This part of craving describes approach motivations that underlie active efforts to cope with stress (discussed in chapter 3). The investigators found another side of craving as well, which they labeled *loss of control*, that includes feelings of intense anxiety and restlessness, as well as lack of control. Here, we find rough parallels with a second dimension of stress response discussed earlier: one focused on avoidance and defense against distress.

What factors increased these two forms of drug craving for the heroin addicts, and what factors decreased craving? The investigators were able to address this question by looking across the many observations to see what was happening when craving increased and when craving decreased. It turned out that the absence of positive emotion increased both types of craving. When feeling low, the heroin addicts were much more likely to report strong needs for their drugs and also less control over their feelings.

The social situation mattered. When alone, cravings for heroin and cocaine were at the highest levels. Apparently, Janis Joplin was on target in her song about "Mary Jane" (a street name for marijuana):

> Oh, when I'm feeling lonesome and I'm feeling blue
> There's only one way to change
> Now I walk down the street now lookin' for a man
> One that knows my Mary Jane.

Feelings of loneliness and lack of positive emotion are a primary source of craving. The investigators also looked to see if craving was reduced after getting a "fix." Although the findings here are complicated by the type of drug, there was clear evidence that heroin use did not extinguish the craving, even for a single beep (Kaplan, 1992).

Substances of abuse are not all alike in how they influence and are influenced by our emotions. Not only do different drugs yield different physiological responses, but also the social context that shapes the patterns of use may also differ. In contrast to heroin and cocaine, alcohol use is legal, readily accessible, socially sanctioned, and promoted in our culture. Our expectations for benefits and costs of using alcohol as opposed to other drugs also vary dramatically.

Howard Tennen and his colleagues have launched a series of diary studies of men and women who drink regularly and heavily on occasion.[7] In their studies, they signaled these men and women three times a day for 30 days, giving them hand-held computers with which to respond to a series of questions about how they were feeling at the time, whether they were drinking, and how much they craved a drink. To assess everyday life stressors, as well as positive events, they used our Inventory of Small Life Events,[8] asking their participants to report on daily positive and negative events at work and home, with friends and with family.

Tennen et al.'s studies have yielded a rich set of findings about the everyday lives of frequent drinkers. First, when participants were nervous, they drank more that night and also craved a drink more than when they were not nervous. This finding fit the authors' "self-medication" hypothesis. But that was not the only emotional state that predicted alcohol consumption. The participants who reported that they were happier during the day also drank more during the evening. We note in passing that this finding differs from what the Netherlands' researchers (Kaplan, 1992) found for heroin users: an absence of positive emotions leading to drug use. We suspect different type of drug (alcohol versus heroin), as well as different levels of dependency, may account for the differences. Getting back to the alcohol studies, one daily mood appeared to have the strongest effect on subsequent drinking at night, and that effect was to *reduce* the likelihood of drinking. On days in which the participants were in a calm mood, they drank less. Emotional days, whether positive or negative, prompted more drinking from these men and women.

Separate studies from this same team of investigators (Carney, Armeli, Tennen, Affleck, & O'Neil, 2000) examined the role of stressful events. Again, the findings for negative events were consistent with the standard model of alcohol use as a stress-dampening strategy. When participants had stressful days, they craved a drink more and also drank more than on days that were relatively hassle free. Both stressors at work and at home led to a greater desire for alcohol. But parallel to the results for mood, positive events also were associated with increased craving and consumption of alcohol. "Let the good times roll," you might say. There are a couple of qualifications that apply to this last finding. Positive work events did not increase drinking, nor did positive health-promoting events such as exercise. If anything, these events led to less drinking on the days on which they occurred. Only positive events in the social arena stimulated the desire to celebrate by drinking.

What are the implications of these results for our understanding of addictive behaviors and of how to help people who have cravings for addictive substances? First, it would be fair to say that substance use and abuse do not arise from just pleasure seeking or harm avoidance. It is not just too much of a good thing or just a need to escape personal troubles that promotes craving. The reasons vary by drug and by individual need. Many people drink both to promote the positive and suppress the negative emotions. In any case, the desire to regulate one's own emotional state is pivotal in the decision to use and perhaps also to abuse substances. The pattern that emerges from Tennen et al.'s studies suggests that any emotion and most events can stimulate the need for a drink. If these drinkers progress to dependency and addiction, however, these results might look different. When people become drug dependent or addicted, there may be little room for feelings in between the highs and lows, no space for complex emotions.

From a dynamic perspective, the emotional problems of those suffering from drug dependency and addiction arise gradually as the person begins to substitute feelings in one affective domain for those that belong in another. In essence, they get their emotional wires crossed. In general, positive emotions are gained through approach behaviors. Yet, in addiction, the person is approaching repeatedly, but he or she is no longer doing so for a lift within the positive domain of emotions. The results of the studies by Bechara and his colleagues (Bechara & van der Kooy, 1992; Nader, Bechara, & van der Kooy, 1997; Nader & van der Kooy, 1997) indicate that the function of this chronic pursuit of drugs is converted from pleasure seeking to a reduction in the pain of deprivation. A cruel joke has been played on people who become addicted: They start out thinking they are getting pleasure from the drug and end up running in circles trying to avoid the negative feelings that come from being without it.

Berridge and Robinson (1995, 1998; Robinson & Berridge, 1993) offer yet another view that involves the detachment of incentives from outcomes. Interest and excitement are part of the joy of seeking something pleasurable, and attaining those positive affects clearly motivates us to seek more. If we fail to get much pleasure from these pursuits, why continue? Berridge and Robinson might reply that addicted people misinterpret their cravings, taking them as evidence that what they desire actually brings pleasure. Take the group of heroin addicts in the Netherlands reported by Kaplan (1992). Suppose you showed them proof that their cocaine use really did little to stave off the strong cravings that signify addiction. Further, suppose you asked them to keep careful track of how much pleasure they actually derived from "shooting up." Would their self-examination make a difference in terms of their drug use? I think it would, for they would learn that they were seeking after something that no longer brought them any pleasure.

There is another side to this story. Changing by trying to detach oneself from these cravings still implies loss. Anyone who goes through the end of a close relationship knows this. Adaptation to loss is painful emotionally, whether the person is absent physically or emotionally. Some people continue to seek the person they lost, ignoring the fact that the individual they miss is no longer present, just to avoid acknowledging the loss. This is the contribution of Bechara's team. Addictive behavior may represent responses to a state of deprivation: a fear, even panic, over the possibility of being without. These are powerful emotions, but they are not describing a simple hedonism run amuck. This avoidance of the pain of withdrawal, combined with the misinterpretation that feelings of wanting are feelings of liking, may be what actually underlies the hedonic treadmill of addiction.

A Very Brief History of "Crack"

Let us analyze one recent drug epidemic from the point of view of positive and negative emotions: the "crack" epidemic. Just the name sounds dangerous. Since the mid-1980's, crack has been synonymous with a potent smokable form of cocaine. The actual number of "crack-heads" that emerged from the 1980s addicted to cocaine remains elusive, but it was in the millions. The crack epidemic nearly brought New York City to its knees (Egan, 1999). According to Egan (1999), the New York subways were failing 10 years ago. In one incident, 149 trains stopped on their tracks all at the same time due to an electrical short-circuit during rush hour. The cause of the power outage was traced to missing electrical conduits at several substations throughout Manhattan. It seems that pawnbrokers were offering top dollar for copper wiring at the time, and crack addicts were ripping out the 2-inch-thick copper wires that conducted electricity for the subways and selling them to the pawn shops. It looked as though a drug had been created that literally might bring New York City to a screeching halt. The problems were not confined to copper wiring, either. Families suffered enormous losses due to the drug. Recalling her experience at the tender age of 10, one Harlem resident reported that, "We were eating cornmeal pancakes without syrup for dinner, crack vials all over the floor. I was like, 'Hello! Mom! Don't you know you have a daughter?' " (Egan, 1999).

What is it about this drug and others like it that led people to abandon even their own children? The short answer is that the drug was so efficient in generating strong positive emotions that it overwhelmed all other motivations.

Intense emotions are usually not entirely under our control. It is very difficult to conjure up fear and anger, for example. We may be able to convince ourselves that we are angry, but without a person or an event to blame, it is nearly impossible to generate a powerful visceral response. We can learn to control, even undo, our emotions, in a manner of speaking. By this I mean that we can learn to recover rapidly from negative emotions, to reduce anxiety by using relaxation and imagery techniques, to lower pain through redeploying our attention, and to dissipate angry mood by manipulating our own cognitive sets. For example, we can say things to ourselves such as, "They did not mean to hurt me intentionally; it was an honest mistake." Thus we are able to reduce the intensity and duration of emotional episodes through our coping efforts. But it is very difficult to create the mood that we are trying to be rid of in the first place.

The same is true of positive emotions. One cannot simply will oneself to be happy (though millions of people probably try to do this every day). What we can do is put ourselves in situations that generate positive emotions. For example, we might choose to see a comedy film because we know it will make us laugh, and laughter feels good. Most methods of generating enjoyment propel us forward into some form of engagement with life, with others, with our work, or even within ourselves. We direct ourselves to act, knowing that such engagements are likely to bring rewarding feelings as a consequence.

Relationships are a primary source of joy and other strong positive feelings. Yet these relationships are complicated by many mixes of emotions, many not entirely positive. With drugs such as crack, we try to purify the highs, simplifying our emotional world, or, more likely, simply blinding ourselves to the complexities of our emotional attachments. With alcohol, we may simply fog over our awareness of these complexities to make our pursuit of relationships less daunting. We might feel carefree, at least for a while.

The problem with cocaine and other substances of abuse, however, is that, when ingested repeatedly, these drugs change the neurochemical mix that underlies the response to the drug. The brain has its own ecology. Introducing new neurostimulatory agents into that ecology changes things, sometimes quite dramatically. Basic ecological principles, such as "Everything is related to everything else" and, as the saying goes, "You can't do just one thing," still apply. If you introduce chemicals into the brain that are very similar to those normally released within the nervous system, these chemicals will give rise to new adaptations as the brain responds to the new inputs and strives to regain homeostasis. These responses mimic the neurological accommodations made to the chemical agents that came from within the body. Unfortunately, those new chemicals actually come from outside the body, so they are not readily available from internal resources. The body now has a new source of uncertainty that it must contend with as it turns itself inside out searching for the drug it needs to sustain a balance of chemical forces.

Stress: When Less Is More

A number of studies have been conducted on the effects of cocaine and opiate addictions on brain function. Some of the most startling findings come from investigations of the stress responses of people who are addicted. Weiss, Parsons, and Markou (1995) have studied the brains of rodents before and after bouts of self-administered cocaine. The brains of these animals become hypersensitive to stress during withdrawal, showing abnormally high CRF responses and abnormally low dopamine levels. According to Weiss et al. (1995), these changes in brain chemistry can make it exceedingly difficult for the animal to cope successfully and recover emotionally from even small disruptions in everyday lifestyle routines.

Kreek and Koob (1998) link this increased stress sensitivity to relapse.[9] They note that, following successful withdrawal from cocaine or heroin addiction, the precipitating events leading to a return to illicit drug use are often quite minor stressors. An argument with a supervisor at work can be enough to provoke a relapse if the person feels he or she cannot successfully handle the discord without a "fix." According to Kreek and Koob (1998), opioid drugs inhibit the stress response but increase stress reactivity during withdrawal. A person using opioids such as heroin will experience withdrawal three or four times a day, which, over time, sensitizes the brain to react in anticipation of withdrawal.

Crack cocaine abuse appears to be even worse in this respect. Smoking crack actually stimulates the stress response, leading to elevations in both CRF and ACTH. However, the negative affective consequences of the stress response are masked by the release of dopamine. Because withdrawal also increases stress, there is a "double whammy" for the cocaine user: stress from the drug and then stress on withdrawal. This could explain why many crack users have a "hair trigger." Even everyday hassles can provoke a major stress response.

One way in which Kreek and Koob (1998) have studied these effects has been through the administration of a drug called metyrapone. Metyrapone blocks the secretion of cortisol from the adrenal glands. Cortisol is important because it is the major hormone released during stress from the adrenal cortex, and it is critical to the down-regulation of the stress response. Cortisol finds its way back into the brain and cools down the release of CRF and ACTH. The normal response to an injection of metyrapone is a rise in ACTH levels in the blood. Kreek tried this on people addicted to heroin who were in withdrawal, and the addicts showed double the normal ACTH increase.[10] Those people addicted to cocaine showed similarly hyperactive stress responses. Though they may feel no pain when taking these drugs, their bodies experience just the opposite: an increased sensitization to stress. There is "cross-sensitization" as well. Provide an animal with a highly stressful environment, such as a course of electric shock treatment, and guess what? The animal's physiology reacts with much greater enthusiasm to cocaine availability. So stress and addiction to crack go hand in hand, increasing reactivity to stress from cocaine use and increasing responsiveness to cocaine use following stress.

Will, Watkins, and Maier (1998) demonstrated this phenomenon in a series of experiments on laboratory rodents exposed to inescapable shock. They used a place-preference paradigm similar to the one I described earlier. The animals receive either a series of uncontrollable electric shocks or no shock. A few days later, they are injected with morphine while in one of two chambers that have been decorated by distinctive patterns of black electrical tape. A day or so later, the animals are allowed to roam in and out of each chamber, and the experimenter records how much time they spend in each. The morphine is thought to have the stronger impact if the animal spends more time in the chamber in which it got the injection than in the other chamber.

The animals receiving the shocks spent considerably more time in the chamber in which they received the morphine, a difference that was about double the magnitude of the effect of the morphine on place preferences of the animals that received no shock (see Piazza & Moal, 1998; Stewart, 1999). In another study, Will et al. (1998) tested what happened when they varied the controllability of the shock. The experimenters gave half the animals a way to escape the shocks. The other half had no means of escape but received the same amount of shock as the animals in the controllable condition by a procedure called *yoking*. Yoking means that, for each animal run through the escapable shock, another animal was given inescapable shock lasting just as long as the shock lasted for the animal that could escape. Only the animals given uncontrollable shock showed an increased preference for the place in which they were given a morphine injection. Even in rodents, it is not the negative experience itself but the lack of an effective response that has such troubling effects. The uncertainty created by this lack of control makes the morphine all the more appealing.

In terms of emotional dynamics, a key aspect of addictive behavior is the abnormal coupling of an increase in positive and a decrease in negative emotions. Increased stress is also a catalyst for the coupling of affective experiences. Both a reduction in anxiety and an increase in pleasurable emotions appear to be unleashed by opiates taken during times of stress, strengthening the reward value of the drug and increasing its hold on the drug user.

But the story does not end there. The drug itself also appears to put the person in an affective condition that he or she usually experiences only during times of stress. In normal circumstances, negative affects usually predominate during a stressful episode, but with drugs of abuse, the affective state is accompanied by high rather than low feelings, thereby reinforcing the actions that led up to the stress experience. There is single-mindedness in addictive behavior and a narrowness of vision, as well. These are the by-products of stress. What I am suggesting is that drug addiction fuses the emotions by making relief from the pain of withdrawal misunderstood as an experience of pleasure. As a consequence, a tight web is spun around the motivations of the person addicted to substances such as cocaine. The drug is a "fix" of the emotions. The mother on crack does not even see her daughter's needs. The warmth that comes from her relationship with her child is undervalued currency in one-dimensional emotional systems.

What has happened since the crack epidemic of the mid-1980s? According to Egan (1999), the drug has now run its course and is no longer the threat it was to public health. The numbers of abusers has decreased, both in the so-called "zero tolerance" zones such as New York City in which many drug users were arrested and also in more permissive urban areas such as Washington, D.C.[11] The increased surveillance did not send the drug lords packing. Instead, interest just seemed to die off. Why would this be so? Is there something about the dynamics of emotions that can explain disengagement from a drug such as crack, as well as attachment to it?

There are many possible answers to this question, and in one sense there are as many answers as there are drug users who have turned away from this highly addicting substance. Here are three. First, the drug can fool the emotion systems for just so long. Sooner or later, the addicted person comes to understand that the drug is not really offering much pleasure but is only useful to alleviate the pain of withdrawal. Inevitably, the drug user grasps the faulty logic of staying in that "marriage." In short, the drug user simply gets bored with the whole enterprise. Drug treatment programs should investigate how they might speed up this process of adaptation.

Second, the drug no longer seems "sexy" to the new cohort of potential users. The media attention paid to crack, with their many stories of family neglect and damaged lives, has had an effect. People growing up in neighborhoods in which crack addiction flourished have witnessed how unappealing the lives of crack users are. As one of my students remarked, a new young generation is interested in looking good, and these "crack-heads" just had no fashion sense.

Third and most important, social conditions have changed within the neighborhoods that have been breeding grounds for crack users. People have gone back to work. Since 1993, the unemployment rate in the country has dropped to 6% or less. Although these rates are higher in impoverished communities, they still are substantially lower than they were in the 1980s, when more than one-third of young men and women in our inner cities were unemployed. Work provides a viable alternative activity to drug use, provides positive meaning, and lowers the level of economic stress on the family. In this context, drug use comes to represent little more than a form of recreation rather than the centerpiece of a person's emotional life.

Although I have focused on drug addiction research in this chapter, the principles apply much more broadly. The dangers of addiction to any repetitive activity increase dramatically under conditions that narrow the scope of our emotional experience. During stressful and other uncertain times, we may think we are acting out of desire, when in fact we have found a place to hide from adversity. It is under such conditions that we are likely to find ourselves on a hedonic treadmill of one kind or another,[12] whether it be drug dependence, chat rooms on the Internet, or falling into another unfulfilling but nonetheless habit-forming routine.

The successes of programs such as Alcoholics Anonymous (AA; Alcoholics Anonymous World Services, 1976) provide us with insight into the antidotes to the madness of addiction. Although many commentators in the social sciences are critical of aspects of the AA model, it is important not to overlook some of the social and psychological benefits of AA's 12-step programs. AA, above all else, provides a means of reentry into meaningful social relations. By encouraging self-disclosure, admission of failure, and acceptance of self, the program fosters close ties among group members. These common bonds offer a steady source of authentic social engagement to many who attend. The person forges an even more personal bond with his or her sponsor. The sponsor is another member of the AA community who is further along in his or her own recovery from addiction and who agrees to provide daily support. These ties are often as close as those developed in combat. The stakes are just as high. By encouraging disclosure of personal failings within a framework of social support, the program guides its members toward a more complex emotional life, one in which feelings of sorrow and shame do not diminish the experience of joy from those who embrace the close social ties and a sense of community that are offered there.

There are other ways to combat addiction besides attending 12-step programs. And *abstinence* is not the only method of staying sober (Fletcher, 2001).[13] Cognitive methods of challenging the mistaken belief that substance use is out of one's control are also successful—surprisingly so, given that this challenge seems to contradict a fundamental tenet of AA.[14] Such apparent contradictions suggest that we need to go beyond each program's specific principles and narrow rhetoric to find the active ingredients that these opposing therapies share.

The place to look for these deeper truths may be in the emotional meanings evolving over time from the use of drugs and alcohol. There is nothing inherently wrong with these substances, nor with the motives that lead us to the well. When we "toast to our health," our enjoyment of the moment is real, not fiction, and we are not in denial of the negative every time we indulge. There is much good that comes from feeling good, even when it must be primed a bit by mind-altering substances.

If we lose sight of the initial intent, though, our use may take on a different purpose: Tto forestall feelings of deprivation rather than to facilitate social engagement. Full awareness of this turn of events may be the key to recovery from dependency and addiction. The longer we stay under the spell of the drug, the narrower the window of understanding of the complexity of our own needs. The answer, at least in part, is to find ways to reclaim the richness of the human experience through awareness of our emotions in all their complexity.

11   Emotions Abused

> You stand at the blackboard, daddy,
> In the picture I have of you,
> A cleft in your chin instead of your foot
> But no less a devil for that.
>   —Sylvia Plath, "Daddy"

Children are special in the way they communicate emotions. Their expressions have a purity of form that connects right to our hearts every time. Think of a child's delight when at play. Nothing in adult life comes through so clearly and unambiguously positive as that. Now picture for a moment another scene. A 3-year-old boy standing alone in an aisle of a department store. You spot him there just as he realizes that his mom is not at his side. His lips begin to quiver; he spins around anxiously, looks all around, and then begins to sob. My heart breaks when I see this.

Children do not enter this world with such a fully developed set of emotions as these. Their emotions arrive as a work in progress. As new parents, we will stand on our heads to get a smile. But the first smiles often take weeks. It is usually 2 months before a child smiles in response to our smiles, and a full 4 months before we hear a child laugh. Anger develops gradually as well. It will take the child 4 to 6 months before he or she develops an expression of anger that is distinct from other forms of distress. And infants are born fearless. Not until 6 months do parents notice the child displaying apprehension when introduced to people outside the immediate family circle, a phenomenon commonly referred to as stranger anxiety.

It takes about half a year of life for children to acquire these basic emotions and to distinguish among negative feelings such as fear, anger, and sadness. On the positive side, basic expressions of curiosity seem present at birth, but joy takes a while longer (Denham, 1998; Lewis, 1989). The more the child develops a concept of self, the more complex and differentiated the emotions become. Emotions that depend on self-consciousness, such as embarrassment and envy, do not arise until 15 or 18 months, and emotions that depend on self-evaluations, such as pride and shame, do not appear until the child is 3 years of age or older. A child's emotional capacities continue to develop throughout childhood and adolescence. I asked my 14-year-old son how he would describe the emotions of a teenager. He saw in himself not only more intensity but also many more emotions. Indeed, teens do have new feelings to understand within themselves and their friends. Although they are present before adolescence, sexual urges, rebelliousness, feelings of defiance, depression, and low self-esteem are suddenly much more evident in the emotional profiles of teenagers. Regulation of these emotions is very demanding indeed (Eisenberg & Fabes, 1992). Normal development of these capacities requires a social context that is alert and responsive to the emotional actions and reactions of the child. Now suppose we throw an abusive relationship into this mix. What might we expect to happen to the child's emotional development?

This chapter examines this question, relating it to the major themes developed thus far. I discuss how abuse influences the development of positive, as well as negative, emotion systems and how the stress associated with abuse harms emotional development. In prior chapters on depression, anxiety, and substance abuse, I focused on how some people respond abnormally to stress, resulting in mental disorder and addiction. Now I discuss a situation that is painfully abnormal. Indeed, abuse poses grave threats to the adaptive capacities of all those who experience it.

Infant brains start out with a wide range of options for localizing various functions. This neural plasticity in infants allows them flexibility in the development of a behavioral and an emotional repertoire, but it also makes them vulnerable physiologically, as well as psychologically, to the long-term effects of abuse (Bell, Baldwin, Russek, Schwartz, & Hardin, 1998).[1] Although inhumane actions can be harmful to people of all ages, the abuse of children and teenagers is especially egregious. How can an adolescent girl who is just learning to understand her own feelings of sexuality possibly avoid feeling stressed by unwanted demands for sexual favors from a member of her family?

If abuse were rare, we might find it to be a curious phenomenon to study, just as any extreme case would be. Unfortunately, these abuses are altogether too common among families in the United States. Every year, there are more than 1.5 million cases of child abuse reported in the United States (Wissow, 1995). More than half of these cases involve neglect. Another 22% are counted as physical abuse, and 8% as sexual abuse. McCauley and her colleagues (1997) provide one estimate of the rates of abuse for women. They found that 22% of women patients who were seen in primary care practices reported physical or sexual abuse or both as a child or adolescent.

The health consequences of abuse can be severe. McCauley and her colleagues (1997) refer to these abusive experiences as "unhealed wounds." Compared with women without a history of abuse, these abused women were four times more likely to report multiple physical health problems, four times more likely to have attempted suicide, and three times more likely to have been hospitalized for psychiatric conditions.

Types of Abuse

Three types of traumas are defined as child abuse. Each of them maps onto a different domain of emotional regulation. Most obvious are the physical abuses, marked by the severity and chronicity of the child's pain and the child's fear of harm, arising from feeling defenseless against the physical force of the parental figure. This abuse affects the child's capacity to regulate negative emotional states, one of the two principal dimensions of emotional experience.

In emotion terms, a very different abuse experience arises from a pattern of parental neglect. In this case, the parental failing is in not responding to the child's needs for shared positive experience and the secure attachments that are patterned after those experiences. The long-term impact of neglect is likely to be qualitatively different from that of physical abuse. Here the abuse is defined more in terms of the absence of the positive than the presence of negative interactions. This form of abuse is more insidious, and for that reason it may actually be more harmful to the developing child in the long run.

Bryon Egeland (1996), examined the lives of 267 high-risk mothers and their children. This study is one of the most comprehensive studies of abuse conducted to date. Unique to this study, the investigators began interviews with each family 6 months before the child was born and then continued with follow-up interviews as the child matured. Collecting early data in this way allowed the measurement of outcomes of mother-child interactions prospectively. Nearly all prior research has been retrospective. Such studies suffer from one very strong potential bias: a propensity to recall harmful events in one's past to justify suffering from a current emotional problem.[2] By avoiding that bias, Egeland (1996) was in a position to provide some of most accurate accounts of the risks of child abuse yet available.

The research team identified 44 cases of abuse within the sample. The rate of abuse was expected to be higher than average—the mothers had few financial resources, most were teenagers, and few were married. The usual groups—physical abuse, neglect, and sexual abuse—were used, along with another category of abuse called "psychological availability." In the latter cases, the mothers were often present physically but detached emotionally from their children. They might cook a meal but be so inattentive that they do not hear the child ask for a fork. Some of these mothers were passively rejecting their children; others were simply too preoccupied with themselves.

Egeland (1996) showed that there was no doubt that physical abuse took its toll on child development. Physically abused children showed little tolerance for frustration and often responded with angry outbursts, some aimed directly at their mothers. The children with mothers who were psychologically unavailable appeared even more devastated emotionally. Nearly three-fourths of these children showed profound insecurities in their attachments, often denying that they even needed a close relationship with their mothers. They were angry, frustrated, and uninterested in life. They showed little or no positive emotion. The lack of interest from their mothers blunted the development of the child's capacity for close positive relationships (Egeland, 1996).

These results are surprising only if abuse is understood in terms of a single dimension of emotional harm. Certainly, physical abuse hurts more than neglect. But regulation of negative affective experience is only one challenge for the child to master. A second challenge is to find and sustain positive affective experiences that satisfy a separate set of needs for the child. What children lose from parents who are otherwise engaged is attention to their needs for lasting positive bonds. Children (and adults) need to share emotional experiences, not only to half the sorrows that arise from painful experiences but also to double the joys that come from moments of accomplishment.

Some striking results have been uncovered from experimental investigations of the impact of abuse. This work is done by manipulating the care and treatment of animals because intentionally inflicting abuse on humans is strictly forbidden. Even the rats in these studies deserve better treatment.

The common laboratory procedure is to separate rat pups from their mothers, usually for 3 hours a day for 10 days, during the first weeks of life. After being returned, the animals are treated like those in the control conditions from then on. When the animal is an adult, some 20 weeks later, its responses to stress are studied in detail and compared with the responses of the animals that were not separated from their mothers.

Heim and Nemeroff (1999) have used this method to investigate the effects of maternal separation on the health of the pups once they reached adulthood (see also Heim, Owens, & Nemeroff, 1997). The rodents that were separated from their mothers showed many signs of increased stress reactivity compared with the control animals, who were not separated. When the experimenters piped in unpredictable puffs of air, a mildly stressful event for laboratory animals, they showed an exaggerated startle response, a persistent elevation in ACTH, and a greater CRF response. Interestingly, these animals also showed considerably less interest in the sweet taste of sugar water than other adult rats did. In short, not only did they appear to be on edge physiologically, but they also were unresponsive to potentially pleasurable events. They were anhedonic, to use a human diagnosis.

Hodgson, Rosengren, and Walker (2000) took this approach even further. Sixty days after the separation procedures, the experimenters tested how well the animals' immune systems were functioning. To do this, they put the animals in a restraint harness for 10 hours a day, every other day. They injected the pups with tumor cells on the days in between and then examined how well the animals' immune systems mobilized in response to the invasion of tumor cells. Not only did the stress lead to higher cortisol levels in the animals who were separated from the mothers at an early age, but also those animals showed more rapid tumor development, indicating that the cancer-fighting immune processes were less effective.

At first, scientists interpreted these studies as evidence of critical periods in development at which the animals were especially susceptible to parental influence. Although there may be a critical period, scientists have converged on a different explanation for the aversive consequences observed when the mother is taken away from the infant pups. Researchers now believe that what is disturbed is the mother's emotional bond with the infant pup. When the experimenter takes the pup away from the mother, he or she changes the pup's relationship with the mother, leading the mother to neglect the pup from that point forward. It is the pattern of neglect provoked by the 10-day separation that is the culprit, not the 10 days themselves. To understand why scientists have embraced a neglect hypothesis, rather than the critical period, as an explanation for these effects, we turn to the work of another research team.

Meaney and his colleagues (see Francis & Meany, 1999) have introduced a second dimension into the studies of how the mother's behavior influences an infant's development of emotional responses. Instead of studying neglect exclusively, these researchers provided an enriching experience for some randomly selected pups. They enriched these environments by quite simple means: They reached into the animals' cages and petted the mothers and babies (officially called "handling" in the scientific literature). Why would this be beneficial? To start with, the cages in which the rats typically live are anything but enriched. If you introduce a hand into the cage, that, in itself, livens things up a bit. Add to the intervention a hand that is grooming, and you have also provided very pleasing physical contact.

By introducing pleasing physical contact through handling, Meany and colleagues (Francis & Meany, 1999) found that they altered the interactions between mothers and pups in simple yet profound ways. One way in which rodent mothers engage their children is by licking and grooming. The investigators found that the mother licked and groomed her pups more if she and her pups were handled. And when the mothers licked and groomed more, their pups became more interested in suckling. Furthermore, the pups who were licked and groomed ate faster. As adults, they had lower ACTH responses to stressors. They also spent more time exploring open fields as adults than did pups without the extra mothering.

The researchers had found a way to encourage mothering. The extra care could reverse the harmful effects of separation from the mother (thus showing that there was not a critical period). These changes in the mother-child relationship also led to more curious and resilient adults.

Meaney and his colleagues (Francis & Meany, 1999) extended their experimentation in a brilliant way. They studied the *next generation* of animals to see how the pup that was groomed later acted toward her own pups. They found that pups who were licked and groomed early in life did more licking and grooming of their own infants, passing along that nurturing family environment. As a consequence, their offspring were also less fearful, more eager to explore their environments, and less stress reactive as adults. Handling also broke the pattern of neglect for those pups who were rarely licked and groomed. After being handled, they would care for their own young with more licking and grooming than they had received as pups (Liu et al., 1997; Caldji et al., 1998). Consequently, their pups were no longer scarred by neglect.

There are interesting parallels between Meaney's work (Francis & Meany, 1999) and our two-dimensional view of emotions, especially in his model for understanding the results. Meaney suggests that there are two separate mechanisms governing the effects of maternal behavior, each mediated by different neurohormones. One mechanism is the neurocircuitry for fear. Here his work parallels that of neuroscientists such as LeDoux (1996), Nemeroff, (Heim & Nemeroff, 1999; Heim et al., 1997; Heim, Owens, Plotsky, & Nemeroff, 1997; Graham et al., 1999) and Charney (Charney, Grillon, & Bremner, 1993a, 1998b). Increase the degree of fear in the pups or the mothers in mother-infant interactions through separation or some other method, and the animals will avoid one another. The consequences include increased stress reactivity in adulthood, manifested by heightened CRF in the cerebrospinal fluid that bathes the nervous system. CRF is anxiogenic, which means that it leads to greater anxiety in the animal. Increased anxiety in adult animals leads to poorer maternal care, and, we may presume, poorer paternal care as well.

But that is not the whole story. Meaney (Francis & Meaney, 1999) postulates the presence of another mechanism that exerts its effects through an entirely different set of neural circuits. This is a circuitry of social engagement, stimulated by increases in oxytocin, a hormone known to be released in the brains of mammals during the act of mothering. This second circuit appears to regulate feelings of social attraction and other positive emotions associated with maternal behavior. Unlike CRF, oxytocin is anxiolytic, which means that it leads to lowered anxiety. This neuropeptide also leads to lower blood pressure, lower cortisol in response to stress, and enhanced tone in the vagus nerve, which promotes feelings of calm, warmth, and tolerance for pain (Uvnas-Moberg, 1997).

These adaptive responses to stress appear to be transmitted from the mother to the offspring. According to Meaney (Francis & Meaney, 1999), young animals need both protection from fear-arousing situations and the attention that comes from parents interested in licking and grooming and other positive interactions (Kraemer, 1999).[3] Otherwise, the young may fall prey to what Meaney has called a "pessimistic pattern" of neural development.

There is ample evidence that physical abuse and other fear-arousing negative behaviors harm the pup's ability to cope with stress. Is there any evidence to support the relationship between positive parental behaviors and the health and well-being of humans? To investigate such potential long-term health effects of parental care, Russek and Schwartz (1997a, 1997b) tracked down participants from the Harvard mastery of stress study, conducted in the 1950s. In that study, college students were asked a series of questions about their mothers' and fathers' parenting styles. From the students' answers, Russek and Schwartz (1997a, 1997b) rated six positive caring responses: loving, just, fair, strong, clever, and hardworking. A separate scale was constructed from the eight negative attributes that they rated: severe, stingy, brutal, mean, nervous, poor, drunk, and frequently punitive. In addition to these ratings, participants had also been asked, "What kind of person is your mother (and father)." Tallies of the number of positive remarks and the number of negative remarks were used as another method of assessing parent-child relations from the child's perspective.

Russek and Schwartz (1997a, 1997b) conducted detailed personal and family health histories with these participants 35 years later. They also obtained blood work and physical exam results from participants' doctors so that they could confirm the presence or absence of a number of medical problems, including cardiovascular disease, alcoholism, and duodenal ulcers. With all this information, they asked whether there was a relationship between how the college students characterized their parents 35 years before and the presence of major health problems.

Those who rated both mother and father as uncaring had rates of illness that were 3 ½ times higher than those who rated both parents high in caring. Both fathers and mothers mattered to kids; those who stayed healthy had either caring fathers or caring mothers or both.

The more surprising result is that only the positive ratings mattered. The extent of parents' negative attributes did not discriminate between those who stayed healthy and those who were ill by midlife. Although it would be presumptuous to claim that the presence of positive attributes mattered more than the absence of negative ones, this study shows clearly that caring parental relations play a key role in the preservation of health across the life span, independent of negative parent-child relations. Had the researchers focused only on the harms incurred by parental excesses, they would have missed finding significant relationships between positive parent-child relations and the child's health at midlife.

Sexual Abuse

Sexual abuse is a third form of child abuse, and it is perhaps the most troubling of all. This form of abuse represents a fundamental emotional betrayal. Physical abuse may provoke abnormally intense fear responses that adversely affect the development of the regulatory system for negative emotions. Neglect may fail to nurture positive emotional development, adversely affecting the development of that system. In contrast, sexual abuse conflates positive with negative emotions, hopelessly entangling one emotion system with the other. Following the theory of emotion dynamics I introduced in chapter 4, interwoven emotional domains would constrict experience, severely constraining the abused person's capacity to experience positive emotions independently of negative emotions. Most likely, this form of abuse occurs when sexual favors are sought from the child under the guise of caring. The child may experience warmth and loving but at the cost of humiliation. This is true of some physical abuse as well, but sexual abuse is even more likely to cross affective domains. The child not only learns to distrust the perpetrator but also the accompanying shame and humiliation teach the child not to trust some of the most tender feelings he or she has ever experienced.

Heim and Nemeroff (1999) conducted one of the most comprehensive studies to date of the problems of adults who were sexually abused as children.[4] Heim's research team recruited three groups of adults. Those with a history of sexual abuse as children who were depressed made up one group. Those who were abused but not currently depressed constituted a second group. A third matched group had not been abused as children and were not currently depressed.

All participants were subjected to a laboratory procedure called the Trier Social Stress Test. One of the laboratory tasks calls for participants to talk about themselves in front of a class. Posing as students in the classroom, research assistants acted openly hostile, making the experience quite stressful. There were also other aspects of the Trier test, such as arithmetic problems that were impossible to solve correctly. The whole procedure lasted about 1½ hours. During the session, all participants were wired to record cardiovascular activity, and blood was drawn from their arms at set intervals throughout the stress test.

All groups showed increases in heart rate, ACTH, and cortisol during the stress test, but the elevations were highest for participants in two of the three groups: those currently depressed who had a history of sexual abuse and those not depressed who had been abused as children. These results indicate that stress responses are profoundly disturbed among those people who have suffered childhood sexual abuse. Even if they never became depressed, they remain highly stress reactive.

The evidence is now accumulating that early childhood trauma, particularly abusive relationships with parental figures, places a person at grave risk for developing a chronic pain syndrome. Walker and his collaborators (1997) investigated whether child abuse precipitates a pain disorder called fibromyalgia.[5] People with this pain disorder (about 2% of the adult population and 4.5% of women) exhibit pain in soft tissue across all four quadrants of the body. These patients literally hurt all over. Walker et al. (1997) found evidence of abuse in 42% of the cases of fibromyalgia that they investigated. This figure compared with 16.7% among those with rheumatoid arthritis, a painful condition with a known pathological disease process that underlies the painful symptoms.

How could early trauma of this sort contribute to the development of chronic health problems such as fibromyalgia? This question has yet to be answered definitively, but the evidence at present points to a profound disturbance in the normal development of the stress response system, a neural sensitization that leaves the person vulnerable to experiencing pain even when exposed to stimuli that are not painful to others. There is little question that abuse can unravel us emotionally. The resulting stress may also play a key role in the maintenance of pain and other symptoms of chronic illness.

To explore the dynamics of specific emotions involved in abuse, Dickerson, Kemeny, Aziz, Kim, and Fahey (2001) have engaged in a series of studies on the physiological costs of the experience of shame. Their results identify biological correlates of shame that may prove to be the key mechanisms that underlie the health problems that result from abuse. In one of their studies, the researchers asked a randomly selected group of participants to write about a traumatic experience for 3 days and compared their responses with those of a group who wrote about mundane events for 3 days (Dickerson et al., 2001). This method replicated the approach used by Pennebaker (1990; reviewed in chapter 6), but with one important difference. In this study the researchers asked participants in the high "shame" condition to write about negative experiences for which they blamed themselves. To get a sense of this experimental condition, try following the instructions the researchers gave to participants: "to write about one of the most traumatic and upsetting experiences of your life; please focus on an experience that made you feel bad about yourself or that you were to blame for."

How would you feel after writing about such a traumatic experience? Would you feel ashamed? The participants in the study did. They reported feeling significantly more shame than those participants in the control condition did. Moreover, those people in the shame condition had elevations in cytokines associated with potentially harmful proinflammatory actions. Furthermore, those in the experimental condition who experienced greater shame showed the largest elevations in proinflammatory cytokines. The results of this study indicated that shame was the key emotional experience associated with immune changes that could be unhealthy. This emotion is one of the most common reactions to sexual abuse.

I suspect that the risk of adverse outcomes from sexual abuse are greatest for those children who most need the caring that accompanies the unwanted sexual attention. Those contexts may be more likely to elicit shame than contexts in which the child had not sought attention from the abuser. But more research is needed to unravel these crossed transactions, especially studies that compassionately examine the full range of emotions experienced by the child and that thoroughly explore the nature of the emotional attachment formed between abused and abuser.

Playwright Paula Vogel (1998) was asked to describe the subtext of her critically acclaimed play, "How I Learned to Drive." In the play, the lead character recalls her sexually abusive relationship with her uncle. In an interview conducted by Arthur Holmberg (1998)[6] the literary director of the American Repertory Theatre, offered his interpretation, saying, "The play is about how we receive harm from the people who love us." Ms. Vogel corrected him, stating, "I would say rather that, 'We receive great love from the people who harm us.' " From this standpoint, it is the character's great love for her Uncle Peck and ultimately, her understanding of his troubled psyche that propels the protagonist forward with her story and strengthens her resolve to move beyond the experience. Vogel went on to observe that many modern dramatic treatments of the same theme fail to contend with "the victim's responsibility to look the experience squarely in the eye." Vogel wants us to disentangle the emotional experiences embedded within these abusive relationships, allowing us to see not only the victimization but any benefits that arose independently of the emotional double-cross.

Two-dimensional thinking about these relationships is particularly difficult. It requires us to think more broadly about abuse than we normally would allow ourselves to do. We often forget that the loudest protest comes not from those who see things for what they are but from those who see things as simply black or white. Two-dimensional thinking requires us to look at all the emotional responses of the people involved to fully understand the nature of and the effects of abuse.

Sexual abuse is perhaps the most difficult topic to study without bias. There are many reasons for that, not the least of which are the strong emotional reactions that abuse provokes. Anger, disgust, even rage can easily preempt calm, resolute examination of the evidence. Society does not permit much freedom of discourse on this subject. Rind, Tromovich, and Bauserman (1998) reviewed empirical research and declared that there was little conclusive evidence of severe emotional harm arising from sexual abuse. The review's conclusions were picked up by a Web site catering to pedophiles and used to promote "man-child" relations. From there, news of the article came to a conservative host of a talk-radio show in Phoenix, Arizona. The United States House of Representatives denounced the article within a week and prompted the initiation of a costly independent evaluation of the peer review processes used by one of psychology's most prestigious journals.[7]

The question is not whether sexual relations between adults and children are harmful. What we need to know is how this form of abuse disturbs normal development. Sometimes we are prevented from seeing the complexity of emotional responses to events, whether from forces outside ourselves or from forces within. The stress of ambiguity is sometimes impossible to tolerate, and strong emotions of one kind or another rush to fill the vacuum. If we can remain open to complex, and even contradictory emotions within ourselves, we will allow ourselves to see the complexity in the hearts of others whose behavior attracts our strongest rebuke. Then the more fully and honestly we can live within the world and help those most troubled by actions that have sent daggers through our hearts and the hearts of those whom we hold most dear.

12 Marriage and Other Close Relationships

A Two-Dimensional Look

Waste me not, I beg you, waste
Not the inner night.
—D. H. Lawrence,
"Liaison"

" 'My nerves are bad to-night. Yes, bad. Stay with me.
'Speak to me. Why do you never speak. Speak.
  'What are you thinking of? What thinking? What?
'I never know what you are thinking. Think.' "
—T. S. Eliot, *The Waste Land*

Behavioral scientists are like most people; they tend to think of relationships as either good for you or bad for you. In truth, relationships defy such simple classification. They can be, and usually are, both healthy and unhealthy. The evidence that divorce leads to health problems is strong, especially for men. Higher rates of depression, and alcoholism, and a twofold increase in suicides are typically found among divorced and separated men compared with married and single men (Bruce & Kim, 1992; Kposowa, 2000; Power, Rodgers, & Hope, 1999). Women are also at risk, with high rates of depressive disorders following marital dissolution. But these statistics do little to dissuade people from marriage and other risky intimate partnerships. A close relationship is indeed a double-edged sword. This chapter examines these two sides of the emotional life of marriage and similar bonds, relying on the two-dimensional framework developed thus far in this book.

John Neale and Arthur Stone (Stone, 1981; Stone & Neale, 1982) were among the first to discover dualism in everyday conjugal relations.[1] They recruited couples who answered their advertisements in the local newspapers and asked them to complete daily diaries. Partners recorded the positive and negative interactions with their spouses for 30 days. What immediately surprised the investigators was that couples varied widely in their reports of positive interaction, regardless of the extent of negative interaction. Those who had many conflicts with their spouses were unhappy with their marriages and were more likely to have sought or to currently be receiving marital counseling. But they were neither more nor less likely to have many positive social interactions with their spouses. Some couples were both very happy and very unhappy with married life. Others found little exceptional either way. In short, the everyday course of marital relationships unfolds in two separate domains: a positive one and a negative one. I suspect that these results would generalize to other close relationships, as well.

This result is not really surprising once we think about it. People seek many types of fulfillment from their partners. Pleasure, joy, and intimacy are on the list of positives, but so are safety and security as deterrents to negative states. Nor is it surprising that marital difficulties are so common.[2] Each partner not only has to satisfy his or her own many needs but also has to coordinate the satisfaction of his or her needs with that of the different needs of another person. These complexities characterize all meaningful romantic relationships, whether they are between heterosexual, gay, or lesbian couples. Take the situation in which one partner is trying to resolve conflicts that are the source of negative feelings and the other partner is looking for ways to enhance shared positive feelings. Both partners will feel misunderstood. Sometimes it can seem as if one's partner is not even on the same planet. One partner wants to make love, and the other cannot believe his or her partner could even be considering that. There are times at which even the closest couples find themselves in entirely different emotional worlds.

The first time I witnessed this type of disconnection was not in a clinical setting. It was with a couple who stopped to give me a lift when I was hitchhiking across the country in the 1970s. I got in the back seat of their Chevy Camaro in Salt Lake City, headed for Cheyenne, Wyoming.

The man loved to drive and was behind the wheel. He also loved speed. In fact, he had a very specific goal for this leg of their trip: Salt Lake City to Cheyenne in 6 hours. Never mind that it was 440 miles away. He was determined.

But speeding made the woman anxious. Thus, the faster they went, the more nervous she became. It appeared at first that she blunted those feelings with chatter and drugs, but I think that her nerves were more an excuse than the cause for her loquaciousness. Besides, her anxiety also had a specific physiological effect: less bladder control, or at least the fear of less bladder control. So the faster he went, the more often she felt she had to relieve herself.

He never complained once about pulling over for the rest rooms, but as he steered us back onto the highway after each pit stop, he would remind us that he would have to make up for the lost time. Two parallel dimensions, his and hers, were propelling us forward down the open road at some pretty dangerous speeds.

John Gray (1992) has written about differences between men and women euphemistically as differences between Mars and Venus: war and love, competition versus communion.[3] From the perspective of emotional dynamics, this might mean that war games are less complicated for boys and that tender emotions introduce a riskier form of engagement for them than for girls. Socialization practices may also lead men to value personal achievement as a source of positive emotion more than women do, and women to value a sense of community more than men do.

Whatever the gender-specific emotional roles in our culture, close relationships are complicated by the many choices open to men and women in how to behave toward one another. Uncertainties about the partner's motivation can lead to some difficult challenges in developing and sustaining closeness. There is no single best way to promote a close lasting relationship. Further, there is no guarantee that your bids for closeness will be understood in the way they were meant. So, for example, a bid for intimacy might be seen as a ploy for power and control, and a desire for solitude might be perceived as another form of rejection.

We gain some clarity by applying a two-dimensional view of the emotional worlds of the partners struggling to communicate their needs and to understand one another. We can inquire whether the partners are relating on the same dimension. A principal source of conflict for couples is their differences in the relative attention each gives to the promotion of positive emotions versus protection against threat and other negative states. Most meaningful activities that couples engage in together can be threatening, as well as potentially gratifying, and the relative amounts of fear and excitement may vary extensively between partners.

Are men and women different in the amount of time and attention that they give to protecting themselves versus reaching out? There is some evidence of such gender differences. Peter Lang (Bradley & Lang, 2000; Lang et al., 1998) recorded the neural activity in the visual cortex and surrounding structures in the brains of a sample of men and women while they looked at either pleasant or unpleasant pictures. Women showed significantly greater brain activity when looking at unpleasant pictures than at pleasant pictures. For men, it was the opposite. Their occipital lobes lit up when viewing pleasant pictures. Their brains responded to unpleasant stimuli, too, but not to the same extent. From inside the brain it would appear that women are more attuned to potential harms and that men are keying on ways to experience more pleasure. We should not consider these differences in brain activity as irrefutable evidence that men are hardwired to attend to pleasure more than women are or that women are always more attentive to potential threat. These differences in brain activation are likely shaped by differences in how men and women are socialized to respond and thus may reflect cultural learning, as well as genetic propensities.

We find culturally derived expectations for how men and women should respond emotionally wherever we look. Most TV situation comedies with married couples seem built on a simple premise: Men seek pleasure, and women avoid harm. A day does not go by that Homer Simpson does not blunder his way into trouble due to his inexhaustible capacity for flights of fancy. This trend can be traced back to one of the first sitcoms, *Life of Riley*, and also to Ralph Kramden in *The Honeymooners*. Why is this so? Is there some hidden truth in these sitcoms about men's and women's motivational styles? Or are we observing the reification of cultural stereotypes of how people behave in relationships? Perhaps a little of both.

On the one hand, women are more vulnerable physically and so, by necessity, may be more attuned to situations that might require quick defensive action.[4] Posttraumatic adaptations due to childhood abuse might also leave many women much more vigilant in protecting themselves from potential harm throughout their adult lives. But men are also vulnerable in many ways. Physically, he may be more powerful than a woman, but there is always another man who can make him feel like a 170-pound weakling. That vulnerability runs so deep that men often must resort to dangerous displays of fearlessness to hide those weaknesses from rivals.

One way to think about gender differences in emotion is to examine different types of responses to threatening situations. A useful dichotomy exists between what are called *internalizing responses*, such as depression, fear and nervousness, and *externalizing responses*, such as substance use and anger and aggression (Kring & Gordon, 1998; Nolen-Hoeksema & Rusting, 1997). Whereas women tend to show more internalizing of negative emotions in the face of difficult situations, men show more externalizing. Recent statistics on domestic violence confirm that men are more often the perpetrators of physical abuse.

What has alarmed many, though, is that the ratio of men to women under arrest for violence against the spouse or partner is just 2 to 1 and not 10 to 1, as expected. In over 30% of the cases of domestic violence, the woman is the abuser. A number of commentators note that the numbers may also reflect a bias in reporting the man as the wrongdoer. There is probably no sign of submissiveness for a man that is worse than admitting that he is physically intimidated by his wife. In any case, it should be clear from these statistics that one cannot make men the only aggressors and women the only defenders. It is more complicated than that, if for no other reason than that both genders are equipped with a full range of emotions. Neither gender is unidimensional.

But why do so many men have the reputation of behaving as if they are interested only in themselves or, even more narrowly, in sexual pleasures? Perhaps they behave so as to stay cued in to a positive dimension and to tune out the substantial anxiety and fear that they may sense, but do not fully understand, about other aspects of themselves and their relationships. Indeed, recent studies support the conventional wisdom that men are not as aware of the emotional complexities in everyday situations as women are and that they are more likely to interpret their feelings as black or white. They do not see that rich tapestry of emotions that women find when looking beneath the surface.[5]

The intimacy that couples seek requires honesty in identifying and communicating to one another both the needs to defend against harm and the needs for love, something not easy for either partner. Both men and women are likely to hide from communicating that which is most threatening to them and may even disguise those fears by engaging in what appear to be positive strivings but that subtly serve the purpose of protecting against harm. These are crossed transactions that lead to the most profound misunderstandings in married life. Indeed, the bidimensional model would suggest that intimate relationships are especially at risk when members engage in activities that bring pleasure as a salve for what hurts. This is peddling snake oil, and anger and recriminations are bound to follow.

Are women as guilty of crossing the wires between pleasure and fear as men? Perhaps. Taylor and her colleagues (2000) suggest that the classic "fight or flight" responses do not always offer realistic options for women, particularly in physically threatening situations. According to Taylor et al., the social bonding that we observe among women may constitute a means of protection from threat. In stressful situations, men may engage in fights and flight, but women may not be able to run, let alone stand and fight if the aggressor is bigger, stronger, and faster. Furthermore, women often have someone else in mind besides themselves. They may have children or other loved ones to care for, and as much as they might relish a good fight or feel the urge to flee, they cannot risk harming their young. So, according to Taylor et al. (2000), they may adopt other strategies. They may "tend and befriend" instead. For example, they may offer a helping hand to someone who frightens them as a means of defusing a potentially explosive situation, or they may gather a group of people together by forming alliances against a common threat. These strategies would appear to be an advanced adaptation strategy, requiring more thoughtfulness and self-regulation than taking a swing at someone.

From the perspective of emotional communication, the use of tend-and-befriend strategies in the face of danger may add another troubling twist to the relationships between men and women. If Taylor and her colleagues (2000) are right that many women use these strategies as a means of coping with threatening situations, then women are as guilty as men of crossing up the dimensions of emotional expression. The tend-and-befriend activities are normally associated with the generation of positive emotions. When women use those activities to protect themselves from harm, they inadvertently introduce another source of misunderstanding in their relationships, a misunderstanding that is not easily corrected. For when men provide support and guidance to their partners, they also enhance their own positive feelings toward that partner, which may even increase their desire for intimacy. What they may not realize, though, is that when a woman provides support and offers friendship, she may be doing so only as a means of defending herself against harm.

The strategies that men and women adopt as methods for dealing with stress have physiological consequences, as well. Direct fight-or-flight reactions may allow for a quicker physiological resolution than secondary strategies for protection against harm. More circuitous routes of resolution may be safer but less optimal physiologically. And this, too, is a common complaint. One partner wonders why the other person seems to hold on to "hurts," whereas the other reacts with incredulity to the suggestion that they engage in lovemaking right after a major conflict.

One standard pattern of nonresolution of conflicts in close relationships has been withdrawal. According to marital researchers, the male is most often the one who runs away (Gottman & Levenson, 1988). But it is a pattern of negative emotional engagement followed by disengagement, a pattern perpetuated by both partners, that characterizes unhappy marriages. One partner is the "nag," always harping on the unpleasant, and the other partner is either out the door or has a hand on the knob, ready to take flight.[6]

This is not the only pattern that characterizes marriages that are failing. Another, even more obvious, sign of unhappiness is the expression of angry words and the escalation of angry exchanges. When researchers study couples in order to distinguish happy from unhappy marriages, they typically find that negative emotions overwhelm the interactions in troubled marriages. Does marriage success depend most strongly on the management of negative emotions? Can we ignore the positive emotions in understanding how people attain harmonious relationships with their partners?

If we rely only on the study of relationships after they have developed their own characteristic emotional rhythms, perhaps only the frequency and intensity of negative emotional exchanges are sufficient to identify relationships that are failing. But we are not so much interested in knowing that fighting and other expressions of negative emotion characterize unhappy bonds between people. This is obvious. The important question is. How did the couple come to be that way? One way to investigate relationships in greater depth is to study newly formed bonds between partners to see how they fare over time. It turns out that, when we look deeper at the roots of troubled relationships, we find that relationship problems arise when couples are unable to reach beyond their conflicts and broaden the emotional dialogue to include positive, as well as negative, emotional domains.

One of the best studies to tackle the prediction of marital success was conducted by Gottman, Coan, Carrere, and Swanson (1998).[7] They located newlywed couples through local advertisements, eventually recruiting 130 couples who had been married 6 months or less and for the first time. They assessed marital status and satisfaction each year for 6 years after the initial interviews to determine the condition of those marriages. Over that time period there were 17 divorces, so one of the contrasts was between those still married and those divorced. They also formed two contrasting groups within the stable marriages: 20 happy couples and 20 unhappy couples, based on the couples' ratings of their marital satisfaction.

Gottman et al. (1998) attempted to predict who ended up with happy marriages versus unhappy or "broken" marital bonds based on the way the newlywed couple expressed positive and negative emotions while talking to one another. To gather the necessary data, they brought each of the couples into a room wired for sound and videotape recording and asked them to discuss a problem they had identified as a source of marital conflict.

This interaction methodology has become the gold standard for the study of close relations. In essence, the investigators create a stressful situation and observe the partners' responses to one another. The videotape recordings of the interactions allow the investigators to score the behaviors of the partners on a number of dimensions, including the number of positive and negative statements made to one another when discussing the conflict. By analyzing facial expression and tone of voice, the researchers can also determine the degree of positive and negative affect expressed nonverbally during the session. Further, they can analyze these responses as a sequence to identify the timing of the actions and reactions of each member of the dyad: a sophisticated "he said, she said" scenario. Gottman et al. (1998) coded the interactions to identify five different positive emotions, including interest, validation, affection, humor, and joy, and ten different negative exchanges, including disgust, contempt, anger, fear, defensiveness, and "stonewalling."

What interactions laid the foundation for happy versus unhappy relationships? It turned out that one variable was the strongest predictor of marriages that stayed together and were happy as opposed to troubled: the degree of positive affect expressed during the stress of the conflict interview. In the happy marriages, positive affect was expressed as part of "de-escalation" sequences: times at which one partner does not respond to anger with anger but instead finds a way to lighten the tension. In doing so, the partners succeed in reclaiming the richness and complexity of their emotional lives together.

Interestingly enough, the degree of anger the partners expressed to one another did not predict long-term unhappiness in the marriage. A related yet different emotion, contempt, was a marker for future divorce to be sure, but it did not predict whether couples who stayed together were unhappy. And run-of-the-mill negativity during the stress interview did not predict anything of consequence. Instead, it was soothing positive regard during these stressful transactions that characterized those couples who had more lasting and happy marriages. Newlyweds who did not get embroiled in negative emotional exchanges but found sources of pleasing interaction with each other along the way were the ones who most often succeeded in staying happily engaged with each other (Gottman et al., 1998).

Stress and Marital Relations

There are many sources of stress in married life, and relationships outside the home have a strong influence on the stresses experienced inside marriages and other close and committed relationships. What has been missing in the analysis of many close relationships to date is attention to the quality of the positive support couples provide one another for problems that arise outside the relationship. Support of this kind can make partners more affectionate and also ease the burden of stressful encounters outside the relationship. These external stressors also pose challenges to the integrity of the relationship. A couple's inability to work together to resolve these problems coming from the outside may erode intimacy within the relationship.

Pasch and Bradbury (1998) investigated whether supportive interactions concerning problems outside the home protect the couple from future marital dysfunction in the home.[8] They noted that most investigations of marital satisfaction and dysfunction have focused on how well (or poorly) couples resolve their own conflicts. They reasoned that these conflicts are only one type of stress that tests the quality of the marital bond. Couples also must contend with problems that have their origins elsewhere. How partners support one another during discussions of such troubles may reveal an inner strength of the relationship not detected when examining conflicts within the marriage.

To investigate these questions, Pasch and Bradbury (1998) recruited 60 newlywed couples from the Los Angeles area for a videotaped interview. In addition to asking couples to discuss a conflict between them, these researchers asked the couples to discuss another type of situation: problems each was having outside the home, either at work or in other family relations. Highly trained observers viewed the videotapes of the sessions and recorded both the positive and negative behaviors of the husbands and wives during these discussions. A positive supportive remark might be, "Well, you know I'm on your side, no matter what you decide to do." A negative or nonsupportive comment might be, "You need to stop complaining about this, and do something."

Two years later Pasch and Bradbury (1998) recontacted the couples, asking them to report on their satisfaction with their marriages. Nine couples who were either separated or divorced since the initial assessment were placed in the marital-distressed group, along with those couples still together who scored very low on marital harmony. The investigators also defined a middle group that they called "satisfied" and a third group whom they referred to as "very satisfied" based on their reports of marital adjustment at the 2-year follow-up.

The findings were intriguing. During the conflict situation, the husbands' expressions of negative affect, particularly anger and disgust, were strong warning signs that the marriage was not going to be satisfying. The wives' negative affect was also important, but less so. During discussions of problems outside the marriage, supportiveness turned out to be an equally important predictor of future marital satisfaction. Here the wives' behaviors mattered most. The wives who expressed more positive regard and made fewer critical statements during the husbands' discussion of a problem outside of the home had happier marriages 2 years later. These predictors of future marital harmony had effects independent of one another. The wives' supportiveness did not diminish the dangers of the negative emotional displays of the husbands. Likewise, the negative reactions of the husbands did not compromise the contribution of the wives' supportiveness. The results indicate that both positive and negative emotional displays influenced the courses of the relationships. Both fewer scowls from the husbands and more caring gestures from the wives predicted better marriages (Pasch & Bradbury, 1998).

How can we understand the gender differences found among the couples in this study? Why were the wives' negative affects during conflict less damaging than the husbands', and why were the wives' supportive behaviors more helpful than the husbands' were? On some fundamental level, are women really needed more than men to "soothe the beast"? Perhaps it is a matter of gender-specific hormonal profiles. Some evolutionary psychologists might point to the male's higher levels of testosterone and the female's greater capacity for oxytocin release as evidence of a biologically based predisposition for men to ignite sympathetic nervous system activity and for women to rekindle warmth by stimulating parasympathetic responses.

Such conjectures are easy to pose but impossible to confirm. It would be premature to embrace biological explanations when strong social forces are at work in shaping the distinctions we make in defining the roles of men and women within our society. Pasch and Bradbury (1998) suggest one nonbiological explanation for the gender differences in their findings about support. Women may have more sources of support than their husbands do, so they may rely less on their husbands for support than their husbands rely on them. Thus men who do not gain support from their wives may be in a much more desperate state than women who do not have the support they need from their husbands.

Why would a husband's expression of discontent be more meaningful? It appears that male expressions of negative emotions have more powerful effects than female expressions. In a study of physiological responses to facial expressions of men and women depicting various emotions, participants showed significantly greater changes in heart rate when rating angry expressions on male faces than when rating angry faces of females (Johnsen, Thayer, & Hugdahl, 1995; Thayer & Johnsen, 2000).[9] Perhaps men just can look more menacing.

In a short story by James Joyce (1925) titled "Counterparts," a man humiliated at work hurts those he loves at home. Supportive ties can interrupt such a cascade of harmful interactions and allow a marriage to breathe without constant intrusion from forces outside the relationship. Historically, pressures on men at work have been a more frequent threat to marriages than work pressures on women. Yet the same vulnerabilities exist for women who are dedicated to their work. A supportive husband is likely to be critical to the survival of modern marriages in which both partners have obligations and ambitions outside the home.

Modern society offers many complex choices for relating. Our reluctance to adhere to traditional forms, with their strict cultural guidelines, has freed us further from prescribed roles. These freedoms are a mixed blessing, however. They increase uncertainty about how to relate to those closest to us. In times of relative calm in our social worlds, the relaxation of gender roles allows us to explore new emotional domains with our partners that we would not have attempted otherwise. Assigning an early draft of this chapter to my class, I asked my students how the "Can't live with them, can't live without them" adage applied in modern relationships. In reply, one student wrote:

> I feel closest to my husband when we relate as two naked souls rather than as a woman and a man. I am free with him to be angry or independent. He is free to cry or feel dependent on me as well. If we would always operate within our gender roles, I think I could definitely live without him. However, because at times we can experience our whole selves without constraints, I find I cannot live without him.[10]

The stresses that surround us pose fundamental threats to this level of openness and intimacy in our relationships. As threats and uncertainties increase in our lives, our capacity to experience and share our emotional selves may be diminished. We tend to gravitate to standard, even stereotypical, ways of relating during challenging times. Embracing culturally prescribed roles for ourselves and others may calm the storm of uncertainty over how to behave, but the resulting centripetal force casts us further away from one another as we retreat to our respective corners. If there is a challenge in relating that is unique to the modern era, it is this: how to preserve the emotional richness in our closest relationships when faced with uncertainty about how to weather the many storms outside and within ourselves.

A Changing Therapeutic Focus

What advances might be forthcoming from the helping professions that might benefit couples? Until recently, counseling for troubled couples focused primarily on their communication difficulties. Communication is an important problem to be sure, particularly given how easy it is for people in close relationships to misunderstand one another's emotional needs. The therapist would often instruct the couple on how they should talk to each other. Combative couples would be told that they needed to edit out the provocative language that they used. Alternatively, overly nice couples, who tended to avoid dealing with important conflicts, would be taught to level with each other more. In short, couples would be treated as if the key to their problems could be found in the grammar of their relating rather in the relationship itself.

Couples' sessions are still punctuated by therapists interrupting the arguments to correct the couples' methods of conflict resolution, or lack thereof. The hallmark of this approach has been what behavior therapy advocates have called "active listening." Each partner is taught to repeat (some would say "parrot") the essence of his or her partner's point of view about the issues between them before offering his or her own point of view. This process slows the tempo and intensity of the arguments between couples and alleviates the most frequent complaint heard in marital therapy: that he or she does not listen. In general, this and related methods provide a means of rational conflict resolution.

The only problem with these techniques is that they actually do little to promote happy marriages. After painstakingly careful analysis of reams of data collected on the use of active listening and its consequences in close relationships, one of the founders of behavior therapy for couples, Neil Jacobson (1992), reported that the approach he had been advocating for many years was flawed. Couples in successful relationships were not using this kind of listening any more or any less than distressed couples.

It was a stunning reversal for the field of couples' therapy. According to Jacobson, what practitioners have been missing in their attentiveness to the behavioral mechanics of the relationship is the need to encourage a different emotional orientation. He urged greater attention to the means by which partners in close relationships can acknowledge their differences uncritically and *accept* each other. We have searched far and wide for technical answers to human relations, only to find ourselves back to the basic human equation for sustaining a life with an intimate partner: understanding and support for threats from without and acceptance of differences in each partner's needs that arise from within. Conflict is inevitable when two individuals face one another directly without feeling ashamed to ask for what they need. But excitement, even joy, are also natural consequences of promises kept in a relationship that acknowledges the many differences in emotional experiencing between even the closest partners.

In this chapter I have applied a two-dimensional view of emotions to see if this approach could help unravel some of the puzzles of intimate relationships. The number of studies with relevant findings is still small. Nevertheless, the evidence from those studies shows that it is useful to examine the positive, as well as the negative, aspects of close relationships. The absence of positive interactions is a key predictor of future marital difficulties, independent of any risk of harm from negative interactions.

Indeed, many conflicts arise as a consequence of partners having separate emotional agendas in mind when relating to each other. Partners who understand these complexities and who adopt an accepting attitude toward each other's difficulties have the best chance of sustaining close romantic ties during the stressful times within the relationship and troubles brought into the home from outside. In the next chapter, I turn to a discussion of one of the central areas of our lives outside the home: our work. I explore how we can better understand our emotional attachments to the workplace by adopting a two-dimensional framework.

13   The Quality of Emotional Life at Work

Things men have made with wakened hands, and put soft
    life into
Are awake through years with transferred touch, and go on
    glowing
For long years.
           —D. H. Lawrence. "Things Men Have Made"

When you ask people why they work, you often hear comments such as, "It puts food on the table," or "It keeps me busy," or "To get out of the house." These comments disguise the strong emotional attachments that most of us have to our jobs, the way that troubles at work can preoccupy us, or the profound sense of loss that we feel when we leave a job, whether we choose to go or are asked to leave. Most people still find contentment at work, even when their jobs are so taxing physically and psychologically that their activities are truly harmful to their health.[1] There is no experience other than marriage and family that involves us so fully.[2]

How can we begin to understand our emotional attachments to employment in a way that can account for the fundamental contribution that the work experience makes to our lives? Marie Jahoda (1981)[3] identified what she called "latent" or hidden purposes underlying work. A job imposes a time structure on the waking day, allows for shared experiences with people outside the home, links an individual to goals and purposes that transcend one's own, defines key components of personal identity, and, perhaps fundamentally, requires activity. Elizabeth Yerxa (1998) summed up these purposes in a single word: *engagement*. It is engagement that breathes meaning into the work and sustains us, even in the face of mistreatment in the workplace.

Though attitude polling may not capture these "latent" purposes of work, one does not have to dig far below the surface to identify key dimensions of emotional life on the job. This chapter examines how positive and negative emotions inform those key dimensions of working life.

One approach to assessing emotionally salient aspects of work has been to ask individuals the following question: "Think of a time when you felt exceptionally good or exceptionally bad about your job—either your present job or any other job you have had. Tell me what happened." Two questions are embedded within this one. One question asks you to recall a time when you were feeling exceptionally good about work. But a time and place are also requested for occasions when you felt exceptionally bad about your job.

Herzberg, Mausner, and Snyderman (1959) first used these questions to survey job attitudes among middle-level managers in the Pittsburgh metropolitan area. The method of inquiry is called the *critical incident survey*, developed during World War II by John Flanagan, a pioneer in attitude research. The idea behind asking about critical events is that many of our core beliefs are shaped by times in our lives that were truly exceptional. There is another advantage as well. By focusing on meaningful events, this method is less likely to detect and score attitudes that are not based on personal experience. We all carry around beliefs that are only skin deep. These "throwaway" attitudes are constructed from many sources, sometimes even from on-the-spot assessments of what the interviewer wants to hear. Herzberg et al. (1959) focused instead on critical events and, in doing so, grounded his search for workers' attitudes about their jobs in their recall of actual experiences that changed how they felt about their work (cf. Grigaliunas & Wiener, 1974; King, 1970).

Herzberg et al. (1959) collected descriptions of both exceptionally good and exceptionally bad experiences at work, with no particular preference for one or the other description. However, he asked every participant to provide at least one positive and one negative job experience. In addition to descriptions, the interview continued with questions such as, "How long did those feelings last?" "What specifically made the change in feelings begin?" and "What did these events mean to you?" To get a feel for this, take a few minutes to answer these questions for yourself. What past work experience would you describe as exceptionally good or bad? You can use the broadest definition of work including schoolwork, housework, volunteering, and sustained efforts in any other sphere of life.

Herzberg and his colleagues (1959) dutifully recorded, read, and classified each of the descriptions based on 10 basic aspects of working life: achievement, recognition for achievement, salary, working conditions, supervision, company policy and procedures, interpersonal relations, responsibility, advancement, and personal growth. By tallying the number of times the managers mentioned each of those aspects as a chief cause of either an exceptionally good or exceptionally bad experience, the researchers could estimate how frequently each job aspect played a part in exceptionally good or bad episodes at work. To depict these results, they drew up a chart that provided a profile of the key job components for the managers they interviewed. I have reproduced a prototype of their results in Figure 13.1.

What Herzberg et al. (1959) found was that fundamentally different aspects of the job were associated with times of positive and negative emotions at work. Exceptionally negative times were related to those difficulties with contextual features of the job such as outdated and/or unfair company policies, poor supervision, adverse working conditions, and interpersonal conflicts. These factors were described in sequences that produced exceptionally bad feelings, but they were rarely mentioned in descriptions of exceptionally good work experiences.[4] When the managers talked about highly positive experiences, they described experiences not with the job context but with the work itself. Factors such as achievement, recognition for one's achievements, increased work responsibility, job advancement, and personal growth were the defining features of critically positive job experiences. These findings have now been replicated many times in studies of the quality of work life in companies and also in countless graduate and undergraduate classes in human resources management.

Based on these results, Herzberg (1966) developed what he called the motivation-hygiene theory of worker motivation. In his model, people have two distinct sets of needs at work: the need for fulfillment through satisfying work and the need to protect themselves from harmful social and physical contexts that surround the job.

Herzberg et al. (1959) anticipated the harsh criticism that his theory received from some members of the academic community soon after his work was published, criticism that continues unabated to the present day.[5] He wrote:

One of the basic habits of scientific thinking is to conceive of variables as operating on a continuum. According to this, a factor that influences job attitudes should influence them in such a way that the positive or negative impact of the same factor should lead to a corresponding increase or decrease in morale. Perhaps some of

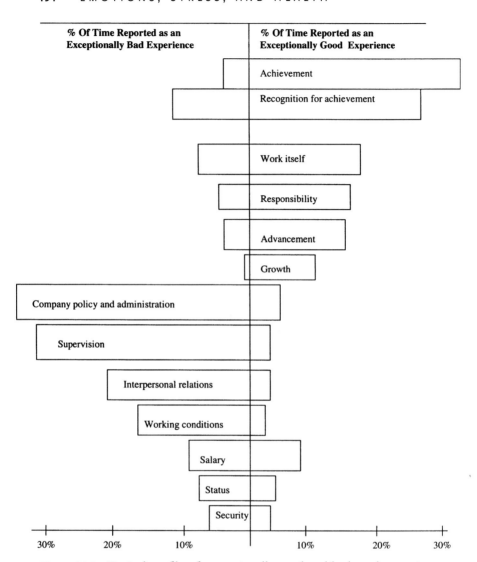

Figure 13.1. Typical profile of exceptionally good and bad work experiences.

the confusion as to what workers want from their jobs stems from the habit of thinking that factors influencing job attitudes operate along such a continuum. But what if they don't? What if there are some factors that affect job attitudes only in the positive direction? (Herzberg et al., 1959, p. 111)

This is, of course, precisely the point. We benefit greatly in understanding our work experiences if we allow our positive and negative emotional responses to fall along two continua rather than one. If you answered the questions about exceptionally good and bad work experiences for yourself, then you have some personal experience with this way of thinking. Did you report qualitatively different experiences as the sources of positive emotions at work compared with those that led to negative emotions? If so, then you join countless others who find that the sources of job satisfaction are often independent of the sources of job dissatisfaction in the workplace.

Rose, Jenkins, and Hurst (1978) are among those social scientists who must have been surprised to find patterns of work life that did not correspond to a standard one-motivation-fits-all model classification scheme. They sought to study people in occupational settings that were especially stressful. One occupation that seemed to fit the bill was air traffic control. Controllers are highly skilled radar screen operators who monitor the flight paths of incoming and outbound aircraft from airport radio towers. It is their job to make sure that each plane has a clear path to the runway and that there is sufficient space between airplanes to render the chances of midair collisions remote. These men and women perform this work under considerable time pressure. The aircraft they follow are flying at high speeds and often coming in from different directions simultaneously. If the controllers make a mistake, they can cause the deaths of hundreds of people. This surely sounds stressful.

Rose and his colleagues (1978) conducted interviews, hoping to document these stressors within the work of air traffic controllers itself. This is not what they found, however. What the researchers had thought would be stressful, the air traffic controllers reported enjoying. They liked the technical demands of reading and interpreting radar and were proud of having responsibility for the safety of the passengers and crew of the aircraft they guided.

Were these employees then free of job dissatisfactions? No. It turned out that air traffic controllers had many exceptionally bad experiences, but they did not stem from the actual work, but rather from company policy and administration, not to mention interpersonal conflicts with supervisory staff. The Federal Aeronautics Administration (FAA) stood out in the interviews as particularly demonic. The controllers reported excess paperwork, arbitrary rules and regulations, and questionable hiring and promotion decisions as key sources of pain at work. Rose et al. (1978) could not have known at the time that they were witnessing the strong undercurrents of labor unrest among the controllers that would eventually lead to a bitter strike by air traffic controllers against the FAA. Nevertheless, through all this discontent with contextual features that surrounded the job, the controllers still found self-confidence and satisfaction from meeting the challenges inherent in the work itself.[6]

I once was asked to examine the quality of work life for another group of employees in a highly demanding work environment: engineers responsible for power transmission and distribution for one of the local electric companies in the Southwest. My task was to evaluate the level of job stress among these employees. On the surface the work looked stressful. From mid-July through September, thunderstorms roll into the Valley of the Sun, bringing high winds, dust, and hail, as well as torrential downpours. Power outages caused by downed transmission lines and surges of electrical current from the lightning required quick reflexes on the part of this crew to reroute the electrical transmission. They also had to turn power on and off at various substations to permit linemen to make necessary repairs safely. Every so often a communication failure would lead to power being turned back on prematurely while the lineman was still repairing the fault, causing injury, even death.

There was indeed evidence of job stress among these employees. Seventy-seven percent of the employees reported nervousness at work, 40% had rapid heartbeat, 25% reported breaking out into a cold sweat, and 23% reported gastrointestinal upset during three days of self-monitoring while at work. But interestingly enough, the stresses they reported were not from the demands that the rainstorms brought but rather from the conflicts with supervisors and upper-level management about how the employees were treated at work.

The two examples I have just given you are of jobs that are fulfilling, even though they are stressful. A different problem arises when the work is seen as unfulfilling or lacking in meaning and purpose, even if it is safe, secure, and easy to perform. In those cases, Herzberg focused on changing the structure of the job by means of "job enrichment," a method of adding challenge and interest to the work itself to improve productivity and the quality of work life (Herzberg, 1976; see also Herzberg, 1968, 1974). In Herzberg's words: "You cannot expect people to do a good job unless you give them a good job to do."

Herzberg contrasted his methods of motivating workers with the more common practices involving the manipulation of incentive systems to create new external rewards and punishments. His approach was to keep these positive and negative motivational systems separate and not attempt to conflate the two needs by using the carrot or stick as a means of gaining greater investment in the work itself. He even coined a phrase that became so popular in the world of work that it showed up as a new word in the Oxford American Dictionary. That word was "KITA," which stood for "kick-in-the-(pants)" management. As he put it, KITA methods promote movement but not motivation. Without satisfying work, there is no "internal generator" that produces a motivated worker, and without that self-perpetuating motivational force, wages and other incentives spiral out of control in attempts to keep up with rising expectations of employees for even greater external rewards for their performances.

A number of principles govern how job enrichment is accomplished, but the focus is clearly on increasing the challenge of the work, enlarging opportunities for growth and new learning. In one project conducted at Hill Air Force Base in Utah, a job enrichment team worked with a crew of avionics engineers responsible for the maintenance and repair of F-15s, jet fighter aircraft with the capacity to fly 2½ times the speed of sound (Herzberg & Rafalko, 1976). In avionics at the time, there were three production lines. Prior to job enrichment, mechanics on each of these lines did the initial checkup and repair of the aircraft. After that, the plane was wheeled to the flight test bay, where other mechanics, the so-called "glory boys," made the final adjustments. The job enrichment change was to have one avionics line follow their plane out of the hangar and work with the flight test crew to make the final repairs.

Several things happened as a result of this modification. From a production point of view, the avionics repairs were done more efficiently. The planes going through the enrichment sequence had significantly fewer retest flights than those on other lines, resulting in substantial cost savings. And as a result, management decided to adopt the changes on all three lines.

How did the employees feel about the changes? Did the change improve the quality of their work lives, or was it seen as just another management ploy? As a postdoctoral fellow in industrial mental health in Utah at the time, I was asked to interview the employees at Hill as part of an evaluation of the program (Herzberg & Zautra, 1976).[7] Employees reported that many of the changes were beneficial to them personally. One employee on avionics noted, for example, that, "It's more of a challenge. You get vague troubles that are hard to analyze, and it isn't obvious where the problem is. This makes it more interesting than it would (be) otherwise." Overall, 12 of the 15 people I interviewed in avionics reported increases in job satisfaction. However, it was a change, and that also brought with it some irritations. Some employees were uncomfortable with the conflicts that stemmed from their newly elevated status as part of the flight test crew. Two older employees did not like the increased responsibility. In other words, there were some negative emotions that arose along with the positives.

My favorite quotation, gleaned from the Hill assessments, comes not from avionics but from a more loquacious group of contract negotiators whose jobs were also enriched as part of the Hill Air Force Base experience. This group was given more authority to sign off on deals they struck with various companies for providing their services at the base. When I asked one of these negotiators if the job redesign had affected him personally, he said this: "Yeah, my general level of energy increased in all areas. I accomplished more at home. Got along with my knot-headed kids better. Generally, in being happier, I sleep better. I worry about more positive things like how to get the job done rather than how to get out of the job." This could be an anecdote from a depressed person after a course of anti-depressive therapy with a serotonin reuptake inhibitor such as Zoloft. But Zoloft had not yet been discovered when this interview was conducted, and perhaps the Hill project was all the better for that. This change improved both the employees' mental health, and the efficiency of procurement operations at the base.

Are highly motivating jobs always healthier? Those interested in the promotion of a healthier workplace have urged that greater attention be paid to the many sources of emotional turmoil that stem from how people are treated on the job and relatively less attention to how enriched the work is. For example, the National Institute for Occupational Safety and Health has been interested in identifying sources of dissatisfaction from poor treatment in the workplace and has attempted to relate these dissatisfactions to increases in physical health problems.

What still surprises many is that level of effort does not, by itself, increase risk of health problems (Hanson, 2000).[8] High job demands surely increase physiological arousal while at work, firing up the cardiovascular system and other functions linked to epinephrine and other chemical messengers of the sympathetic nervous system. Marie Frankenhauser (1989) devoted much of her career to charting changes in these arousal patterns as a function of stress at work. After many years of careful research, she concluded that the increases in heart rate and other indicators of cardiovascular load were unhealthy only if the person did not return to normal levels after work.

Repetitive work has been one type of labor that places the person at risk, not because it raises epinephrine levels but because those levels do not recover rapidly enough after work. What makes these repetitive tasks particularly stressful? Robert Karasek (1981) proposed an intriguing way of classifying work that helped define which jobs were actually harmful to the employees' health. He defined work along two dimensions: the task demands and decision-making latitude. It turned out that these dimensions identified those occupations that suffered higher risks of cardiovascular illness.[9]

I have reproduced one of Karasek's classic diagrams in Figure 13.2. Karasek (1981) reasoned that it was loss of control over the work that was the key to job stress. If we work long, hard, and late at night, we may suffer from lack of sleep, not to mention poor nutrition, but the work itself

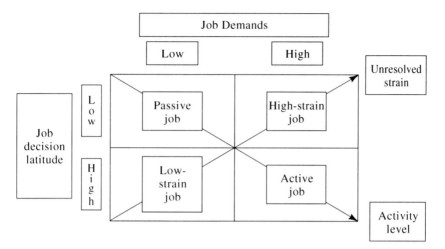

Figure 13.2. Karasek's job characteristics.

would not necessarily be stressful.[10] Only if someone else dictates the methods and flow of the work would we be likely to suffer adverse health consequences. He classified professions based on the degree of work demand and decision latitude and then tested to see which jobs were associated with high rates of cardiovascular disease. Only those occupations characterized by both high effort and low choice, identified in Figure 13.2 as causing unresolved strain, placed the employee at greater risk for a heart attack.

This makes sense from the perspective of our model of how stress affects emotional awareness. Lack of decision-making latitude increases uncertainty over key aspects of job performance, disturbing the natural rhythms of working environment. This uncertainty over features such as the pace and flow of the work creates a pressure-cooker environment. Success and failure and their matching emotional states become linked closely together in an either-or, win-lose fashion under these conditions. Authority over key aspects of the work not only bolsters self-esteem but also reduces key sources of stress in the workplace, stresses that both raise job dissatisfaction, and narrow the emotional experience.

The study of the everyday lives of white-collar employees by Nancy Nicolson and her colleagues found just this sort of pattern (van Eck, Nicolson, & Berkhof, 1998; Zautra, Berkhof, & Nicolson, 2002). As I discussed in Chapter 4, even minor stressors within a workday increased negative feelings and constricted emotional space, leaving the employee with a more uni-dimensional frame of reference through which to judge the quality of work life.

In another diary study of working men, Arthur Stone and his colleagues (Stone et al., 1994) examined the health consequences of everyday events. Their study focused on the body's production of sIgA antibodies. This antibody, found in saliva, is one of the body's first defenses against invading organisms, including bacteria and viruses responsible for the common cold. IgA antibody production is stimulated by the presence of foreign substances (antigens), and its task is to surround, engulf, and remove those substances before they take up residence in our bodies. High levels of antibodies found in saliva samples after the introduction of an antigen is one indicator of a responsive immune system.

Stone et al. (1994) instructed their participants to ingest rabbit albumin each morning, record their daily activities, and take saliva samples each night for 12 weeks. The albumin cocktail contains a harmless but foreign protein that stimulates IgA antibody production. The reports of daily events provided accounts of both undesirable and desirable events that might affect antibody production, and the amount of sIgA in the men's saliva at night served as the outcome measure of the body's capacity to defend itself against invading organisms.

Two findings stand out from this research. First, on days punctuated by many work stressors, the participants' immune systems produced less sIgA antibody. Of all the various types of undesirable events assessed, work hassles had the largest effect on IgA production. The second finding was even more compelling evidence that quality of daily life was related to immune functioning for these men. Days filled with many desirable events led to the highest antibody production. In fact, these effects were more powerful than those for undesirable events. The beneficial effects of desirable events on sIgA levels lasted longer, with significant effects for up to 2 days beyond those of undesirable events. The positive effects also overrode the negative effects of work stressors. As long as the men had a sufficient daily diet of desirable experiences, the stressful workdays had no substantial effect on sIgA levels.

Stone et al. (1994) found that stressful workdays can be unhealthy, but their methods allowed them to go further. By investigating daily life with a wider lens, one that spotted positive events, as well as negative ones, the research provided a fuller picture of the influences of daily life on health. They identified protective and restorative factors on health that derived from leisure and otherwise desirable everyday life experiences for working people. Without examining both positive and negative dimensions of emotional life in the daily lives of these men, they would have missed discovering that positive experiences can provide the antidote for stressful days at work.

When Work Is Play

It is interesting as well to examine the other extreme, namely situations in which the person is fully engaged at work, has much to do, feels challenged by the task at hand, and has the freedom to set his or her own pace and to select the methods he or she finds most useful to get the job done. One can extend this engagement scenario further by having the person select his or her own pursuits. For a faculty member, that might be writing a paper or teaching one's own course. For a bioengineer, that might be building a mechanical elbow; for a physician, investigating new treatments for a rare disease; and for an auto mechanic, rebuilding the engine on his '57 Chevy.

Mihaly Csikszentmihalyi (1990) has studied engagements of these sorts extensively. He refers to the underlying experience as "flow": a very special state of seamless concentration on a chosen task in which self-awareness, even awareness of time, fall away from the person who is focused with whole body and mind on his or her work. The work may be strenuous, even painful, but the person perceives the work as almost effortless. In sports such as basketball it is called being "in the zone." Optimal experiencing depends on how one's state of mind coheres with activity. Successful completion of the task must be attainable, and the working conditions need to allow the person to focus on the task with all his or her cognitive and emotional energies. This experience is the foundation for positive emotional life at work.

In highly stressful job environments, flow is repeatedly interrupted by other exigencies. The employees may be left with a work life that has little emotional depth and to which they have little attachment or commitment. Every organization has times during which it functions in crisis mode. These are special times of high stress that may even help shape camaraderie among employees.

The problem is that an increasing number of jobs in the American economy never seem to make it out of crisis mode. The challenges at work to make a deadline or beat out the competition can generate a highly engaged and motivated work force. Institutionalizing that kind of challenge as a way of life in the organization, however, risks the emotional health of the most highly motivated employees. From our dynamic two-dimensional model of emotion, these win-lose stresses link positive emotions such as interest and excitement with negative emotions such as anxiety and fear. These practices result in a narrowing of emotional experiencing. After an initial surge, employee motivation declines as positive strivings to achieve are repeatedly crossed with needs to defend against failure. The company knows that it has gone too far when its latest campaign to best the competition promotes not joie de vivre among its employees but feelings of alienation, contempt, and the quiet desperation of chronic fatigue.

Social changes in the nature of the work experience portend an ever-increasing degree of uncertainty over some fundamental aspects of the work experience. In a look to the future of occupational medicine in the twenty-first century, Jenny Firth-Cozens (2000) alerts us to an almost two-fold increase in levels of worker stress over the past 10 years. Even when unemployment rates are relatively low, increases in pressures to work longer, harder, and faster have injected more uncontrollability into everyday work life. Although much attention within industry has focused on trying to weed out those employees who are more vulnerable to the effects of stress, this effort misses the point. Firth-Cozens notes that companies in the United Kingdom vary widely in the degree of distress reported by their employees and suggests that management practices themselves are a principal source of stress-related illnesses.

In the United States, similar comparisons have been made between companies that promote compassion at the workplace and those that treat the world of work as a game of *Survivor* (O'Boyle, 1998).[11] According to the model of stress and health introduced in chapter 4, the consequences of fostering uncertainty over such basic aspects as job security may increase performance initially but also increase the risk of illness and injury by disturbing emotional awareness and regulation. Unfortunately, companies are rarely held accountable for the development of health problems of their employees. Indeed, it may take years to see the adverse consequences of stress-related changes in cardiovascular function and cortisol regulation. The situation parallels that of attempts to regulate environmental hazards. Tobacco is a case in point. Even with direct links between tobacco and disease, companies in the nicotine delivery business argued effectively that individuals chose to smoke and thus were solely responsible for whatever health consequences arose as a result. Only by taking persistent legal action that spanned many years were prosecutors able to force some companies to pay the piper for violating the community's trust. Perhaps by means of a similar process of legal action and debate, we will gain greater corporate attention to job stresses and their effects on employee health problems.

Some far-sighted companies are already fostering ways to reduce health risks of job-related stressors. Some of the best methods have been based on evidence from carefully designed research on emotions and health. For example, one firm has introduced autobiographical writing in their work with employees who have lost their jobs. Following the research of James Pennebaker (1990; see chapter 6 for more details), this company advises unemployed workers to write about the experiences surrounding their job loss as part of their outplacement counseling program. This intervention is likely to benefit emotional adjustment and reduce stress-related health problems for employees fired or laid off from work. There is also strong evidence that this intervention pays dividends in other ways, as well. In one study, laid-off employees randomly assigned to writing about their experiences found new jobs significantly faster than those laid-off employees who were not assigned to write about their experiences (Spera, Buhrfeind, & Pennebaker, 1994).

In this chapter I have focused on the design of jobs as one fundamental determinant of the emotional lives of employees. This approach, of necessity, treats all people alike when estimating the effects of the workplace. Not everyone responds in the same way to their job assignments, and by focusing on each individual's wants and needs, management reforms can have more powerful effects, though on smaller groups of employees[12] Important, too, has been the influence of a new breed of managerial consultants who have introduced practical guides for self-governance, mixed with an appeal for the application of values, even spirituality, to the management of oneself and one's relations at work. *The One-Minute-Manager* (Blanchard & Johnson, 1982) exemplifies the emphasis on technique. Other approaches teach executives more intelligent ways to manage their emotions at work (Goleman, 1999). Steven Covey's (1989) writings about the habits of highly effective people have been highly influential. He addresses the central role of values and moral principles in guiding people in their search for meaning and purpose in the work world.

Csikszentmihalyi (1990) tells us that there is much we can do ourselves to promote optimal experiences such as flow within our own lives. This is indeed refreshing to hear. The message is a positive one from the point of view of psychology, and to say that stress is also an experience of the mind frees us to develop mindful strategies tailored to our unique emotional needs. These freedoms do not extend proportionately across every occupation, however, and the organizational culture establishes the boundaries and thus sets the constraints on self-actualization and growth-producing engagement at work.

In this chapter I have revived some principles of management first introduced in the 1960s that offer a two-dimensional perspective on employees' needs at work. The focus at that time was on promoting positive striving through programs such as job enrichment. Attention to those forces that strengthen positive engagement needs to be balanced with concern for the many potential sources of stress and distress in the workplace. Giving exclusive attention to the potential for harm from personnel practices also misses the point. Improvements in work life quality require attention to both sets of emotional needs. Job involvement can be one of the greatest sustainable sources of joy and fulfillment in our lives. However, for work to flow, we need more time unencumbered by production crises, office politics, and the other potential sources of distress at work. We would benefit, as well, by looking inward, understanding our positive and not-so-positive emotional attachments at work. To enjoy enriching occupations, many people need to develop better ways to calm those inner anxieties that arise from a compulsive drive to produce. By attending to our own feelings during the process of work and staying aware of the value of our goals, we remain mindful of our interests in both emotional domains.

14 The Preservation of Quality of Emotional Life as We Age

Tho' much is taken, much abides; and tho'
We are not now that strength which in old days
Moved earth and heaven; that which we are, we are.
—Alfred, Lord Tennyson, "Ulysses"

My aim in this chapter is to examine the quality of the emotional lives of older adults with lenses focused on both positive and negative dimensions of emotional experience. But first, I think it is important to address a bias that pervades much of our thinking about aging populations. Many people maintain that we have more important concerns than attending to the quality of life of older adults. For them, nurturing the mental health of children provides us with the best hope for the future. They subscribe to the belief that what happens early in life shapes our futures to a great extent. In contrast, the ways of older adults are already set, as if their stories have been foretold, forecast by events earlier in life. Another commonly held belief is that biological processes play a greater role in determining the health and well-being of older adults than of young children. Collectively, these attitudes add up to restatements of the adage about "old dogs" not being able to learn and of the futility of our attempts to improve the lives of our elders. Even if older adults could be influenced by new experiences to the same extent as young adults and children, the balance of years favors investing in children and their mothers first, does it not? So many years are wasted when a child dies or is wounded psychologically; fewer years are lost for the person already past his or her "prime." These are the arguments I hear about the relative unimportance of enriching the quality of life of our elders.

Allow me to pose the counter-argument. The lives of children and young adults are unfolding, with many significant experiences still ahead. In contrast, the future is now for older adults. They do not have decades to consider how to improve their lives. For older adults, every troubled year represents a significant proportion of remaining life lost to those troubles. Not many young people think about lost chances this way. Most people live as if they will go on forever. Perhaps more of us would change the way we live earlier in life if we thought we could improve things, if we had the resources to do so, and if we also realized that we do not have as much time as we think. Sometimes it does not dawn on us until late just how precious our lives are.

Consider the last few weeks of life for those who have some very important unfinished business. It is indeed a tragedy for someone to die without gaining resolution of a lifelong problem. How profoundly sad to observe someone suffer from guilt and fail to receive absolution from a loved one who refuses to forgive in those final minutes before death. That last bit of time is so important; those last hours promise and also threaten to become the defining moments of an entire life. As we age, these defining moments challenge us to transform our lives before it slips away forever. A child's fortunes can be reversed, except perhaps in the most extreme cases of abuse of fundamental needs. An older adult increasingly faces doors closing around him or her, doors that cannot be reopened.

Laura Carstensen (1993) has proposed an intriguing model of how awareness of having a finite time to live changes our approach to life in very fundamental ways. She suggests that older adults attend to and regulate their emotions much more than younger adults do because they are more cognizant of the collapse of time. She writes, "Awareness of limited time provides the sense of perspective that softens the experience of negative affects (Carstensen, Isaacowitz, & Charles, 1999, p. 171)." Unlike someone younger, the older adult is more likely to ask himself, "Why get angry now?" As people age, they attend to what she calls "emotion motives" in their social interactions to a greater extent than younger adults do. They do not want to waste time engaged in lengthy bitter disputes, and they steer clear of others who are sources of negative affective engagement. Further, they are more likely to try to transform painful experiences into occasions for gaining meaning and a sense of coherence about themselves and their lives.

The data from several studies support Cartsensen's (1993) theory. The older a person gets, the lower the frequency of his or her negative emotions

(Mroczek & Kolarz, 1998). This downward linear trend is sustained at least to age 80. Carstensen (1993) attributes this trend to better emotional regulation. Older people know what they like, and they are not going to be bothered so much by those things they do not like. Are older adults happier? There is no clear evidence that positive feelings are more frequent for elders, and even some evidence of loss in the sheer number of positive events. However, these losses have more to do with fewer opportunities than with changes in older adults' capacity to enjoy life. In fact, there is evidence from both the laboratory and field studies of everyday life that older adults do experience emotions just as intensely as younger adults do.

Reminger, Kaszniak, and Dalby (2002) asked the following question: To what extent do older adults react to emotional displays with the same or less intensity than younger adults?[1] To address this question, they presented a slide show to two groups of people: young adults and older adults. A third of the slides were very positive. They had pictures of a child playing with her dog and other heartwarming images. A third were very negative, such as fighting or grieving at a funeral for a young child. There were also many slides that were neutral in emotional tone. The investigators asked their participants to report how they felt when they looked at these pictures and analyzed these self-reports to see if people of varying ages reported their emotions with different degrees of intensity. They added another feature to their study that made the findings altogether more convincing. They secured electrodes on the facial musculature of their young and old volunteers. From the brow, electrodes on the corrugator muscles recorded the magnitude of the person's frowns during the slide show. Smiles were also quantified by placing electrodes on the zygomatic muscles.

When people looked at the pictures that were negative they frowned more, along with reporting more negative emotions. Similarly, when people looked at positive scenes, they smiled more and reported experiencing more positive emotions compared with their reactions to slides that were relatively neutral. But age did not influence the extent of these reactions. Older and younger adults not only reported the same degree of emotional response to the pictures but also showed the same magnitude of facial response: the same amount of smiling at joyful photos and the same degree of consternation when viewing unhappy ones.

As noted before, laboratory studies are valuable because of the experimental control that is possible. But these benefits come at a cost. The lab setting is somewhat artificial, so the experimenter does not know, based on those studies, whether the same results would be observed in real life. To address whether there are age differences in everyday life emotions, Cartsensen, Pasupathi, Mayr, and Nesselroade (2000; see also Carstensen, et al., 1999) sampled the daily experiences of emotion among adults ranging in age from 18 to 95. Each person wore a beeper for a week, and at 35 randomly selected intervals, the beeper signaled them to record their emotions at that moment. The researchers collected information on both the frequency and intensity of the participants' emotions at each of the 35 beeps.

Older adults had fewer experiences of negative emotions and the same number of positive emotions as younger adults.[2] On the whole, though, their emotional experiences carried the same amount of intensity (Carstensen et al., 2000).

Another difference between groups was particularly revealing. When the investigators looked at how long negative feelings lasted, they again found differences between younger and older adults. Older adults let go of those feelings more rapidly than younger participants. In sum, the older adults in Cartsensen et al.'s study were less distressed than the younger adults were because they managed their negative affective experiences better. Not only did they have fewer negative experiences but they also did not let those events affect them as much.

What about the degree of relationship between the emotions, a key indicator of emotional complexity? Cartsensen et al. (2000) looked at this question as well. They found more evidence for uncoupling of emotions among the elders in their sample. The participants were more likely to report some positive emotions, along with negative emotions, and showed significantly more complexity in their ratings of their feelings. Younger adults tended to be more unidimensional in their appraisals of their feelings and less differentiated overall in their views of how they felt at any given moment in time. In one comparison, the investigators computed the degree of interrelationship between negative and positive affects for people of different ages. The overlap between high negative emotions and fewer positive emotions was 3 times larger for younger adults. The greater emotional differentiation among the older adults may derive from several factors. Older adults have less stress in their lives, are more attentive to how they feel, and are better able to manage stressful situations compared with younger people.

Not all older adults fit this glowing profile of emotional health in aging, however. Indeed, the compression of time may also compress the emotional experiences of those people who suffer from anxiety over their health and well-being as they age. These anxieties can adversely affect their capacity to understand the complexities of their emotional experiences. That tension appears to be especially prevalent among those babyboomers who are ill prepared to accept finite limits on their lifetimes. At age 50 in the United States, everyone with a social security number is invited to become a card-carrying member of the American Association of Retired Persons (AARP). This is a day of reckoning for many people. Some boomers worry that if they are not doing what it is they desire most to do, they will never get to it. The AARP letter brings on feelings of dread for those people who feel unfulfilled. One cannot live fully or well under the duress of this much existential anxiety.

As the Body Slows: The Impact of Arthritis and Other Chronic Disablements

Many elders face daily challenges to their hopes for happiness, and often these challenges threaten both dimensions of emotional life. Chronic illnesses such as arthritis are a case in point. These health problems carry with them threats to well-being in both dimensions. Arthritis not only causes joint pain due to swelling and the destruction of cartilage and bone in our joints, but the illness also interferes with a person's capacity to act. Even the simplest actions can become ordeals for those with joint damage due to the disease. Difficulties opening car doors, untwisting bottle caps, or walking out to the curb to get the newspaper add up to diminish the person's physical means of sustaining positive emotional health.

For these reasons, arthritis is one of the most troubling illnesses for people of any age. It is also the most frequent cause of disability in the population. Nearly one of every six people in the United States has some form of arthritis. That amounts to 43 million Americans. As our population ages, these numbers will grow; current estimates are that by the year 2020, 60 million people will have some form of arthritis, and 11.6 million of those people will suffer from arthritis-related disability (Lawrence et al., 1998).

Disability and pain are the twin perils of arthritis, and they can influence psychological health in different ways. A group of health psychology researchers and I studied the emotional consequences of arthritis pain and disability using data from three community studies of rheumatoid arthritis patients (Zautra et al., 1995). We asked whether arthritis affected the quality of life of older adults, and if it did, whether it primarily influenced positive emotions, negative emotions, or both aspects of psychological well-being.

Here is a summary of what we found. Arthritis patients with the most pain felt negative emotions more often and with more intensity than those with less pain. This in itself comes as no surprise. More surprising was our finding that the amount of pain had little influence on positive emotions. By and large, feelings of excitement, pride, and enthusiasm were unaffected by pain level. What did erode this positive side of well-being were physical limitations that accompanied the disease. Those arthritis patients who have many activity limitations had the greatest difficulty sustaining positive affective health. They did not necessarily feel any more distress, but something was definitely missing in the quality of their everyday lives. These results did not apply just to the first sample of 210 rheumatoid arthritis patients but also held for two other samples of rheumatoid arthritis patients: over 500 patients altogether.

The Stress of Caregiving

There are other sources of chronic stress besides health declines that challenge older adults' abilities to maintain psychological and physical well-being. One of these stressors—prevalent among older adults—is the burden of caring for a spouse or other family member who is disabled. The work of those caring for a disabled spouse or parent has been euphemistically called "the 36-hour day" (Mace & Rabins, 1981). The everyday strains on caregivers can be enormous and unrelenting. Further, when caring for those with Alzheimer's disease and other forms of dementia, the family member simultaneously experiences the loss of the loved one he or she is caring for, as the disease increasingly erodes the patient's intellectual and emotional capacities. In one carefully controlled study, the rates of depression for 86 older adults who were caring for a spouse with progressive dementia were compared with the rates of 86 older adults who had healthy spouses (Dura, Stukenberg, & Kiecolt-Glaser, 1990). Thirty percent of the caregivers experienced a depressive disorder during the years they provided for their spouses, compared with only 1% of the matched control sample.

The problems extend into the physical health arena, as well. In one recent study (Schulz & Beach, 1999), distressed caregivers were at 64% greater risk of death over a 4-year period while caring for their spouses than noncaregivers were. Why would these people have a higher risk of mortality than noncaregivers? The evidence is mounting that significant alterations in immune function occur for these caregivers. One of the important functions of the immune system is to generate antibodies following exposure to bacteria and viruses. Antibodies serve as cellular memories to cue a rapid immune response to future invasions by the same or similar foreign tissue that might threaten the body's health. Vaccines work by stimulating the production of these antibodies, thus preparing the body for future exposures to more virulent pathogens.

In one study, Ron Glaser and his colleagues (Glaser, Sheridan, Malarkey, MacCallum, & Kiecolt-Glaser, 2000) investigated the immune responses to vaccinations for pneumonia and influenza for elders who were caring for their spouses and compared them with a matched sample of elders who were not caregivers. The antibody production of caregivers was not different from that of controls at first, but by 6 months after vaccination, there was clear evidence that the caregivers were less well prepared immunologically for future exposure to strains of flu virus and pneumonia bacteria. This finding takes on even more significance when considering that the fourth leading cause of death among elders is exposure to just these types of pathogens.

Not everyone who has this burden of care is adversely affected, however. Though 30% of caregivers become depressed during the time in which they are taking care of a disabled spouse, 70% do not. Even among those who do have severe depressive reactions, there is considerable variability in the length of time it takes to recover. The higher risk of mortality found for caregivers also did not hold for everyone. Only those elders who reported considerable distress when caring for their spouses had higher mortality rates than elders without caregiving responsibilities (Schulz & Beach, 1999).

What makes the difference? A two-dimensional perspective on emotions offers an approach to answering this question. That approach does not focus exclusively on reducing the pain of caregiving but rather directs our attention to those emotional forces that can sustain life amidst suffering. The caregiving elders who are able to preserve their own health may be those who are able to sustain emotionally satisfying activities even when suffering from the daily burdens of providing life support for their spouses. Those who give up on themselves and disengage from their own lives during this time may be the ones most at risk. This depressive response has been the single most consistent source of vulnerability in studies of survival, as well as quality of life, among older adults.

Studies of immune responses suggest that the body's resistance to illness is greatest among those elders who are able to preserve vitality and other positive emotions in the face of the chronic stress of caregiving. Stowell, Kiecolt-Glaser, and Glaser (2000) studied the immune responses of 102 caregivers whose spouses were suffering from dementia. For comparison purposes, they also recorded immune system reactions of 83 noncaregiving elders. Each of the participants gave blood that was then prepared for analysis and placed on a small shallow (petri) dish. The authors measured the rate at which certain immune cells originating in the thymus (T-cells) multiplied in response to a pathogen introduced into the petri dish. The researchers reasoned that rapid proliferation of these immune cells was an indication of the capacity of the person's immune system to provide timely protection against the consequences of exposure to real-life pathogens.

As expected, caregivers had considerably more stress in their lives than noncaregivers did. The elevations of stress levels in themselves did not alter immune responses. What did make a difference was the coping styles of the caregivers. Those caregivers with active coping styles showed rapid immune cell division and proliferation in response to the pathogen. Their responses were similar to those of the noncaregiving samples. The T-cell proliferation of those caregivers with less proactive responses was in slow motion by comparison.[3]

There are many paths to successful adaptation to caregiver burden. Simply responding well to stressors does not capture all the options available for sustaining well-being. Our two-dimensional approach invites us to extend our understanding of adaptation beyond coping. Take the work on self-efficacy as an example. In an earlier chapter, I discussed Albert Bandura's (1992) model of human striving that is based on this term, and that model has been a very successful one in predicting who copes best during times of stress. In essence, his approach focuses on how our beliefs in our abilities play a key role in determining our success in performing difficult tasks. Belief in one's efficacy in coping with life's difficulties is critical to the mental health of older adults. The evidence is strong that their beliefs in their own abilities to handle stress are among the best predictors of sustained psychological well-being. That confidence in being able to "take what comes" allows older adults to experience even severe losses in functional abilities without increases in the depression and anxiety that otherwise accompany disabling chronic illnesses.

But this type of efficacy only goes halfway in defining our beliefs in our adaptive capacities. Another set of beliefs surrounds our capacities for sustaining positive engagements in life, not just adjustments to stressful events. Few studies inquire about this form of efficacy.

When we asked a sample of 265 older adults about this second form of efficacy, we discovered two things (Zautra, Hoffman, & Reich, 1997).[4] First, we learned that efficacy beliefs concerning obtaining positive experiences were unrelated to beliefs about the capacity to cope successfully with problematic life experiences. Some people were good at one but not the other, some were good at both, and some had little confidence in their abilities in either quarter. Efficacy expectations for positive outcomes defined a dimension of beliefs about oneself separate from expectations for negative outcomes. As we have found in our studies of coping, our beliefs about own abilities are also organized around our emotions; one set of beliefs corresponds to positive feeling states, and another corresponds to how well we believe we can cope with the negative.

The study we conducted (Zautra et al., 1997) allowed us to ask about the long-term benefits of these two kinds of efficacy beliefs on health and mental health among older adults. In interviews conducted 4½ years later, we collected information about the levels of depression and anxiety of the elders and also about their changes in physical functioning. We found that those elders who believed in their abilities to cope with stress were able to preserve their mental health in the face of losses in functional ability over time. Beliefs in the ability to sustain positive engagements did not protect the elders from mental health downturns. But in a way, the effects that we did find for positive event efficacy were more fundamental. Those with strong beliefs in their ability to make things happen showed fewer decrements in their physical abilities.

Which is more important to well-being—mental health or physical functioning? Both are important. We need to encourage efficacy beliefs in both realms; joy does not protect us from sorrow, but those ramparts that defend against sorrow do not, in themselves, bring us joy.

Can these efficacy beliefs be taught? And can elders acquire these habits of thought, or is it too late for such learning? Rodin and Langer (1977) tackled this question in a study of nursing home residents. They encouraged residents on one floor of the facility to take a more active role in caring for themselves and contrasted the effects of that intervention with a comparison group who resided on other floors of the same nursing home but who did not receive instructions to take more control over their lives. The results were astounding. Through follow-up assessments made 18 months later, Rodin and Langer found that the elders who took more responsibility for themselves were more vigorous, actively engaged and social, and healthier, according to ratings by the nurses caring for them. Further, the results suggested that the active-intervention group had a 25% greater chance of still being alive than the comparison group. To further our understanding of the needs of older adults, we need to allow ourselves to think outside the box and broaden our inquiry beyond coping with distress when searching for keys to successful aging.

Stress and Cognitive Decline

The illness feared most by older adults is Alzheimer's disease. This condition, along with other forms of dementia, represents a catastrophic defeat in the struggle to preserve quality of life. It erodes the very quality of our consciousness. Not many elders are afflicted early—around 5% before the age of 80—but 20% over 80 years of age show evidence of some form of dementia. There are many biochemical causes of the decay in memory and attention that characterize dementias such as Alzheimer's disease, and many are beyond the reach of our model of stress and emotional health. Nevertheless, it has become increasingly evident that physiological responses to stress play a prominent role in the development of cognitive impairments among older adults.

The focus of this work has been on a region of the brain called the hippocampus that is essential for the storage and retrieval of memories. This structure straddles the thalamus and undergirds all the cortical regions responsible for the integration of sensory input and motor output. With damage to this region, people cannot remember their birthdays, how many children they had, or even if they were ever married. The area is responsible for storage and retrieval of fundamental bits of knowledge about ourselves.

The hippocampus plays a major part in down-regulating hormone levels by sending signals to the hypothalamus to lower CRH secretion, stemming the tide of glucocorticoids released from the adrenal cortex. In essence, the hippocampus is responsible for saying, "enough already," thereby ending the cortisol secretions that characterize HPA-axis responses to stress. There is a crowd of receptors for cortisol and other glucocorticoids in the hippocampus to guarantee that the brain detects the flow of stress hormones and shuts the system down before a "meltdown" occurs from an overload of stress hormones in the brain.

The system works well, except for one rather troubling side effect. Glucocorticoids such as cortisol can kill hippocampal neurons (Sapolsky, 1998). The mechanisms are still under investigation, and it looks as though overexposure can lead directly to cell death but also work indirectly by weakening the cell's resistance to other harmful agents. The level and length of exposure figure in when trying to determine the conditions that make glucocorticoids harmful to hippocampal cells. With fewer hippocampal cells, the capacity to regulate the HPA-axis and its secretions of glucocorticoids is blunted, leading to even more cell damage. Sapolsky (1998) has called this the "glucocortioid cascade" and has offered strong evidence that this downward spiral in hippocampal functioning is responsible for a significant portion of the decline in memory that accompanies aging.

Michael Meaney and his colleagues (Meaney et al., 1995) suggest that the memory impairments are due in part to lifelong patterns of stress reactivity in which cortisol elevations are both higher and last longer than normal. Everyone does not develop dementia, and Meaney and colleagues suggest that those animals reared in relatively more enriched home environments are less susceptible. He used his handling versus nonhandling paradigm to explore this question (Meaney, Aitken, van Berkel, Bhatnagar, & Sapolsky, 1988). Handled infant rats had lower physiological reactivity to stress as adult rats compared with the nonhandled rats in his experiments.

Aging rats, like some of their human counterparts, show a hormonal response to stress that is longer in duration than younger rats. Meaney and colleagues (1998) have shown that this difference in hormonal reactivity is present primarily in the nonhandled rats, not the handled rats. He also tested the cognitive skills of these groups of rats by putting each of them into a tank of water. The animals had to find a platform submerged under water in order to climb out of the water. The animals that had been handled as pups navigated the waters with the same skill regardless of age. But aging nonhandled rats took 3 to 4 times longer to locate that platform than younger rats. Meaney et al. (1998) concluded that handling renders these animals less susceptible to cognitive decline by setting off a series of stimulating events that cascade in their own way to produce a less reactive and more inquisitive animal.

Can we interrupt those stress processes that cause premature aging in humans? This is a "Fountain of Youth" question, in part. And some hold out for some sort of pharmaceutical wonder drug that can arrest the aging process. Perhaps it will be a testosterone cocktail, a kind of Viagra for the mind. Aside from a miracle drug, it is fair to look at what else might interrupt the harmful aspects of the stress response.

Laura Fratiglioni and her colleagues (Fratiglioni, Wang, Ericsson, Maytan, & Winblad, 2000) provided strong evidence that positive social ties are protective factors in the onset of dementia. They examined the social networks of citizens in Stockholm, Sweden, who were over the age of 75 and then used those data as predictors of who developed dementia, determined by follow-up assessments conducted 3 years later. Those older adults who were married or living with someone and who had a friend or two and a good relationship with children were least likely to develop dementia. Those without these types of social ties were 60% more likely to show signs of dementia at follow-up, even when accounting for any differences in dementia symptoms at the initial assessment.

There are only a few published studies like Fratiglioni et al.'s that have focused on factors, such as social integration, that may increase resistance to cognitive decline. Most of the work thus far has focused on those processes that are harmful to recovery from stress rather than those that make us more resilient. Nonetheless, they are instructive even if limited in the scope of their analysis.

Depression, for good reason, is often cited for its contribution to cognitive decline. Among older adults, a significant number of those who are depressed also show a hypercortisol response to stressful events. These chronic cortisol elevations can do some real damage to the hippocampus.

One recent study found a way to measure the size of the hippocampus in the brains of women with and without a history of major depression (Sheline, Sanghavi, Mintun, & Gado, 1999).[5] Apart from their depression, these women were physically healthy. The longer and more severe these women's depression, the smaller the hippocampus: about 12% shrinkage in the depressed women compared with those not depressed. In fact, there was a correlation of −.60 between total number of days depressed across one's lifetime and hippocampal volume. The connection between depression and cognitive decline is so striking that some scientists suggest that antidepressive medications might provide the best protection against cell death in the hippocampus.

Depression is a label that carries with it many different meanings. We need to know which aspect of depression plays the central role in cognitive decline. Depression is characterized by both the presence of certain negative emotional states and the absence of positive emotions. Some early evidence suggests that the absence of key elements from positive emotional domains may carry special risks. There is evidence that older adults react less physiologically to stressful situations when their esteem for themselves is relatively high. In one recent study, Teresa Seeman and her colleagues (Seeman et al., 1995) found that self-esteem altered the connection between a stressful event and cortisol elevations in older adults. In their study, older adults reported on their own self-worth and then participated in a stress reactivity experiment. In the laboratory, the elders climbed into a driving simulator that had the look and feel of a real automobile. During a resting phase, they "drove" after watching a video about how to drive safely. But during the second film, they had to follow taped instructions that demanded their keenest driving skills to evade oncoming cars and other challenging situations that appeared on the videotape. While they were driving, a catheter drew blood from their veins at periodic intervals, taking samples when they were at rest and also when they were under stress.

As expected, cortisol increased significantly during the stressful episodes compared with the initial period, but not for everyone. Seeman et al. (1995) analyzed cortisol levels during the driving simulation challenge for those people who were high, medium, and low in self-esteem. As predicted, those participants who had high self-esteem did not show elevations in cortisol, the medium self-esteem group showed modest increases, and those low in self-esteem showed large increases.

Earlier, I reviewed how depression in combination with anxiety might create emotional constriction that clouds over adaptation efforts. How do we help older adults feel that they are not under a constant state of siege of body and mind? The defensive mindset that is characterized by depres-

sion and anxiety leads to retreat from emotional life. Und
person may easily mistake any relief from sorrow and pai
happiness. Without the presence of mind to recognize t!
perience more than one emotion and feel good even without ᴎᴗ
feeling better, the aging person with chronic ills may find no alternativᴇ
helplessness.

What Can We Do?

How can older adults overcome their depression? The simple answer has
been to take a pill, and the psychiatrist's arsenal of effective medications
to fight against depression is growing monthly. What we do not know is
whether these approaches are opening the mind to emotional complexity,
as well as closing down intense negative emotions. Some alternative approaches rely on physical activity rather than biochemistry to improve the
emotional well-being of older adults. James Blumenthal and his colleagues
(Blumenthal et al., 1999) have pursued this line of research with astonish-
ing results. In one of the most extensive studies of the mental health benefits of exercise to date, these investigators recruited 156 older adult men
and women into treatment for major depression. They then randomly assigned the older adults to one of three treatments: a standard course of
antidepressive medication (they used Zoloft), a 16-week aerobic exercise-
training program, or both medication and exercise training. A psychiatrist
met with each patient who received medication periodically throughout
the course of the study to establish a therapeutic dose and maintain the
drug regimen. The exercise intervention consisted of three supervised exercise sessions each week. The regimen required the participant to walk or
jog at a mild training level for cardiovascular conditioning during each session.

   The investigators monitored levels of depression by scheduling clinical
interviews throughout the study. Over 60% of all participants no longer
met criteria for depression at the end of the study, with no differences
between groups. By the end of the study, those in the exercise condition
showed improvements comparable to those taking Zoloft. There was one
difference that favored the medication group: Their depression subsided
somewhat more quickly than it did for those in the exercise condition.
There was also one difference that favored the depressed elders who received exercise: They were not only psychologically healthier, but they
were also more physically fit by the end of the study (Blumenthal et al.,
1999).

   This finding is intriguing. On the one hand, we have a drug that targets the actions at specific neural synapses. Years of research and clinical testing preceded the entry of this drug into the marketplace as a means of altering the biochemistry of the brain. By comparison, we have this blunt instrument, aerobic exercise, which is thought to elevate positive emotions and increase self-efficacy, along with increasing cardiovascular conditioning. Both work. The chemistry of emotional health is mutable by behavioral, as well as biochemical, methods. What we do not know is if they both work in the same way. As was discussed earlier, depression means deficits in positive affective health, as well as elevations in negative affects, and includes pervasive thoughts of helplessness. From Blumenthal et al.'s (1999) study, we do not know which of these components of depression were influenced by the two treatments. Still, these results inform us of one important principle: There is more than one way for elders to fend off depression.

What about cognitive decline? There is direct evidence that physical exercise can improve cognitive performance, as well. Kramer et al. (1999) recruited a group of 124 older adult men and women who might be classified loosely as couch potatoes. After pretesting, half were randomly assigned to a simple walking program. The other half did nonaerobic stretching exercises. Six months later, the investigators readministered cognitive tests that probed what is sometimes called "executive functioning." These tasks involved planning, making and remembering choices, and switching choices rapidly when necessary. Those elders in the walking intervention showed a 25% improvement on those tasks. Those elders in the other condition showed no gains in cognitive performance.

Liepert, Bauder, Miltner, Taub, and Weiller (2000) provided one of the most dramatic demonstrations of how our behavior can enhance our gray matter. These investigators did brain scans of 13 stroke patients who had sustained significant damage to a portion of the motor cortex responsible for the use of one of their hands. The images of the patients' brains revealed that the regions responsible for muscle movement in the paralyzed hands had shrunk due to the stroke and were considerably smaller in size than the region responsible for muscle movement in the nonparalyzed limb. Then they tied the stroke patients' good hands down during a 12-day "restraint treatment." The patients could use only their paralyzed hands during the treatment.

The stroke patients treated with the restraint harness showed substantial improvement in the use of the paralyzed hands, but the really interesting finding was uncovered in the new images of the brain taken after the intervention. A new scan of their damaged motor cortexes revealed a significant increase in the size of the area, as well as recruitment of new brain areas: All of this resulted from preventing the patients from taking the easy way out and using their good hands. This study shows that the brain ought not to be regarded as static, but as a dynamic, even somewhat malleable, part of us that can grow, as well as decay.

People have also become increasingly interested in meditative approaches, both as a way to reduce anxiety and as a means of allowing a more natural flow of contemplative and pleasant emotions. Guidance through imagery training is also used to direct the person's thinking toward positive affective memories instead of negative affects. The alternative music of today that is so appealing to those approaching older adult life combines sweet simple melodies with a gentle rhythm that reduces stress and promotes openness to contemplation.

Mindfulness meditation, an approach to meditation that I discussed earlier in reference to the management of chronic pain, is gaining many adherents as well. What is unique about this method is that it encourages awareness of all emotions, not just positive ones. Most Western stress-reduction programs encourage a Promethean-like stance by fostering active problem solving, focused attention, physical exercise, and other ways of empowerment. In contrast, mindfulness emphasizes acceptance of all feelings, including painful ones, and teaches methods of releasing the mind from the all-consuming efforts to fend off negative emotions. In doing so, the approach allows us to experience our lives more fully and, at the same time, protects us from feeling helpless over those events that we cannot control. By encouraging emotional awareness and lowering stress through meditative methods, mindfulness offers people the opportunity to expand their capacities for sensing and responding to emotions in both dimensions.

For some, meditative approaches are anxiety-provoking, however, for they allow images of past emotional turmoil to surface in consciousness. The people may be ill equipped to listen to themselves reliving those past traumas without support. Viney (1993) has developed a model of psychotherapy for older adults that encourages repair in self-esteem damaged by past experiences. She advocates life course review[6] for older adults, and there is good reason to suspect that such a review could yield many emotional benefits for older adults. Talking about the past was once considered ill advised for fear that telling one's story would encourage people to live in the past or reawaken feelings of regret. Now there are workshops around the country that guide older adults in writing their autobiographies (Rimer, 2000). The topics of these writings range from deeply troubling events to the recall of the daily texture of important relationships at an earlier time. The outcomes of these stories appear much less important than the process of reconnection with the whole of one's emotional life. It is a process that allows us to see the continuity and change in our lives at a deeper, more fundamental level of discourse.

Here is an example. A renowned clinical psychologist, Ernst Beier,[7] is leading the way by writing his autobiography after a long successful career as an educator, clinician, and behavioral scientist at the University of Utah. Beier's theory of emotional communication in psychotherapy was mentioned in chapter 8 (Beier & Young, 1998). His therapeutic model focuses on our use of overt and covert emotional messages. We use these messages to shape the responses of significant others in our lives. By keeping messages covert, according to Beier, we can persuade people to do our bidding without them being aware of how they are influenced. He uses the example of the emotional tugs on our pocketbooks from TV ads such as Virginia Slims' "You've come a long way baby!" that target the needs for autonomy among adolescent girls.

According to Beier, we may also hide from aspects of ourselves and our own needs and desires that we find impossible to acknowledge openly. These "forbidden wishes" lead us to send covert messages about our intentions that we are not even aware of. Consider, for example, a woman taught to be always caring and deferential to others' needs and demands, who secretly feels imprisoned at home but cannot acknowledge the source of those feelings. As a consequence, she finds herself quick to anger over the slightest offense and constantly at odds with several members of her family. Psychotherapy, according to Beier, is a process by which people come to greater awareness and acceptance of those aspects of themselves that have been hidden from view.

In his autobiography, Beier writes about his flight from Hitler's Germany prior to World War II to escape persecution and his return as a prisoner of war after he was captured while fighting as an American soldier against his former countrymen. By far the most dramatic aspect of the autobiography is his retelling of his encounter with a savage German commander in charge of the POW camp. Like other suspected Jewish prisoners in the camp, he was called to meet the commander, a meeting from which few, if any, prisoners ever returned. Beier found a way to save himself, however. He noticed a book on the commander's desk by Johann Wolfgang von Goethe, arguably the greatest of all German writers. As a student and an intellectual growing up in Germany, Beier was well versed in Goethe's writings, and he struck up a conversation with the commander about this great German philosopher. That conversation saved his life. That conversation was also the starting point for the development of his theories about covert communication. In a book that traces the currents and crosscurrents of development as a psychologist and as a person, he provides us with an illustration of the power of autobiography for all, even the experts.

Can retelling of our own stories heal, as well as serve to foster emotional growth? In the stream of life there can develop many eddies and backwaters. Patient review of the darkest waters is difficult to do, often impossible to do alone. We all have trouble facing our own errors of judgment and coming to terms with the consequences of those mistakes. For many, it is the fear of these memories that stands in the way of adaptation, and those barriers to health can last a lifetime. With listening and acceptance from a supportive other, a detailed inquiry into the events of one's life can reveal passions and energy for life long buried. Themes of redemption and new hope for a higher quality of life can result from the uncoupling of events from a one-dimensional world of pain and sorrow. By finding meaning and purpose within the fault lines of life, we restore the richness of emotional experience of past events, and in doing so open ourselves to a full emotional life in the future. For many, this is the soundest approach to ending the siege and regaining a quality of consciousness. Perhaps, too, some of the young will listen. They would learn much about emotional complexity if they do.

15 The Emotional Community

"He who would do good to another, must do it in Minute
    Particulars
General Good is the plea of the scoundrel hypocrite, and
    flatterer:
For Art and Science cannot exist but in minutely organized
    Particulars
And not in generalizing Demonstrations of Rational Power."
                                        —William Blake, *Jerusalem*

The Greene family was driving through Sicily at night when
they were attacked. A group of bandits brandishing firearms pulled alongside the Greenes' car. As the family tried to flee, the bandits opened fire.
After a chase, the bandits pulled away, and the Greenes came upon an
automobile accident with police and ambulance present. At first relieved,
they stopped their car to report their brush with lawlessness. When they
opened the back door, however, they found that a bullet had pierced the
skull of their 6-year-old son, Nicholas. Two days of intensive care did not
reverse the fact that their child was brain dead. When they told this story
on National Public Radio,[1] 3 years after the event, few of the millions of
listeners could hold back tears.

Mr. and Mrs. Greene lost a life very precious to them on that Sicilian
highway. But what happened next seems nothing short of miraculous. By
donating their son's organs, the Greenes ignited an international movement

that has saved the lives of countless people. Their story provides a dramatic illustration of the opportunities for positive thought and emotion that are embedded within even the most tragic circumstances. And when you hear them tell it, as a simple matter of fact, an attitude of, "Well, wouldn't anyone have done the same?" we know that the warmth we feel is not due to the way they told the story but from how the story itself touches us.

When Diane Reeve, their interviewer, asked them whether they had hesitated to donate their son's organs, their reply was soft-spoken yet decisive. It was the easiest decision there was to make, they said. Reeve persisted: "Were you not angry at the Italians, at their country, for the death of your son?"

Mrs. Greene answered, thoughtfully, "You know, we had two days after he was shot, and that might have made a difference. During those two days, the people there surrounded us with so much concern, so much caring and support. Everyone we came into contact with would have done anything to bring our son back. It wasn't the Italian people who did this to our family, it was just five men."

Then they told the stories of some of the people who had received their son's organs. A teenage girl without a functioning liver, who was in the hospital waiting to die with family and an entourage of relatives, suddenly had a new liver and a new life because of the Greenes. The girl lived, married, and gave birth to a son. They named their child Nicholas. Listening to them telling this story, those of us who were in tears before suddenly were breathless, overwhelmed with joy over this turn of events.

In all, seven children received life-saving organs from Nicholas's body. And the response from the people of Italy was remarkable, as well. Though Italian customs forbade removing organs to serve as transplants, thousands of new donors came forward in Italy alone to offer organs to save people's lives. The Greenes themselves have played a prominent role in developing charitable groups around the globe dedicated to encouraging organ donations. The number of lives saved due to these events is inestimable. Nor is it possible to fully gauge the strength of the positive emotions these events have generated, but I think it is safe to say that the emotional gains on the positive side of the ledger have been enormous.

Would we try to weigh these events to see if the scales tilted in favor of good or bad? No, there is no counterweight that justifies a murder such as that. The parents' profound sadness over this death remains, and no amount of consequential "good" makes up for that loss. The Greenes do not appear to be particularly religious; they may even have no belief that these events had a special purpose or were divined in some way. They remain in tears and in joy over the events of that day, events that propelled them into the work of saving lives, both with their son's body and by telling their story and inviting others to emulate them.

Contained within this story of the Greenes is a great lesson in the building of community. Hidden within even the most distressing experiences lie potential acts of kindness that foster the strongest communal ties. These ties are not fortified by sharing sorrows alone. The shared experiences of joy that follow successful resolution of the tragedy are also part of the community equation. The development of community requires sharing of emotions in both dimensions. In this chapter I explore how both positive and negative emotions aid in the development of ties within the community. As the story of the Greene family reveals, stressful events often serve as catalysts for the formation of these ties. We need to examine closely how stress narrows our choices for relating, choices that turn out to be crucial to the development of community ties.

The loss of a sense of community has been a frequent theme of critiques of life in the United States and other highly industrialized nations. How can a two-dimensional analysis of emotions help us understand the problems of our Western culture in sustaining a connectedness among people? One place to look is at the way culture encourages certain pursuits of the positive and, in doing so, discourages others that might be equally or even more satisfying. Some have argued persuasively, for instance, that within our society strong positive emotions have been seen as arising primarily from individual achievement, what Vicki Helgeson (1994) refers to as needs for agency, and not from social relations: the fulfillment of needs for communion.[2] It is not that needs for personal agency should be ignored, but only that unmitigated attention to those needs leads to unhappiness and ill health, according to Helgeson.

These cultural prerogatives also influence the frameworks for social science research. Social ties are often studied as resources that protect and defend us against loss. Rarely are they appreciated for their most obvious contribution: as a means to promote well-being. Indeed, social scientists study the value of social ties nearly exclusively because of their protective value as buffers against mental and physical upset. But social support is not just a means to an end. It is an end in itself.

To understand community, we need to acknowledge to a greater extent the advantages of social engagement as a source of positive affective health, regardless of its powers as a buffer against negative emotions. The evidence is quite striking in showing that high levels of social integration, especially for men, lead to lower heart rate, serum cholesterol, systolic blood pressure, and cortisol levels (Seeman, 1996). These findings, coupled with epidemiological evidence, clearly favor social ties as a significant key to health and long life. It has typically been assumed that social relations are protective because they reduce negative emotions and buffer the person against stress. What if the underlying mechanism has more to do with the contrast between those who are able to fulfill their needs for attachment and those lonely individuals who suffer from an absence of positive social engagement? Perhaps too many in our society have unfulfilled needs to belong, and that is the source of our collective loss of community.

Kerstin Uvnas-Moberg (1998) has investigated physiological mechanisms that link positive social relations to better health. In her work, she has put special emphasis on the neuropeptide oxytocin. Oxytocin is released from the hypothalamus during one fundamentally important social exchange, breast feeding. Lower blood pressure and cortisol levels are associated with oxytocin release, along with higher levels of growth hormone and increases in energy storage activity. Other forms of nonstressful touch, besides breast feeding, also stimulate the secretion of oxytocin; massage, for example, stimulates oxytocin. But consider breast feeding itself for a moment. Here is one of the purest acts of loving between two people. And the giving is mutual: Not only is the mother giving life-sustaining nutrients to the baby and giving warmth and safety with her body, but the mother also receives back warmth and touch, as well as life-sustaining physiological responses that arise from within her own body. Oxytocin promotes lower blood pressure, enhances motility in the gut, stimulates sexual appetite, and raises pain tolerance thresholds. Uvnas-Moberg (1998) notes that women who breast feed often undergo a personality transformation of sorts. They become more sociable, calmer, and generally more tolerant and accepting. These appear to be natural consequences of hormonal changes that take place when breast feeding.

Oxytocin does not accomplish all these changes by itself. Rather, the hormone appears to set off a chain of events that favor less anxiety and more enjoyment of life. The effects on pain threshold, for example, appear to be a result of changes in beta-endorphin levels that are stimulated by oxytocin. There is evidence of quicker wound healing and less stress reactivity to a physical stressor. These effects may be due to repeated spikes of oxytocin that, over time, reduce secretions of cortisol under stress. Oxytocin itself has a relatively short half-life and does not linger in the bloodstream more than a few minutes. Nevertheless, it stimulates many other physiological systems to encourage adaptive responses.

One of the most intriguing studies of oxytocin suggests that its antistress effects are contagious as well. Agren, Uvnas-Moberg, and Lundberg (1997) injected rats with oxytocin and observed lowered temperature in the rats' tails and a greater tolerance for heat applied to the tails than was evidenced with control animals in other cages. Then they looked at the performance of rats paired up with the oxytocin-injected rats. These were rats that did not get the injection but that were in the same cages as those that did. Those rats showed the same lower temperature and tolerance for heat stress as their cage-mates, even though they did not get an injection of the hormone. How could this be? The researchers tested another group of rats coupled in cages, one of which was injected with oxytocin and the other not, but this time they blocked the animals' sense of smell with some zinc sulphate. Without the capacity to smell, the rats without oxytocin no longer showed the same effects as those with oxytocin. The effects of oxytocin appear to be communicable via olfaction. What a provocative model for us to consider. Sense of community may be transferable, provided we stay close enough to one another to stimulate our olfactory senses.[3]

How well must we know our neighbors to benefit from our contact with them? Many undergraduate texts in social psychology refer to a commonly held belief that people react less favorably toward strangers under stressful conditions. The idea is that the negative emotions generated by the stressful conditions of life color the evaluations of people, especially those about whom little is known. Racial prejudice is thought to arise in just this way: through the formation of negative evaluations of strangers during stressful times.

Kenrick and Johnson (1979) have challenged that popular notion in an elegant study of attraction. In their study, women undergraduate participants were subjected to either loud blasts of noise or mild noise through earphones and then were asked to rate the attractiveness of another person. By random assignment, some women rated a stranger, someone whom they had never met and whom they would be unlikely to ever meet. This condition replicated the way other studies had introduced a stranger. Alternatively, some women were randomly assigned to a separate condition. In the new condition they rated the attractiveness of someone they met at the site of the experiment for the first time and who (they were told) would also experience the same stressful blasts of noise.

Under stress, the women rated the stranger they had never met as unattractive, as in prior studies. In contrast, they showed significantly more affinity for the stranger whom they had met just before receiving the stressor. Stress can bring people together, as well as drive them apart emotionally.

Is oxytocin involved in increasing the affiliative responses of those under stress? Maybe. Laboratory studies do suggest that we are drawn to one another in difficult times (Carter, 1998) and that there are strong hormonal changes during stress, such as increases in oxytocin, that could provide the mechanism that underlies increases in affiliation. There may be a catch, however. This pull toward affiliation may be present only with those people with whom we have had face-to-face contact. According to Kenrick and Johnson (1979), under stress, people will still disparage the strangers they have never met.[4]

When Uncertainty Reigns

Warm and supportive relationships develop best in stable environments, and stressful environments can disrupt these normal patterns of mutual caring. One of the most interesting studies on the effects of uncertainty on mothering and child development was conducted on troops of macaques (Rosenblum & Andrews, 1994). The investigators varied both the availability of food and the predictability of the food for mother and baby macaques. There were three conditions, with each troop assigned randomly to one of them. In the first condition, the mothers were given food easily within reach. In a second condition, mothers had to forage long and hard for their food, but if they put in the effort, they would always succeed. The third condition was the most stressful, if we define stress as uncertainty. Their food was sometimes readily available, as with the first group, but sometimes they would have to search, like the second group. Which condition was in force at any given time was varied at random so that on any given day, the mothers would not know how difficult a time they would have finding food.

This third condition was most disruptive to mother macaques and their infants. In that condition, mother and offspring fought with one another more, and the infants acted depressed, similar to the way macaques behave when separated from their mothers. Further, as adolescents, these young monkeys were more fearful and played less with other young monkeys. Rosenblum and Andrews also followed the offspring into adulthood. Those raised in highly variable food availability conditions had higher levels of corticotropin releasing factor. They were more prone to anxiety and gave more intense fear responses to stress, including elevations in downstream stress hormones such as cortisol. In these ways, the stress effects of an unpredictable environment can be transmitted from parent to child. These macaques needed a coherent, predictable resource community within which to find food and raise their young. Without it, the young develop less effective responses to stressful situations, leading to a progressive deterioration in the quality of relating among kith and kin.[5]

Violence Erupts

One of most disturbing cases of social unrest in the United States occurred in the suburban community of Littleton, Colorado, in April 1999. Two boys, dressed in Gothic black, gunned down 13 of their classmates at the local high school and then shot themselves. Can the dynamic two-dimensional framework introduced in this book help us understand what happened in Littleton? There are complex social processes at work in any community crisis, so it would be presumptuous to claim that the answer may be found in any one model of human behavior. Nevertheless, an analysis of emotions under stress may reveal some hidden forces at work in the minds of those troubled boys

From the confluence of violent acts, there are two streams to follow back to their source as we seek to understand the emotional forces responsible. One stream to follow is the course of the development of alienation. From this perspective, we seek to identify the source of a detachment from community so perverse that the person feels no concern for the welfare of others. The other stream to trace is that of the violence itself. How did such nihilistic impulses develop in the first place? What is the genesis of such intense interest in actions that have the power to end another person's life?

To address the first question, we need to study the positive emotional forces that underlie attachment to community to see what may be missing in modern society. Schiff (1999) wrote a piece for *The New York Times* about a week after the shootings that offers some clues about the source of estrangement from community. Schiff grew up in Littleton 30 years before the shootings, when it was a small rural town, not the middle-class suburb of Denver it is today. He sees the difference between then and now as a difference in a "sense of place." Although he suffered from some of the same verbal taunts from the "jock-oriented" high school culture as the gunmen did, he and his friends never would have considered engaging in vengeful acts of violence as a response to being treated as second class by their peers. Schiff and his friends knew that they had a place in the scheme of things. According to Schiff, that sense of place in Littleton got lost in the miles and miles of shopping malls constructed since he was a boy. The anonymous "mall-lands" do not provide us with any borders to defend together, nor do they give us a shared sense of identity to protect.

In psychological terms, what Schiff is taking about is a sense of community.[6] Fulfillment of the need to belong may indeed be the glue that could hold communities together. Its absence may be what makes them fall apart and increases their vulnerability to random acts of violence. Sociologists have begun to study this characteristic of communities, referring to it as *social capital* (Kawachi & Kennedy, 1999). Social capital has two critical features: a high level of trust among citizens and a high level of participation in voluntary associations and local organizations. Within the U.S. cities of Baltimore and New York, those social areas that scored high on social capital had the lowest rates of violent crime. It was not just "neighborhood crime watch" memberships. People in these communities participated in social organizations because they enjoyed the interactions with members of their community for their own sake.

A study conducted by Lynn Simons and me of the mental health of neighborhoods in Salt Lake City may help illustrate the importance of social capital (Zautra & Simons, 1979).[7] Lynn was developing models of need for mental health services in Salt Lake City, and I was developing ways to depict the quality of life in that community from survey data we had collected from a sample of 454 men and women living there. Our interests converged in trying to classify the well-being of the census tract neighborhoods within the community.

Census tracts are geographically defined regions within the city that the census bureau has demarcated. There were 26 contiguous tracts that defined the boundaries of the community mental health center's service area. A considerable amount of demographic data had been compiled for each of these census tracts from prior United States census surveys. Contained within those data were indicators of social capital, or lack thereof, such as median family income, percent of high school graduates, and percent divorced. We conducted the quality of life survey with a representative sample of adults from those same census tracts. In that survey we inquired about recent stressful events, such as being laid off at work and marital separation. We also asked about the number of positive experiences in people's lives, such as making new friends, marriage or reconciliation with a partner, and a new job or promotion at work. By averaging the scores on these positive and negative events for everyone who lived within the boundaries of the census tract, we constructed estimates of the average number of positive and negative events that occurred to adults in each census tract.

What we found was that in those census neighborhoods with higher social capital, residents had more positive and fewer negative events in their lives. Income predicted both fewer negative and more positive events, as did high school completion rates. Divorce rates did not predict more negative events, but this indicator of social disharmony did predict significantly fewer positive events in the lives of the residents.

Of what significance were the positive experiences within census neighborhoods? Simons investigated whether event rates predicted service utilization at the community mental health center. He found that those neighborhoods with residents engaged in more positive experiences used mental health services at significantly lower rates than those with a relative absence of positive experiences. The well-being of community seems to depend greatly on the presence of the positive, as well as protection from the negative. And stress ups the ante even further, making positive engagement with others all the more critical to community life.

A close look at modern community life reveals many people seeking positive interactions but with fewer and fewer behavior settings for meaningful social exchange. Churches are becoming increasingly important in maintaining community life by providing a place for purposeful interactions with others. An increase in religious participation over the past decade is one of the few healthy signs of life within our communities. Much positive interaction takes place in economic activity, but it is worth questioning the extent of the depth and meaning of those interpersonal exchanges. Movie theaters and the Internet are packed with people finding images of interaction but not actual face-to-face contact with others in real time. Virtual relationships keep us from real-life entanglements but do not allow us to engage others with all our senses.

Many people appear to be starving for meaningful social relations but without knowing what they are missing. Have we, growing up with the belief that individual interests hold sway over interpersonal bonds, unwittingly created a nation of people at sea, each living on his or her own island of thought, action, and emotion?

In one of the most important sociological works since David Riesman's *The Lonely Crowd* (1950), Bellah, Madsen, Sullivan, Swidler, and Tipton (1985) have endeavored to capture the essence of contemporary community life in America in their book, *Habits of the Heart*. "Habits of the heart" refers to cultural mores that govern how we permit ourselves and one another to find meaning and purpose in our lives. The authors argue persuasively that the cultural mores within America pose special difficulties for participation in community life because of the emphasis on individualism and an inattention to the merits of collective action for the good of the group. If people do not recognize the validity of actions performed for the common good, it is difficult to sustain positive emotional attachment to social commitments that do not serve some immediate personal need. The loneliness many feel is a symptom of the times. Our culture's offer of self-centered goods whets our appetites but does not fulfill our interests for meaningful social ties. These are the social conditions that underlie the detachment and alienation from the community found in Littleton.

Is Man a Wolf to Man?

Turning to the question of violence itself, what do we find upstream of the river of anger and aggression that seems to flow into our lives so persistently? Indeed, there is a dark side of community life that needs to be acknowledged. Freud (1930) was among the first to characterize the psychology of aggression. But Freud found these dark reaches within the soul of man and saw community, with its rules and laws, as a necessary step to control man's naturally aggressive instincts. As Freud saw it, "Men are not gentle creatures who want to be loved, and who at the most can defend themselves if they are attacked; they are, on the contrary, creatures among whose instinctual endowments is to be reckoned a powerful share of agressiveness" (p. 58).

This picture of evil within us is not the modern view, however, and for good reason. Destructive behavior is not the norm of society but an aberration. People appear naturally inclined to like, rather than dislike, one another and are willing to cooperate, at least at first, rather than compete (Axelrod, 1984).[8]

What then does give rise to the spread of hostility and other negative affects across a community that can produce an event such as that in Littleton, Colorado? Sociologists have identified a second key element that distinguishes those communities with high crime rates: a strong sense of inequality, or lack of fairness in the distribution of social and economic resources. Those same community studies that found social capital to be a valuable crime deterrent also found that the extent of income inequality was associated with high levels of violent crime (Kawachi, Kennedy, & Wilkinson, 1999). They found that a greater range of incomes in households was associated with a greater sense of relative deprivation and a higher crime rate. How does this fit within our paradigm?

To answer that question, we need to focus on the emotional reactions of those people who are not permitted full participation in the community. One emotional response that is overdue for more careful examination in this context is the feeling of envy. Envy is a powerful hurt that arises from feelings of unfair exclusion from the social exchange of positive emotions (Baumeister & Leary, 1995). So it may come down to this: no sense of community normally fostered through positive engagement and much negative affect engendered through social inequality.

The inner life of a violent person is impossible to know fully, nor is it possible to predict with any degree of accuracy that first act of outward aggression that harms another human being (see O'Toole, 2000). Repeated small acts of aggression, in themselves minor violations of social norms, are likely to harden the wax that shapes the person's future potential for violence. These first acts of hostility can evolve into a whole set of aggressive behaviors. In addition to reducing anxiety and feelings of vulnerability, aggression activates positive emotions. Violence then may build on itself as a habitual response that in a single stroke appears to solve two problems at once: the frustration from unfulfilled and impoverished social relationships and anger over being unjustly deprived of the social riches that those with more social capital have acquired (Bohart & Stipek, 2001).

What does the person do who sees others enjoying one other while he is feeling ignored? A child would make noise to be heard. A child with a gun might make a louder noise. And what if the person watching others at play is feeling shunned, even ridiculed, by some of those around him? If, peering in as through a department store window, the person sees those on the inside as unfeeling, glassy-eyed mannequins, what then are the chances of violence?

Difficult conditions can provoke anger. A popular social psychological model would make a single distressing event the trigger, the match that ignites the tinderbox. This model makes sense and explains when tempers are most likely to flare. Indeed, the affect compression that occurs during stressful times is incendiary, particularly among those prone to flashes of rage.

Two researchers have found experimental evidence that stressful situations can lead to an escalation in the intensity and rigidity of habitual interaction patterns. Todd Van Denburg and Donald Kiesler (1993) noted that what distinguishes the behavior of abnormal persons from that of normal people is their extremes of interpersonal behavior and the rigidity with which they cling to their beliefs about others.[9] They reasoned further that the inner stress of the abnormal person may be re-created to some extent by exposing normal people to external stressors and testing to see if the stresses lead them to behavioral extremes, as well as rigidity in their thinking. It is not that the person will suddenly behave irrationally under stress, but rather that the person will conform to usual patterns of behavior and thinking but in more extreme form.

In one of Van Denburg and Kiesler's (1993) studies, they gathered a group of 30 college women who exhibited the same interpersonal style: friendliness and submissiveness. The question they asked was whether these women would increase their use of this style of relating or switch to another style when under stress.

The stressful situation was an interesting one, and, by random assignment, half of the 30 women were subjected to it. Following 10 minutes of a nonstressful interview with a female experimenter, they were faced with a series of unexpected and rather penetrating questions, such as, "What things do you dislike about your mother?" and "What things in your past are you ashamed of or feel guilty about?" Those in the low-stress condition were just asked a series of innocuous questions such as, "What are your favorite movies?"

Van Denburg and Kiesler (1993) increased uncertainty in the high-stress group in another way, as well. The interviewer behaved in a way that was "anticomplementary" to the participant's manner. What this means in this case is that the interviewer behaved in a style that rejects the preferred interpersonal style of the person. Instead of being friendly, the interviewer became hostile, and instead of showing dominance (which would complement a submissive style), the interviewer was submissive. In sum, the interviewer appeared to be aloof, self-doubting, inhibited, and detached, as well as hostile. The complementary style was used in the low-stress condition. It was friendly-dominant, which translates into sociable, warm, friendly, and outgoing. The authors made sure that the interviewers behaved as intended by providing them with considerable training before-hand and also by tape-recording their interactions and rating them on those dimensions.

How did the women react to the stress condition? To determine this, all the interviews were videotaped and rated for interpersonal style by five highly trained raters using an elaborate but well-established coding scheme. At issue was whether the women who started out as friendly-submissive became more or less friendly and submissive and whether they became more or less rigid in their styles, demonstrated by showing fewer (or more) interpersonal behaviors that did not fit their initial styles. One might expect, for example, that when faced with hostility, the women would begin to react with hostility as well, which would be contrary to the authors' "same but more extreme" hypothesis.

Consistent with Van Denburg and Kiesler's (1993) predictions, the women in the high-stress condition reacted with more extreme friendly-submissive behavior. And they appeared more rigid in their responses by being less sociable, dominant, and assured. They also showed more, rather than less, distrust. This reaction adds another disturbing element to what happens during stressful times in community life. What the study suggests is that stress is not a catalyst for new behavior but rather provokes more extreme forms of the community's typical behavior. Increases in stress in a community may tend to narrow the people's choices of ways to behave toward one another. Those who tend to express aggression and hostility during the best of times will be prompted to explode with violence when provoked during a stressful time. If mistrust is added to the equation, along with a relative lack of good will that might have been engendered by past positive social engagements, is there any reason not to expect social unrest?

Six months after the catastrophe in Littleton, there were some rays of hope, but also some distressing signs of continued struggle. Two reports stand out. In October of that year, Carla June Hochhalter, the mother of one of the shooting victims at Littleton, walked into a pawnshop and asked to see a revolver. Her daughter had survived the shooting but was paralyzed from the waist down as a result. Dad and daughter were out raising money, asking for donations for the child's rehabilitation. Indeed, the first signs of movement in the girl's legs since the shootings had appeared just a week or so before. At the pawnshop, Mrs. Hochhalter pointed to a .38-caliber revolver behind the glass counter and asked the shopkeeper to get it out for her. As he did, she slipped two bullets from her purse into the gun left out on the counter, fired one into the wall as a test, and the second into her own head. She died instantly. As one of her friends remarked, "Six months of being heartbroken just got to her" (Janofsky, 1999).

Why did the mother do this? Why did she not interpret the small but meaningful improvements in her daughter's life as cause for rejoicing, as some would? How could she allow herself to inflict more pain and suffering on her family by committing suicide? We do not know the reasons for her self-destructive behavior, but one observation is warranted. Without the stresses that arose out of those shootings 6 months before, she would not have gone to such extremes of despair.

On October 30th, 1999, the *New York Times Magazine* carried another story (Belkin, 1999). This one began with a front-page cover picture of the mother and father of Isaiah, the only black victim of the shooting at Columbine High School in Littleton. Their faces showed anger mixed with profound sorrow. The caption on the cover repeated something they said: "They ask us if we blame the parents? Who else do we blame?" They are suing the parents of the teenager shooters for the loss of their son's life. The parents of one of the shooters is also filing suit. They are suing local law enforcement officials for not informing them of rumors heard around the school that their children were bent on attacking their classmates. What kind of relief from their suffering will these lawsuits bring? What are the chances for building a greater sense of community around a bonfire of retribution? Very little chance, I am afraid. But what alternatives are open to a parent to resolve the sorrow and the anger that come from the death of a child? Does a two-dimensional model of emotions provide any insight into the nature of recovery?

Our understanding of the complexities of emotional experiences teaches us that there are no simple answers. Yet during highly stressful times, we gravitate toward simplicity in our emotional responses. The contractions that emotions undergo under conditions of uncertainty create one of the greatest challenges we face in recovery from traumas: how to retain the ability to see events in all their complexity. As stress narrows our field of vision, precluding the possibility of positive emotion, recovery may require finding some positive emotional consequence that lies outside the domains of sorrow and anger that we feel. Only by finding a source of light outside the darkness will we be able to repair our consciousness.

There is no single prescription for breaking free of a blind passion for retribution, but the following illustration does offer some provocative ideas. This quotation comes from the father of a boy who was beaten and left to die on a wooden fence outside of Laramie, Wyoming, because he was a homosexual. The crime was a hideous one, and the convicted killers were facing a death sentence when the jury convened to hear testimony concerning the sentence to give to those convicted. The victim's father spoke at the hearing, and here is an excerpt of what he said to his son's murderers:

> I would like nothing better than to see you die. . . . However, this is a time to begin the healing process, to show mercy, to use this as the first step in my own closure about losing Matt. I'm going to grant you life, as hard as it is for me to do so, because of Matthew. . . . You robbed me of something very precious and I will never forgive you for that. I give you life in the memory of one who no longer lives. May you have a long life and thank Matthew every day for it.[10]

These responses are more complex than those of retribution, and they offer resolutions that serve not only the individual but the good of the community as well. Indeed, the act of forgiveness appeals to us as a means of healing that extends far beyond the individual case. To live compassionately, however, we need to move away from the purely agentic forms of relating with others that are promoted so heavily in our culture and allow ourselves to also embrace communal concerns. In advising how to dissolve feelings of aggression and fear, Pema Chödrön (2000) puts it best: "The basic idea of generosity is to train in thinking bigger, to do ourselves the world's biggest favor and stop cultivating our own scheme" (p. 101).[11] By looking beyond ourselves, we can more readily find a way to broaden our emotional experiences during stressful times and see life's events as they are, rather than as we wish them to be.

We may need to look no further for a model to guide us than Nelson Mandela, the first black leader to be elected president of a nation in a multiracial election. Mandela served 20 years in prison for his efforts to free South Africa from the racial bigotry wrought by apartheid. Yet during his inauguration, he had the band play the national anthems of both the black and the former all-white apartheid government. Unity, reconciliation, and an end to vengeance have been the themes of his governance.

Indeed, he personifies this approach to the resolution of conflict and the end of violence. His truth commission sought out all those who committed crimes against humanity during the reign of apartheid and struck the following deal with those who testified: Tell the truth about what you did, and we shall forgive, and spare the harshest punishments. This approach embraces both the pain of knowledge of the atrocities and also the best of human emotions: understanding and absolution. It is a sense of community that does not hide from both sides of the human condition. There may be no better model for human and community consciousness for the next millennium.

16   Some Conclusions

Behold'st thou not two shapes from the east and west
Come, as two doves to one beloved nest . . . ?
And, hark! their sweet sad voices! 't is despair
Mingled with love and then dissolved in sound.
　　　　—Percy B. Shelley, *Prometheus Unbound*

A group of behavioral scientists within the American Psychological Association have been advocating for a new "positive psychology." At the start of the twenty-first century, a special issue of the *American Psychologist* (see Seligman & Csikszentmihalyi, 2000) has been devoted to this topic, a voluminous *Handbook of Positive Psychology* (Snyder & Lopez, 2001) has been published, and fairly large cash prizes, previously unheard of in our profession, have been given out to a number of researchers for advancing this field of inquiry. Is this advocacy of the positive just more ballyhoo? Are we recycling threadbare slogans from Norman Vincent Peale, or does our discipline have something new to offer?

I confess that my initial reaction to this new psychology was not enthusiastic. I behaved like Bartleby in Melville's tale. Looking up from my computer monitor, I considered joining in, but muttered to myself, "No, I'd rather not," and went back to scrivening. Some of my colleagues, and even some of you, may be similarly underwhelmed by the prospects of this new approach: "Chasing rainbows," one of my professors once called it. After all, many great writers have been scornful of positive emotions. To hear George Bernard Shaw tell it, "A lifetime of happiness! No man alive could bear it: it would be hell on earth." Or as Goethe proclaimed, "Nothing could be more miserable than a succession of sunny days!"

Perhaps living in Arizona, with its more than 300 sunny days a year, has me hoodwinked, but I think there is good reason to search for value in that which feels good. Although we often are reluctant to admit it, our positive emotions, along with the interests, plans, hopes, and desires that lead us to those states, help define who we are. They are worthy of study in their own right for their contribution to our health and well-being. Two of the nation's scientific panels, commissioned by the National Academy of Sciences, agree. The Institute of Medicine's report (Brandt & Pope, 1997) contains forceful appeals to behavioral scientists to devote more attention to positive emotional health. In another monograph (Singer & Ryff, 2001), the National Research Council urges biological and social scientists to work together to develop new models of positive health.

In preparing this book, I have uncovered much compelling evidence to support this rising tide of enthusiasm for the study of positive emotions. Whether it be in our attempts to understand others or just in living our own lives, the take-home message is clear and irrefutable: Stay alert to moments of joy, as well as periods of distress. Hear both the sweet and the sad voices that surround us.

Two basic ideas about emotions underlie this message. First, human emotional experiences do not fall onto a single continuum from bad to good, happy to sad, or delighted to terrible. At least two dimensions are needed to fully classify human emotions, one that gauges the nature and extent of negative affects and accompanying motivations of defense and another that gauges the extent of positive emotion and the accompanying motivations to create and extend. Both the East Coast theories of vulnerability and West Coast theories of psychological growth hold truths for us that we cannot ignore.

These two dimensions of emotional experience operate independently of one another much of the time. The full implications of this point are not always self-evident. In the previous few chapters I have described how a two-dimensional model may help us understand human behavior better across a wide variety of human endeavors, including work, marriage, aging, and community. For instance, having two emotion systems explains why people may continue to work even when they are mistreated on the job, stay married even with considerable discord, and age gracefully even while suffering from chronic and painful illness.

This bi-dimensional view also helps us understand some of the difficulties behavioral scientists have encountered in classifying and treating people with emotional difficulties. By examining the emotional dynamics that underlie three of the most common psychiatric disorders, depression, anxiety, and substance abuse, I have tried to show the clinical utility of adopting a two-factor view of emotional adaptation. Depression, for example, is a label used to characterize two different disorders of mood: the presence of unrelenting and intense negative affects and the absence of positive affects. To best understand and treat this disorder, we need to know which emotion systems are disturbed. As for substance abuse, we may understand the nature of drug dependence better by considering how the emotional dynamics that are stimulated by ingesting drugs change over time, particularly regarding the behavioral shift from finding comfort and pleasure to avoiding the pain of withdrawal.

Despite the benefits we gain from awareness of dual systems of emotion, several factors conspire to encourage one-dimensional thinking. Cultural mores often press us to adopt simplifications of our emotional experiences. For example, with incantations such as "Embrace the pain," some popular self-help writings urge us to use joy to extinguish suffering. Such declarations are part of a well-established tradition within American culture that emphasizes action-oriented styles of coping with adversity. A more brutal example of treating separate affective systems as if they were interchangeable is the cry, "In revenge, there is life!" This deplorable exhortation was recorded from the shouts of an Afghan crowd watching a public execution at a soccer stadium during the reign of the Taliban in Afghanistan. This invitation to cultivate violent acts of retribution as a way of feeling alive constitutes an emotional meltdown. The one-dimensional thinking fostered by such sloganeering is harmful to individuals, families, and even whole nations.

When calling on one set of emotional forces to resolve another, we infect the dynamics of the pursuit of the positive with the dynamics of defense against the negative. This co-mingling of affective purposes provides a quick fix when applied to problems that have simple solutions. But when attempting to resolve recurring troubles, shifting attention away from our suffering by focusing on the positive only creates new difficulties. Consider the people who count their blessings instead of taking action to end an abusive relationship. We need not ask twice, "Where have all the flowers gone?" in those lives.

We often forge links between positive and negative emotional forces in our attempts to integrate the divergent feelings we observe within the same person. Here is a real-life example. During the dress rehearsal for his high school play, my oldest son asked his 6-year-old brother to join him on stage by taking a walk-on part as the child of one of the characters. At first the younger brother agreed, but on the drive up to his first (and last) rehearsal, he backed down. With no peers his age in the production, he felt alone and afraid. He was not going up on stage, no matter what. As we sat in the wings watching the other actors rehearse, he reiterated his position: "I'm not going out there, Dad. No way. Never."

Somehow his brother convinced him to visit backstage during a break in rehearsal. He peeked around the curtains at the then empty seats in the theater. His brother walked him to the place he would stand on stage. His "mother" in the play took his hand and said hello. Then they rehearsed his part with the whole ensemble, he walked on, and they cheered him afterward, even called him a star. Now beaming with delight, he could not wait to get back on stage the next day to face a full house.

When I came home to report what had happened that night, I exclaimed with pleasure, "Freud was right all along! We fear most that which we most secretly desire." I put together his excitement and his fear, inferring that both arose from a single source. It sounded good as a depth interpretation that could unify my son's motives. But in truth, he responded with two separate emotions: first stage fright and then delight. Each competed for his attention and governed his choices. When we merge emotional domains the way I did, we unify disparate elements and reach what we believe to be a greater truth. In doing so we simplify complex situations and ignore the many competing emotional responses contained therein.

Another point I have emphasized throughout this book is that our awareness of these emotional complexities varies as a function of stress. In times of uncertainty, when the outcomes at stake are important to us, our focus narrows, and the two-dimensional space that we use to map our emotions begins to fold onto itself, compressing negative and positive emotions into a single bipolar dimension. Indeed, when conditions call for decisive action, it is most adaptive to speak with one voice. In chapter 4, I called these moments "turning points." They give direction to our lives and new meaning to our relationships.

The temporary fusion of emotional states can be highly adaptive, both in fostering a sense of personal efficacy that we carry with us long after the crisis is over and in improving close relationships. But we need to be careful not to view our everyday lives as an ever-unfolding drama of good versus evil or negative versus positive emotions. Doing so leads us to miss the complexities and underestimate the richness of our lives and the lives of the people closest to us.

We also do not make our emotional lives less painful by simply accentuating the positive. As I explained in chapter 5, a careful review of the empirical evidence reveals that finding positive meaning in adversity does little to reduce psychological distress. However, when we allow ourselves to see positive outcomes alongside the negative, we imbue our life experiences with images of personal accomplishment and social connection. The surprising point is that this more balanced view of life's difficulties appears to have benefits for physical health, even when there is no improvement in the standard indices of mental health. In chapter 6, I cited findings from study after study that uncovered significant gains in health and recovery from illness for those people who are able to sustain positive affective engagements in life.

Resiliency in Two Dimensions as a Model of Health

Most mind-body theories link mental with physical health through mechanisms associated with psychological upset. Psychosocial research on cardiovascular illness, for example, has focused on hostility. Anxiety is studied because of its contribution to asthma, and depression is seen as a risk factor in disease progression for a number of illnesses. Solutions are offered that attempt to tame the anger, calm anxiety, and lift the dark moods that characterize depression. Path diagrams that model how these psychological forces affect physiological processes introduce stressors as the catalysts that provoke the upset and active coping responses as the keys to successful adaptation. These are useful models, to be sure, but they do not extend beyond a single dimension of adjustment. We need more than a coping theory to fully appreciate the dynamics of human striving that make us resilient. We do not live by bread alone.

This book begins the work of developing a model of resilience in two dimensions. At the core of this model of resilience is emotional awareness, the capacity for seeing the complexity of emotions and motivations that underlie many situations. Our success in managing our emotional lives depends on our willingness to look at the apparent contradictions within our own feelings and the feelings of others. Of course, awareness is not enough. As I suggest in chapter 7 in regard to emotional intelligences, we need to be able to regulate our actions and reactions in ways that protect and defend ourselves from harm and also to work to sustain and extend our chances for fulfillment. Some of us succeed perfectly well in managing our distress but forsake our hopes and dreams. We look mentally healthy, but our ship remains in the harbor. Some of us suffer daily from being unable to defend ourselves from life's sorrows but find happiness nonetheless. Failure in one emotional realm does not keep us from success in the other. And it is possible to show intelligence in both worlds.

The key to resilience is keeping these two emotional realms separate and affording each sufficient attention. There may even be an optimal ratio in the allocation of psychological resources to each agenda. Perhaps a 5:1 rule of thumb would do. Optimally, we might attend to our positive emotions on average 5 times as much as we attend to our negative emotions.

A principle like this may not be difficult to follow when each day predictably follows the next. But life is not so predictable. Stressful events, both large and small, inevitably disturb our equilibrium, posing both threats to current adjustment and opportunities for personal growth. As I showed in chapter 3, the uncertainty that underlies these upending experiences provokes physiological changes that can threaten physical health, as well as psychological adjustment. Indeed, a thorough understanding of the body's response to stress is needed to build a sturdy bridge between physical and emotional health.

In storybooks, resilient people may appear to walk on water, but in truth, their reactions to threat and uncertainty are not so different from those of non-resilient people, at least initially. The key difference between these two groups is in the duration of their responses to stress. Resilience is the capacity to bounce back, to carry on in the face of tremendous difficulties, and to recover one's balance quickly after losing it. This capacity may be measured physiologically, not by the lack of a blood pressure change under stress but by how quickly a person's blood pressure returns to normal afterward. It is also revealed by psychological indicators, such as stability in self-esteem, and rapid recovery of positive affect following a failure experience, even when negative affect remains elevated significantly.

According to the model of stress and health I have presented, what distinguishes resilient people is their ability to retain perspective during stressful events. Resiliency does not provide immunity from the constraints that stress imposes on our openness to experience, but it does allow the person to make a more rapid recovery of emotional depth. To be resilient is to show flexibility in our cognitive maps of emotions and mindfulness when taking action in response to our feelings. Our dynamic two-dimensional model of emotions uses these building blocks to guide the construction of a new understanding of resilience.

Resilient qualities do not emerge without the scaffolding of support. Emotional development is social, and, as I discussed in chapter 11, abusive relationships can do great harm to the capacity for emotional awareness. One of the surest ways to begin to enhance positive mood is to take some action that leads to feelings of personal mastery, but without a reinforcing social environment, we would not feel self-reliant for long. In chapter 15, I elaborated on the importance of communal forms of participation as a counterweight to our rush for personal fulfillment.

We are born connected. Indeed, the strongest emotions we feel arise from our interactions with others. Positive emotions that derive from close relationships have health benefits that we have only begun to appreciate. Physiological markers such as oxytocin and vasopressin begin to identify the mechanisms of action through which positive states influence health. But we still are only scratching the surface. Underneath lies a cascade of neurohormonal processes that need to be examined for their role in sustaining both psychological and physical well-being.

On the other side of the ledger are the costs of social alienation. The dangers that arise from acts of violence fueled by anger and envy are increasingly apparent in our communities. Stressful events often function as triggers that ignite aggression among those who feel mistreated. The physiological components of the stress response have been studied more thoroughly than their counterparts for positive emotion. Still, there is much that is not known, particularly how certain emotional responses lead to a rapid recovery, whereas others provoke prolonged and recurrent stress reactivity that is harmful to health and social relations. Resilience in the face of aggression is apparent in the person who searches for an adaptive response that extends beyond the simplifying emotions of vengefulness and bitterness. A dynamic two-dimensional framework provides a way of understanding how emotional complexity can collapse and spark violence and how people can regain perspective without resorting to strategies of retribution that add fuel to the flames.

Further work is needed to develop these ideas and to build new methods to identify complex patterns of emotional response. More contributions are needed from neuroscientists, as well. We have still not mapped our neural circuitry in sufficient detail to visualize how the brain cordons off positive emotional responses from negative emotions. We need to do more careful work on neural imaging of emotions to capture the distinctive patterns of each emotion. We also need to examine the mechanisms at work during stress that lead to the breakdown of the boundaries that separate different classes of emotional response.

We must stay attuned to the influence of social context when studying the role of emotions in health. No map of the brain's responses can replace careful analysis of social-cultural influences on emotions (Nussbaum, 2001). The emotions we experience and express are shaped by neurolinguistic programs that owe as much to our social interactions as to our neurophysiology. Even the relative value placed on emotional complexity versus single-mindedness is informed by social and cultural mores.

The recent discovery that positive emotions can play a role in healing has led to innovations in treatment and prevention and to rumblings of a paradigm shift in our thinking about how to improve the mind's work within the body. I have highlighted some of these new approaches in each of the chapters that address a social problem. Among the most promising are those interventions that urge us to look beyond fight-or-flight for a second, often hidden, positive dimension within all experience. Mindfulness meditation provides one method that enlarges this kind of awareness. It promotes daily practice of openness to how the mind responds to both external events and internal states. The practice encourages the development of an unhurried kindness toward our own emotional struggles and the struggles of the people around us.

Whether used to ease chronic pain or other long-term emotional difficulties, methods that encourage openness offer a means to enhance awareness of all feelings. In managing chronic pain, learning to be mindful can reduce anticipatory anxiety and open the person's experience to other feelings besides those involved in the struggles with pain. For substance abusers, increasing awareness of the actual emotional highs and lows experienced when taking a controlled substance may be particularly beneficial. This awareness may reveal central disturbances in the underlying motivations that result from ingesting substances that boost positive mood dramatically and artificially. These principles extend to interventions with those in close relationships, as well. A central problem that successful interpersonal interventions address is the hardening of the mind to the potential for shared positive experiences with those who have disappointed us. Acceptance is a central theme in the repair of intimate relations and forgiveness is a prerequisite for the restoration of community.

With compassion, these approaches coax us toward greater openness to both the negative and the positive features of life experience. Retelling one's story without holding back allows recovery of the full dimensions of emotional expression. The healing comes perhaps most swiftly when we release ourselves from the constraining backwaters of defense and allow ourselves to playfully embrace the positive that resides within us and throughout our social worlds.

Notes

Chapter 1

1. Although a number of emotion theorists may be identified with this position, the foremost among them are the late Silvan Tomkins (1984), who viewed emotions as amplifications of motivational states, and his frequent collaborator, Carroll Izard (1977).

2. Their model is known as the James-Lange theory of emotion, and it may be undergoing somewhat of a revival of late. See Lange and James (1922/1967).

3. The Cannon-Bard model (Cannon, 1927) introduces the role of brain structures such as the thalamus in the experience of emotions. Some success in identifying specific autonomic nervous system signatures for specific emotions has been reported. For one recent review, see Cacioppo and colleagues (2000).

4. In chapter 8 of this book, I review this classic experiment and offer another interpretation of their findings based on a dynamic model of emotion. For a critique of their experiments and the cognitive approach to emotions in general, see Griffiths (1997).

5. By "appraisal," Lazarus (1982,1984) refers to a number of processes by which the person judges the meaning of events. This judgment is critical to the experience of emotions in his model. Although Lazarus's models are the best known, Magda Arnold (1960a) also developed cognitive approaches to understanding emotion that focused on appraisal processes, along with perceptual processes, in the shaping of an emotional response.

6. In addition to demonstrating that emotions may influence behavior without our awareness, Zajonc has also pursued his own theories of emotion, often referred to as a theory of facial efference. In this model, emotions arise in part from the physiological consequences of various facial expressions. He has dem-

onstrated, for instance, that blood flow, and with it, the temperatures of brain structures responsible for regulating emotional behavior, are modified by smiles and also by frowns.

7. Some current cognitive theories of emotion distinguish between *emotion* and *affect* and, by doing so, argue persuasively that appraisal is involved in all emotional states. Gerald Clore and Andrew Ortony (2000) suggest that emotion, unlike affect, is always directed at someone or something. In linking affect to object, we evaluate the situation in light of our personal goals, standards, and attitudes.

8. In my first research project in graduate school, I studied the degree to which vocal expressions of emotion could be understood by people from different cultures. In that study we had college students express emotions using words such as "Hello" and varying the length of the expression, as well as the underlying emotion expressed. We made audiotapes of these emotional expressions and sent them to members of the faculty at two universities abroad: one in Japan and another in Poland. These professors agreed to play the tapes to their classes and ask students to guess the emotion displayed in each utterance. We then compared how accurate the students from Poland and Japan were compared with college students in the United States. It turned out that students at those universities decoded the basic emotions of anger, fear, sadness, and joy with about the same degree of accuracy as students in the United States, if the phrase was long enough. More complex expressions such as guilt and flirtation do not show universal rules of display; they are shaped by cultural rules to some extent. Although there was some agreement, there was also disagreement between cultures on the more complex emotions. But fear, joy, anger, and sadness all can be spoken without words through the language of sounds. See Beier and Zautra (1972) for further details.

9. There were 111 books on the right brain on January 29, 2000, when I searched Amazon.com's Internet bookstore. Robert Ornstein (1997) is one author most often cited in reference to right- versus left-brain thinking.

10. If you have seen Jeff Bridges in the movie *Fearless*, you would know how dangerous this state could be. In one scene in the movie, our fearless hero intentionally drives into a brick wall going about 60 miles an hour.

11. Richard Lane (2000) and his colleagues found that specific patterns of neural activity were associated with positive emotions and negative emotions through an examination of PET images from human participants who were induced to experience either a positive or a negative emotion while their brain's cortical activity was being mapped.

12. Damasio's (1994) book begins with an insightful discussion of what happens to those who lose emotional reasoning power even though they retain full intellectual capacities. Most recently, Damasio (1999) has examined the role of emotion in consciousness.

13. Ekman has added a valuable afterword on the twentieth-century debates concerning the universalities of emotional expression.

14. This particular kind of smile has been named the Duchenne smile, to honor the nineteenth-century French anatomist Duchenne de Boulogne, who discovered that the crinkling around the eyes, or crows' feet, occur only with authentic smiles.

15. Lazarus maintains that cognitive appraisals are a prerequisite for emotion, but he has broadened his conceptualization of these processes to allow for rapid, unconscious appraisals. These appraisals may then ignite emotional programs that are biologically determined, at least in part.

Chapter 2

1. Many researchers are involved in this pursuit. One of the leaders in this field has been Ed Diener. He and his colleagues Daniel Kahneman, and Norbert Schwarz (Kahneman, Diener, & Schwarz, 1999) have urged the development of a "hedonic psychology" dedicated to the empirical study of psychological well-being. Diener and his colleagues have also been instrumental in creating a new international research society dedicated to the study of quality of life.

2. James Russell (1980; Russell & Carroll, 1999a, 1999b; Russell & Feldman-Barrett, 1999) is the heir apparent of Osgood's approach.

3. I elaborate on Herzberg's work in a later chapter on the quality of work life.

4. Frederick and Loewenstein (1999) point out some of the strengths and weaknesses of adaptation-level models of hedonic states.

5. Herzberg (1966) actually proposed that different dynamics would apply to satisfying and dissatisfying experiences. He saw satisfying events as predominately those that promoted personal growth and development. Such events would build on one another rather than weakening each other's impact. He viewed dissatisfying work events as those involving environmental changes and saw them following dynamics similar to those of AL theory. Even positive environmental changes were seen as those that reduced sources of dissatisfaction, and those changes would establish higher expectations for similar improvements. This aspect of his model has never been adequately tested.

6. Westbrook has examined this question in other contexts as well.

7. These kinds of biases have provided the basis for challenges to a two-factor model of affects. Green, Goldman, and Salovey (1993) and Green, Salovey, and Truax (1999) have argued that shared-questionnaire methods promote positive correlations between items, which could lead to the empirical result of no correlation between items that are opposites. Thus, the Bradburn scale might yield no correlation between positive and negative facets, not because the affects are independent but because the inverse correlation between the affects is disguised by the "yes-saying" tendencies of participants in the study.

8. This work includes a confirmatory factor analysis of mood adjectives that revealed clear evidence for distinct emotions within the broad domains of positive and negative emotions. The authors saw those findings as evidence in support of biological theories of affect and as inconsistent with the view that emotions were social constructions.

9. It is interesting to see what happens in the analysis of emotions that arise from the absence of another emotion. Church et al. (1999) found a substantial number of affect adjectives that were worded as the negation of an emotion. When

they factor-analyzed ratings of emotional experience using these words, along with the other emotion adjectives gleaned from the Filipino language, these negation words formed a separate factor. On this factor loaded both the absence of positive and the absence of negative emotions.

10. The number of articles published on this topic in 1999 alone is astounding. On the circumplex side of the debate are Feldman-Barrett and Russell (1999), Green and Salovey (1999), and Russell and Carroll (1999a, b). Watson and Tellegen (1999) and Tellegen, Watson, and Clark (1999a, b) present the bidimensional view. Also, a special section of an issue of the *Journal of Personality and Social Psychology* is devoted to the controversy. Diener (1999) introduces the various arguments in that issue.

11. There are two notable exceptions that are very different states of mind: religious reverie and sexual ecstasy.

12. Panksepp provides a richly textured account of the neurochemistry of emotions and the evidence for a "seeking system" emanating out of the lateral hypothalamus. This system is a fundamental part of much of our human strivings, our frustrations, and even our despair over failure, according to Panksepp.

13. Actually, the right anterior medial thalamus, bilateral pallidum, and bilateral subgenual cingulate were involved in winning during winning streaks. Bilateral activity in the hippocampus characterized losing during losing streaks.

14. Research on psychological well-being has been uneven in studying positive versus negative affective health. Highly sophisticated models exist for the assessment of negative states, including the designation of levels and types of psychopathology, but nothing comparable exists for the assessment of positive states. More to the point is the frequent failure of investigators to assess positive affective states in addition to negative affective states when studying outcomes of treatments. It is not surprising, therefore, to see studies continue to show up in the literature that claim no beneficial effects of positive life experiences on the person's adjustment. Inspection of the study measures typically shows either that only negative affective outcomes were assessed or that the participants were not assessed during times at which, and in situations in which, positive states were relevant.

15. Carver and Scheier (1998) examine how optimistic beliefs can shape our futures. The scale they developed is fast becoming one of the most popular scales with which to study expectancies for health, as well as mental health outcomes. The authors have maintained that the underlying structure of their scale is bipolar, and they see optimism as the polar opposite of pessimism.

16. The level of correlation between optimism and pessimism varies considerably, depending on which questions are used to assess optimism and pessimism and, as is noted later, who is doing the ratings.

Chapter 3

1. A renowned researcher, Sheldon Cohen developed one of the best-known scales of this type about 25 years ago as a quick way to measure stress in health-related research. He is now researching better ways to define and measure stress.

2. Dohrenwend, Raphale, Stueve, and Skodol (1993) provide a cogent argument against exclusive reliance on subjective ratings in the measurement of stress.

3. Apart from thumbing through issues of *Psychosomatic Medicine* and the *Journal of Psychosomatic Research*, the interested reader can find a particularly useful description of this model in Creed (1993). Additionally, Laborit (1993) discusses the physiological consequences of behavioral inhibition.

4 This troubling paradox characterizes many studies of psychological distress and health.

5. This point of view may be found in many scholoarly treatments of the stress concept including Cohen, Kessler, and Gordon's (1995) *Measuring Stress*, Sanford and Salmons's (1993) *Stress: From Synapse to Syndrome*, and Goldberger and Breznitz's (1993) *Handbook of Stress: Theoretical and Clinical Aspects*. These edited texts are not the only useful treatments of the subject, but they are representative of the best comprehensive reviews of the subject.

6. The role of unexpected events in our lives has been extended to the study of what have been referred to as "off-time" events: those experiences that were not supposed to happen when they did in the course of a person's life. Death of a spouse early in marriage or the death of a child at any time in a person's life may be thought of as especially stressful because they are not expected to occur. Our spouses may die, but not until after the children are raised; and our children are supposed to be at our gravesites, not we at theirs. Lowenthal and Chiriboga (1973) have written about the impact of such unexpected events. Goodhart and Zautra (1984) developed this line of reasoning as a means of characterizing the levels of stress in communities.

7. Our work on assessment of everyday life events has appeared in a series of papers beginning with studies of college students (Zautra, Guarnaccia, & Dohrenwend (1986; Reich & Zautra, 1988), and then extending that work to the examination of the everyday life of older adults (Zautra, 1996; Zuatra, Guarnaccia, Reich, & Dohrenwend, 1988; Zautra, Guarnaccia, & Reich, 1989; Zautra, Reich, & Guarnaccia, 1990; Zautra, Finch, Reich, & Guarnaccia, 1991; Zautra, Schultz, & Reich, 2000). We have also applied these methods to chronically ill patients with fibromyalgia, rheumatoid arthritis, and osteoarthritis to examine the role of stress in flare-ups of chronic pain (Davis, Zautra, & Reich, 2001; Potter & Zautra, 1997; Zautra, Burelson, Matt, Roth, & Burrows, 1994; Zautra, Hamilton, Potter, & Smith, 1999; Zautra & Smith, 2001). Arthur Stone and John Neale's (1982) work provided us with a foundation from which to construct our measures.

8. There are many descriptions of these stress responses, and each new rendering adds additional physiological systems as part of the stress response as our knowledge advances on the many neuroendocrine interactions that shape and are shaped by stress. One of my favorite descriptions is that of Stratakis and Chrousos (1995). Another is that provided by John Cacioppo (1994) in his 1993 presidential address to the Society for Psychophysiological Research.

9. Bruce McEwen is one of those renaissance scholars who understands stress and stress responses not only at the level of molecules but also at the level of the mind and society.

10. Ron Glaser, Janice Kiecolt-Glaser, Phil Marucha, Robert MacCullum, By-

ron Laskowski, and William Malarkey (1999) used suction to create blisters on the fore arms of postmenopausal women. Phil Marucha, Janice Kiecolt-Glaser, and M. Favagehi (1998) studied the effects of examination stress on wounds to the harm palate of dental students. Janice Kiecolt-Glaser, Phil Marucha, and Ron Glaser (1995) conducted the study on fore arm wound healing among caregivers of Alzheimer's patients.

11. A key psychological component to the stress response is the degree of helplessness the person feels in response to stressful events. Martin Seligman (1975) and his colleagues developed a theory of learned helplessness to explain the development of maladaptive responses to stress. In his early formulations of this model, repeated exposure to unpredictable and uncontrollable stressors were thought to lead to individuals' learning that there was no effective response to the stressor. They would give up trying and show signs of chronic distress, including depression. The model held well for lower mammals, but not all humans in helpless situations lost motivation and became depressed. How the person understood the reasons for his or her helplessness appears to make all the difference (see Abramson, Seligman, & Teasdale, 1978). If the person sees that everyone can have similar problems and that any personal failure is limited only to this specific situation, the stressor has little adverse effect. On the other hand, if the person focuses on his or her own failure as a chronic problem that happens not just in one but across a wide range of situations, then motivation, affect, and cognitive abilities are all depressed. Seligman (1975) provides one classic description of his model, and Lyn Abramson, Gerald Metalsky, and Lauren Alloy (1989) provide a revised model that they refer to as a "hopelessness theory of depression." In a later chapter I further discuss the learned-helplessness model and its contributions to understanding psychiatric conditions such as depression.

12. I review the evidence on this point in chapter 5.

13. In this paper my colleagues Virgil Sheets, Irwin Sandler, and I argued this point, examining the role of coping in reducing distress among mothers coping with divorce. In that study, higher distress predicted greater use of avoidant coping 4 months later, but more avoidant coping did not predict more distress over time.

14. Mardi Horowitz (Horowitz et al., 1993) has developed his theory of stress response syndromes from both clinical observations and experimental studies of stress reactivity. He and his colleagues have devised a scale to measure two chief components of this syndrome: intrusive and avoidant thoughts. Those with post-traumatic stress disorder show substantially higher scores on his scale than those without that condition.

Chapter 4

1. A narrowing of vision may be taken quite literally. Jean Williams, Phyllis Tonymon, and Mark Anderson (1990) teamed up to examine why athletes are at greater risk for physical injury during stressful periods in their lives. They hypothesized that under stress, athletes would have a narrower field of vision, making

them less aware of potential harms at the periphery, such as a 250-pound line-backer rushing running toward them at breakneck speed. They had student athletes engage in a stressful task called the Stroop Color Word Test, with pre- and post-assessments of field of vision. After exposure to the laboratory stressor, the participants were much less aware of events occurring at the periphery of their field of vision. The experimenters also administered a standard life stress inventory to these athletes. Those reporting many recent life stressors had the most dramatic narrowing of their vision.

2. Paulhus and Lim (1994) refer to their approach as a dynamic complexity model of social judgments.

3. One of the complexities in studies such as this is that the measure used to detect shrinkage in affective space is a change in the level of correlation between positive and negative emotions. Although conceptually this makes perfect sense, the measure of correlation is not always reliable. The size of a correlation can be affected by a number of things, including the range and shape of the distribution of scores on the various measures and similarities in the wording of items from different scales. To rule out these kinds of confounds in this study, we used a hierarchical linear modeling approach to data analysis.

4. The measure used here was the *Profile of Mood States*, or POMS, which was developed by McNair, Lorr, and Droppleman (1971). The measure is designed to assess current mood across a number of dimensions. In order to confirm that there were separate positive and negative dimensions within the POMS, we conducted factor analyses of the ratings both at baseline and at the high-stress week. Both of those analyses revealed two factors, with positive mood items loading on one factor and negative mood items loading on the other.

5. There are a number of studies that support our hypothesis, even though the authors of those studies did not report their data with our model in mind. This type of evidence is often tucked away within the correlation tables. One such study comes research on caregiving partners of HIV-positive men (Folkman, 1997). The investigation called for periodic interviews over 2 years. During the course of Folkman's study, a number of people who were HIV-positive died. When Folkman examined the caregiver's emotional states, she found little evidence that positive affect levels dropped as their partners became increasingly ill, although there was clear evidence that these caregivers were beset by many emotional trials that heightened their anxiety and depression. Further, Folkman found that the correlation between her indices of positive and negative affect, although inverse, was of only modest size. But one period of time showed a different pattern. The exception was during the 6 months surrounding the partner's death. During the month just prior to bereavement and up to 5 months thereafter, positive affect dropped significantly, whereas negative affect increased significantly, revealing a strong inverse relationship.

6. Rod Martin (2001) reviews this literature with a critical eye, urging more rigorous research on the health benefits of humor. Robert Provine (2001) examines naturally occurring episodes of laughter from several angles, including social context and the evolutionary significance of comedy.

7. Derks, Gillikin, Bartolome-Rull, and Bogart (1997) have identified actual changes in electrical activity in the brain when a person recognizes this incongruity within humor.

8. Berk et al. (1989) provide some support for the Balinese point of view. They found that laughter appears to have effects on the neuroendocrine system that are the reverse of most of the effects of stress. Men who watched a 60-minute humorous video showed reductions in cortisol and epinephrine and higher levels of growth hormone than controls who did not watch the film.

9. Another analysis of data from the same study is reported by Keltner and Bonanno (1997). In that study the authors looked carefully at the kind of positive emotions that appeared to be the most powerful means of undoing negative emotions during grief work. The full-bodied laugh won out over the more cautious smile of contentment.

Chapter 5

1. Potter and Zautra (1997) show that although the major calamities this woman suffered were associated with a reduction in her illness, the everyday stresses and strains that she reported throughout the year were associated with more rather than less pain from her arthritis.

2. Guarnaccia (1990) examined the evidence for this theory through a longitudinal study of older adults who had recently lost a spouse. In the monthly interviews, he recorded other losses due to death of close friends or family members for those whose spouses had died. He then compared their adjustment following the new loss with that of a matched control group who had not lost their spouses. Although he did not find incontrovertible evidence of an inoculation effect, he did detect one important difference. Those elders who had lost spouses reported fewer negative changes as a consequence of the new loss than the comparison group who had not lost spouses.

3. Investigators interested in the health consequences of bereavement have studied this question from a number of angles. Reviews of the relationship between bereavement and immune function (Herbert & Cohen, 1993; Stein, Miller, & Trestman, 1991) suggest that a decrease in certain immune parameters often accompany death in the family. Other researchers have demonstrated that the risk of death increases markedly during the first 6 months after the spouse has died.

4. The term *learned resourcefulness* is a more recent construction, usually associated with the research and theoretical contributions of Charles Peterson, Steven Maier, and Marty Seligman (1993). Michael Rosenbaum (1983) was the first to broaden the idea from an earlier and more limited conception to include a behavioral repetoire of coping skills.

5. There was major motion picture titled *The Turning Point.* In it two women who were talented dancers review the course of their lives after one decided to give up her career for a family and the other forged ahead to fame. The story pivoted on the choices and regrets of both women as they meet and talk over their

successes and their failures in life. Sheehy (1976) reviews the life stories of a number of men and women faced with such turning points.

6. Barbara Dohrenwend (1978) may be credited with one of the clearest statements of this model to date as part of her work in defining the key factors in community studies of mental health. The crisis model itself has a long history in clinical psychology and in public health. Gerald Caplan (1964) was among the first and most influential proponents of this model of mental health.

7. Finkel (1975) and Finkel and Jacobsen (1977) analyzed data from children, adolescents, and young and middle-aged adults to determine how many people who experienced a traumatic sequence of events in their lives converted the experience into what he called a "stren": a stressful event that gives rise to feelings of strength, growth and/or new learning. In his work, he estimated that less than 10% of children but over 25% of adults reported making such transformations in the meaning of those traumatic experiences.

8. Christopher Davis, Susan Nolen-Hoeksema, and Judith Larson (1998) presented evidence to suggest that positive construals of meaning can reduce psychological distress among those who have experienced the death of a loved one. In their study of the same sample as Folkman et al.'s (1996), the mental health outcome was a composite of three measures, including depression, low positive affect, and symptoms of posttraumatic stress syndrome. It is difficult to distinguish whether they were observing an increase in positive emotions or a decrease in negative feelings among those finding some benefit from the experience.

9. Bruce Smith (2000) performed a meta-analysis on all published studies dealing with the question of whether those people who found benefits from their stressful experiences were better off. He studied several different outcomes, including psychological distress, psychological well-being, overall mental health, and physical health. He also examined a subset of studies that had longitudinal data. After pooling data from various studies of psychological distress, he found that the average effect size was a meager −062: This amounts to less than 1% of the variance in individual differences in distress that could be accounted for by whether the person found benefit from major stressors.

10. Smith (2000) calculated the effect size for four studies that examined a concurrent relationship between perceived benefits and well-being. The weighted mean effect was .275, which he showed was a stronger relationship than that between benefits and distress.

11. Craig Smith, Ken Wallston, Kathleen Dwyer, and Sharon Dowdy (1997), my colleagues, Virgil Sheets, Irwin Sandler, and I (1996), and Barbara Felton and Tracey Revenson (1984) found these relationships between active coping and mental health.

12. Robert White (1959) went against the prevailing models at the time concerning drive reduction and psychoanalytic principles. He saw these models as lacking an appreciation for the separable needs of the person to explore and master the environment, whether through direct action or through understanding.

13. Albert Bandura, one of the world's leading learning theorists, introduced the idea of self-efficacy when he found that beliefs in one's abilities to perform

stressful tasks were better predictors of future performance than one's past performance. Previously it had always been assumed that past behavior was the single best predictor of future behavior.

14. The best predictor of mental health for those who became disabled was a strong belief in one's abilities to cope successfully with life stresses assessed prior to disablement.

15. In one of the most comprehensive reviews to date, Carter (1998) discusses the role of the neuroendocrine system in attachment and love. She presents evidence from a number of studies that have demonstrated increases in social bonding during and just following stressful experiences. She attributes these effects in part to increased levels of oxytocin following HPA-axis activation, a hormone known to both facilitate social attachment and also to down-regulate cortisol secretions through inhibiting stress reactivity. Thus there appear to be neurological mechanisms that underlie stress-related coupling of negative affective experiences with the positive emotions generated through social bonding and attachment.

16. This speech was given on October 2, 2001, to the Labour Party's congress in Brighton, England.

Chapter 6

1. Japanese skier Yuichiro Miura was the adventurist who attempted this feat in the 1975 documentary. One of the single best accounts of the human drive to conquer Everest, in spite of the pain and agony associated with such a climb, is Jon Krakauer's (1997) account of a fated 1996 expedition to the summit. The book reveals the extraordinary degree of suffering and loss of life that can result from these human strivings.

2. Brown's book was meant as a then modern-day interpretation of Freud's work but mixed in was the sexual revolution of the 1960s and other apparent excesses in beliefs that the positive, in itself, was a source of goodness.

3. Herzberg (1966) argued that Judaic principles were founded on the fundamental question of how man (and woman) ought to live. He saw the human need to address this question of how to participate in life as creating the basis for the best of human motivation. I discuss Herzberg's contributions in more detail in chapter 13.

4. Csikszentmihalyi has published a number of scholarly works that attest to the human potential for creative thought and action. He has developed a concept of optimal functioning in everyday life, which he refers to as *flow* (Csikszentmihalyi & Larson, 1990). I discuss his contributions further in chapter 13.

5. Rod Dishman has done extensive work developing animal models of the effects of exercise on brain chemistry. His work included examination of the role of voluntary versus involuntary exercise in the production of norepinephrine (NE) in various brain regions. Higher cortical centers appear to be innervated by NE following voluntary exercise to a greater degree than involuntary exercise. Further, the depletion of NE following the stress of foot shock is abated. This finding may

have special significance for the physiological underpinnings of the development of learned helplessness and depression.

6. The Psychoneuroimmunology Research Society has a Web address (pnirs.org) and a healthy skepticism. During a visit to that society's annual meetings, I found the society members engaged in building new models of health that include attention to neuropeptides and hormonal interactions that extend well beyond cortisol to include oxytocin and vasopressin, to name a few.

7. A study by Lutgendorf, Vitaliano, Tripp-Reimer, Harvey, and Lubaroff (1999) found that the positive emotion, "vigor," taken from an established measure of mood profiles, was associated with higher natural killer (NK) cell activity among older adults. The study focused on the stress of an impending move on the immune system activity of older adults. Evidence from that study suggested that the move led to less joie de vivre, which in turn led to less NK cell activity. Of interest also was the contrast with negative mood. There was the lack of any significant effects of negative mood per se on immune function for this group.

8. Our own studies support this relationship between positive events and lower disease activity in patients with rheumatoid arthritis (see Zautra & Smith, 2001). We have found that on stressful weeks, patients reported greater pain unless they also experienced rewarding social interaction.

Chapter 7

1. Peter Salovey and John Mayer (1990) were among the first to develop this concept. Daniel Goleman (1995) put emotional intelligence on the map with his best-selling book on the topic. Goleman's success has led some of the top book publishers to be increasingly interested in the topic of emotions. Mayer and Salovey (1997) have recently revised their model and developed a performance test that measures four "branches" of emotional intelligence: perception, understanding emotions, managing emotions, and facilitating thought through emotion. The September 2001 issue of the journal *Emotion* provides research and commentary on this performance test and on the construct validity of emotional intelligence overall.

2. Ryff and Singer make the case that health is not simply the absence of illness and that psychological well-being extends beyond simply the capacity to cope with life's difficulties.

3. One representative study on the stability of affective states in adult life was conducted by Susan Turk-Charles (1998) and her colleagues. They interviewed men and women periodically beginning in 1970, asking them to report on their positive and negative emotions.

4. Watson, Clark, McIntyre, and Hamaker (1992) found a correlation of .56 between neuroticism and stable levels of negative affect. Still, much of one variable is not fully accounted for by the other.

5. The affective reaction does not necessarily include more autonomic reactivity to stressors for neurotics compared with nonneurotics. Rather, it appears to be at the level of interpretation of events that most of the troubles arise for this

group. David Schwebel and Jerry Suls (1999) conducted a careful study of cardio-vascular reactivity among neurotic and nonneurotic comparison groups. No differ-ences were observed in blood pressure between groups in either the laboratory stress protocol or the ambulatory assessment of blood pressure throughout a normal day.

6. In order to test the separate influences of resilience and vulnerability, Smith (2002) analyzed the effects of each cluster of dispositions on emotional health while holding constant the effects of the other cluster statistically.

7. Carver and White's scale is longer than this. I have listed here only the top three items loading on the two factors. The BAS scale actually consists of three subscales: Reward Responsiveness, Drive, and Fun Seeking. I have listed the top item in each of the three scales here.

8. It is interesting to speculate on the degree to which stress was manipulated in these studies. The game undoubtedly generated some uncertainty in the punish-ment condition. In the high-reward condition, it is less clear whether uncertainty was created, because participants were given the (false) impression that they were performing well.

9. The Gable et al. (2000) study also involves stressful circumstances, but the data were not analyzed in a way that would permit an examination of the rela-tionship between positive and negative affects during nonstressful and highly stress-ful days or whether that relationship varied as a function of behavioral inhibition or behavioral activation.

10. DeVellis et al. (1998) point out the differential effects of mood clarity, which supports the framework advocated here: that positive and negative emotions need to be considered separately.

11. Interested readers may wish to consult Showers and Kling (1996) on re-covery from sad mood.

12. See the January 2000 issue of *American Psychologist*, which is devoted to themes of "Happiness, excellence, and optimal human functioning."

Chapter 8

1. Forgas (1995) provides a through review of his own theoretical model, the affect infusion model, which differs from Bower's model in that it integrates a number of mechanisms thought to be responsible for the influence of affect on cognitive processes.

2. Richards and Gross (2000) did not interpret their results in exactly the same way that I have done here. They argued that suppression of negative emotions was more costly cognitively, leading to more errors in verbal recall than restruc-turing.

3. Ashby, Isen, and Turken (1999) present a neuropsychological model of how positive affect influences cognition. They discuss the role of dopamine as a principal chemical messenger responsible for the effects of positive affect on cognitive pro-cesses, including attention and working memory, as well as incentive motivation.

4. Melzack and Wall's model was the single most influential work on neural

mechanisms of pain modulation to date. Although the model has undergone many revisions since it was first introduced, the central features of the model continue to guide research in the area.

5. Ploghaus, Tracey, Gati, Clare, Menon, Matthews, and Rawlins (1999) report on a functional magnetic resonance imaging study of healthy participants. They found that anticipation of pain was associated with changes in neural activity in locations close to but not the same as those parts of the brain activated when the pain was applied.

6. We conducted a study to test whether the use of pain medications influenced these key psychological components (Zautra, Smith, & Reder, 2001). We randomly assigned a group of 109 osteoarthritis patients with moderate to severe pain to one of two conditions—a time-release morphine drug (CR oxycodone) or a placebo—and followed their adjustment for 90 days. Those on the pain medication reported significant gains in coping efficacy and reductions in helplessness and passive coping, along with reductions in pain, compared with the placebo control group.

7. Bandura has examined the role of agency, that is, beliefs in one's abilities, in the reduction in anxiety and other states of distress associated with poor mental and physical health. His work may be contrasted with the work of other investigators in studying optimism and pessimism, which identifies more generalized expectations for positive and negative outcomes. One key issue is the extent to which it matters whether the person's positive outlook is linked to self-efficacy or is just a rosy perspective on future events. Bandura (1992) reviewed how self-efficacy influences physiological processes.

8. Nicassio and Greenberg (2001) conducted an exhaustive review of the efficacy of cognitive-behavioral treatments and also of psychoeducational programs on arthritis patients. They found benefits in pain reduction and self-efficacy due to these programs, but little evidence of improvement in depression.

9. The number of adherents to this model of adaptation to chronic pain, as well as other sources of life difficulty, is growing exponentially.

10. Kabat-Zinn (1990) also reviews evidence in favor of mindfulness as a means of reducing the suffering associated with chronic pain. Several studies conducted in the author's pain clinic have shown sizable reductions in the level of pain and in the degree of interference that pain causes in their abilities to engage in normal activities.

11. Kushner's book was in part inspired by the author's profound experience of loss following the death of his son. Though he sees himself as more sensitive and understanding to the needs of his congregation as a result of his son's death, he makes the central point that he would give all that up to have his son still with him.

Chapter 9

1. Wells, Golding, and Burman (1989) examined rates of chronic medical conditions in a sample of 2,554 adults with and without psychiatric disorders. They

found higher rates among those with depression, anxiety, and substance abuse. The adverse influences on physiological mechanisms is broad in scope, ranging from adverse effects on cellular immunity among older adults (Schleifer, Keller, Bond, Cohen, & Stein, 1989) to reduced bone mineral density in women (Michelson et al., 1996).

2. The effects of hopelessness on all-cause mortality held even after controlling for a number of other risk factors, including age, ethnic background, number of health conditions, perceived health, smoking, and number of social contacts. The residents who reported depressive symptoms from a geriatric depression scale and who said "no" when asked if they were hopeful had the greatest chance of dying in the 10 years that ensued between the initial survey and the follow-up.

3. In Musselman et al.'s (1998) review, effects ranged from nonsignificant to an odds ratio of 4.54 among those diagnosed with major depression. Frasure-Smith, Lesperance, and Talajic (1993, 1995) conducted the study of increased mortality risk among depressed heart patients.

4. Of special interest to us was a construct that Denollet and Brutsaert (1998) referred to as Type D personality. Type D was used to label those high in psychiatric distress and also high in social inhibition, a factor that suggests a lack of positive affective engagement in the social world. This personality type was the strongest predictor of future cardiac events and 6-year mortality for the study population.

5. Everson et al. (2000) also found that hopelessness was a better predictor of hypertension than symptoms of depressed affect. This was the first study to show that hopelessness could predict a significant rise in blood pressure.

6. For platelet activation, changing densities of serotonin have been implicated.

7. For a discussion of the endocrine and immune responses following loss of a loved one see Carter (1998) and on depression more generally see Herbert and Cohen's (1993) review as well as Stein, Miller, and Trestman (1991).

8. Pincus and colleagues (1996) provide one conservative estimate: 15% of rheumatoid arthritis patients with a current depressive disorder. Katz and Yelin (1993) report substantially higher rates. In either case, these rates are significantly higher than those within the general population.

9. Watson, Clark, and Carey (1988) have proposed that depression is best characterized by an absence of positive affect rather than the presence of negative affect.

10. See Maier (1984) for an overview of these animal models.

11. Abramson, Metalsky, and Alloy (1989) provide a revised model that they refer to as a "hopelessness theory of depression," building on the earlier work by Martin Seligman (1975). The initial work on depressive attributional style may be found in Seligman, Abramson, Semmel, and von Baeyer (1979).

12. More evidence of the role of positive emotion in recovery from depression was found by Rottenberg, Kasch, Gross, and Gotlib (2002). The authors played film clips of sad, fearful, and amusing scenes and compared the emotional reactions of patients with major depressive disorder to non-depressed controls. As expected,

the depressed patients showed much greater sadness to the sad film than the controls. The level of positive emotional response to the amusing film was not different between groups. However, when the researchers reexamined the depressed patients 6 months later to assess any clinical improvement, they did find that positive emotional reactions predicted recovery. Patients with greater heart rate acceleration and more smiles when watching a movie clip of "Mr. Bean" putting on his pants while driving to work in his Austin Cooper had a higher likelihood or recovery from depression 6 months later than patients less responsive.

13. Constance Hammen (1991) provides some of the most convincing evidence that depression itself is a cause of stress in that it increases the frequency of stressful interpersonal interactions.

14. Wells et al.'s (1989) epidemiological study indicates that the effects of anxiety on developing medical conditions are more rapid than those of other psychiatric conditions.

15. In a series of recent experiments, Doug Derryberry and Marjorie Reed (1997) have examined the role of anxiety in attention. The results of their studies suggest that anxious persons, as opposed to those who are not anxious, are more likely to focus on negative cues and to sustain attention to those cues that are laden with negative affect. The researchers interpret their findings as evidence of a shrinking of attentional focus but not of a change in the architecture of emotional experience.

16. In this study we used a statistical method commonly referred to as confirmatory factor analysis. Using that method we estimated the correlation between latent constructs formed from multiple indicators of positive and negative affects. Separate constructs were formed for the anxious and depressed groups. We then tested the goodness of fit of the model we proposed to the actual data. We tested whether the correlation between positive and negative affect was different for the two groups, using another goodness-of-fit test. Our analyses revealed an excellent fit for the two latent factors in both groups and a significantly different correlation between the two affects between groups. The reports of positive and negative affect had a strong inverse correlation for the anxious group, unlike the depressed group.

17. Susan Wiser and Marvin Goldfried (1998) have begun the task of identifying when therapists broaden the emotional experiences of their clients and when they seem to constrict that experience. It appears that the type of therapy matters little in comparison with the kind of therapist. Both cognitive-behavioral therapists and psychodynamic-interpersonal therapists often enrich the emotional experience of their clients so long as they are also understanding, nonjudgmental, and noncontrolling.

Chapter 10

1. Alan Lang, Christopher Patrick, and Werner Stritzke (1999) call this alcohol-as-medicine model a time-honored theory of why people drink.

2. In addition to mortality and morbidity figures, McGinnis and Foege (1999) also provide an estimate of the economic toll of addiction, which they estimate to be $400 billion a year. They also discuss the social costs to the families and the health effects of passive exposure.

3. Lindman, Sjoholm, and Lang (2000) provide cross-cultural evidence of the great expectations that people have for a boost in positive affective states following alcohol consumption. Interestingly enough, American students seem to have the highest hopes for positive outcomes of drinking when compared with students from several European countries. One experimental test of the effects of positive expectancies on drinking is provided by Johnson and Fromme (1994).

4. Solomon and Corbit (1974) claim this process also explains the loss of strong emotional highs from interactions with our romantic partners, and the irritability, even contempt, that some older couples appear have for one another much of the time.

5. There are a number of reasons that animal studies have contributed so much to this field. Among the most important is the ability of the scientists to manipulate the administration of the drug and to study the animal's addictive behaviors under controlled experimental conditions. Such could not be done ethically with human participants. Some have argued cogently that such studies should not be performed on any animal.

6. A last group of animals landed in one compartment following morphine and another compartment following saline. The results, not shown here, were mixed for this condition, as expected.

7. The work of this research team may be found in several places, including articles by Tennen, Affleck, Armeli, and Carney (2000), Swendsen, Tennen, Carney, Affleck, Willard, and Hromi (2000), Carney, Armeli, Tennen, and O'Neil (2000), and Armeli, Carney, Tennen, Affleck, and O'Neil (2000).

8. Some sample items from this scale are given in chapter 4 in table 4.1.

9. This and other work on this subject are discussed by Steven Stocker (1999).

10. Kreek demonstrated that drug treatment does have some beneficial physiological effects on these processes. After 3 months or more of methadone treatment, those with heroin addiction showed ACTH responses back to normal levels.

11. One reference to data on patterns of drug use comes from the U.S. Department of Health and Human Services (2000) 1999 national household survey on drug abuse. In the most recent survey, some encouraging news was the emergence of a pattern of lower rates of drug use among those 12 to 17 years of age. Early drug use is one of the strong predictors of later dependency and addiction.

12. Philip Brickman and Donald Campbell (1971) produced a rather pessimistic view of our society in their classic paper on hedonic relativism. The model they applied, though, was one-dimensional in its treatment of emotion.

13. Fletcher (2001) provides engaging accounts from people who have succeeded in solving their drinking problems without relying exclusively on AA programs.

14. The most comprehensive study to date, conducted by the Project MATCH Research Group (1997), attempted to compare the success of a 12-step program with that of cognitive-behavioral treatment for alcohol dependence and

of a motivational enhancement program. The purpose of the study was to test the "match" hypothesis: that people with certain personality features were more likely to succeed in one or another model. After random assignment of 1,766 men and women to one of the three treatment conditions and 12 weeks of counseling for each group, no support for the matching hypothesis was found. In fact, the three therapies were about equally effective in treating alcohol dependence.

Chapter 11

1. Bell (1998) and her colleagues have developed a model of adaptation to traumatic events that they refer to as "neural sensitization." This sensitization arises from experiences with abusive parental figures and is often manifested by an amplification of bodily responses to stress. A dysfunctional response to stress increases risks of abnormalities in behavior, mood, and endocrine and immune function in adult life.

2. This problem becomes all the more salient in disorders for which there is no known cause, including chronic pain syndromes like fibromyalgia and multiple chemical sensitivity. The absence of a physical abnormality could encourage those with the illness to search for an explanation in what they perceive as abnormal childhood experiences. Of course, it is also possible, even likely, that the absence of a manifest physical disease is consistent with a dysfunctional HPA-axis stress response such as Rachel Yehuda (1997) has detailed for posttraumatic stress disorders.

3. Kraemer (1999) reviews evidence of the effects of parental separation in studies of rhesus monkeys. Of particular interest is his discussion of differences between those monkeys raised by their mothers and those monkeys raised by their peers. Although the two groups have comparable levels of tactile stimulation from others during development, the peer-raised rhesus simians showed more severe responses to separation, more inflexibility in problem solving, and less frequent but more pronounced aggression compared with those raised by their mothers. He sees this as evidence for a basic need for secure attachment that may be most often provided by the mother, and not by peer relations, in the young.

4. Heim and Nemeroff (1999) describe this study and related research in their reviews of the impact of early childhood experiences on the development of the stress response. Their work has centered on sensitization of CRF in the hypothalamus, amygdala, and other brain mechanisms that regulate the HPA axis and other stress response systems.

5. Of interest also were the high rates of abuse as adults that those with fibromyalgia reported. When they added the reports together to estimate reports of lifetime victimization from any sexual or physical assault, 91.7% of those patients with fibromyalgia reported one or more events, compared with 66.7% of those with rheumatoid arthritis.

6. For more information, see the Web site http://hipp.gator.net/drive_perspectives_vogel.html.

7. The March 2002 issue of the *American Psychologist* is devoted to a discus-

sion of the controversies surrounding the scientific review and publication of the Rind et al (1998) paper.

Chapter 12

1. Stone was one of the first researchers to employ daily diaries in the study of stress. The findings reported by Stone and Neale have since been replicated in other investigations of married life.

2. J. Haskey (1996) recently estimated that two of every five marriages in the United States would end in divorce.

3. Deborah Tannen (1990) also wrote in the same vein. Both books provide a wealth of examples of how men and women often appear to be living on different planets. The authors offer some useful guidance for overcoming these perplexing problems.

4. Bagozzi, Wong, and Yi (1999) recently conducted a multinational study of gender differences in the relationship between positive and negative emotions. They found that women in Western cultures shown less affective differentiation than men as revealed by a stronger inverse correlation between positive and negative emotions. Women from cultures such as China that cultivate more interdependent lifestyles showed more complex emotional responses.

5. One of the most compelling studies of gender differences in emotional awareness was conducted by Barrett, Lane, Sechrest, and Schwartz (2000). The authors drew seven separate samples of men and women from around the country and gave them the emotional awareness scale developed by Lane, Quinlan, Schwartz, Walker, and Zeitlin (1990). In all samples, women outscored men on emotional awareness. On average, this difference was about a half a standard deviation. The findings held up as well after controlling for verbal intelligence differences between men and women in the various samples.

6. Heavey, Layne, and Christensen (1993) have focused on this pattern of relationship as particularly destructive. There is evidence from their recent work that the wife-demanding, husband-withdrawing style is the most damaging to the well-being of the marriage.

7. This study provides an exceptionally thorough examination of newlywed couples' emotional styles of relating using methods unsurpassed in methodological rigor.

8. In addition to the findings I have reported in text, Pasch and Bradbury (1998) also found that the affective responses to the conflict situation predicted marital outcomes significantly. The amount of positive affect displayed in discussions of conflict had no predictive power. However, the expression of negative affect, particularly anger and disgust by the husbands, were strong warning signs that the marriage was not going to be blissful. The wife's negative affect was also important, but less so. These findings differ from those by Gottman et al. (1998). One major difference between the studies, however, is the length of the follow-up period. In the study by Gottman and his colleagues, the follow-up period was 6 years, as opposed to 2 years in this study.

9. This study had many facets and included a test of the degree of complexity in the ratings of emotions by the men and women in the study. Their findings suggested that women, on the whole, were more discerning of the various nuances in the expression of emotion. This point has been raised in other studies (see Thayer & Johnsen, 2000).

10. This quotation is from Jennifer Sander, made during my seminar, "Emotions, Stress, and Health," held in the fall 2000 semester.

Chapter 13

1. The story told of an employee of the Penobscot Poultry Company (Chatterley, Rouverol, & Cole, 2000) perhaps illustrates this point best. The worker, Linda Lord, suffered egregious harm from her labors at the factory, yet held steadfast to her job until the meat processing plant was closed.

2. Ashforth and Humphrey (1995) put it best when they wrote, "The experience of work is saturated with feeling" (p. 98).

3. Marie Jahoda was an early proponent of greater attention to positive mental health. I In this research she examined the world of work in an attempt to address some of the hidden values of employment to the human experience.

4. The type of work that the person does can affect the relative distribution of interpersonal events reported as good versus bad work experiences. Many occupations demand what Hochschild (1983) has called "emotional labor." People who are in service occupations, such as flight attendants and restaurant servers, and also those in the helping professions, such as clinical psychologists and nurses, are successful in their jobs when they are able to effectively manage their relationships with their customers. Thus the work itself is interpersonal, and these kinds of events show up as a major source of job satisfaction, as well as job dissatisfaction. In a recent examination of the linkages between emotions and job events, John Basch and Cynthia Fisher (2000) documented this shift in the role of interpersonal events when they interviewed employees who had more complex social roles at work. These employees reported interpersonal experiences when they described times at work at which they were happy, as well as those at which they experienced negative emotions such as frustration and anger.

5. See Joseph McGrath (1970) and Frank Landy (1978), who exemplify the academic approach Herzberg is referring to.

6. It was indeed tragic how the government handled the demands of these striking workers. Newly elected President Ronald Reagan found it useful at the time to distinguish himself from former President Jimmy Carter by firing all striking employees who refused to return to work. Those fired were not allowed to return to work for the FAA for several years, thereby all but barring the strikers from working as air traffic controllers again.

7. Herzberg and I discuss the changes in job satisfaction reported by 98 staff members from nine job enrichment projects and compared those results with interviews of 40 employees in jobs slated for enrichment but in which no job redesign had begun prior to the assessment.

8. Hanson used electronic pagers to chart the influence of work demands several times a day for a week with 77 Finnish workers, half of whom were health care professionals and half clerical workers. The author found that workers reported more positive affect when they were busy and showed increases in cortisol (as measured by swabs of saliva taken periodically at work) only when negative affects increased.

9. When I interviewed Karasek, he was convinced that Herzberg could not be right in thinking that boring work would not necessarily be harmful to the person's health. Indeed, the absence of positive emotions associated with work invites greater dissatisfaction with work life, especially under stress. Herzberg's theory does not address such propositions.

10. Katharine Parkes (1999) has shown rather convincingly that shift work, in itself, can pose substantial risks to physical health.

11. O'Boyle (1998) writes of the ruthlessness of managerial practices at General Electric over the past decade and a half under the leadership of CEO Jack Welch. In contrast, he cites how companies with similar products, such as Motorola, foster job security, as well as commitment to the company, with more humane management practices.

12. Though not a focus of this chapter on work, there are significant individual differences in level of interest and motivation at work. In one highly influential article, Barry Straw, Nancy Bell, and John Clausen (1986) demonstrated that employee differences in job satisfaction are a function of the person, as well as the job he or she is doing. These authors found strong evidence that personality factors assessed at adolescence can predict job satisfaction more than 20 years later. Hackman and Oldham (1975) have taken another approach to the study of individual differences through the measurement of what they have called "growth need strength." In a recent study of middle managers from 26 work organizations by Saavedra and Kwun (2000), employees with enriched jobs reported more positive emotion. Those managers with stronger growth needs showed the greatest gains in positive feelings from more challenging and responsible work. Although such personal dispositions are important to attend to in understanding emotional reactions at work, it would be inaccurate to say that the organizational environment does not matter very much or that the aspects of work that generate excitement and enthusiasm on the job cannot be defined for most, if not all, employees.

Chapter 14

1. Reminger, Kaszniak, and Dalby used pictures from Peter Lang's International Affective Picture System (Lang, Bradley, & Cuthbert, 1999). These pictures have extensive normative ratings on the degree of positive and negative affect they generate. They also have established ratings of the degree of arousability of the pictures. Some of the most arousing pictures in this inventory were not used here. Specifically, the pictures with blood and pictures of nudes were not shown in the study described.

2. The actual relationship between negative affect and age was nonlinear. A steady reduction in negative emotions until age 80 was reported, at which time there was a slight upturn. However, the frequency of negative affect does not return to the high levels reported by the young adults.

3. Another study of caregivers of spouses with dementia showed that depressive symptoms followed similar patterns. Kav Vedhara, Nola Shanks, Stephen Anderson, and Stafford Lightman (2000) assessed "reactive" and "proactive" coping among 50 caregivers. Those caregivers with greater depression levels were both more reactive and less proactive in their attempts to resolve stressful situations.

4. The study took place over 4½ years so that we could chart the increase in disabling illnesses among a group of elderly who had no physical limitations at the start of the study.

5. Of interest also in this study was that the authors had hypothesized that older women would show the greatest loss in hippocampal volume. Once history of depression was accounted for, however, there were no effects of age on cell death in that region of the brain.

6. Robert Butler (1974) may have been the first to introduce the term *life course review* to describe this natural process of reclaiming one's personal history through autobiographical accounts. These forms are also referred to as *narrative therapies*.

7. An excerpt of Ernst Beier's forthcoming book may be found on his Web page, www.aros.net/~bernst/

Chapter 15

1. This show was broadcast on National Public Radio on May 20, 1999.

2. Earlier work by David Bakan (1966) was seminal in the development of the ideas of agency and communion.

3. This finding has obvious implications for Internet communication and how our relationships with one another may become increasingly fragile within a work world in which, 80% or more of the time, the employees are dealing with people in hyperspace.

4. This study was conducted prior to the popularization of the Internet as the primary means of communication. It remains to be seen whether Internet strangers are viewed as more or less attractive during stressful times.

5. We have found evidence of similar patterns in human communities when we conducted door-to-door interviews of men and women in Salt Lake City. Those people living in difficult social circumstances were at greatest risk for mental health problems. We also found evidence that the scope of their evaluations of the quality of their own lives narrowed significantly under stress. When stresses were relatively low, the community residents' evaluations of themselves was related to, but also in part separate from, their evaluations of the quality of their family lives, their standard of living, health, work and leisure time satisfactions. But for those with highly stressful lives, there was a disturbing constriction in their ratings of the

quality of their lives such that their evaluations of their own goodness seemed completely determined by their ratings of their successes and failures in the social world (Zautra & Beier, 1978).

6. Seymour Sarason (1974) introduced the term *psychological sense of community*. It is that sense that I am using here in an attempt to understand what went wrong in Littleton.

7. The results of this study should be regarded as somewhat tentative given the small number of census tracts involved and the problems of interpretation that arise when aggregating data into geographic units prior to computing the correlations. As an interesting side note, I conducted a similar study in the Tri-City area in Arizona and found similar results. Rates of utilization of mental health services was inversely correlated with the number of positive events reported by residents surveyed in those census tracts.

8. Axelrod demonstrated that the strategy of social exchange in which the person cooperates first, punishes, but then forgives dishonesty may indeed be the most successful approach from an evolutionary standpoint. In a series of simulation games, he discovered that this simple approach to social exchanges garnered more resources in the long run compared with other approaches that would attempt to "trick" their opponents into trusting them in order to gain greater rewards.

9. Van Denburg and Kiesler adopted a system for classifying how people were relating to one another as belonging in one of four quadrants of a two-dimensional space based on how friendly versus hostile the person was and how dominant versus submissive. These four types resulted: friendly-dominant, friendly-submissive, hostile-dominant, and hostile-submissive. This system has been found useful in characterizing individual styles of interacting with others in a vast number of prior studies. Here, they used this interpersonal grid to find women who came across as friendly-submissive.

10. Dennis Shepard, father of Matthew Shepard, at the sentencing of Aaron J. McKinney on November 5, 1999, as recorded by the Albany County Attorney's Office, in Laramie, Wyoming.

11. Pema Chödrön is an American Buddhist nun and resident teacher at Gampo Abbey in Nova Scotia.

References

Preface

Herzberg, F. (1966). *Work and the nature of man.* Cleveland, OH: Cleveland World Publishing.

Maslow, A. H. (1968). *Toward a psychology of being* (2d ed.). Princeton, NJ: Van Nostrand.

Chapter 1

Arnold, M. B. (1960a). *Emotion and personality: Vol. 1. Psychological aspects.* New York: Columbia University Press.

Arnold, M. B. (1960b). *Emotion and personality: Vol. 2. Neurological and physiological aspects.* New York: Columbia University Press.

Beier, E., & Zautra, A. J. (1972). The identification of vocal expressions of emotion across cultures. *Journal of Consulting and Clinical Psychology, 40,* 560.

Berntson, G. C., Cacioppo, J. T., & Gardner, W. L. (1999). The affect system has parallel and integrative processing components: Form follows function. *Journal of Personality and Social Psychology, 76,* 839–855.

Cacioppo, John T., & Berntson, G. G. (1994). Relationship between attitudes and evaluative space: A critical review, with emphasis on the separability of positive and negative substrates. *Psychological Bulletin, 115,* 401–423.

Cacioppo, J. T., Berntson, G. G., Larsen, J. T., Poehlmann, K. M., & Ito, T. A. (2000). The psychophysiology of emotion. In M. Lewis & R. J. M. Haviland-Jones (Eds.), *The handbook of emotions* (2d ed.; pp. 173–191). New York: Guilford Press.

Cannon, W. B. (1927). The James-Lange theory of emotion: A critical examination and alternative theory. *American Journal of Psychology, 39,* 106–124.

Clore, G. L., & Ortony, A. (2000). Cognition in emotion: Always, sometimes, or never? In R. D. Lane & L. Nadel (Eds.), *Cognitive neuroscience of emotion* (pp. 24–61). New York: Oxford University Press.

Clynes, M. (1978). *Sentics: The touch of emotions.* Garden City, NY: Anchor Books.

Clynes, M. (1982). *Music, mind, and brain: The neuropsychology of music.* New York: Plenum Press.

Damasio, A. R. (1994). *Descartes' error: Emotion, reason, and the human brain.* New York: Putman.

Damasio, A. R. (1999). *The feeling of what happens: Body and emotion in the making of consciousness.* New York: Harcourt Brace.

Darwin, C. (1998). *The expression of the emotions in man and animals.* London: HarperCollins. (Original work published 1872)

Ekman, P. (1982). *Emotion in the human face* (2d ed.). Cambridge, England: Cambridge University Press.

Ekman, P. (1994a). All emotions are basic. In P. Ekman & R. J. Davidson (Eds.), *The nature of emotion: Fundamental questions* (pp. 15–19). New York: Oxford University Press.

Ekman, P. (1994b). Strong evidence for universals in facial expression: A reply to Russell's mistaken critique. *Psychological Bulletin, 115,* 268–287.

Frijda, N. H. (1993). Appraisal and beyond: The issue of cognitive determinants of emotion. *Cognition and Emotion, 7,* 357–388.

Griffiths, P. E. (1997). *What emotions really are: The problem of psychological categories.* Chicago: University of Chicago Press.

Hesse, H. (1972). Inside and Outside. In T. Ziolkowski (Ed.), *Stories of five decades.* New York: Farrar, Straus, & Giroux.

Izard, C. E. (1971). *The face of emotion.* New York: Appleton-Century-Crofts.

Izard, C. E. (1994). Innate and universal facial expressions: Evidence from developmental and cross-cultural research. *Psychological Bulletin, 115,* 288–299.

Izard, C. E. (1977). *Human emotions.* New York: Plenum.

Lane, R. D. (2000). Neural correlates of conscious emotional experience. In R. D. Lane & L. Nadel (Eds.), *Cognitive neuroscience of emotion* (pp. 345–370). New York: Oxford University Press.

Lange, C. G., & James, W. (1967). *The emotions.* New York: Hafner Publishing (original work published 1922).Lazarus, R. S. (1982). Thoughts on the relations between emotion and cognition. *American Psychologist, 37,* 1019–1024.

Lazarus, R. S. (1984). On the primacy of cognition. *American Psychologist, 39,* 124–129.

Lazarus, R. S. (1991). *Emotion and adaptation.* New York: Oxford University Press.

LeDoux, J. (1996). *The emotional brain: The mysterious underpinnings of emotional life.* New York: Simon & Schuster.

Ornstein, R. (1997). *The right brain: Making sense of the hemispheres.* New York: Harcourt Brace.

Russell, J. A. (1994). Is there universal recognition of emotion from facial expression? A review of the cross-cultural studies. *Psychological Bulletin, 115,* 102–141.

Sapolsky, R. M. (1998). *Why zebras don't get ulcers: A guide to stress, stress-related disease, and coping* (2d ed.). New York: Freeman Press.

Schachter, S., & Singer, J. (1962). Cognitive, social and physiological determinants of emotional state. *Psychological Review, 69,* 379–399.

Scherer, K. R. (1986). Vocal affect expression: A review and a model for future research. *Psychological Bulletin, 99,* 143–165.

Stein, N. L., Trabasso, T., & Liwag, M. (1993). The representation and organization of emotional experience: Unfolding the emotion episode. In M. Lewis & J. M. Haviland (Eds.), *Handbook of emotions* (pp. 279–300). New York: Guilford Press.

Tomkins, S. S. (1962). *Affect, imagery, and consciousness: Vol. 1. The positive affects.* New York: Springer-Verlag.

Tomkins, S. S. (1963). *Affect, imagery, and consciousness: Vol. 2. The negative affects.* New York: Springer-Verlag.

Tomkins, S. S. (1984). Affect theory. In K. R. Scherer & P. Ekman (Eds.), *Approaches to emotion* (pp. 163–196). Hillsdale, NJ: Erlbaum.

Tomkins, S. S. (1991). *Affect, imagery, and consciousness: Vol. 3. The negative affects; anger and fear.* New York: Springer-Verlag.

Zajonc, R. B. (1980). Feeling and thinking: Preferences need no inferences. *American Psychologist, 35,* 151–175.

Zajonc, R. B. (1985). Emotion and facial efference: A theory reclaimed. *Science, 228,* 15–21.

Chapter 2

Auden, W. H., & Kallman, C. (1993). *The complete works of W. H. Auden.* Princeton, NJ: Princeton University Press.

Bradburn, N. M. (1969). *The structure of psychological well-being.* Chicago: Aldine.
Bradburn, N. M., & Caplovitz, D. (1965). *Reports on happiness: A pilot study of behavior related to mental health.* Chicago: Aldine.

Brickman, P., Coates, D., & Janoff-Bulman, R. (1978). Lottery winners and accident victims: Is happiness relative? *Journal of Personality and Social Psychology, 36,* 917–927.

Carver, C. S., & Scheier, M. (1998). *On the self-regulation of behavior.* New York: Cambridge University Press.

Church, A. T., Katigbak, M. S., Reyes, J. A. S., & Jensen, S. M. (1999). The structure of affect in a non-Western culture: Evidence for cross-cultural comparability. *Journal of Personality, 67,* 505–534.

Clynes, M. (1978). *Sentics: The touch of emotion.* Garden City, NY: Doubleday Anchor.

Davidson, R. J. (1992). Emotion and affective style: Hemispheric substrates. *Psychological Science, 3,* 39–43.

Davidson, R. J. (2000). The functional neuroanatomy of affective style. In R. D. Lane & L. Nadel (Eds.), *Cognitive neuroscience of emotion* (pp. 371–388). New York: Oxford University Press.

Diener, E. (1999). Introduction to the special section of the structure of emotion. *Journal of Personality and Social Psychology, 76,* 803–804.

Dimond, S., Farrington, L., & Johnson, P. (1976). Differing emotional response from right and left hemispheres. *Nature, 261,* 690–692.

Ekman, P. (1982). *Emotion in the human face* (2d ed.). Cambridge: Cambridge University Press.

Elliot, R., Fristo, K. J., & Dolan, R. J. (2000). Dissociable neural responses in human reward systems. *Journal of Neuroscience, 20,* 6159–6165.

Feldman-Barrett, L., & Russell, J. A. (1999). The structure of current affect: Controversies and emerging consensus. *Psychological Bulletin, 8,* 10–14.

Frederick, S., & Loewenstein, G. (1999). Hedonic Aadaptation. In D. Kahneman, E. Diener, & N. Schwarz (Eds.), *Well-being: The foundations of hedonic psychology.* New York: Russell Sage Foundation.

Gray, J. A. (1982). *The neuropsychology of anxiety.* New York: Oxford University Press.

Green, D. P., Goldman, S. L., & Salovey, P. (1993). Measurement error masks biopolarity in affect ratings. *Journal of Personality and Social Psychology, 64,* 1029–1041.

Green, D. P., & Salovey, P. (1999). In what sense are positive and negative affect independent? *Psychological Science, 10,* 304–306.

Green, D. P., Salovey, P., & Truax, K. M. (1999). Static, dynamic, and causative biopolarity of affect. *Journal of Personality and Social Psychology, 76,* 856–867.

Helson, H. (1964). *Adaptation-level theory: An experimental and systematic approach to behavior.* New York: Harper.

Herzberg, F. (1966). *Work and the nature of man.* New York: Crowell.

Herzberg, F., Mausner, B., & Snyderman, B. (1959). *The motivation to work.* New York: Wiley.

Kahneman, D., Diener, E., & Schwarz, N. (Eds.). (1999). *Well-being: The foundations of hedonic psychology.* New York: Russell Sage Foundation.

Lang, P. J., Bradley, M. M., & Cuthbert, B. N. (1998). Emotion, motivation, and anxiety: Brain mechanisms and psychophysiology. *Biological Psychiatry, 44,* 1248–1263.

Malenka, R. C., Hamblin, M. W., & Barchas, J. D. (1989). Biochemical hypothesis of affective disorders and anxiety. In G. J. Siegel, B. W. Agranoff, R. W. Albers, & P. B. Molinoff (Eds.), *Basic neurochemistry: Molecular, cellular and medical aspects* (4th ed.). New York: Raven Press.

Osgood, C. E., Suci, G. J., & Tannenbaum, P. H. (1957). *The measurement of meaning.* Urbana: University of Illinois Press.

Panksepp, J. (1998). *Affective neuroscience: The foundation of human and animal emotions.* New York: Oxford University Press.

Robinson-Whelen, S., Kim, C., MacCallum, R. C., & Kiecolt-Glaser, J. K. (1997).

Distinguishing optimism from pessimism in older adults: Is it more important to be optimistic or not to be pessimistic? *Journal of Personality and Social Psychology, 73,* 1345–1353.

Russell, J. A. (1980). A circumplex model of affect. *Journal of Personality and Social Psychology, 39,* 1161–1178.

Russell, J. A., & Carroll, J. M. (1999a). On the bi-polarity of positive and negative affect. *Psychological Bulletin, 125,* 3–30.

Russell, J. A., & Carroll, J. M. (1999b). The phoenix of bi-polarity: Reply to Watson and Tellegen. *Psychological Bulletin, 125,* 611–617.

Russell, J. A., & Feldman-Barrett, L. (1999). Affect and prototypical emotion episodes. *Journal of Personality and Social Psychology, 76,* 805–809.

Star Tribune (1998). Pessimism harms more than optimism helps (Gordon Slavot). March 4, p. E3.

Tellegen, A., Watson, D., & Clark, L. A. (1999b). On the dimensional and hierarchical structure of affect. *Psychological Bulletin, 10,* 297–309.

Tucker, D. M. (1981). Lateral brain function, emotion, and conceptualization. *Psychological Bulletin, 89,* 19–46.

Watson, D., & Tellegen, A. (1985). Toward a consensual structure of mood. *Psychological Bulletin, 98,* 219–235.

Watson, D., & Tellegen, A. (1999). Issues in dimensional structure of affect: Effects of descriptors, measurement error, and response formats: Comment on Russell and Carroll. *Psychological Bulletin, 125,* 5601–5610.

Watson, D., Weise, D., Vaidya, J., & Tellegen, A. (1999). The two general activation systems of affect: Structural findings, evolutionary consideration, and psychobiological evidence. *Journal of Personality and Social Psychology, 76,* 820–838.

Westbrook, M. T. (1976). Positive affect: A method of content analysis for verbal samples. *Journal of Consulting and Clinical Psychology, 44,* 715–719.

Wise, R. A., & Hoffman, D. C. (1992). Localization of drug reward mechanisms by intracranial injections. *Synapse, 10,* 247–263.

Zajonc, R. B. (1980). Feeling and thinking: Preferences need no inferences. *American Psychologist, 35,* 151–175.

Chapter 3

Abbott, E. A. (1994). *Flatland: A romance of many dimensions.* New York: HarperCollins.

Abramson, L. Y., Alloy, L. B., & Metalsky, G. J. (1989). Hopelessness depression: A theory-based subtype of depression. *Psychological Review, 96,* 358–372.

Abramson, L. Y., Seligman, M. E. P., & Teasdale, J. D. (1978). Learned helplessness in humans: Critique and reformulation. *Journal of Abnormal Psychology, 87,* 49–74.

Brown, G. (1989). Life events and measurement. In G. Brown & T. O. Harris (Eds.), *Life events and illness* (pp. 3–45). New York: Guilford Press.

Cacioppo, J. T. (1994). Social neuroscience: Autonomic, neuroendocrine, and immune responses to stress. *Psychophysiology, 31,* 113–128.

Cassel, J. (1975). Social science in epidemiology: Psychosocial processes and "stress" theoretical formulation. In E. L. Struening & M. Guttentag (Eds.), *Handbook of evaluation research* (pp. 537–553). Beverly Hills, CA: Sage.

Charney, D., Grillon, C., & Bremner, D. (1998a). The neurobiological basis of anxiety and fear: Circuits, mechanisms, and neurochemical interactions: Part 1. *Neuroscientist, 4,* 35–44.

Charney, D. S., Grillon, C. C. G., & Bremner, J. D. (1998b). The neurobiological basis of anxiety and fear: Circuits, mechanisms, and neurochemical interactions: Part 2. *Neuroscientist, 4,* 122–132.

Chrousos, G., & Gold, P. W. (1992). The concepts of stress and stress system disorders. *Journal of the American Medical Association, 257,* 1244–1252.

Cohen, S., Kessler, R. C., & Gordon, L. U. (1995). *Measuring stress.* New York: Oxford University Press.

Creed, F. (1993). Stress and psychosomatic disorders. In L. Goldberger. & S. Breznitz (Eds.), *Handbook of stress: Theoretical and clinical aspects* (pp. 496–510). New York: Free Press.

Davis, M. C., Zautra, A. J., & Reich, J. W. (2001). Vulnerability to stress differs in older women with fibomyalgia vs. osteoarthritis. *Annuals of Behavioral Medicine, 23,* 2150–226.

Dohrenwend, B. P., Raphael, K. G., Stueve, A., & Skodol, A. (1993). The structured event probe and narrative rating method for measuring stressful life events, In L. Goldberger & S. Breznitz (Eds.), *Handbook of stress: Theoretical and clinical aspects* (pp. 174–199). New York: Free Press.

Folkow, B. (1993). Physiological organization of neurohormonal responses to psychosocial stimuli: Implications for health and disease. *Annals of Behavioral Medicine, 15,* 236–244.

Glaser, R., Kiecolt-Glaser, J. K., Marucha, P. T., MacCallum, R. C., Laskowski, B. F., & Malarkey, W. B. (1999). Stress-related changes in proinflammatory cytokine production in wounds. *Archives of General Psychiatry, 56,* 450–456.

Glass, D. C., Singer, J. E., & Friedman, L. N. (1969). Psychic cost of adaptation to an environmental stressor. *Journal of Personality and Social Psychology, 12,* 200–210.

Goldberger, L. & Breznitz, S. (Eds.) (1993). *Handbook of stress: Theoretical and clinical aspects.* New York: Free Press.

Goodhart, D. E., & Zautra, A. J. (1984). Assessing quality of life in the community: An ecological approach. In W. R. O'Connor & B. Lubin (Eds)., *Ecological approaches to clinical and community psychology* (pp. 251–291). New York: Wiley.

Horowitz, M. J., Field, N. P., & Classen, C. C. (1993). Stress response syndromes and their treatment. In L. Goldberger. & S. Breznitz (Eds.), *Handbook of stress: Theoretical and clinical aspects* (pp. 757–774). New York: Free Press.

Kasl, S. V. (1987). Methodologies in stress and health: Past difficulties, present dilimmas, future directions. In S. V. Kasl & C. L. Cooper (Eds.), *Stress and health: Issues in research methodology* (pp. 307–318). New York: John Wiley & Sons.

Kelley, K. W., & Dantzer, R. (1991). Growth hormone and prolactin as natural antagonists of glucoccorticoids in immuneregulation. In N. Plotnikoff, A. Murgo, R. Faith, & J. Wybran (Eds.), *Stress and immunity* (pp. 433–452). Boca Raton, FL: CRC Press.

Kiecolt-Glaser, J. K., Marucha, P. T., & Glaser, R. (1995). Slowing of wound healing by psychological stress. *Lancet, 346,* 1194–1196.

Klinger, E. (1975). Consequences of commitment to and disengagement from incentives. *Psychological Review, 82,* 1–25.

Laborit, H. (1993). Inhibition of action: Interdisciplinary approach to its mechanism and physiopathology. In H. C. Traue & J. W. Pennebaker (Eds)., *Emotion, inhibition and health* (pp. 57–79). Seattle, WA: Hogrefe & Huber.

Lowenthal, M. F., & Chiriboga, D. (1973). Social stress and adaptation.: Toward the life course perspective. In C. Eisdorfer & M. P. Lawton (Eds.), *The psychology of adult development and aging* (pp. 281–310). Washington, DC: American Psychological Association.

Marucha, P. T., Kiecolt-Glaser, J. K., & Favagehi, M. (1998). Mucosal wound healing is impaired by examination stress. *Psychosomatic Medicine, 60,* 362–365.

McEwen, B. S. (1998). Protective and damaging effects of stress mediators. *New England Journal of Medicine, 338,* 171–179.

Potter, P. T. & Zautra, A. J. (1997). Effects of major and minor stressors on disease activity in rheumatoid arthritis patients. *Journal of Consulting and Clinical Psychology, 65,* 319–323.

Reich, J. W. & Zautra, A. J. (1988). Direct and moderating effects of positive life events. In L. N. Cohen (Ed.), *Advances in research on stressful life events* (pp. 149–181). Beverly Hills, CA: Sage Publications.

Rotenberg, V. S., Sirota, P., & Eilzur, A. (1996). Psychoneuroimmunology: Searching for the main deteriorating psychobehavioral factor. *Genetic, Social and General Psychology Monographs, 122,* 331–345.

Roth, S., & Cohen, L. J. (1986). Approach, avoidance, and coping with stress. *American Psychologist, 41,* 813–819.

Rothbaum, F., Weisz, J. R., & Snyder, S. S. (1982). Changing the world and changing the self: A two-process model of perceived control. *Journal of Personality and Social Psychology, 42,* 5–37.

Sanford, S., & Salmon, P. (Eds.). (1993). *Stress: From synapse to syndrome.* New York: Academic Press.

Sapolsky, R. M. (1998). *Why zebras don't get ulcers: A guide to stress, stress-related disease, and coping* (2d ed.). New York: Freeman.

Seligman, M. E. P. (1975). *Helplessness: On depression, development, and death.* San Francisco: Freeman.

Selye, H. (1973). The evolution of the stress concept. *American Scientist, 61,* 692–699.

Sternberg, E. (1992). The stress response and the regulation of inflammatory disease. *Annals of Internal Medicine, 117,* 854–866.

Stone, A. A., & Neale, J. M. (1982). Development of a methodology for assessing daily experiences. In A. Baum & J. Singh (Eds.), *Environment and health* (pp. 49–83). Hillsdale, NJ: Erlbaum.

Stratakis, C. A. & Chrousos, G. P. (1995). Neuroendocrinology and pathophysiology of the stress system. *Annals of New York Academy of Sciences, 771,* 1–17.

Thoits, P. (1983). Dimensions of life events that influence psychological distress: An evaluation and synthesis of the literature. In H. B. Kaplan (Ed.), *Psychological stress: Trends in theory and research* (pp. 33–103). New York: Academic Press.

Ursin, H., & Olff, M. (1993). The stress response. In S. Sanford & P. Salmon (Eds.). (1993). *Stress: From synapse to syndrome* (pp. 3–22). New York: Academic Press.

van Eck, M., Nicolson, N. A., & Berkhof, J. (1998). Effects of stressful daily events on mood states: Relationship to global perceived stress. *Journal of Personality and Social Psychology, 75,* 1572–1585.

Zautra, A. J. (1996). Investigations of the ongoing stressful situations among those with chronic illness. *American Journal of Community Psychology, 24,* 698–719.

Zautra, A. J., Burelson, M., Matt, K., Roth, S., & Burrows, L. (1994). Interpersonal stress and disease activity in rheumatoid arthritis. *Health Psychology, 13,* 139–148.

Zautra, A. J., Finch, J. Reich, J. W., & Guarnaccia, C. A. (1991). Predicting the everyday events of older adults. *Journal of Personality, 59,* 507–538.

Zautra, A. J., Guarnaccia, C. A., & Dohrenwend, D. P. (1986). The measurement of small events. *American Journal of Community Psychology, 14,* 629–655.

Zautra, A. J., Guarnaccia, C. A., & Reich, J. W. (1989). The contribution of daily life events to negative affective states. In P. C. Kendall & D. Watson (Eds.), Anxiety and depression: Distinctive and overlapping features (pp. 225–251). New York: Academic Press.

Zautra, A. J., Guarnaccia, C. A., Reich, J. W., & Dohrenwend, B. P. (1988). The contribution of small events to stress and distress. In L. N. Cohen (Ed.), *Advances in research on stressful life events* (pp. 123–148). Beverly Hills, CA: Sage Publications.

Zautra, A. J., Hamilton, N. A., & Burke, H. M. (1999). Comparison of stress responses in women with two types of chronic pain: Fibromyalgia and osteoarthritis. *Cognitive Therapy and Research, 23,* 209–230.

Zautra, A. J., Hamilton, N. A., Potter, P., & Smith, B. (1999). Field research on the relationships between stress and disease activity in rheumatoid arthritis. *New York Academy of Sciences, 879,* 397–412.

Zautra, A. J., Okun, M. A., Robinson, S. E., Lee, D., Roth, S. H., & Emmanual, J. (1989). Life stress and lymphocyte alteratons among rheumatoid arthritis patients. *Health Psychology, 8,* 1–14.

Zautra, A. J., Reich, J. W., & Guarnaccia, C. A. (1990). Some everyday life consequences of disability and bereavement for older adults. *Journal of Personality and Social Psychology, 59,* 550–561.

Zautra, A. J., Schultz, A. S., & Reich, J. W. (2000). The role of everyday events in depressive symptoms for older adults. In G. M. Williamson, P. A. Parmelee, & D. R. Shaffer (Eds.), *Physical illness and depression: A handbook of theory, research, and practice* (pp. 65–92). New York: Plenum.

Zautra, A. J., Sheets, V. L., & Sandler, I. N. (1996). An examination of the construct validity of coping dispositions for a sample of recently divorced mothers. *Psychological Assessment, 8,* 1–8.

Zautra, A. J. & Smith, B. W. (2001). Depression and reactivity to stress in older women with rheumatoid arthritis and osteoarthritis. *Psychosomatic Medicine, 63,* 687–696.

Chapter 4

Armstrong, J. (1999). *Monument to a summer hat.* Kalamazoo, MI: New Issues Press.

Berk, L. S., Tan, S. A., Fry, W. F., Napier, B. J., Lee, J. W., Hubbard, R. W., et al., (1989). Neuroendocrine and stress hormone changes during mirthful laughter. *American Journal of the Medical Science, 298,* 390–396.

Bonanno, G. A., & Keltner, D. (1997). Facial expressions of emotion and the course of conjugal bereavement. *Journal of Abnormal Psychology, 106,* 126–137.

Cousins, N. (1981). *Anatomy of an illness as perceived by the patient.* New York: Bantam.

Derks, P., Gillikin, L. S., Bartolome-Rull, D. S., & Bogart, E. H. (1997). Laughter and electroencephalographic activity. *Humor, 10,* 285–300.

Folkman, S. (1997). Positive psychological states and coping with severe stress. *Social Science and Medicine, 45,* 1207–1221.

Fredrickson, B. L., & Levenson, R. W. (1998). Positive emotions speed recovery from the cardiovascular sequelae of negative emotions. *Cognition and Emotion, 12,* 191–220.

Keltner, D., & Bonanno, G. A. (1997). A study of laughter and dissociation: Distinct correlates of laughter and smiling during bereavement. *Journal of Personality and Social Psychology, 73,* 687–702.

Kuiper, N. A., & Martin, R. A. (1998). Laughter and stress in daily life: Relation to positive and negative affect. *Motivation and Emotion, 22,* 133–154.

Martin, R. (2001). Humor, laughter, and physical health: Methodological issues, and research findings. *Psychological Bulletin, 127,* 504–519.

McNair, D. M., Lorr, M., & Droppleman, L. F. (1971). *EITS Manual for the Profile of Mood States.* San Diego, CA: Educational and Industrial Testing Service.

Paulhus, D. L., & Lim, D. T. (1994). Arousal and evaluative extremity in social judgments: A dynamic complexity model. *European Journal of Social Psychology, 24,* 89–99.

Potter, P. T. (1999). *Stressful events and the internal structure of affect: Implications for health psychology.* Tempe, AZ: Arizona State University.

Provine, R. R. (2001). *Laughter: A scientific investigation:* New York: Penguin Books.

Reich, J. & Zautra, A. J. (1981). Life Events and personal causation: Some relationships with satisfaction and distress. *Journal of Personality Social Psychology, 41,* 1002–1012.

Wikan, U. (1989). Managing the heart to brighten face and soul: Emotions in Balinese morality and health. *American Ethnologist*, 16, 294–312.

Williams, J. M., Tonymon, P., & Andersen, M. B. (1990). The effects of life-event stress on anxiety and peripheral narrowing. *Behavioral Science*, 16, 174–181.

Zautra, A. J., Berkhof, J., & Nicolson, N. A. (2002). Changes in affect interrelations as a function of stressful events. *Cognition and Emotion*, 16, 309–318.

Zautra, A. J., Potter, P. T., & Reich, J. W. (1997) The independence of affects is context-dependent: An integrative model of the relationship between positive and negative affect. In M. P. Lawton (Series Ed.) & K. W. Schaie & M. P. Lawton, M. P. (Vol. Eds.), *Annual review of gerontology and geriatrics: Vol. 17. Focus on adult development* (pp. 75–103). New York: Springer.

Zautra, A. J., Reich, J. W., Davis, M. C., Nicolson, N. A., & Potter, P. T. (2000). The role of stressful events in the relationship between positive and negative affects: Evidence from field and experimental studies. *Journal of Personality*, 68, 927–951.

Chapter 5

Bandura, A. (1992a). Exercise of personal agency through the self-efficacy mechanism. In R. Schwarzer (Ed.), *Self-Efficacy: Thought control of action* (pp. 3–37). Washington, DC: Hemisphere.

Bandura, A. (1992b). Self-efficacy mechanism in psychobiological functioning. In R. Schwarzer (Ed.), *Self-Efficacy: Thought control of action* (pp. 355–392). Washington, DC : Hemisphere.

Caplan, G. (1964). *Principles of preventive psychiatry*. New York: Basic Books.

Carter, C. S. (1998). Neuroendocrine perspectives on social attachment and love. *Psychoeneuroendocrinology*, 23, 779–818.

Davis, C. G., Nolen-Hoeksema, S., & Larson, J. (1998). Making sense of loss and benefiting from the experience: Two construals of meaning. *Journal of Personality and Social Psychology*, 75, 561–574.

Dohrenwend, B. S. (1978). Social stress and community psychology. *American Journal of Community Psychology*, 6, 1–14.

Elder, G. H., Jr., & Clipp, E. C. (1988). Wartime losses and social bonding: Influences across 40 years in men's lives. *Psychiatry*, 51, 177–198.

Eysenck, H. J. (1983). Stress, disease, and personality: The "inoculation effect." In C. L. Cooper (Ed.), *Stress research* (pp. 121–146). New York: Wiley.

Felton, B. J., & Revenson, T. A. (1984). Coping with chronic illness: A study of illness controllability and the influence of coping strategies on psychological adjustment. *Journal of Consulting and Clinical Psychology*, 52, 343–353.

Finkel, N. J. (1975). Strens, traumas, and trauma resolution. *American Journal of Community Psychology*, 3, 173–178.

Finkel, N. J., & Jacobsen, C. A. (1977). Significant life experiences in an adult sample. *American Journal of Community Psychology*, 5, 165–175.

Folkman, S., Chesney, M., Collette, L., & Boccellari. C. M. & Cooke, M. (1996). Postbereavement depressive mood and its prebereavement predictors in HIV + and HIV-gay men. *Journal of Personality and Social Psychology, 70*, 336–348.

Frankl, V. E. (1963). *Man's search for meaning: An introduction to logotherapy.* Boston: Beacon Press.

Goodhart, D. E. (1985). Some psychological effects associated with positive and negative thinking about stressful event outcomes: Was Pollyanna right? *Journal of Personality and Social Psychology, 48*, 216–232.

Guarnaccia, C. A. (1990). An alternative perspective on the effects of conjugal bereavement and general fateful loss: Stress innoculation. Unpublished dissertation, Arizona State University, Tempe.

Herbert, T. B., & Cohen, S. (1993). Depression and immunity: A meta-analytic review. *Psychological Bulletin, 113*, 472–486.

Lehman, D. R., Davis, C. G., Delongis, A., Wortman, C., Bluck, S., Mandel, D. R., & Ellard, J. H. (1993). Positive and negative life changes following bereavement and their relations to adjustment. *Journal of Social and Clinical Psychology, 12*, 90–112.

Peterson, C., Maier, S. F., & Seligman, M. E. P. (1993). *Learned helplessness: A theory for the age of personal control.* New York: Oxford University Press.

Piper, W. (1984). *The little engine that could.* Racine, WI: Platt & Munk.

Potter, P., Engel, C., Hamilton, N. A. & Zautra, A. J. (2002). Impact of two types of expectancy on recovery from total knee replacement surgery in adults with osteoarthritis. Unpublished manuscript.

Potter, P. T., & Zautra, A. J. (1997). Effects of major and minor stressors on disease activity in rheumatoid arthritis patients. *Journal of Consulting and Clinical Psychology, 65*, 319–323.

Roethke, T. (1975). *The collected poems of Theodore Roethke.* New York: Anchor.

Rosenbaum, M. (1983). Learned resourcefulness as a behavioral repertoire for the self-regulation of internal events: Issues and speculations. In M. Rosenbaum, C. M. Franks, & Y. Jaffe (Eds.), *Perspective on behavior therapy in the eighties* (pp. 54–73). New York: Springer.

Schaefer, J. A., & Moos, R. H. (1998). Life crises and personal growth. In B. N. Carpenter (Ed.), *Personal coping: Theory, research, and application* (pp. 149–170). Westport, CT: Praeger.

Selye, H. (1973). The evolution of the stress concept. *American Scientist, 61*, 692–699.

Sheehy, G. (1976). *Passages: Predictable crises in adult life.* New York: Dutton.

Simpson, J. A., & Rholes, W. S. (1994). Stress and secure base relationships in adulthood. *Advances in Personal Relationships, 5*, 181–204.

Smith, B. W. (2000). Is perceiving benefits in stressful events related to health? A meta-analytic review and research synthesis. Unpublished manuscript, Arizona State University, Tempe.

Smith, B. W., & Zautra, A. J. (2000). Purpose in life and coping with knee replacement surgery. *Occupational Therapy Journal of Research, 20*, 96–99.

Smith, C. A., Wallston, K. A., Dwyer, K. A., & Dowdy, S. W. (1997). Beyond good and bad coping: A multidimensional examination of coping with pain in persons with rheumatoid arthritis. *Annals of Behavioral Medicine, 19,* 11–21.

Solzhenitsyn, A. I. (1974). *The gulag archipelago: An experiment in literary investigation* (Vols. 3–4). New York: Harper & Row.

Stein, M., Miller, A., & Trestman, R. L. (1991). Depression, the immune system, and health and illness. *Archives of General Psychiatry, 48,* 171–177.

White, R. W. (1959). Motivation reconsidered: The concept of competence. *Psychological Review, 66,* 297–333.

Zautra, A. J., Hoffman, J., & Reich, J. W. (1997). Two kinds of efficacy beliefs and the preservation of well-being among older adults. In B. Gottlieb (Ed.), *Coping with chronic stress* (pp. 269–292). New York: Plenum Press.

Zautra, A. J., Reich, J. W., & Newsom, J. T. (1995). Autonomy and sense of control among older adults: An examination of their effects on mental health. In L. Bond, S. Cutler, A. Grams (Eds.), *Promoting successful and productive aging* (pp. 153–170). Newbury Park, CA.: Sage.

Zautra, A. J., Sheets, V. L., & Sandler, I. S. (1996). An examination of the construct validity of coping dispositions for a sample of recently divorced mothers. *Psychological Assessment, 8,* 256–264.

Chapter 6

Affleck, G., Tennen, H., & Croog, S. (1987). Casual attribution, perceived benefits, and morbidity after a heart attack: An 8-year study. *Journal of Consulting and Clinical Psychology, 55,* 29–35.

Bower, J. R., Kemeny, M. E., Taylor, S. E., & Fahey, J. L. (1998). Cognitive processing, discovery of meaning, CD4 decline, and AIDs-related mortality among bereaved HIV seropositive men. *Journal of Consulting and Clinical Psychology, 60,* 979–986.

Brown, N. O. (1959). *Life against death: The psychoanalytical meaning of history.* Middletown, CT: Wesleyan University Press.

Cohen, S., Doyle, W. J., Turner, R. B., Alper, C. M., & Skoner, D. P. (2002). Emotional style and susceptibility to the common cold. Unpublished manuscript.

Cruess, D. G., Antoni, M. H., McGregor, B. A., Kilbourn, K. M., Boyers, A. E., Alferi, S. M., Carver, C. S., & Kumar, M. (2000). Cognitive-behavioral stress management reduces benefit finding among women being treated for early stage breast cancer. *Psychosomatic Medicine, 62,* 304–308.

Csikszentmihalyi, M. (1975). *Beyond boredom and anxiety.* San Francisco: Jossey-Bass.

Csikszentmihalyi, M., & Larson, R. (1990). *Flow: The psychology of optimal experience.* New York: Harper & Row.

Cunningham, M. (1998). *The hours.* New York: Farrar, Straus, & Giroux.

Danner, D. D., Snowdon, D. A., & Friesen, W. V. (2001). Positive emotions in early life and longevity: Findings from the nun study. *Journal of Personality and Social Psychology, 80*, 804–813.

Dishman, R. K. (1996). Brain: Monoamines, exercise, and behavioral stress: Animal models. *Medicine and Science in Sports and Exercise, 18*, 63–74.

Folkman, S., Chesney, M., Collette, L., & Boccellari, C. M. (1996). Postbereavement depressive mood and its prebereavement predictors in HIV+ and HIV− gay men. *Journal of Personality and Social Psychology, 70*, 336–348.

Folkman, S., & Moskowitz, T. (2000). Positive affect and the other side of coping. *American Psychologist, 55*, 647–654.

Helgeson, V. S., & Fritz, H. L. (1999). Cognitive adaptation as a predictor of new coronary events after percutaneous transluminal coronary angioplasty. *Psychosomatic Medicine, 61*, 488–495.

Hershey, R. D. (2000, January 15). Rise in death rate after New Year is tied to the will to see 2000. *New York Times*, p. A1.

Herzberg, F. (1966). *Work and the nature of man*. New York: Crowell.

Janoff-Bulman, R. (1992). *Shattered assumptions: Toward a new psychology of trauma*. New York: Free Press.

Krakauer, J. (1997). *Into thin air*. New York: Anchor Books/Doubleday.

Lutgendorf, S. K., Vitaliano, P. P., Tripp-Reimer, T., Harvey, J. H., & Lubaroff, D. M. (1999). Sense of coherence moderates in relationship between life stress and natural killer cell activity in healthy older adults. *Psychology and Aging, 14*, 552–563.

McCubbin, J. A. (1993). Stress and endogenous opioids: Behavioral and circulatory interactions. *Biological Psychiatry, 35*, 91–122.

McCubbin, J. A., Wilson, J. F., Bruehl, S., Ibarra, P., Carlson, C. R., Norton, J. A., & Colcough, G. W. (1996). Relaxation training and opioid inhibition of blood pressure response to stress. *Journal of Consulting and Clinical Psychology, 64*, 593–601.

McEwen, B. S. (1998). Protective and damaging effects of stress mediators. *New England Journal of Medicine, 338*, 171–179.

Melnuchuk, T. (1988). Emotions, brain, immunity, and health: A review. In M. Clynes (Ed.)., *Emotions and psychopathology* (pp. 181–247). New York: Plenum Press.

Nakajima, A., Hirai, H., & Yoshino, S. (1999). Reassessment of mirthful laughter in rheumatoid arthritis [Letter to the editor]. *Journal of Rheumatology, 26*, 512–513.

Panskepp, J. (1993). *Neurochemical control of moods and emotions: Amino acids to neuropeptides*. In M. Lewis (Ed.), *Handbook of emotions* (pp. 87–107). New York: Guilford Press.

Pennebaker, J. W. (1990). *Opening up: The healing power of confiding in others*. New York: Morrow.

Pennebaker, J. W., Mayne, T, & Francis, M. E. (1997). Linguistic predictors of adaptive bereavement. *Journal of Personality and Social Psychology, 72*, 863–871.

Segerstrom, S. C., Taylor, S. E., Kemeny, M. E., & Fahey, J. L. (1998). Optimism is associated with mood, coping, and immune change in response to stress. *Journal of Personality and Social Psychology, 74,* 1646–1655.

Valdimarsdottir, H. B., & Bovbjerg, D. H. (1997). Positive and negative mood: Association with natural killer cell activity. *Psychology and Health, 12,* 319–327.

Yoshino, S., Fujimori, J., & Kohda, M. (1996). Effects of mirthful laughter on neuroendocrine and immune systems in patients with rheumatoid arthritis. [Letter to the editor]. *Journal of Rheumatology, 23,* 793–794.

Zautra, A. J., & Smith, B. W. (2001). Depression and reactivity to stress in older women with rheumatoid arthritis and osteoarthritis. *Psychosomatic Medicine, 63,* 687–696.

Zukowska-Grojec, Z. (1995). Neuropeptide Y: A novel sympathetic stress hormone and more. *Annals of the New York Academy of Sciences 771,* 219–233.

Chapter 7

Bauer, J., & Bonanno, G. A. (2001). Doing well and being well (for the most part): Adaptive patterns of narrative self-evaluation during bereavement. *Journal of Personality, 69,* 451–482.

Canli, T., Zhao, Z., Desmond, J. E., Kang, E., Gross, J., & Gabrieli, J. E. (2001). An fMRI study of personality influences on brain reactivity to emotional stimuli. *Behavioral Neuroscience, 115,* 33–42.

Carver, C. S., & White, T. L. (1994). Behavioral inhibition, behavioral activation, and affective responses to impending reward and punishment: The BIS/BAS scales. *Journal of Personality and Social Psychology, 67,* 319–333.

Cole, S. W., Kemeny, M. E., Fahey, J. L., & Naliboff, B. D. (2000). Psychosocial and autonomic predictors of immunologic recovery following HAART therapy for HIV-1 infection: The role of openness/inhibition. *Brain, Behavior, and Immunity, 14,* 85–86.

Davidson, R. J. (2000). The functional neuroanatomy of affective style. In R. D. Lane & L. Nadel (Eds.), *Cognitive neuroscience of emotion* (pp. 371–388). New York: Oxford University Press.

Depue, R. A., & Collins, P. F. (1999). Neurobiology of the structure of personality: Dopamine, facilitation of incentive motivation, and extraversion. *Behavioral and Brain Sciences, 22,* 491–569.

DeVellis, R. F., Carl, K. L., DeVellis, B. M., Blalock, S. J., & Patterson, C. C. (1998). Correlates of changes in mood following a mood induction in osteoarthritis patients. *Arthritis Care and Research, 11,* 234–242.

Epel, E. S., McEwen, B. S., & Ickovics, J. R. (1998). Embodying psychological thriving: Physical thriving in response to stress. *Journal of Social Issues, 54,* 301–322.

Eysenck, H. J. (1967). *The Biological Basis of Personality.* Springfield, IL: Thomas.

Fitzgerald, F. Scott (1945). *The crack-up*. New York: Laughlin.

Gable, S. L., Reis, H. T., & Elliot, A. J. (2000). Behavioral activation and inhibition in everyday life. *Journal of Personality and Social Psychology, 78,* 1135–1149.

Goleman, D. (1995). *Emotional intelligence*. New York: Bantam.

Gray, J. A. (1982). *The neuropsychology of anxiety: An inquiry into the functions of the septo-hippocampal system*. New York: Oxford University Press.

Gross, J. J., Sutton, S. K., & Ketelaar, T. (1998). Relations between affect and personality: Support for the affect-level and affective-reactivity views. *Personality and Social Psychology Bulletin, 24,* 279–288.

Keats, J. (1899). *The complete poetical works and letters of John Keats*. New York: Houghton Mifflin.

Lane, R. D. (2000). Neural correlates of conscious emotional experience. In R. D. Lane & L. Nadel (Eds.), *Cognitive neuroscience of emotion* (pp. 345–370). New York: Oxford University Press.

Lane, R. D. & Schwartz, G. E. (1987). Levels of emotional awareness: A cognitive-developmental theory and its application to psychopathology. *American Journal of Psychiatry, 144,* 133–143.

Lang, P. J., Bradley, M. M., Fitzsimmons, J. R., Cuthbert, B. N., Scott, J. D., Moulder, B., &Nangia, V. (1998). Emotional arousal and activation of the visual cortex: An fMRI analysis. *Psychophysiology, 35,* 1–13.

Linville, P. W. (1985). Self-complexity and affective extremity: Don't put all of your eggs in one cognitive basket. *Social Cognition, 3,* 94–120.

Mayer, J. D., & Salovey, P. (1997). What is emotional intelligence? In P. Salovey & D. J. Sluyter (Eds.), *Emotional development and emotional intelligence* (pp. 3–31). New York: Basic Books.

Neuberg, S. L., & Newsom, J. T. (1993). Personal need for structure: Individual differences in the desire for simple structure. *Journal of Personality and Social Psychology, 65,* 113–131.

Reich, J. W., Zautra, A. J., & Potter, P. T. (2001). Cognitive structure and the independence of positive and negative affect. *Journal of Social and Clinical Psychology. 20,* 105–122.

Rusting, C. L., & Larsen, R. L. (1998). Personality and cognitive processing of affective information. *Personality and Social Psychology Bulletin, 24,* 200–213.

Ryff, C. D., & Singer, B. (1998). The contours of positive human health. *Psychological Inquiry, 9,* 1–28.

Salovey, P., & Mayer, J. D. (1990). Emotional intelligence. *Imagination, Cognition, and Personality, 9,* 185–211.

Salovey, P., & Sluyter, D. J. (1997). *Emotional development and emotional intelligence*. New York: Basic Books.

Schwebel, D. C., & Suls, J. (1999). Cardiovascular reactivity and neuroticism: Results from a laboratory and controlled ambulatory stress protocol. *Journal of Personality, 67,* 67–92.

Showers, C. J. (1992). The compartmentalization of positive and negative self-knowledge. *Journal of Personality and Social Psychology, 62,* 1036–1049.

Showers, C. J., & Kling, K. C. (1996). Organization of self-knowledge: Implications for recovery from sad mood. *Journal of Personality and Social Psychology, 70,* 578–590.

Smith, B. W. (2002). Vulnerability and resilience as predictors of pain and affect in women with arthritis. Unpublished doctoral dissertation, Arizona State University, Tempe.

Sutton, S. K., & Davidson, R. J. (1997). Prefrontal brain asymmetry: A biological substrate of the behavioral approach and inhibition systems. *Psychological Science, 8,* 204–210.

Tedeschi, R. C., & Calhoun, L. G. (1995). *Trauma and transformation: Growing in the aftermath of suffering.* Thousand Oaks, CA: Sage.

Tedeschi, R. C., & Calhoun, L. G. (1996). The posttraumatic growth inventory: Measuring the positive legacy of trauma. *Journal of Truamatic Stress, 9,* 455–469.

Turk-Charles, S. (1998). Age differences in psychological well-being. Paper presented at Arizona State University, Tempe.

Watson, D., Clark, L. A., McIntyre, C. W., & Hamaker, S. (1992). Affect, personality, and social activity. *Journal of Personality and Social Psychology, 63,* 1011–1025.

Wilkinson, R. G. (1996). *Unhealthy societies: The afflictions of inequality.* London: Routledge.

Zautra, A. J., Potter, P. T., & Reich, J. W. (1997) The independence of affects is context-dependent: An integrative model of the relationship between positive and negative affect. In M. P. Lawton (Series Ed.) & K. W. Schaie & M. P. Lawton (Vol. Eds.), *Annual review of gerontology and geriatrics: Vol. 17. Focus on adult development* (pp. 75–103). New York: Springer.

Zautra, A. J., Smith, B., Affleck, G., & Tennen, H. (2001). Examinations of chronic pain and affect relationships: Applications of a dynamic model of affect. *Journal of Consulting and Clinical Psychology.*

Chapter 8

Ashby, F. G., Isen, A. M., & Turken, A. U. (1999). A neuropsychological theory of positive affect and its influence of cognition. *Psychological Review, 106,* 529–550.

Bandura, A., Cioffi, D., Taylor, C. B., & Brouillard, M. E. (1988). Perceived self-efficacy in coping with cognitive stressors and opioid activation. *Journal of Personality and Social Psychology, 55,* 479–488.

Beier, E. G., & Young, D. (1998). *The silent language of psychotherapy: Social reinforcement of unconscious processes.* New York: Aldine.

Bower, G. H. (1995). *Emotion and social judgments.* Washington, DC: Federation of Behavioral, Psychological and Cognitive Sciences.

Clore, G. L., & Ortony, A. (2000). Cognition in emotion: Always, sometimes, or never? In R. D. Lane & L. Nadel (Eds.), *Cognitive neuroscience of emotion* (pp. 24–61). New York: Oxford University Press.

Forgas, J. P. (1995). Mood and judgement: The affect infusion model (AIM). *Psychological Bulletin, 117*, 39–66.

Forgas, J. P., & Bower, G. H. (1987). Mood effects on personal perception judgements. *Journal of Personality and Social Psychology, 51*, 53–60.

Grau, J. W., & Meagher, M. W. (1999, May/June). Pain modulation: It's a two-way street. *Science Briefs*, 10–12.

Griffiths, P. E. (1997). *What emotions really are.* Chicago: University of Chicago Press.

Harman, C., Rothbart, M. K., & Posner, M. I. (1997). Distress and attention interactions in early infancy. *Motivation and Emotion, 21*, 27–43.

Isen, A. M., Daubman, K. A., & Nowicki, G. P. (1987). Positive affect facilitates creative problem solving. *Journal of Personality and Social Psychology, 52*, 1122–1131.

Junghaenel, D., & Broderick, J. E. (2001). The arthritis foundation self-management program for fibromyalgia: Efficacy and success of incorporating written emotional disclosure. (Abstract available from the authors, Department of Psychiatry and Behavioral Science, State University of New York, Stony Brook, NY 11794-8790).

Kabat-Zinn, J. (1982). An out-patient program in behavioral medicine for chronic pain patients based on the practice of mindfulness meditation: Theoretical considerations and preliminary results. *General Hospital Psychiatry, 4*, 33–47.

Kabat-Zinn, J. (1990). *Full catastrophe living: Using the wisdom of your body and mind to face stress, pain, and illness.* New York: Dell.

Ketelaar, T., & Clore, G. L. (1997). Emotion and reason: The proximate effects and ultimate functions of emotions. In G. Matthews (Ed.), *Cognitive science perspectives on personality and emotion* (pp. 355–396). New York: Elsevier.

Kushner, H. S. (1981). *When bad things happen to good people.* New York: Schocken Books.

Lewis, C. S. (1996). *The problem of pain.* New York: Simon & Schuster. (Original work published 1962).

McCracken, L. M. (1998). Learning to live with the pain: Acceptance of pain predicts adjustment in persons with chronic pain. *International Association for the Study of Pain, 74*, 21–27.

Melzack, R. (1993). Pain: Past, present and future. *Canadian Journal of Experimental Psychology, 47*, 615–629.

Melzack, R., & Wall, P. (1965). Pain mechanisms: A new theory. *Science, 50*, 971–979.

Nicassio, P. M., & Greenberg, M. A. (2001). The effectiveness of cognitive-behavioral and psychoeducational interventions in the management of arthritis. In M. H. Weisman, M. E. Weinblatt, & J. S. Louie (Eds.), *Treatment of the rheumatic diseases: Companion to Kelley's textbook of rheumatology* (pp. 147–161). New York: Saunders.

Ploghaus, A., Tracey, I., Gati, J. S., Clare, S., Menon, R. S., Matthews, P. M., & Rawlins, J. N. P. (1999). Dissociating pain from its anticipation in the human brain. *Science, 284,* 1979–1981.

Posner, M. I., & Rothbart, M. K. (1998). Attention, self-regulation and consciousness. *Philosophical Transactions of the Royal Society of London,* 1915–1927.

Richards, J. M., & Gross, J. J. (2000). Emotion regulation and memory: The cognitive costs of keeping one's cool. *Journal of Personality and Social Psychology, 79,* 410–424.

Schachter, S., & Singer, J. (1962). Cognitive, social and physiological determinants of emotional state. *Psychological Review, 69,* 379–399.

Shannon, C. E., & Weaver, W. (1949). *The mathematical theory of communication.* Urbana, IL: The University of Illinois Press.

Turk, D. C., Meichenbaum, D., & Genest, M. (1983). *Pain and behavioral medicine: A cognitive-behavioral perspective.* New York: Guilford Press.

Watkins, L. R., & Mayer, D. J. (1982). Organization of endogenous opiate and nonopioid pain control systems. *Science, 216,* 1185–1192.

Zautra, A. J., Smith, B. W., & Reder, R. (2001). Effectiveness of controlled-release oxycontin on cognitive-behavioral dimensions of quality of life in osteoarthritis patients with uncontrolled pain. *Journal of Pain, 2* (Suppl. 1), 44.

Chapter 9

Abramson, L. Y., Alloy, L. B., & Metalsky, G. J. (1989). Hopelessness depression: A theory-based subtype of depression. *Psychological Review, 96,* 358–372.

Bandura, A. (1992). Exercise of personal agency through the self-efficacy mechanism. In Schwarzer, R. (Ed.) *Self-Efficacy: Thought control of action.* (pp. 3–37). Washington DC: Hemisphere Publishing Company.

Barlow, D. H., Chorpita, B. F., & Turovsky, J. (1996). Fear, panic, anxiety, and disorders of emotion. In D. A. Hope (Ed.) *Nebraska Symposium on Motivation: Vol. 43.* Perspectives on anxiety, panic, and fear (pp. 251–328). Lincoln: University of Nebraska Press.

Carter, C. S. (1998). Neuroendocrine perspectives on social attachment and love. *Psychoeneuroendocrinology, 23,* 779–818.

Checkley, S. (1996). The neuroendocrinology of depression and chronic stress. *British Medical Bulletin, 52,* 597–617.

Denollet, J., & Brutsaert, D. L. (1998). Personality, disease severity, and the risk of long-term cardiac events in patients with a decreased ejection fraction after myocardial infarction. *Circulation, 97,* 167–173.

Derryberry, D., & Reed, M. A. (1997). Motivational and attentional components of personality. In G. Matthews (Ed.), *Cognitive science perspectives on personality and emotion* (pp. 443–473). New York: Elsevier Science.

Everson, S. A., Kaplan, G. A., Goldberg, D. E., & Salonen, J. T. (2000). Hypertension incidence is predicted by high levels of hopelessness in Finnish men. *Hypertension, 35,* 561–576.

Fava, G. A., Rafanelli, C., Cazzaro, S., Conti, S., & Grandi, S. (1998). Well-being therapy: A novel psychotherapeutic approach for residual symptoms of affective disorders. *Psychological Medicine, 28,* 475–480.

Fitzgerald, F. Scott. (1945). Letter first published in Esquire (New York, Feb. 1936). In E. Wilson (Ed.) *The crack-up.* New York: J. Laughlin.

Frasure-Smith, N., Lesperance, F., & Talajic, M. (1993). Depression following myocardial infarction: Impact on 6-month survival. *Journal of the American Medical Association, 270,* 1819–1825.

Frasure-Smith, N., Lesperance, F., & Talajic, M. (1995). Depression and 18-month prognosis after myocardial infarction. *Circulation, 91,* 999–1005.

Frost, R. (1996) *Collected poems of Robert Frost.* New York: Amarron.

Hammen, C. (1991). Generation of stress in the course of unipolar depression. *Journal of Abnormal Psychology, 100,* 555–561.

Herbert, T., & Cohen, S. (1993). Depression and immunity: A meta-analytic review. *Psychological Bulletin, 113,* 472–486.

Johnson, J. G., Crofton, A., & Feinstein, S. B. (1996). Enhancing attributional style and positive life events predict increased hopefulness among depressed psychiatric inpatients. *Motivation and Emotion, 20,* 295–297.

Katz, P. P., & Yelin, E. H. (1993). Prevalence and correlates of depressive symptoms among persons with rheumatoid arthritis. *Journal of Rheumatology, 20,* 790–796.

Kessler, R. C., DuPont, R. L., & Wittchen, H.-U. (1999). Impairment in pure and comorbid generalized anxiety disorder and major depression at 12 months in two national surveys. *American Journal of Psychiatry, 156,* 1915.

Kessler, R. C., McGonagle, K. A., Zhao, S., Nelson, C. B., Hughes, M., Eshleman, S., et al. (1994). Lifetime and 12-month prevalence of DSM-III psychiatric disorders in the United States: Results from the National Co-Morbidity Survey. *Archives of General Psychiatry, 51,* 8–19.

Knutson, B., Wolkowitz, O. M., Cole, S. W., Chan, T., Moore, E. A., Johnson, R. C., et al. (1998). Selective alteration of personality and social behavior by serotonergic intervention. *American Journal of Psychiatry, 155,* 373–379.

Lepore, S. J. (1997). Expressive writing moderates the relation between intrusive thoughts and depressive symptoms. *Journal of Personality and Social Psychology, 73,* 1030–1037.

Maes, M., Lambrechts, J., Bosmans, E., Jacobs, J., Suy, E., Vandervorst, C., et al. (1992). Evidence for a systemic immune activation during depression: Results of leukocyte enumeration by flow cytometry in conjunction with monoclonal antibody staining. *Psychological Medicine, 22,* 45–53.

Maier, S. F. (1984). Learned helplessness and animal models of depression: Progress in neuropsychopharmacology. *Biological Psychiatry, 8,* 435–446.

Michelson, D., Stratakis, C., Hill, L., Reynolds, J., Galliven, E., Chrousoe, G., & Gold, P. (1996). Bone mineral density in women with depression. *New England Journal of Medicine, 35,* 1176–1181.

Musselman, D. L., Evans, D. L., & Nemeroff, C. B. (1998). The relationship of depression to cardiovascular disease. *Archives of General Psychiatry, 55,* 580–592.

Needles, D. J., & Abramson, L. Y. (1990). Positive life events, attributional style, and hopefulness: Testing a model of recovery from depression. *Journal of Abnormal Psychology, 99*, 156–165.

Nemeroff, C. G. (1998). A decade of serotonin research: Looking toward the future: Psychopharmacology of affective disorders in the 21st century. *Society of Biological Psychiatry, 44*, 517–525.

Pennebaker, J. W. (Ed.). (1995). *Emotions, disclosures and health.* Washington, DC: American Psychological Association,

Pincus, T., Griffith, J., Pearce, S., & Isenberg, D. (1996). Prevalence of self-reported depression in patients with rheumatoid arthritis. *British Journal of Rheumatology, 35*, 879–883.

Rottenberg, J., Kasch, K. L., Gross, J. J., & Gotlib, I. H. (2002). Sadness and amusement reactivity differentially predict concurrent and prospective functioning in major depressive disorder. *Emotion, 2*, 135–146.

Schleifer, S. J., Keller, S. E., Bond, R. N., Cohen, J., & Stein, M. (1989). Major depressive disorder and immunity. *Archive of General Psychiatry, 46*, 81–87.

Schwarzer, R., & Leppitt, A. (1992). Possible impact of social ties and support on morbidity and mortality. In H. O. E. Veiel & U. Baumann (Eds.), *The meaning and measurement of social support* (pp. 65–83). New York: Hemisphere.

Seligman, M. E. P. (1975). *Helplessness: On depression, development, and death.* San Francisco: Freeman.

Seligman, M. E. P., Abramson, L. Y., Semmel, A., & von Baeyer, C. (1979). Depressive attributional style. *Journal of Abnormal Psychology, 88*, 242–247.

Stein, M., Miller, A. H., & Trestman, R. L. (1991). Depression, the immune system, and health and illness. *Archives of General Psychiatry, 48*, 171–177.

Stern, S., Dhanda, R., & Hazuda, H. P. (2001). Hopelessness predicts mortality in older Mexican and European Americans. *Psychosomatic Medicine, 63*, 344–351.

Watson, D., Clark, L. A., & Carey, G. (1988). Positive and negative affectivity and their relation to anxiety and depressive disorders. *Journal of Abnormal Psychology, 97*, 346–353.

Wells, K. B., Golding, J. M., & Burman, M. A. (1989). Chronic medical conditions in a sample of the general population with anxiety, affective, and substance use disorders. *American Journal of Psychiatry, 146*, 1440–1446.

Williams, J., Peeters, F., & Zautra, A. J. (2002). Differential affect structure in depressive and anxiety disorders. Unpublished manuscript.

Willner, P. (1997). Validity, reliability, and utility of the chronic mild stress model of depression: A 10-year review and evaluation. *Psychopharmacology, 134*, 319–329.

Wiser, S., & Goldfried, M. R. (1998). Therapist interventions and client emotional experiencing in expert psychodynamic-interpersonal and cognitive-behavioral therapies. *Journal of Consulting and Clinical Psychology, 66*, 634–640.

Zautra, A. J., Guenther, R. T., & Chartier, G. M. (1985). Attributions for real and hypothetical events: Their relation to self-esteem and depression. *Journal of Abnormal Psychology, 94*, 530–540.

Zautra, A. J., Hamilton, N. A., Potter, P., & Smith, B. (1999). Field research on the relationships between stress and disease activity in rheumatoid arthritis. *Proceedings of the New York Academy of Sciences, 879,* 397–412.

Chapter 10

Alcoholics Anonymous World Services. (1976). *Alcoholics anonymous* (3rd ed.). New York: Author.

Armeli, S., Carney, M. A., Tennen, H., Affleck, G., & O'Neil, T. P. (2000). Stress and alcohol use: A daily process examination of the stressor-vulnerability model. *Journal of Personality and Social Psychology, 78,* 979–994.

Bechara, A., & van der Kooy, D. (1992). A single brain stem substrate mediates the motivational effects of both opiates and food in non-deprived rats but not in deprived rats. *Behavioral Neuroscience, 106,* 351–363.

Berridge, K. C., & Robinson, T. E. (1995). The mind of an addicted brain: Neural sensitization of wanting versus liking. *Psychological Science, 4,* 71–76.

Berridge, K. C., & Robinson, T. E. (1998). What is the role of dopamine in reward: Hedonic impact, reward learning, or incentive salience? *Brain Research Reviews, 28,* 309–369.

Brickman, P., & Campbell, D. T. (1971). Hedonic relativism and planning the good society. In M. H. Appley (Ed.), *Adaptation level theory: A symposium* (pp. 287–302). New York: Academic Press.

Burns, J. F. (1999, September 19). Khat-chewing Yemen told to break ancient habit. *The New York Times,* p. Y3.

Carney, M. A., Armeli, S., Tennen, H., Affleck, G., & O'Neil, T. P. (2000). Positive and negative daily events, perceived stress, and alcohol use: A diary study. *Journal of Consulting and Clinical Psychology, 68,* 788–798.

Cohen, I. A. (1995). *The high-low trap.* New York: Health Press.

Egan, T. (1999, September 19). A drug ran its course, then hid with its users. *The New York Times,* p. Y1.

Fletcher, A. M. (2001). *Sober for good: New solutions for drinking problems.* New York: Houghton Mifflin.

Frederick, S., Loewenstein, G. (1999). Hedonic adaptation. In D. Kahneman, E. Diener, & N. Schwarz (Eds.). *Well-being: The foundations of hedonic psychology.* New York: Russell Sage Foundation.

Helson, H. (1964). *Adaptation-level theory: An experimental and systematic approach to behavior.* New York: Harper.

Johnson, C. N., & Fromme, K. (1994). An experimental test of affect, subjective craving, and alcohol outcome expectations as motivators of young adult drinking. *Addictive Behaviors, 19,* 631–641.

Kaplan, C. (1992). Drug craving and drug use in the daily life of heroin addicts. In M. W. deVries (Ed.), *The experience of psychopathology: Investigating mental disorders in their natural settings* (pp. 193–218). New York: Cambridge University Press.

Kreek, M. J., & Koob, G. F. (1998). Drug dependence: Stress and dysregulation of brain reward pathways. *Drug and Alcohol Dependence, 51,* 23–47.

Lang, A. R., Patrick, C. J., & Stritzke, W. G. K. (1999). *Alcohol and emotional response: A multidimensional-multilevel analysis.* In K. E. Leonard & H. T. Blane (Eds.), *Psychological theories of drinking and alcoholism* (2nd ed., pp. 328–371). New York: Guilford Press.

Lindman, R. E., Sjoholm, B. A., & Lang, A. R. (2000). Expectations of alcohol-induced positive affect: A cross-cultural comparison. *Journal of Studies in Alcohol, 61,* 681–687.

Masefield, J. (1953). *Poems.* New York: Macmillan.

McGinnis, J. M., & Foege, W. H. (1999). Mortality and morbidity attributable to use of addictive substances in the United States. *Proceedings of the Association of American Physicians, 2,* 109–180.

Milkman, H., & Sunderwirth, S. G. (1998). *Craving for ecstasy: How our passions become addictions and what we can do about them.* San Francisco: Jossey-Bass.

Nader, K., Bechara, A., & van der Kooy, D. (1997). Neurobiological constraints of behavioral models of motivation. *Annual Review of Psychology, 48,* 85–114.

Nader, K., & van der Kooy, D. (1997). Deprivation state switches the neurobiological substrates mediating opiate reward in the ventral tegmental area. *Journal of Neuroscience, 17,* 383–390.

Panksepp, J. (1998). *The foundation of human and animal emotions.* New York: Oxford University Press.

Piazza, P. V., & Moal, M. L. (1998). The role of stress in drug administration. *Trends in Pharmacological Sciences, 19,* 67–74.

Project MATCH Research Group. (1997). Matching alcoholism treatments to client heterogeneity: Project MATCH posttreatment drinking outcomes. *Journal of Studies on Alcohol, 58,* 7–29.

Robinson, T. E., & Berridge, K. C. (1993). The neural basis of drug craving: An incentive-sensitization theory of addiction. *Brain Research Reviews, 18,* 247–291.

Solomon, R. L., & Corbit, J. D. (1974). An opponent-process theory of motivation: Temporal dynamics of affect. *Psychological Review, 81,* 119–145.

Stewart, J. (2000). Pathways to relapse: The neurobiology of drug- and stress-induced relapse to drug-taking. *Journal of Psychiatry Neuroscience, 25,* 125–136.

Stocker, S. (1999). Studies link stress and drug addiction. *NIDA Notes, 14,* 1–4. Available from National Institute on Drug Abuse web site, http://www.nida.nih.gov/NIDA_Notes/NNVol14N1/stress.html

Swendsen, J. D., Tennen, H., Carney, M. A., Affleck, G., Willard, A., & Hromi, A. (2000). Mood and alcohol consumption: An experience sampling test of the self-medication hypothesis. *Journal of Abnormal Psychology, 109,* 198–204.

Tennen, H., Affleck, G., Armeli, S., & Carney, M.A. (2000). A daily process approach to coping. *American Psychologist, 55,* 626–636.

U.S. Department of Health and Human Services. (2000). *Summary of findings from the 1999 National Household Survey on Drug Abuse.* Rockville, MD: National Clearinghouse for Alcohol and Drug Information.

Weiss, F., Parsons, L. H., & Markou, A. (1995). A neurochemistry of cocaine with-drawal. In R. L. Hammer, Jr. (Ed.), *The neurobiology of cocaine: Cellular and molecular mechanisms* (pp. 163–180). Boca Raton, FL: CRC Press.

Will, M. J., Watkins, L. R., & Maier, S. F. (1998). Uncontrollable stress potentiates morphine's rewarding properties. *Pharmacology Biochemistry and Behavior, 60,* 655–664.

Chapter 11

Bell, I. R., Baldwin, C. M., Russek, L. G. S., Schwartz, G. E. R., & Hardin, E. E. (1998). Early life stress, negative paternal relationships, and chemical intolerance in middle-aged women: Support for a neural sensitization model. *Journal of Women's Health, 7,* 1135–1147.

Caldji, C., Tannebaum, B., Sharma, S., Francis, D., Plotsky, D., & Meaney, M. J. (1998). Maternal care during infancy regulates the development of neural systems mediating the expression of behavioral fearfulness in adulthood in the rat. *Proceedings of the National Academy of Sciences, 95,* 5335–5340.

Denham, S. A. (1998). *Emotional development in young children.* New York: Guilford Press.

Dickerson, S. S., Kemeny, M. E., Aziz, N., Kim, K. H., & Fahey, J. L. (2001). Immunological effects of induced shame and guilt. Unpublished manuscript.

Egeland, B. (1996). Looking backward and forward for the causes and consequences of child maltreatment. In M. R. Merrens & G. C. Brannigan (Eds.), *The Developmental Psychologists* (pp. 53–67). New York: McGraw-Hill.

Eisenberg, N., & Fabes, R. A. (1992). Emotion, regulation, and the development of social competence. In M. S. Clark (Ed.), *Review of personality and social psychology: Vol. 14. Emotion and social behavior* (pp. 119–150). Newbury Park, CA: Sage.

Francis, D. D., & Meaney, M. J. (1999). Maternal care and the development of stress responses. *Current Opinion in Neurobiology, 9,* 128–134.

Graham, Y. P., Heim, C., Goodman, S. H., Miller, A. H., & Nemeroff, C. B. (1999). The effects of neonatal stress on brain development: Implications for psychopathology. *Development and Psychopathology, 11,* 545–565.

Heim, C., & Nemeroff, C. B. (1999). The impact of early adverse experiences on brain systems involved in the pathophysiology of anxiety and affective disorders. *Society of Biological Psychiatry, 46,* 1509–1522.

Heim, C., Owens, M. J., Plotsky, P. M., & Nemeroff, C. B. (1997). The role of early adverse life events in the etiology of depression and posttraumatic stress disorder. *Annals of the New York Academy of Sciences, 821,* 194–207.

Heim, C., Owens, M. J., Plotsky, P. M., & Nemeroff, C. B. (1997). Endocrine factors in the pathophysiology of mental disorders. *Psychopharmacology Bulletin, 33,* 185–192.

Hodgson, D. M., Rosengren, S., & Walker, F. (2000). Neonatal stress potentiates hypothalamic-pituitary-adrenal responsivity and impairs wound healing and tumor resistance in the adult rat. *Brain, Behavior, and Immunity, 14,* 101.

Holmberg, A. (1998). Through the eyes of Lolita. An interview with Pulitzer Prize-winning playright Paula Vogel. American Repertory Theatre. Web address: http://www.amrep.org/past/drive/drive1.html

Kraemer, G. W. (1999). Psychobiology of early social attachment in rhesus monkeys: Clinical applications. In C. S. Carter, I. L. Lederhendler, & B. Kirkpatrick (Eds.), *The Integrative Neurobiology of Affiliation* (pp. 373–390). MA: Bradford.

Lewis, M. (1989). Emotional development in the preschool child. *Pediatric Annuals, 18*, 317–326.

Liu, D., Tannebaum, B., Caldji, C., Francis, D., Freedman, A., Sharma, S., et al. (1997). Maternal care, hippocampal, glucocorticoid receptor gene expression and hypothalamic-pituitary-adrenal responses to stress. *Science, 277*, 1859–1882.

McCauley, J., Kern, D. E., Kolodner, K., Dill, L., Schroeder, A. F., Dechant, H. K., et al. (1997). Clinical characteristics of women with a history of childhood abuse. *Journal of the American Medical Association, 277*, 1362–1368.

Plath, S. (1981). *The collected poems.* New York: Harper & Row.

Rind, B., Tromovich, P., & Bauserman, R. (1998). A meta-analytic examination of assumed properties of child sexual abuse using college samples. *Psychological Bulletin, 124*, 22–53.

Russek, L. G., & Schwartz, G. E. (1997a). Perceptions of parental caring predict health status in midlife: A 35-year follow-up of the Harvard mastery of stress study. *Psychosomatic Medicine, 59*, 144–149.

Russek, L. G., & Schwartz, G. E. (1997b). Feelings of parental caring predict health status in midlife: A 35-year follow-up of the Harvard mastery of stress study. *Journal of Behavioral Medicine, 20*, 1–13.

Uvnas-Moberg, K. (1997). Physiological and endocrine effects of social contact. *Annals New York Academy of Sciences, 807*, 146–163.

Vogel, P. (1998). *The mammary plays: How I learned to drive* and *The Mineola Twins.* New York: Theatre Communications Group.

Walker, E. A., Keegan, D., Gardner, G., Sullivan, M., Bernstein, D., & Katon, W. J. (1997). Psychosocial factors in fibromyalgia compared with rheumatoid arthritis: 2. Sexual, physical, and emotional abuse and neglect. *Psychosomatic Medicine, 59*, 572–577.

Wissow, L. S. (1995). Child abuse and neglect. *New England Journal of Medicine, 332*, 1425–1431.

Yehuda, R. (1997). Sensitization of the hypothalamic-pituitary-adrenal axis in posttraumatic stress disorder. *Annals of the New York Academy of Sciences, 821*, 57–75.

Chapter 12

Bagozzi, R. P., Wong, N., & Yi, Y. (1999). The role of culture and gender in the relationship between positive and negative affect. *Cognition and Emotion, 6*, 641–672.

Barrett, L. F., Lane, Sechrest, & Schwartz (2000). Sex differences in emotional awareness. *Personality and Social Psychology Bulletin, 26,* 1027–1035.

Bradley, M. M., & Lang, P. J. (2000). Measuring emotion: Behavior, feeling, and physiology. In R.D Lane & L. Nadel (Eds.), *Cognitive neuroscience of emotion* (pp. 242–276). New York: Oxford University Press.

Bruce, M. L., & Kim, K. M. (1992). Differences in the effects of divorce on major depression in men and women. *American Journal of Psychiatry, 7,* 914–917.

Eliot, T. S. (1963). *Collected poems.* New York: Harcourt.

Gottman, J. M., Coan, J., Carrere, S., & Swanson, C. (1998). Predicting marital happiness and stability from newlywed interactions. *Journal of Marriage and the Family, 60,* 5–22.

Gottman, J. M., & Levenson, R. W. (1988). The social psychophysiology of marriage. In P. Noller & M. A. Fitzpatrick (Eds.), *Perspectives on marital interaction* (pp. 182–200). Philadelphia: Multilingual Matters.

Gray, J. (1992). *Men are from Mars, women are from Venus: A practical guide for improving communication and getting what you want in your relationships.* New York: HarperCollins.

Haskey, J. (1996). The proportion of married couples who divorce: Past patterns and current prospects. *Popular Trends, 83,* 25–36.

Heavey, C. L., Layne, C., & Christensen, A. (1993). Gender and conflict structure in marital interaction: A replication and extension. *Journal of Consulting and Clinical Psychology, 61,* 16–27.

Jacobson, N. S. (1992). Behavioral couple therapy: A new beginning. *Behavior Therapy, 23,* 493–506.

Johnsen, B. H., Thayer, J. F., & Hugdahl, K. (1995). Affective judgment of the Ekman faces: A dimensional approach. *Journal of Psychophysiology, 9,* 193–202.

Joyce, J. (1925). *Dubliners.* New York: Huebsch.

Kposowa, A. J. (2000, April). Marital status and suicide in the national longitudinal mortality study. *Journal of Epidemiology and Community Health, 4,* 254–261.

Kring, A. M., & Gordon, A. H. (1998). Sex differences in emotion: Expression, experience, and physiology. *Journal of Personality and Social Psychology, 74,* 686–703.

Lane, R. D., Quinlan, D.M., Schwartz, G.E., Walker, P.A., & Zeitlin, S.B. (1990). The levels of emotional awareness scale: A cognitive-development measure of emotion. *Journal of Personality Assessment, 55,* 124–134.

Lang, P. J., Bradley, M. M., Fitzsimmons, J. R., Cuthbert, B. N., Scott, J. D., Moulder, B., & Nangia, V. (1998). Emotional arousal and activation of the visual cortex: An fMRI analysis. *Psychophysiology, 35,* 1–13.

Lawrence, D. H. (1994). *Complete poems* (V. De Sola Pinto & W. Roberts, Eds.). London: Penguin.

Nolen-Hoeksma, S., & Rusting, C. L. (1999). In D. Kahneman, E. Diener, & N. Schwarz (Eds.), *Well-being: The foundations of hedonic psychology* (pp. 330–350). New York: Russell Sage Foundation.

Pasch, L. A. & Bradbury, T. N. (1998). Social support, conflict and the development of marital dysfunction. *Journal of Consulting and Clinical Psychology, 66*, 219–230.

Power, C., Rodgers, B., & Hope, S. (1999). Heavy alcohol consumption and marital status: Disentangling the relationship in a national study of young adults. *Addiction, 94*, 1477–1487.

Stone, A. A. (1981). The association between perceptions of daily experiences and self- and spouse-rated mood. *Journal of Research in Personality, 15*, 510–522.

Stone, A. A., & Neale, J. M. (1982). Development of a methodology for assessing daily experiences. In A. Baum & J. Singer (Eds.), *Advances in environmental psychology: Environment and health* (Vol. 4, pp. 49–83). Hillsdale, NJ: Erlbaum.

Tannen, D. (1990). *You just don't understand: Women and men in conversation.* New York: Ballantine Books.

Taylor, S. E., Klein, L. C., Lewis, B. P., Gruenewald, T. L., Grunung, R.A.R., & Updegraff, J. A. (2000). Biobehavioral responses to stress in females: Tend-and-befriend, not fight-or-flight. *Psychological Review, 107*, 411–429.

Thayer, J., & Johnsen, B. H. (2000). Sex differences in judgement of facial affect: A multivariate analysis of recognition errors. *Scandinavian Journal of Psychology, 41*, 243–246.

Chapter 13

Ashforth, B. E., & Humphrey, R. H. (1995). Emotion in the workplace: A reappraisal. *Human Relations, 48*, 97–125.

Basch, J., & Fisher, C. D. (2000). Affective events-emotions matrix: A classification of work events and associated emotions. In N. M. Ashanasy, C. E. J. Hartel, & W. J. Zerbe (Eds.), *Emotions in the workplace: Research, theory, and practice* (pp. 36–48). Westport, CT: Quorum Books.

Blanchard, K. H., & Johnson, S. (1982) *The one-minute manager.* New York: Morrow.

Chatterley, C. N., Rouverol, A. J., & Cole, S. A. (2000). *I was content and not content.* Carbondale: Southern Illinois University Press.

Covey, S. R. (1989). *The seven habits of highly effective people: Restoring the character ethic.* New York: Simon and Schuster.

Csikszentmihalyi, M. (1990). *Flow: The psychology of optimal experience.* New York: HarperCollins.

Firth-Cozens, J. (2000). New stressors, new remedies. *Occupational Medicine, 50*, 199–201.

Frankenhauser, M. (1989). A biopsychosocial approach to work life issues. *International Journal of Health Sciences, 19*, 747–758.

Goleman, D. (1999). *Working with emotional intelligence.* New York: Bantam Books.

Grigaliunas, B., & Wiener, Y. (1974). Has the research challenge to motivation-hygiene theory been conclusive? An analysis of critical studies. *Human Relations, 27*, 839–871.

Hackman, J. R., & Oldhan, G. R. (1975). Development of the Job Diagnostic Inventory. *Journal of Applied Psychology, 60,* 159–170.

Herzberg, F. (1966). *Work and the nature of man.* Cleveland: Cleveland World Publishing.

Herzberg, F. (1968, January-February) One more time: How do you motivate employees? *Harvard Business Review, 46,* 53–62.

Herzberg, F. (1974, September–October). The wise old Turk. *Harvard Business Review, 52,* 70–80.

Herzberg, F. (Ed.). (1976). *The managerial choice: To be efficient and to be human.* Homewood, IL: Dow Jones-Irwin.

Herzberg, F., Mausner, B., & Snyderman, B. B. (1959). *The motivation to work.* New York: Wiley.

Herzberg, F., & Rafalko, E. A. (1976) Efficiency in the military: The Hill Air Force Base Project. In F. Herzberg (Ed.), *The managerial choice: To be efficient and to be human.* Homewood, IL: Dow Jones-Irwin.

Herzberg, F., & Zautra, A. (1976, September/October). Orthodox job enrichment and job satisfaction. *Personnel, 53,* 54–68.

Hochschild, A. R. (1983). *The managed heart.* Los Angeles: University of California Press.

Jahoda, M. (1981). Work, employment, and unemployment. *American Psychologist, 36,* 184–191.

Karasek, R. A. (1981). Job decision latitude, job design, and coronary heart disease. In G. Salvendy & M. J. Smith (Eds.), *Machine pacing and occupational stress* (pp. 45–55). London: Taylor & Francis.

King, N. (1970). Clarification and evaluation of the two-factor theory of job satisfaction. *Psychological Bulletin, 74,* 18–31.

Landy, F. J. (1978). An opponent process theory of job satisfaction. *Journal of Applied Psychology, 63,* 533–547.

Lawrence, D. H. (1994). *Complete poems* (V. De Sola Pinto & W. Roberts, Eds.). London: Penguin.

McGrath, J. (1970). *Social and psychological factors in stress.* New York: Holt, Rinehart, & Winston.

O'Boyle, T. F. (1998). *At any cost: Jack Welch, General Electric, and the pursuit of profit.* New York: Vintage Books.

Parkes, K. R. (1999). Shiftwork, job type, and the work environment as joint predictors of health-related outcomes. *Journal of Occupational Health Psychology, 4,* 256–268.

Rose, R. M., Jenkins, C. D., & Hurst, M. W. (1978). *Air traffic controller health change study: A prospective investigation of physical, psychological and work-related changes.* Boston, MA: Boston University School of Medicine.

Saavedra, R., & Kwun, S. K. (2000). Affective states in job characteristics theory. *Journal of Organizational Behavior, 21,* 131–146.

Sarason, S. B. (1974). *The psychological sense of community, prospects for a community psychology.* San Francisco: Jossey-Bass.

Spera, S. P., Buhrfeind, E. D., & Pennebaker, J. W. (1994). Expressive writing and coping with job loss. *Academy of Management Journal, 37,* 722–733.

Straw, B. M., Bell, N. E., & Clausen, J. A. (1986). The dispositional approach to job attitudes: A lifetime longitudinal test. *Administrative Science Quarterly, 31,* 56–77.

Stone, A. A., Neale, J. M., Cox, D. S., Napoli, A., Valdimarsdottir, H., & Kennedy-Moore, E. (1994). Daily events are associated with a secretory immune response to an oral antigen in men. *Health Psychology, 13,* 440–446.

Yerxa, E. J. (1998) Health and the human spirit for occupation. *American Journal of Occupational Therapy, 52,* 412–418.

Zautra, A. J., Berkhof, J., & Nicolson, N. A. (2002). Changes in affect interrelations as a function of stressful events. *Cognition and Emotion, 16,* 309–318.

Chapter 14

Blumenthal, J. A., Babyak, M. A., Moore, K. A., Craighead, W. E., Herman, S., Khatri, P., et al. (1999). Effects of exercise training on older patients with major depression. *Archives of Internal Medicine, 159,* 2349–2356.

Butler, R. (1974). Successful aging and the role of life review. *Journal of the American Geriatric Society, 22,* 529–535.

Carstensen, L. L. (1993). Motivation and social contact across the life span: A theory of socioemotional selectivity. In J. E. Jacobs (Ed.), *Nebraska Symposium on Motivation:, Vol. 40.* Developmental perspectives on motivation (pp. 209–254. Lincoln: University of Nebraska Press.

Carstensen, L. L., Isaacowitz, D. M., & Charles, S. T. (1999). Taking time seriously: A theory of socioemotional selectivity. *American Psychologist, 54,* 3.

Carstensen, L. L., Pasupathi, M., Mayr, U., & Nesselroade, J. R. (2000). Emotional experience in everyday life across the life span. *Journal of Personality and Social Psychology, 79,* 644–655.

Dura, J. R., Stukenberg, K. W., & Kiecolt-Glaser, J. K. (1990). Chronic stress and depressive disorders in older adults. *Journal of Abnormal Psychology, 99,* 284–290.

Fratiglioni, F., Wang, H., Ericsson, K., Maytan, M., & Winblad, B. (2000) Influence of social network on occurrence of dementia: A community-based longitudinal study. *Lancet, 355,* 1315–1319.

Glaser, R., Sheridan, J., Malarkey, W., MacCallum, R. C., & Kiecolt-Glaser, J. (2000). Chronic stress modulates the immune response to a pneumococcal pneumonia vaccine. *Psychosomatic Medicine, 62,* 804–807.

Hanson, E. (2000). *Exploring the short-term effects of effort-reward imbalance.* Unpublished doctoral dissertation, Utrecht University, The Netherlands.

Kramer, A. F., Hahn, S., Cohen, N. J., Banich, M. T., McAuley, E., Harrison, C. R., et al. (1999). Ageing, fitness and neurocognitive function. *Nature, 400,* 418–419.

Lang, P. J., Bradley, M. M., & Cuthbert, M. M. (1999). *International affective picture system (IAPS): Technical manual and affective ratings.* Gainsville, FL: The Center for Research in Psychophysiology, University of Florida.

Lawrence, R. C., Helmick, C. G., Arnett, F. C., Deyo, R. A., Felson, D. T., Giannini, E. H., et al. (1998). Estimates of the prevalence of arthritis and selected musculoskeletal disorders in the United States. *Arthritis and Rheumatism, 41*, 778–799.

Liepert, J., Bauder, H., Miltner, W. H., Taub, E., & Weiller, C. (2000). Treatment-induced cortical reorganization after stroke in humans. *Stroke, 6*, 1210–1216.

Mace, N. L., & Rabins, P. V. (1981). *The 36-hour day.* Baltimore and London: The Johns Hopkins University Press.

Meaney, M. J., Aitken, D. H., van Berkel, C., Bhatnagar, S., & Sapolsky, R. M. (1988). Effect of neonatal handling on age-related impairments associated with the hippocampus. *Science, 239*, 766–768.

Meaney, M. J., O'Donnell, D., Rowe, W., Tannenbaum, B.T., Steverman, A., Walker, M., et al. (1995). Individual differences in hypothalamic-pituitary-adrenal activity in later life and hippocampal aging. *Experimental Gerontology, 30*, 229–251.

Mroczek, D. K., & Kolarz, C. M. (1998). The effect of age on positive and negative affect: A developmental perspective on happiness. *Journal of Personality and Social Psychology, 75*, 1333–1349.

Reminger, S. L., Kaszniak, A. W., & Dalby, P. R. (in press). Age-invariance in the asymmetry of stimulus-evoked emotional facial muscle activity. *Aging, Neurospychology and Cognition.*

Rimer, S. (2000, February 9). Turning to autobiography for emotional growth in old age. *New York Times,* p. A12.

Rodin, J., & Langer, E. J. (1977). Long-term effects of a control-relevant intervention with the institutionalized aged. *Journal of Personality and Social Psychology, 35*, 897–902.

Sapolsky, R. M. (1998). *Why zebras don't get ulcers* (2d ed.). New York: Freeman.

Schulz, R., & Beach, S. R. (1999). Caregiving as a risk factor for mortality: The caregiver health effects study. *Journal of Ameirican Medical Association, 282*, 2215–2219.

Seeman, T. E., Berkman, L. F., Gulanski, B. I., Robbins, R. J., Greenspan, S. L., Charpentier, P. A., & Rowes, J. W. (1995). Self-esteem and neuroendocrine response to challenge: Macarthur studies of successful aging. *Journal of Psychosomatic Research, 39*, 69–84.

Sheline, V. I., Sanghavi, M., Mintun, M. A., & Gado, M. H. (1999). Depression duration but not age predicts hippocampal volume loss in medically healthy women with recurrent major depression. *Journal of Neuroscience, 19*, 5034–5043.

Stowell, J. R., Kiecolt-Glaser, J. K., & Glaser, R. (2000). Coping styles, perceived stress levels, and T-lymphocyte responses to mitogens. *Brain, Behavior, and Immunity, 14*, 135–136.

Tennyson, A. (1987). *Idylls of the king and a selection of poems.* New York: New American Library.

Vedhara, K., Shanks, N., Anderson, S., & Lightman, S. (2000). The role of stressors and psychosocial variables in the stress process: A study of chronic caregiver stress. *Psychosomatic Medicine, 62*, 374.

Viney, L. L. (1993). *Life stories: Personal construct therapy with the elderly.* New York: Wiley.

Zautra, A. J., Burleson, M. H., Smith, C. A., Blalock, S. J., Wallston, K. A., DeVellis, R. F., et al. (1995). Arthritis and perceptions of quality of life: An examination of positive and negative affect in rheumatoid arthritis patients. *Health Psychology, 14*, 399–408.

Zautra, A. J., Hoffman, J., & Reich, J. W. (1997). Two kinds of efficacy beliefs and the preservation of well-being among older adults. In B. Gottlieb (Ed.), *Coping with chronic stress* (pp. 269–292). New York: Plenum Press.

Chapter 15

Agren, G., Uvnas-Moberg, K., & Lundberg, T. (1997). Olfactory cues from an oxytocin-injected male rat can induce antinociception in its cage mates. *NeuroReport, 8*, 3073–3076.

Axelrod, R. (1984). *The evolution of cooperation.* New York: Basic Books.

Bakan, D. (1966). *The duality of human existence.* Chicago: Rand McNally.

Baumeister, R. F., & Leary, M. R. (1995). The need to belong: Desire for interpersonal attachments as a fundamental human motivation. *Psychological Bulletin, 117*, 497–529.

Belkin, L. (1999, October 31). "They ask us if we blame the parents? Who else do we blame?" *New York Times Magazine*, pp. 60–67.

Bellah, R. N., Madsen, R., Sullivan, W. H., Swidler, A., & Tipton, S. M. (1985). *Habits of the heart.* Berkeley: University of California Press.

Bohart, A. C., & Stipek, D. J. (Eds.). (2001). *Constructive and destructive behavior: Implications for family, school, and society.* Washington, DC: American Psychological Association.

Carter, C. S. (1998). Neuroendocrine perspectives on social attachment and love. *Psychoeneuroendocrinology, 23*, 779–818.

Chödrön, P. (2000). *When things fall apart: Heart advice for difficult times.* Boston: Shambhala.

Freud, S. (1930). *Civilization and its discontents.* New York: Norton.

Helgeson, V. S. (1994). Relation of agency and communion to well-being: Evidence and potential explanations. *Psychological Bulletin, 116*, 412–428.

Janofsky, M. (1999, October 24). Aftereffects of Columbine are claiming new victims. *The New York Times*, p. Y16.

Kawachi, I., & Kennedy, B. P. (1999). Income inequality and health: Pathways and mechanisms. *Health and Services Research, 34*, 215–227.

Kawachi, I., Kennedy, B. P. & Wilkinson, R. G. (1999). Crime: Social disorganization and relative deprivation. *Social Science and Medicine, 48*, 719–731.

Kenrick, D. T., & Johnson, G. A. (1979). Interpersonal attraction in aversive environments: A problem for the classical conditioning paradigm? *Journal of Personality and Social Psychology, 37*, 572–579.

Keynes, G. (Ed.). (1966). *Blake: The complete writings.* London: Oxford University Press.

O'Toole, M. E. (2000). The school shooter: A threat assessment perspective. Quantico, VA: Federal Bureau of Investigation Academy, National Center for the Analysis of Violent Crime, Critical Incident Response Group.

Riesman, D. (with Glaser, N., & Denney, R.). (1950). *The lonely crowd.* New Haven, CT: Yale University Press.

Rosenblum, L. A., & Andrews, M. W. (1994). Influences of environmental demand on material behavior and infant development. *Acta Paediatric Supplement, 397,* 57–63.

Sarason, S. B. (1974). *The psychological sense of community.* San Francisco: Jossey-Bass

Schiff, S. (1999, April 22). Littleton, then and now. *The New York Times,* p. A-31.

Seeman, T. E. (1996). Social ties and health: The benefits of social integration. *Annals of Epidemiology, 6,* 442–451.

Uvnas-Moberg, K. (1998). Oxytocin may mediate the benefits of positive social interaction and emotions. *Psychoneuroendocrinology, 23,* 819–835.

Van Denburg, T. F., & Kiesler, D. J. (1993). Transactional escalation in rigidity and intensity of interpersonal behavior under stress. *British Journal of Medical Psychology, 66,* 15–31.

Zautra, A., & Beier, E. (1978). The effects of life crisis on psychological adjustment. *American Journal of Community Psychology, 6,* 125–135.

Zautra, A., & Simons, L. (1978). The assessment of a community's mental health needs. *American Journal of Community Psychology, 6,* 351–362.

Chapter 16

Brandt, E. N., & Pope, A. M. (Eds.). (1997). *Enabling America: Assessing the role of rehabilitation science and engineering.* Washington, DC: National Academy Press.

Nussbaum, M. C. (2001). *Upheavals of thought: The intelligence of emotions.* New York: Cambridge University Press.

Seligman, M. E. P., & Csikszentmihalyi, M. (2000). Positive psychology: An introduction. *American Psychologist, 55,* 5–14.

Shelley, P. B. (1960). *The complete poetical works of Percy Bysshe Shelley.* London: Oxford University Press.

Singer, B. H., & Ryff, C. D. (Eds.). (2001). *New horizons in health: An integrative approach.* Washington, DC: National Academy Press.

Snyder, C. R., & Lopez, S. J. (Eds.). (2001). *Handbook of positive psychology.* New York: Oxford University Press.

Index

Lightning Source UK Ltd.
Milton Keynes UK
23 November 2010

163343UK00002B/19/P